CIVIL LIBERTIES 1984

Edited by
Peter Wallington

MARTIN ROBERTSON

© The Cobden Trust, 1984

First published in 1984 by
Martin Robertson & Company Ltd.,
108 Cowley Road, Oxford OX4 1JF.

British Library Cataloguing in Publication Data

Civil liberties 1984.
 1. National Council for Civil Liberties — History
 I. Wallington, Peter
 323.4'0941   JN906

 ISBN 0-85520-701-9
 ISBN 0-85520-702-7pbk

Typeset by Communitype, Leicester
Printed and bound in Great Britain by
Billing and Son Ltd., Worcester

CONTENTS

LIST OF CONTRIBUTORS

JOHN ALDERSON was until 1982 Chief Constable of Devon and Cornwall, and is consultant to the Committee on Education in Human Rights of the Council of Europe.

DUNCAN CAMPBELL is a journalist with the *New Statesman* and author of books on defence, civil defence, surveillance and computers. He was a defendant in the "ABC" secrecy case in 1978.

PAUL CRANE is a solicitor, author of *Gays and the Law* and a co-author of *Trouble with the Law*, which received the Cobden Trust Award for 1979.

NORMAN DORSEN is President of the American Civil Liberties Union and Stokes Professor of Law at New York University Law School. He is editor of the forthcoming *Our Endangered Rights*.

MARTIN ENNALS was General Secretary of the NCCL from 1960 to 1966, subsequently Secretary General of Amnesty International, and currently works with the GLC as Adviser to the Police Committee.

LARRY GRANT is a practising solicitor and a former Legal Officer and Chairman of the NCCL. He is co-author with Ian Martin of *Immigration Law and Practice* (Cobden Trust) and co-editor of *Civil Liberty: the NCCL Guide* (Penguin).

JOHN GRIFFITH is Professor of Public Law at the London School of Economics, and author of *The Politics of the Judiciary*.

PATRICIA HEWITT was General Secretary of the NCCL from 1975 to 1983, and is well known as an author and broadcaster. She is now Press Adviser to the Leader of the Opposition.

1

INTRODUCTION

PETER WALLINGTON

When the founders of the National Council for Civil Liberties first met in the crypt of St Martin-in-the-Fields in February 1934, they could hardly have envisaged the ironic timing their initiative would produce for the celebration of the new body's fiftieth anniversary. Orwell had not yet contemplated *1984*, which was to invest the real 1984 with the special connotations of his fictitious nightmare. Leon Brittan, whose responsibilities as Home Secretary in 1984 are likely to include several more steps towards closing the gap between the fiction and the reality, was not even born. Indeed it is unlikely that it occurred to anybody at that first meeting that there would *be* an NCCL fifty years later. That NCCL has survived, as an independent voice in support of the protection and extension of civil liberties, is in itself an achievement that deserves attention.

It is to mark the fiftieth anniversary of the NCCL that this volume was commissioned. Having been connected in a modest way with NCCL and its Scottish counterpart over the last 14 years, I was privileged and delighted to be asked by Patricia Hewitt to edit a collection of essays. This is not a book *about* the NCCL; a short history of the Council is to be published separately later in 1984. Rather it is a collection of assessments of the state of civil liberty in 1984; there could hardly be a more appropriate year for this.

However a book of this kind would not be complete without acknowledgement of the work and achievements of NCCL. Some of the points I would have wished to make have been made by Patricia Hewitt in her Retrospective (chapter 2), written soon after she retired from the General Secretaryship in the summer of 1983. From that position she did not feel able to blow NCCL's trumpet, but I can be less inhibited. NCCL has made, and is still making, a very real

1

contribution to the preservation of freedom in the UK. The overall view of civil liberties, particularly over the last 5 years, may be depressing, but without NCCL it would have been significantly worse in many areas. Reforms which we now tend to take for granted have in many cases come about largely as a result of the sustained hard work of NCCL's small band of staff and core of active supporters. Individual cases of injustice have been successfully taken up, often without publicity, and the results of less successful cases have contributed to NCCL's ability to speak with the authority of experience about the reality of infringements of liberty.

Some of NCCL's most valuable work in recent years has been on behalf of those without other effective voices to speak for them – mental patients in the 1950s and 1960s; women and the gay community in the years before their respective interests had any effective representation; immigrants, gypsies, boy soldiers. It has been NCCL almost alone of organisations this side of the Irish Sea that has kept the issue of civil liberty in Northern Ireland politically alive. These have not all been popular causes, and it has been one of NCCL's strengths that it has been prepared to argue the case regardless of its popularity. That it has done so has undoubtedly contributed to the image of NCCL as an extremist organisation, a view sustained in some political quarters and fostered by many representatives of the police. It is particularly sad that NCCL should be unthinkingly cast by so many (not all) police officers as an opponent, because the effect is to mask two points. The first is that much of the work of NCCL in the direction of fairer complaints and disciplinary procedures is of value to the individual police officer as much as the complainant. To try to reform the kind of kangaroo justice described by Lord Hailsham in a recent case where a probationary police constable was dismissed on the strength of gossip and unsubstantiated allegations[1] ought not to be regarded as extreme. The second is that polarisation of the civil liberty issues in law enforcement as a police versus civil liberties needle match misrepresents the objectives of civil libertarians. The police have a great deal to learn in terms of increased professionalism and efficiency from greater willingness to acknowledge human rights, as both John Alderson's contribution to this book and Lord Scarman's investigation of the Brixton riots illustrate.

Nor is the image of NCCL that has been fostered by some politicians over Northern Ireland fair either to NCCL or to the people of Northern Ireland. NCCL's position has always been of demands to improve civil liberties not as a *concession* to violence but as a means of removing the genuine grievances that have led many otherwise well-motivated people to see no alternative but violence. If this view had met a response from politicians in the 1960s the resumption of violence in 1968-9 might not have occurred.

Perhaps it is invidious to single out a particular period in NCCL's history for comment, but the achievements of the last decade have been particularly worthy of note. The public impact of NCCL has been substantially increased; its views command more attention in the media and in Parliament. It would be difficult to imagine even a few years ago the alacrity with which the Home Office felt it necessary to respond, in detailed briefings, to the background material NCCL supplied to MPs during the Committee stage of the 1982 Police and Criminal Evidence Bill, or indeed the extent to which MPs drew on NCCL materials in the debate. The coalition of professional bodies that secured the governmental retreat on clause 10 of the Bill (the proposed power to compel the disclosure of confidential information) might well never have been galvanised had not NCCL mounted such an effectively organised initial campaign.

Over the last decade NCCL has built on its skills as a pressure group. There is a greater degree of professionalism in research (much of which is undertaken by NCCL's associated research charity, the Cobden Trust, which is itself celebrating an anniversary in 1984, its 21st) and fundraising, more effective co-ordination of campaigns with other pressure groups, and the development of a test case strategy few other organisations have matched. The latter has been a particularly notable achievement because of the singularly hostile environment offered by the British legal system to anyone attempting reform by litigation; a willingness to persevere with the excruciatingly slow processes of the European Commission and Court of Human Rights has also paid valuable dividends. Above all NCCL (and the Cobden Trust, through such imaginative prog- rammes as its teaching packs to promote civil liberties teaching in schools) has tried to increase civil liberties consciousness through the dissemination of accessible material on individual rights. A great deal of the credit for all this goes to Patricia Hewitt, who followed many distinguished General Secretaries and has in her turn been succeeded by an accomplished campaigner for freedom, Larry

Gostin; some of the latter's achievements in the field of mental health are described elsewhere in this book by Tony Smythe.

However the overall state of liberty is deteriorating in ways which make the efforts of civil liberty organisations both more vital and more depressing to sustain. To attempt an overall estimation of the state of health of civil liberties in Britain is a task beyond this book, let alone this introduction, and the idea of a comparison between 1984 and 1934, with so much that has happened to change the ground rules in between, has a faint air of unreality. The most I can sensibly attempt in taking stock is to identify some of the current trends.

My task in most areas is eased by the discussions of other contributors, but it is in the nature of things not possible to cover the whole spectrum of issues in one book. Two areas in particular receive less attention in the book than I would have liked, had it been possible to arrange contributions: the impact of racism (excluding the specific problem of racism in immigration control, which is the subject of Ian Martin's contribution), and trade union rights. Each deserves some brief comments, before I move to a more general gathering together of the trends highlighted by the book.

Prejudice and discrimination against ethnic minorities are not new phenomena, but both the extent and the consequences of discrimination have had a much graver impact on civil liberty in the last 20 years than hitherto. The rampant anti-semitism of the 1930s has fortunately receded, although there are disturbing signs of an increase in physical attacks on Jews and Jewish-owned premises. Much more serious is the tide of prejudice that has been generated against the West Indian and Asian communities whose families settled in Britain in the 1950s and 1960s.

Evidence of a degree of institutionalised discrimination is easy to point to, ranging from academic studies through official statistics to the all-too-palpable evidence that confronts any visitor to the nation's capital city of the pattern of employment of those members of the black community fortunate enough to be in work. Parliament has legislated three times in the last 20 years to control racial discrimination; the law now covers a wide range of situations. The Race Relations Act of 1976 looks on paper to be an effective weapon against discrimination, but for a variety of reasons – including the practical difficulty of proving discrimination, unwillingness to become involved in litigation, unawareness of the law, and the limited support that the Commission for Racial Equality has been able to give to individuals – the impact of the law has been minimal. Attitudes are too deeply ingrained to be easily or quickly affected by law. The statistics of unemployment among young blacks in particular indicate that the situation in the employment field is if anything getting worse. In other fields discrimination may not be as blatant as in the days of "To Let – No Coloureds" notices, but the more subtle social pressures remain at a level that ought to be regarded as intolerable, especially in the field of housing and in the conduct of the police towards young blacks. Nor are the pressures always subtle; extreme racialist organisations have provoked many acts of violence against members of minority communities and their property, and the response of the law and the police has too often been inadequate.

The difficulties of combating racialism are becoming greater, not less. It is a difficult task to convince many people, especially at a time of slump, not to find scapegoats for their economic misfortunes among those sections of the public who can be differentiated by colour, creed or language. It is precisely *because* the process is so insidious and so difficult to eradicate that a special duty lies on those in positions of power to make an effort to dispel it. With few exceptions the leaders of Britain have not only failed to do so but have helped to sustain and nourish racial ill-will by their actions.

This has occurred, as Ian Martin explains in chapter 14, in the field of immigration control, where successive administrations have constructed a system with racialist elements in its operation that go well beyond any requirement of a policy for restricting net immigration into Britain. It has occurred in the police; at the time this book was going to press in November 1983, the independent study of the Metropolitan Police by the Policy Studies Institute revealed a general tolerance by senior officers of the racist attitudes of their subordinates, and Scotland Yard's lack of sensitivity on the issue of police–black relationships has been illustrated vividly both by Lord Scarman's findings over Brixton and the extraordinary blunder of the Metropolitan Police in publishing a poorly authenticated racial breakdown of street assailants in a manner calculated to hand evidence on a plate to the National Front. Politicians' contributions have too often been in the style of Mrs Thatcher's remarks during the 1979 election campaign, when she referred to people's fears of being "swamped" by immigrants without any attempt to dispel the myths on which those fears rest. Within the ranks of her party, it is now almost fashionable to attack the Commission for Racial Equality as an interfering bureaucracy; the interference with individuals' rights to equal treatment that is the everyday experience of the victims of racial discrimination gets no more than a sanctimonious nod. There are of course many honourable exceptions; but the general picture is of an unwillingness to take a stand or to appear above the parapet. This is one of the basic issues of liberty that will continue to dominate the concerns of NCCL into the foreseeable future.

The freedom of individuals to work for the protection of their collective interests through trade unions is an important component in the civil liberties which NCCL has sought to protect. In many respects the decades since the Second World War have seen a relative strengthening of the position of employees, through their more favourable bargaining position in an expanding economy as well as the specific legal protection accorded to basic employment rights and to freedom to organise and bargain. But a substantial minority of employees have never enjoyed the benefit of these changes. Vulnerable groups, and workers in the least unionised industries (the two categories are synonymous, especially in the case of women workers) have not enjoyed the benefits of protective legislation. Such minimum wage legislation as exists, through the statutory Wages Orders issued by Wages Councils, is systematically ignored by a substantial minority of employers covered – illegal underpayment of wages has been found in up to a quarter of instances in surveys of Wages Council industries – and despite unfair dismissal legislation, job security in industries such as clothing manufacture and catering is at best uncommon.

The return of a period of serious recession and escalating unemployment over the last 4 years has of course undermined the security of both unionised and non-unionised workers, to an extent which underlines the relatively marginal effect of legislation on the protection of conditions of employment. Employment has become subject not just, as Government Ministers are apt to stress, to the discipline of the market place, but also to the financial manipulation of transnational conglomerates and the exploitation that inevitably occurs when there is unequal bargaining power. This is, in short, a time at which workers' rights to seek protection through the collective strength of trade unions are more important, not less.

Over the period since the war, the legal protection given to trade unions has been improved in significant ways. Over the last 5 years not only have many of those improvements been taken away, but some of the basic protection accorded to the liberty to take strike action in the political settlement with the unions of 1906 has been removed. Of course it is a popular belief that trade unions are over-powerful, and in a few sections of the economy this view may be valid. For the broad mass of trade unionists, however, legal protection has been no more than a counterbalance to the collective power of employers.

Some examples of the present state of the law and recent changes may be given. Statutory protection for individual trade unionists from victimisation by their employers, first introduced in 1971, has proved ineffective against employers' blacklists of trade union activists, and in its most recent decision on the scope of the law, the Court of Appeal found itself helpless to prevent an anti-union employer from arbitrarily introducing a redundancy programme in retaliation for a union recognition claim.[2] The limited statutory powers of ACAS to recommend trade union recognition were scrapped at ACAS's own request in 1980 in the face of the judicial battering they had attracted in the Grunwick affair and other cases. An obligation on government contractors to pay recognised union rates of pay, imposed by House of Commons Fair Wages Resolutions since 1893, was revoked in 1983, following the repeal of more general "Fair Wages" legislation in 1980. The Government's response to episodes of mass picketing, which were generally illegal under existing legislation, was to legislate further to restrict freedom of *peaceful* picketing, even by small groups, except at their own workplace. Trade union funds have been exposed to legal action by aggrieved employers twice, under the 1971 Industrial Relations Act and again under Mr Tebbit's Employment Act in 1982, reinstating the notorious *Taff Vale* decision of 1900 which had been reversed by legislation in 1906.

All of the debate on trade union reform has been conducted in the media in terms of trade union privileges or immunities. It is only a historical chance that this is the legal position, because what in many countries on the continent of Europe would be described as the right to strike was relegated to the status of illegality by Victorian judges imbued with the laissez-faire economic doctrines then fashionable. The political neutrality of the law has been achieved by the technical device of immunities, but sadly this labelling has clouded both the balance of discussion and much judicial interpretation of the immunities themselves. The recent changes in the scope of immunities risk dragging the law away from the neutrality towards disputes established early this century.

A final area for comment in this field is the closed shop. This is an emotional subject, often argued (particularly by the present Government) in terms of individuals' freedom of choice. Of course the freedom of individual conscience is important, but it would be more convincingly articulated by a Government which showed an equivalent willingness to protect employees from victimisation on account of their off-duty political activities, or to meet the conscientious objections of many committed pacifists (and others) to financing nuclear weapons.

Moving from these specific areas to a more general overview of the state of freedom as disclosed by the contributors to this book, I would assess the position as follows. On the positive side, considerable advances have been made in extending the necessarily limited freedom of mental patients; a greater public acceptance of the rights of women to equal opportunities and treatment has been achieved (but as yet far from implemented); and the legal and social treatment of the gay community has undergone the first faltering steps on a long road towards tolerance. Freedom of literary expression has become less constrained, the theatre is free of formal censorship and the broadcasting authorities accommodate a wider range of opinion than in earlier days. We are fortunate, for the reasons indicated by Norman Dorsen, no longer to have the death penalty.

On the negative side are all of the losses of freedom which stem from our intolerable level of unemployment and declining standards of public services such as health care and educational amenities. The brooding presence of nuclear power and nuclear weapons has damaged liberty and will continue to do so. Privacy is under an increasing from the threat from technology, and failure to respond to it with effective legal safeguards. Whatever efforts may have been made by the police to secure improvements in policing standards, the reality is of declining public confidence in the police and an increasingly siege-like mentality among the police themselves. The criminal process remains both inefficient and unfair in many aspects of its operation, and our penal institutions are in a state of decay and overcrowding that is a national scandal. We still lack an adequate framework of open government, and despite some welcome reforms on points of detail, the capacity of governments to manipulate information about their activities is growing steadily. In one part of the UK, Northern Ireland, the protection of liberty has been so far relegated to the attempt to control violence that denial of liberty is in danger of becoming the accepted norm, while the creeping extension of the "remedies" of Northern Ireland to the UK has had serious detrimental effects on the balance of criminal procedure.

On the institutional side too there have been gains and losses. Walter Merricks points to the improvements in access to legal services – although the picture is far from rosy. Our adherence to the European Convention on Human Rights has brought positive benefits on our domestic law, but on the negative side it has not yet been incorporated into domestic law to make the remedies it prescribes more effectively available; indeed to incorporate it would be a mixed blessing so long as so few senior British judges can inspire confidence in their capacity to carry out the responsibility for social policy-making that a Bill of Rights entails.

So the picture overall is, as might be expected, a mixed one. 1984 is not likely to be the cataclysm for civil liberties that a morbid attention to fiction might induce us to expect, despite the contribution to the erosion of liberty that the Police and Criminal Evidence Bill will make if it is enacted in its present (November 1983) form. However the omens for civil liberties over the next few years look decidedly worrying. Neither the economic recession nor the level of unemployment show any real signs of easing. This can only mean a continuance or worsening of the ill-effects we have already seen of a polarisation of society: the alienation of young people, opportunities for the fomentation of racism, and an aggravation of the divisions of the country by geography and by class. Such advances as we have seen over recent years in the protection of vulnerable sections of society are easily undone (the example of equal pay for women is particularly clear). Rights, such as legal services, that may depend on a degree of economic prosperity, are similarly vulnerable.

The last few years have also seen the growth of a significant political polarisation over the issues of nuclear weapons and nuclear war. Mass demonstrations and civil disobedience have become the hallmark of protest on these issues in almost all the advanced western democracies; the response of authority has generally been to espouse nuclear power and nuclear deterrence as matters of state interest, not to be trifled with by dissenters. Britain is no exception to this phenomenon, which as Duncan Campbell's essay vividly demonstrates, can lead logically to the ultimate absurdity that the defence of freedom does not admit of the exercise of the freedom purportedly being defended.

The polarisation of society also nurtures a more general intolerance by those in authority, who are more ready to apprehend a threat to the established order from dissent or unorthodoxy. There are plenty of straws in the wind which point to a more repressive response being prevalent already. Some examples can be taken, all of which have attracted publicity during the latter part of 1983. A woman in the West Midlands was visited by the Special Branch after she wrote a letter to a newspaper expressing opposition to Cruise missiles. The Chief Constable, although apologising for the particular way the matter was handled, defended the action as normal police practice. The Manpower Services Commission threatened to withdraw its grant from an unemployment advice centre in Aylesbury if CND or other "political" posters were displayed there again. The Ministry of Defence staged a special military exercise to practise a new system of censorship of reports of military operations. At the Royal Ordnance Factory at Blackburn, managers threatened to take disciplinary action against shop stewards if they publicly opposed proposals for the privatisation of the Royal Ordnance Factories. Each of these examples is the kind of bread and butter problem that NCCL has been dealing with for 50 years. Little has changed to remove the continuing need for its work, and there is every indication that an even stronger and more vigorous NCCL will be needed in the future to maintain the campaign for the protection of essential liberty.

A book of this kind makes demands on many people, and I have been fortunate in the response of everyone who has been involved in writing the book and preparing it for press. In particular I should like to thank the publishers and their staff, who have made remarkable efforts to ensure that the book is available on the date of NCCL's anniversary; the contributors, many of whom had very little time to prepare their essays in between often extremely heavy commitments; Patricia Hewitt, who gave me much invaluable help in selecting contributors; Linda Gage, who as organiser of the fiftieth anniversary celebrations has been an invaluable link with the NCCL and with many of the contributors; Chris Gane, Christine Jackson and Anthony Blond, who read and commented on much of the manuscript; and my wife Barbara, who helped me to avoid an excessive flamboyance in the chapter on freedom of expression, and put up with my neuroses during the more hectic stages of the preparation of the book. Finally I owe a special debt to Joan Kokle, my secretary, who prepared the entire manuscript for the computer typesetting needed to meet our publishing deadline, with sustained efficiency and care and without ever flagging in her enthusiasm. To them all, my thanks.

Masongill   PETER WALLINGTON
November 1983

NOTES

1. *Chief Constable of North Wales* v *Evans* [1982] 3 All England Law Reports, p. 141.

2. *Carrington* v *Therm-a-Stor Ltd* [1983] Industrial Cases Reports, p. 208.

PART I

The National Council for Civil Liberties

2

THE NCCL FIFTY YEARS ON

PATRICIA HEWITT

No-one who has been closely involved with NCCL for ten years, as I have been, can pretend to offer a detached account of its work. Instead in this essay, I shall give a brief outline of NCCL's founding and development – tracing in particular the continuities and changes between its first decade and its fifth – and offer an insider's view, but at the same time a critical one, of the organisation's strengths and weaknesses. In the space available, I cannot provide a comprehensive history, and the reader is referred to Barry Cox's study, *Civil Liberties in Britain*,[1] which covers NCCL's first forty years and on which I have drawn at several points in this essay, and to the brief history to be published by NCCL for its fiftieth anniversary.

NCCL's founding constitution committed the organisation

to assist in the maintenance of hard-won rights, especially freedom of speech, the press and assembly, from all infringements by executive or judicial authority contrary to the due process of law, or infringement by the tendency of governmental or other agencies to use their powers at the expense of the precarious liberties for which citizens of this country have fought

and stated that

the Council shall aid in advancing measures for the recovery or enlargement of these liberties.

NCCL was born at a meeting in the crypt of St Martin-in-the-Fields on 22nd February 1934, called by Ronald Kidd, a journalist and publicist who became the organisation's first General Secretary and whose own observation of police treatment of the Hunger Marches had convinced him of the need for an independent watchdog organisation. On one occasion in late 1932, Kidd was standing in Whitehall as the marchers arrived in London. A police cordon blocked off the march from the entrance to Downing Street. Two of the marchers, wearing "cloth caps and red handkerchiefs", encouraged their mates to attack the police lines and then promptly drew truncheons from their pockets, laid about them and started making arrests.[2] Convinced that he had seen police *agents provocateurs* at work, Kidd swore a statement in front of a JP and proposed to the meeting on 22nd February that a team of respectable, impartial observers should be present when the next march arrived. Amongst that first team were Harold Laski, H G Wells, Claud Cockburn and Victor Gollancz; others who lent their support included Clement Attlee, Nye Bevan, E M Forster, J B Priestley, Vera Brittain, A P Herbert, Aldous Huxley, Storm Jameson, Bertrand Russell and Rebecca West.

From the outset, NCCL saw its activities as belonging to a specific tradition of civil liberties – the defence of civil and political rights, such as freedom of speech and association, rather than economic and social rights, such as the right to education or a minimum standard of living. It was defending the hunger marchers' right to march, not their right to work. That NCCL's founders should have chosen these parameters for the organisation's work is not surprising: they were drawing on the dominant tradition of English political thought concerning the nature of liberty and the definition of the relationship between individuals and the state in terms of rights asserted against a state whose powers are strictly circumscribed. Within that Locke–Mill tradition, economic liberty is seen as the defence of private property, private capital and private enterprise against state interference, rather than the use of state power to guarantee certain economic benefits to all.

In terms of modern international law, the distinction is between the European Convention on Human Rights and Fundamental Freedoms, and the European Economic and Social Charter. Both deal with the rights of citizens and their relationship to government; the United Kingdom is committed to upholding both; but only the former is seen as falling within the definition of civil liberties. This traditional definition has not, of course, gone unchallenged. On an international level, it has given rise to considerable tension between competing definitions of human rights, between the so-called "first generation" of civil and political rights, and the "second generation" of economic and social rights. During the discussions which took place in Britain in the mid-1970s on the possibilities of a new Bill of Rights, it was argued by some, including Cedric Thornberry, former NCCL Executive Committee member and international human rights lawyer, that there were no good reasons for supporting a Bill of Rights which confined itself to the issues covered by the Convention, but omitted those dealt with in the Charter.[3] Nonetheless, there has been no serious attempt to extend the scope of NCCL's work beyond the field of civil and political rights indicated by the 1934 constitution, although the emphasis within NCCL's work has changed dramatically over fifty years, particularly with the recent development of forceful campaigns on women's rights and the rights of homosexuals and lesbians. There appear to be three main reasons for this broad acceptance of the definition of NCCL's purpose.

Firstly, civil and political rights are seen as being above any particular political party or programme; in defending freedom of speech, association and publication, for instance, NCCL's job is to hold the ring for contenders of radically different views, not to choose between those views. Defence of economic and social rights – such as the right to a job, or to a minimum income, or adequate education – would very rapidly, if they were not to remain mere aspirations, involve identification with particular economic and political analyses and programmes.

Secondly, a large part of NCCL's work (and that of civil liberties organisations in other countries) is concerned with justiciable rights, those amenable to being established in a court of law. Although it is clearly possible to think of economic and social rights as being made subject to legal enforcement, it has generally been felt that questions such as the right to a job depend far less on a legal framework than issues such as the right of assembly.

Thirdly, there is the practical question of ensuring that the organisation uses its limited resources as effectively as possible, without duplicating the work of other groups active in the field of economic and social policy.

That is not to say that the civil liberties tradition embraced by NCCL is without difficulties. NCCL's own history and traditional links with the trade union movement, which forms a substantial part of its affiliated membership, make it wary of embracing whole-heartedly the simple opposition between individual and state which is endemic in the Western liberal tradition. The difficulties of reconciling individual with collective freedoms are well illustrated by the debate within NCCL over the last decade and a half on the question of the closed shop, a debate which has never fully been resolved.

FREEDOM OF ASSEMBLY

From the first month of its work, NCCL established itself as a body able to mount major challenges to the authorities. In those pre-war years, you can find most of the crucial themes which have occupied NCCL now for five decades. You will find also the combination of tactics which continue to make NCCL an effective pressure group: the use of independent observers at demonstrations and marches; the test case strategy, seeking both to expose injustice and to change the law in the courts; the establishment of independent commissions of enquiry (usually where the government itself has refused to intervene); the consistent raising of civil liberties issues in both Houses of Parliament; effective research work, coupled with an ability to generate often embarrassing publicity. Even today, it is rare to find a pressure group which deploys this combination of lobbying, publicity and legal work.

As I have indicated, the impulse for NCCL's establishment came from the urgent need to defend the right of peaceful assembly during the mass unemployment of the early 1930s. NCCL's decision to maintain teams of observers to monitor the actions of police and demonstrators led also to the decision that NCCL should not itself organise marches or demonstrations – a practice which has been maintained, with very few exceptions, to the present. (The frequent caricatures in police journals of banner-waving NCCL demonstrators are, for this reason, without foundation.)

The first appearance of NCCL observers came two days after its founding meeting, which agreed a statement deploring the alarmist nature of warnings given by the Home Secretary about the violence likely to result from the hunger marchers' next arrival in London – fears which proved wholly unfounded. The first Annual Report recorded that it was agreed "in well-informed circles that this statement and its accompanying action had a very salutary effect in official quarters". Claud Cockburn offered the more cynical reflection that since "nothing whatever happened and since nobody could say what on earth might not have happened if our Council had not been on the spot, we became nationally known overnight".[4] Probably the most effective use of NCCL observers came during the Vietnam protests of the late 1960s. In October 1967, March 1968 and again in October 1968, NCCL sent teams of observers to Grosvenor Square. Their reports were analysed in detail to provide an overview of demonstrators' and police tactics. On the first two occasions, NCCL sent reports to the Home Secretary, criticising both the behaviour of many demonstrators and the police strategy and, in particular, the reckless use of police horses at the March demonstration. By the second October demonstration, NCCL was able to pay tribute to the conduct of the majority of both police and demonstrators, and noted that very few horses had been used.

The use of observers represents a highly practical commitment to defending freedom of assembly. Their independent evidence has enabled NCCL on a number of occasions not only to reach conclusions about the actions of individual police officers, and particularly the degree of police violence used in controlling or dispersing a demonstration, but also to make general comments about police strategy. There is some evidence that, although the Home Secretary and the police consistently reject in public the validity of NCCL's criticisms, these reports have helped influence police behaviour. Police handling of the anti-Vietnam protests changed significantly, and mounted policemen (the particular target of NCCL criticism) became far less prominent. In 1978, the Birmingham NCCL prepared extensive criticisms, based on observers' reports, of the handling by West Midlands police of a National Front rally and anti-racist counter-march. The following year, the Group was able to praise the police on a similar occasion for having learnt the lessons of their earlier mistakes.

NCCL's use of observers has, however, declined over the last decade. During the repeated clashes between racist and anti-racist marches of the 1970s – which constituted the most crucial test for freedom of assembly in the period – it proved impossible to organise teams of observers who would have a reasonable chance of being present at the crucial flashpoints between rival demonstrators or between demonstrators and the police, and at the same time be protected from serious risk of injury or arrest. On some occasions, observers would plaintively report that they had simply not been at the "right" place and had seen too little of the demonstration to offer useful information. In such circumstances, journalists' reports and television film provide a much fuller basis for a judgment on the occasion. NCCL nationally, and a number of its local groups, continue to organise and brief observers; it seems likely, however, that they will not regain their earlier importance.

NCCL's first year saw two crucial test cases on freedom of assembly, in both of which NCCL briefed members of its legal panel to represent the defendant. In the case of Mrs Duncan, a member of the Unemployed Workers' Movement who had attempted to hold a meeting outside an unemployed training centre, the court significantly extended police officers' powers of arrest.[5] Similarly, in the case of *Thomas* v *Sawkins*,[6] the court considerably extended the police discretion to enter any meeting where they believed some undefined offence might be committed.

Both cases, therefore, were a defeat for NCCL. Similarly, in 1981, when NCCL represented the Campaign for Nuclear Disarmament (CND) in a challenge to a three-week ban imposed on marches in London, the court refused to review the Metropolitan Police Commissioner's decision, holding instead that the ban would protect CND and other peaceful marchers from "hooligans" and "undesirable elements who wanted to disrupt them". In other words, peaceful marchers were to be "protected" from a non-existent threat by being forbidden to march at all!

The risk of a legal setback must, of course, be carefully weighed before NCCL decides to pursue a court action. But a test case, even if lost, may be of considerable value to the broader campaign. Just as the early cases were used by NCCL to publicise the vulnerability of the "right" of the public to assemble to police discretion, upheld and enlarged by hostile courts, the CND case was an important factor in NCCL's defence of peaceful assembly against the growing use by the police and the Home Secretary of their power to ban marches, conferred by the 1936 Public Order Act.

NCCL itself had warned at the time that the 1936 Act would dangerously weaken civil liberties, and that the authorities already had powers which they had refused to use against Mosley's Blackshirts. NCCL's fears were well-founded. The new banning powers were used extensively after the war to ban processions in

London, including May Day marches, and again in the late 1950s against rent protesters in north London and against the Committee of 100. But the election of the first Thatcher Government in 1979 soon brought an unprecedented use of bans. In 1981, a total of 29 banning orders were imposed – more in one year than the total imposed in the previous thirty years. The justification offered was the risk of serious violence arising from proposed National Front or other neo-fascist marches. But in no case was the banning order confined to the specific march or marches which gave rise to the threat of violence, and the speed with which the bans were imposed suggested that little, if any, thought had been given to the possibility of re-routing the march (as provided for in the 1936 Act) or policing the occasion in a manner which would minimise the risk of a violent confrontation.

Through the CND case, and a sustained campaign of publicity, leafletting and briefing, NCCL was able to expose the danger of bans to freedom of assembly generally. Despite the failure of the case itself, a number of banning orders were lifted, or re-imposed in narrower form. Even more importantly, many in the anti-racist movement who had eagerly sought bans against fascist marches came to appreciate the enormous threat to their own and other protesters' activities from the 1936 Act.

The worst confrontation between police and anti-racist demonstrators came in Southall, in West London, in April 1979, when a young schoolteacher, Blair Peach, was killed and hundreds of protesters and police officers injured. The occasion was a National Front election meeting, held under the provisions of the Representation of the People Act in Southall Town Hall, and a counter-demonstration planned by a number of local Asian community organisations. When the Government refused to establish a public enquiry, despite considerable evidence of wholly unwarranted police violence, NCCL established its own under the chairmanship of Professor Michael Dummett.

The Southall Enquiry was the latest in a long line of NCCL Commissions of Enquiry. The first of these to be published, ironically enough, was established in 1936 to investigate the police attack on a peaceful anti-racist rally in Thurloe Square, Westminster.[7] Both enquiries fulfilled the important function of providing as full and accurate an account of what actually happened as could be managed, thus challenging both the refusal of the authorities to accept the evidence of police misbehaviour and the willingness of the press to publish uncritically the police version of events. The Southall Enquiry, which produced two reports totalling nearly 250 pages, not only made detailed criticisms of the police strategy and offered an alternative approach to the occasion, but also argued for a series of changes in the law relating to election meetings, public order, incitement to racial hatred and the conduct of inquests.[8] English law on public order is commonly described as providing a "right" of peaceful assembly in the gaps between specific prohibitions on violent and disruptive conduct. NCCL's work over five decades itself provides a cogent critique of this view, suggesting instead that freedom of peaceful assembly in Britain is a constantly shifting and uncertain commodity, always at the mercy of the discretion of the police and authorities, and always in need of defence.

NORTHERN IRELAND

I have dealt at some length with NCCL's work on freedom of assembly because it provides a striking example of the continuity both of NCCL's task and of its working methods. There are, of course, many other parallels between NCCL's first decade and its fifth. A few months after its inauguration, NCCL was called on to oppose the Incitement to Disaffection Bill, a measure designed to counter "subversion" of the troops after the Invergordon mutiny of 1931. Uniting unexpected allies against the Bill (which was condemned by a leading conservative lawyer, Sir William Holdsworth, as a "most daring encroachment upon the liberty of the subject . . ."), NCCL forced the Government to amend some of its provisions. It seems likely that the vociferous campaign of opposition, although it did not achieve withdrawal of the Bill, made the authorities cautious in its use, and only one prosecution resulted before the war.

In 1972, however, the Act was revived for the prosecution of opponents of British policy in Northern Ireland, with the prosecution of Michael Tobin and, two years later, Pat Arrowsmith. NCCL's campaign against the revival of the Act failed, however, to gain the broad support it had enjoyed in 1934, J B Priestley for one refusing to take the stand he had taken forty years earlier. In 1974, fourteen members of the British Withdrawal from Northern Ireland Campaign were charged with offences under the Act and with conspiracy, in relation to leaflets which sought to tell soldiers who wished to do so how they could leave the army. NCCL acted as solicitors for two of the defendants in one of the decade's major political trials, which ended in a complete rout of the prosecution. All the defendants were acquitted – and once again, the Act disappeared from use.

In its renewed opposition to the Incitement to Disaffection Act, NCCL stressed the effects of the conflict in Northern Ireland on the standards of civil liberties throughout the United Kingdom. Similarly, in the sustained campaign against the Prevention of Terrorism Acts of 1974 and 1976, NCCL has been able to point to its earlier predictions that emergency powers in Northern Ireland would inevitably corrupt the administration of justice in the entire country. The organisation's experience of abuse of civil liberties in Northern Ireland goes back to 1934, when it established a Commission of Inquiry into the Special Powers Acts. (The secretary was Neil Lawson, later a Law Commissioner and High Court Judge.) The Commission, which reported in 1937, concluded that

through the operation of the Special Powers Acts contempt has been begotten for the representative institutions of government. Secondly, that through the use of Special Powers individual liberty is no longer protected by law, but is at the arbitrary disposition of the Executive. This abrogation of the rule of law has been so practised as to bring the freedom of the subject into contempt. Thirdly, that the Northern Irish Government has used Special Powers towards securing the domination of one particular political faction and, at the same time, towards curtailing the lawful activities of its opponents . . . The Government's policy is thus driving its opponents into the ways of extremists.[9]

The scope for defending civil liberties in Northern Ireland, and the resources devoted to the situation there, have varied considerably. During the 1960s, with a growing civil rights movement seeking to expose institutionalised discrimination against the Catholic minority, NCCL was able to offer considerable assistance, in 1965 organising a conference in London which brought together representatives from all the Stormont parties to discuss the issue, and in 1967 helping to found the Northern Ireland Civil Rights Association.

Originally seen as a non-sectarian group concentrating, through individual casework and lobbying, on electoral and judicial reform, NICRA became rapidly involved in mass mobilisation, organising protest marches for civil rights which soon came under violent attack from the largely Protestant police force.

After British troops went in to Northern Ireland in 1969 to protect the Catholic community against Protestant violence, and as relations between the British authorities and the minority community became increasingly violent, NCCL remained in the forefront of the campaign for civil liberties. The campaign against internment without trial (introduced in August 1971 by the Northern Ireland Government) and against the torture which had been used during the interrogation of several internees became a crucial priority for the organisation, which collated much of the information used by the Dublin Government in its complaint against the UK to the European Human Rights Commission. The following year, when thirteen unarmed civilians were shot and killed by the Army on "Bloody Sunday", NCCL not only compiled eye-witness statements for the official inquiry under Lord Widgery, but – disgusted by his exoneration of the paratroopers involved – sought the help of the International League for Human Rights (of which NCCL is an affiliate) in setting up an independent enquiry by American jurist, Professor Sam Dash. Using exactly the same evidence, Dash's enquiry came to radically different conclusions from Widgery's report, providing Members of Parliament, the press and members of the public in the USA and Ireland as well as in the United Kingdom with a strong basis for challenging the Westminster authorities.

Until 1974, NCCL sought unsuccessfully to establish its own office in Northern Ireland. Fears that NCCL would inevitably become identified with one or other community, together with the risk that NCCL would end up competing with existing organis-ations, such as NICRA, played their part, but the overriding barrier was the organisation's inability to raise the necessary funds either in the United Kingdom or in the USA. Instead, NCCL stressed the need to continue trying to educate the British Parliament, the press and the public to the civil liberties realities of Northern Ireland, and to build a lobby against internment and the Emergency Provisions Act.

By the end of 1975, when internment was finally phased out, civil liberties issues no longer appeared to have the primacy within

Northern Ireland which they had had either during the civil rights movement of the 1960s or the early 1970s. The organisation played little part during the campaign in Northern Ireland for "special category status" for prisoners convicted of scheduled offences. Both NCCL's consistent opposition to terrorist violence in Northern Ireland, and its support for the rights of prisoners generally, led it to refuse support for special status to one group of prisoners.

In 1977, when it became clear that the Government's new policy of obtaining convictions in the courts, coupled with the low standards provided by the Emergency Provisions Act for admissibility of confession statements, was leading police interrogators to use considerable violence against suspected terrorists, NCCL assisted Amnesty International in mounting a mission of enquiry which concluded that many of the allegations were well-founded. The changes in police practice which followed the Amnesty report, and that of the Bennett Committee,[10] established by the Government in response to the Amnesty mission, have been closely monitored for NCCL by the Cobden Trust, which now maintains a studentship at Queen's University, Belfast, engaged in continuing analysis of the operation of emergency powers and the behaviour of the police.

The hunger-strikers' campaign for special category status was marked by increasingly violent clashes between demonstrators and the security services, who had in 1975 introduced plastic bullets into their riot control armoury. Between April 1981 and September 1982, eight people were killed, four of them under the age of 16, often in circumstances where there was no evidence of any serious threat to the security services. NCCL commissioned Lord Gifford QC to investigate one such death, that of 15-year-old Paul Whitters, shot by an RUC officer in April 1981, as well as the deaths, in the same month, of Gary English and James Brown who were run over and killed by an Army Land Rover. His report, *Death on the Streets of Derry*, and the introduction of a case at the European Human Rights Commission on behalf of Kathleen Stewart, whose son Brian was also killed by a plastic bullet, were important landmarks in the campaign for withdrawal of plastic bullets and similar riot control methods from the police and Army. Despite the issuing of plastic bullets to mainland police forces after the rioting in the summer of 1981, a number of chief constables and police authorities have already refused to countenance their use, while in Northern Ireland their use has declined markedly.

The NCCL

CHANGING ISSUES

By no means all of NCCL's present work reflects so closely the organisation's early preoccupations. For nearly two decades now, concern with the administration of justice has been at the heart of NCCL's work. Perhaps surprisingly, the reports of NCCL's work in the 1930s shows much less concern with police powers and the operation of the courts, although the abuse of stop and search powers became an important campaign in 1936 and the use of the "sus" provisions of the Vagrancy Act 1824 also attracted the organisation's early attention. More recently, the rapid extension of the criminal law, rising crime rates and a growing concern amongst the police with public disorder and supposedly "subversive" political activities, together with worsening relations between the police and the black communities and a succession of proven wrongful convictions, have produced for NCCL a steady stream of complaints, on the basis of which the organisation now campaigns consistently for an overhauling of police powers and the trial process.

The persistence of NCCL's work on issues such as freedom of assembly and emergency powers is one of the organisation's strengths. Complementing that is NCCL's ability to move into new areas of work as a fresh injustice is exposed, or as new demands are made on the organisation's resources. In 1947, for instance, NCCL successfully initiated *habeas corpus* proceedings on behalf of a woman who, although never certified, was incarcerated in a mental ward. The woman was no isolated case, but one of thousands of people detained without legal control and with precious little prospect of release. A series of such cases, the publication of NCCL's pamphlet, *50,000 Outside the Law*, and a national conference forced the Government to establish the Royal Commission whose report formed the basis of the 1959 Mental Health Act. For several years afterwards, NCCL provided, through its national office and through local groups near the special hospitals, a service of representation at the Mental Health Review Tribunals established by the Act. By the early 1970s, however, MIND (the National Association for Mental Health), under the new directorship of Tony Smythe, formerly NCCL's general secretary, paid growing attention to the civil liberties of mental patients, and NCCL was able to wind up that area of its work almost entirely.

During the last decade, work against sex discrimination and

discrimination on grounds of sexual orientation has assumed a growing importance. In both cases, it was no specific case which led the organisation to change its priorities: discrimination against women in particular was already well documented, and NCCL itself had played an important part in the postwar campaign for equal pay (partly as a result of the personal commitment of its then general secretary, Elizabeth Allen). But the establishment of a Women's Rights Unit within NCCL was the result of growing pressure from feminists who appreciated NCCL's potential value as a legal and lobbying resource to the new women's movement. Similarly, the growing attention paid by the organisation to gay rights and the later appointment of a gay rights worker came at the insistence of a rapidly growing number of gay organisations affiliated to NCCL and vocal at its annual general meetings.

It has been suggested that the attention paid to these two issues is disproportionate, diverting resources from, for instance, work on Northern Ireland. Such criticisms often misunderstand the extent of work which NCCL has in fact carried out on other issues, particularly using the resources of its legal department, even where no specific campaign worker is involved. But it is also important to appreciate the effects of funding constraints on a pressure group's resources. The unpalatable fact is that it is possible to get additional funding (whether from foundations, statutory bodies or individuals) for some issues and not others. NCCL's women's rights work has in fact been specifically financed by donations raised from individual supporters of the women's rights work and by grants from the Equal Opportunities Commission and private trusts – in other words, money which would not have been available for work on, for instance, Northern Ireland, privacy and data protection, or freedom of assembly. The initial appointment of a gay rights worker was financed by one business supporter and continued briefly by donations raised within the gay community. Given the danger that availability of specific funds will override the organisation's own view of what the priorities should be, it is always essential for NCCL to avoid over-dependence on any one funding source, and to maximise its chief source of independent, general finance – that is, its membership and affiliation fees.

As an independent voluntary organisation, free from statutory duties, working in a broadly-defined area where priorities inevitably shift according to the policies and behaviour of the authorities, and with a small, enthusiastic staff eager to take up new campaigns or cases seen as urgent, NCCL can respond flexibly, and on occasion extremely rapidly, to new issues. But precisely because there is always more that NCCL could do than it has resources to achieve, it is inevitable that the demands placed on the organisation (whether internally by active members and affiliates, or externally by, for instance, a particular piece of legislation), together with the personal commitments of its staff and Executive Committee members (constrained by the fairly general limits of the policies determined by AGMs) will largely determine the allocation of resources from day to day and year to year. The price of being able to take on new campaigns may be a lack of consistency in pursuing old ones. And the ability to respond to members' and affiliates' demands may not be matched by an ability to move in new directions even where no such demands exist.

It is perhaps NCCL's greatest failure that, in a multi-racial society where institutionalised racism continues to be one of the most profound civil liberties issues, the organisation remains almost entirely white and unable to generate a consistent presence in the campaign against racial inequalities. Throughout its history, most of NCCL's staff and Executive Committee members have been white; and despite some changes in the last decade, the vast majority of members and affiliates' delegates attending annual general meetings are also white. Where the women's movement and the gay rights movement have had a forceful presence within NCCL, not only asserting a claim on the organisation's resources but also throwing up the individuals who have largely carried out the work they wanted to see done, the black communities do not exist as a "lobby" within NCCL.

In part, that reflects the absence of a black rights movement in Britain comparable, say, to the civil rights movement in the USA. But there is also an ambivalence, and sometimes hostility, towards NCCL from many black organisations. This is, in part, a product of the organisation's own policies on freedom of speech and assembly. Although NCCL was a leading campaigner in the late 1950s and early 1960s for a law against incitement to racial hatred, it later became ambivalent in its support for the legislation, noting that the law had in practice been used almost as often against black power activists as against white racists. Mindful of the danger of increased police powers and laws which curb the expression of opinions, however offensive, NCCL has consistently refused to endorse proposals for a new power of arrest linked to the incitement offence, or for an extension of the offence to, for instance, advocacy of repatriation.

On the question of banning marches, NCCL has steered a careful line between its traditional defence of freedom of assembly and its recognition that a fascist march may in fact be deliberately designed to provoke violence within a black community; while not adopting the American Civil Liberties Union (ACLU) position of defending without qualification the right of neo-fascist and anti-semitic groups to march in areas of their choice, NCCL has attacked the authorities' willingness to resort to bans, and called instead for more effective policing, and appropriate use of specific, limited bans only as a last resort. This compromise, while enabling NCCL to maintain the coalition of views represented by its members and affiliates, has pleased neither the purist advocates of freedom of speech, nor those anti-racists who believe that in this case free speech must be sacrificed to the rights of the black community.

This does not mean, however, that NCCL has been inactive in defending the civil liberties of the black communities. From 1959 to the mid-1960s, NCCL played a leading role in the alliance of white anti-racists and black community organisations which led to the passage of the laws against racial discrimination and against incitement to racial hatred. (The personal commitment of NCCL's then general secretary, Martin Ennals, who succeeded Elizabeth Allen in 1960, was of considerable importance here.) Since then, NCCL has been consistently active in opposing Britain's increasingly racist and unjust immigration laws: indeed, it was one of the first organisations both to oppose those laws and to defend individuals who suffered under them. Much of its work on police powers, and the need for an independent police complaints procedure, has been based on the experience of the black communities at the hands of the police (summed up, for instance, in NCCL's evidence to the House of Commons Select Committee on Immigration and Nationality in 1972; the Southall reports of 1980; and the evidence to Lord Scarman's enquiry into the events in Brixton in 1981). But the fact remains that NCCL has not developed a continuing and consistent relationship with black organisations; is not regularly seen by them as an important ally; and has not attracted them into active membership.

As an organisation whose national office is in London, NCCL has also been criticised, particularly by active members outside the capital, for its London bias. I have already referred to the unsuccessful efforts to establish an office in Northern Ireland. In Scotland, the organisation's failure over a long period to devote resources to the specific civil liberties problems in that part of the country, or to generate staff expertise on Scots laws, led in February 1975 to the establishment of an independent Scottish Council for Civil Liberties, affiliated to NCCL. Until recently, SCCL was able to obtain local funding to finance its office in Glasgow, and it has carried out a wealth of work based on daily experience of civil liberties problem in Scotland, which NCCL itself had never attempted.

Within England and Wales, NCCL now has 25 local groups, run entirely by voluntary activists and, for that reason, varying considerably in resources and activity. All take up civil liberties cases, while some provide a legal advice service. They campaign on civil liberties issues arising locally (such as the local councils' film censorship issues) and provide a vital dimension to national campaigns (for instance, by monitoring and challenging local Police Committees, or pressing for individual access to personal records held by local councils). Direct representation of NCCL groups on the Executive Committee goes some way towards redressing the over-representation of Londoners on that body. Apart from a brief period in the early 1970s when NCCL had an office base in Birmingham, the organisation has never attempted to run regional offices; such a development, if it were ever financially viable, would considerably strengthen NCCL's work.

NCCL's members and affiliated organisations provide the organisation with its policy-making (through the AGMs and the elected Executive Committee), the largest part of its income, the activists who staff the local groups and, to a lesser extent, the sub-committees and working parties which formulate more detailed policies. The affiliates also give NCCL access to a network of groups throughout the country, the largest of these being trade unions, but also including political groups, community relations councils, churches, humanist groups, peace organisations, gay groups and so on.

But NCCL's clout has never depended on the size of its membership. (An individual membership of 6,000 together with 1,000 affiliates can hardly hope to win by force of numbers.) Instead,

NCCL succeeds, where it does, by the force of its arguments, its identification of individual cases which reveal a general injustice, its ability to generate publicity, to create a conventional wisdom in favour of reform (illustrated, for instance, by growing acceptance of the need for an independent police complaints system), to embarrass the authorities and to build alliances on specific issues. The number of individuals and groups prepared to support NCCL generally is small, but there is enormous potential for winning the support of otherwise critical or indifferent groups on a particular campaign.

The scope for alliances is well illustrated by the organisation's campaign on the Conservative Government's 1982 Police and Criminal Evidence Bill, where NCCL was able to build opposition to important sections of the Bill amongst the churches, the extremely powerful medical profession, lawyers, journalists, black organisations, gay groups and an enormous range of other professional and voluntary organisations. The strategy not only forced the Government to make significant concessions on those clauses which threatened the confidentiality of personal records (to which the medical and other professions were particularly opposed), but also generated nationwide publicity about the Bill which had previously been entirely lacking.

Despite successes of this kind, NCCL's base remains far more limited than that of its sister organisation in the USA, the ACLU. Perceived as a considerably more conservative organisation than NCCL and generally accepted to be operating in defence of the country's constitution, ACLU has been able to build an extremely large and powerful membership, particularly but by no means only amongst the legal profession, which crosses party political affiliations. NCCL has never had the same success in drawing in members or supporters of conservative political views, and even Liberal Party supporters have been surprisingly few in NCCL's active membership. Although the British Conservative Party has a tradition of libertarian anti-statism, as well as a strong strand of tolerant liberalism, which should help to inform the civil liberties movement in Britain, neither tradition has found a home in NCCL. (The year after NCCL was founded, Vyvyan Adams MP was forced by the Conservative Party to resign his membership.) Only rarely (in, for instance, opposing an extension of the power of tax inspectors to enter private premises or the more general need for privacy legislation) have a significant number of Conservative MPs agreed with NCCL on identification of an issue; far more often, many Conservative MPs have identified as a massive threat to liberty a measure such as compulsory seat-belts on which NCCL's AGMs have remained agnostic.

Indeed, NCCL's early recruitment of a wide range of disting-uished supporters did not survive long. By the Cold War years, NCCL was widely regarded as a communist "front", and a number of Communist Party members were indeed prominent on the Executive Committee. (In striking contrast, the ACLU expelled its one communist Board member and one of its senior staff members actively co-operated with the FBI in its surveillance of "subvers-ives".) Detailed analysis of NCCL's record in that period suggests that there was, in fact, no attempt by the Communist Party to run the organisation in its own interests; the main campaign of the period was that on the Mental Health Bill; far more damaging to the organisation's actual work was a general appearance of inefficiency and weakness. But the allegation of communist influence remained alive, particularly within the right wing press and the Conservative Party, for several years.

Nor has NCCL begun to match ACLU's recruitment of lawyers (and, for good reasons, it has not wished to do so). One reason for this is that civil liberties litigation has, in the USA, produced a large number of lawyers committed to and expert in civil liberties (and often extremely wealthy!) for whom ACLU is a natural home. A more important reason is that the English legal profession, compara-tively small in numbers, extremely conservative in its habits, and consisting almost entirely of men from a narrow social background who are dependent on the approval of more senior colleagues for advancement, has been reluctant to identify with an organisation which is often regarded as undesirably radical and wholly lacking in deference to the establishment, if not positively subversive. For such lawyers, a more congenial home is to be found in JUSTICE, the British section of the International Commission of Jurists, whose ability to draw on the great and the good to generate quiet proposals for reform (such as its highly successful proposal for the Ombudsman system), as well as the outstanding work of its recently-retired general secretary, Tom Sargent, on cases of wrongful conviction, have been a valuable complement to NCCL's own approach.

To many members of the public, as well as many police officers, NCCL appears to be an anti-police organisation. It is perhaps an inevitable image for an organisation which often criticises police behaviour and which campaigned for an independent complaints procedure long before that became generally popular. The Police Federation itself has persistently caricatured NCCL as banner-waving, long-haired extremists, and the hostility of many of their members was vividly demonstrated on a *Man Alive* debate between Police Federation delegates and NCCL representatives in 1982. Sir Robert Mark, as Commissioner of the Metropolitan Police, refused to meet NCCL's then general secretary, Tony Smythe, and instructed his officers to cease sending full replies to NCCL correspondence.[11] It is perhaps surprising, therefore, that NCCL has in fact developed useful links with different levels of the police establishment. Since the days of Tony Smythe's general secretary-ship, staff and EC members have addressed courses at Bramshill College for senior inspectors up to assistant chief constables, as well as the training colleges of many forces. Sir Kenneth Newman, former Commandant of Bramshill and now Metropolitan Police Commissioner, has broken with Sir Robert's practice and met NCCL's general secretary shortly before taking up his new post. And NCCL's campaign for a new complaints system which would also protect the civil liberties of police officers – in particular, by guaranteeing legal representation at disciplinary hearings – has led to a fruitful, if limited, alliance with the Police Federation.

NCCL remains one of the few British pressure groups to have developed an effective test case strategy. A group like NCCL is always in danger of being overwhelmed with requests for legal advice. Instead, NCCL has hammered out an approach which allows it, on the one hand, to respond to an extremely large number of such requests (providing basic information and, where possible, referrals) and, on the other hand, to sift out the very small number of cases which will be pursued through the courts.[12] Within the last decade, such cases have been pursued not only through the British courts but increasingly through the European Human Rights Commission. Despite the inordinate length of time which it takes to reach a final decision in the Human Rights Court, and despite the fact that such a decision, although binding under the terms of the Convention, may only be acted on reluctantly, or not at all, by the Government concerned, Convention test cases represent an important source of publicity and, where successful, provide international legitimation of a challenge to British law or government policy.

In the last fifty years, NCCL has established itself as a permanent and important factor in British legal and political life. Its strength has been that of a radical pressure group, constantly challenging and opposing the establishment in the courts, in Parliament and the press. In a country where there is a growing gulf between the lip-service paid to liberty and the rule of law and the reality of daily injustices, abuse of power and the growing curtailment of legal rights, NCCL's commitment to civil liberties is widely perceived as subverting, rather than upholding, constitutional principles. The challenge for NCCL, particularly given the opportunities of its fiftieth anniversary, is to build a far stronger understanding of the meaning of civil liberties and to translate that understanding into active support for the organisation.

NOTES

1. Barry Cox, *Civil Liberties in Britain* (London, Penguin, 1975).
2. *Weekend Review*, 19th August and 28th October 1933.
3. See the unpublished memorandum by Cedric Thornberry, quoted in Peter Wallington and Jeremy McBride, *Civil Liberties and a Bill of Rights* (London, Cobden Trust, 1976).
4. *Punch*, 23rd February 1955.
5. *Duncan v Jones* [1936] 2 King's Bench Reports p. 218.
6. [1935] 2 King's Bench Reports p. 249.
7. *The Thurloe Square Baton Charge*, Report of a Commission of Inquiry (NCCL, 1936).
8. *Southall: 23 April 1979* and *The Death of Blair Peach* (NCCL, 1980).
9. *Report of a Commission of Inquiry into the Special Powers Acts* (NCCL, 1936, republished 1972). See also Dermot Walsh's discussion of the working of the Acts in chapter 19, below.
10. *Report of an Amnesty International Mission to Northern Ireland* (1978); *Report of the Committee of Inquiry into Police Interrogation Procedures in Northern Ireland* (Cmnd. 7497, HMSO, 1979).
11. See Sir Robert Mark, *In the Office of Constable* (Collins, 1978), p. 131.
12. Stephen Sedley's essay, which follows this chapter, provides an account of the approach in one case.

3

PIN MONEY: A TEST CASE ON DISCRIMINATION AGAINST PART-TIME WORKERS

STEPHEN SEDLEY*

Congress notes the increase in part-time working and recognises that this provides valuable opportunities for obtaining employment and for making a contribution to society for persons who might otherwise be denied both. However, Congress believes that the situation has been misused by employers to provide a source of cheap labour, particularly amongst married women.

Congress, therefore, demands . . . that greater job security shall be granted to part-time workers and that they should not be discriminated against in redundancy situations.

Congress calls on all affiliated unions to negotiate agreements to include these points, to endeavour to recruit part-time workers, to monitor their numbers and to campaign for the enactment of all necessary legal backing.

So resolved the 1980 Trades Union Congress.

This chapter is about the struggle to turn the TUC's good intentions into legal reality. Its heroines are fifteen women who, like thousands of other part-time workers, were the first to be sacrificed when redundancies were called for, but who fought back and won. It is about how a small and initially powerless group of people, aided by a campaigning organisation with few resources, can take on and defeat the inertia or opposition of larger and more powerful bodies. And it is about how a leading case on sex discrimination and unfair dismissal came to be decided.[1]

---

* The author owes a heavy debt to Brenda Clarke and Ann Sedley for their help in compiling and drafting this chapter.

In 1978 Eley (IMI) Kynoch Limited celebrated its 150th anniversary as a munitions manufacturer in the West Midlands. Although it was by now a subsidiary of the huge IMI Group, and although the world in 1978 was as riddled as it ever had been with conventional warfare and arms build-ups, Eley Kynoch was facing considerable financial difficulties and future uncertainties. One misfortune was that the technology of war had left it behind: the tracer bullets which it manufactured as direction-finders for the British Army's tanks had been superseded by laser beams. From 1979 it started to trim its workforce, and mobility between jobs within the workforce was heavily restricted. In particular the 300-odd part-timers, all of them women, were no longer able to transfer to full-time jobs when their needs and domestic circumstances made such a move desirable and possible.

In January 1981 the works convener, with the authority of his union, the Transport and General Workers Union, concluded a collective agreement with management on redundancy procedure. Clause 5 of it read: "Part-timers in the unit with redundancies to go before full-timers." After this, Clause 6 provided: "Last in unit first out." There was nothing particularly new in this. At Eley Kynoch, as in many other works, it had been the accepted practice for years to sack part-timers, whatever their length of service, in order to protect full-timers when redundancies arose. Before the agreement was finalised it had been duly put to the vote at a meeting of the TGWU membership of the workforce. The part-timers had been quite clear what Clause 5 meant to them in the impending redundancy situation, but they were in a minority and the clause was voted in. It was a fact which was to be constantly highlighted that the great majority of full-timers were women too. Understandably enough, each one as an individual was more concerned to vote to keep her job than to take a collective stand against a discriminatory mode of selection. It is interesting to note that the AUEW agreement on redundancies, concluded at about the same time, did not contain such a clause. All the production workers and the gatekeepers, both part-time and full-time, were members of the TGWU. The skilled engineering workers, far fewer in number, belonged to the AUEW; so far as was known, they were all men and all full-time.

In the mid-1970s Eley Kynoch had had 330 part-time workers. By January 1981, 200 of them had gone, and during 1981, 70 of those remaining had also been made redundant. The full-time workforce of 340 women and 140 men had, however, remained pretty constant: part-timers had carried the entire brunt of the company's recession. In April 1981 the 60 remaining part-timers, all of them women, were given notice of dismissal for redundancy, together with 46 full-timers, 26 of them women.

Sandra Powell was one of the part-time production workers. A young mother, she divided a long working day between child care, delivery to and collection from a playgroup, and earning the best living she could at the Eley Kynoch works at Witton. Brenda Clarke, a part-time gatekeeper, was in her 40s. Her two sons were now grown up and her husband had been made redundant, leaving her the sole breadwinner in the family. She had applied for a full-time forewoman's job but had not got it, and so she continued to work as a gatekeeper, sharing her hours with another part-time woman worker, Joan Clarke. For much of the time there was plenty of overtime, so that her wage packet was often not far short of full-time worker's.

In the early stages practically nobody perceived the dismissals as involving sex discrimination. At the mass meeting the clause which sacrificed part-timers first had been argued about as an issue not of sex discrimination but of basic unfairness. Both the union, at works, local and national level, and the management, persisted in the view that there was nothing sexually discriminatory in the collective agreement right up until the time when the courts held that they were wrong. And for Brenda Clarke the most striking facts were that she was being made redundant when her job was still going to exist, and that she was being dismissed after 14 years of service so that a full-timer who might have been there for less than a year could be protected. It made her angry. She telephoned ACAS (the official Arbitration Conciliation and Advisory Service) and was told that there was plenty of case law which held that she could lawfully be dismissed for redundancy even though her own job was still required. That was correct as far as it went, but it entirely missed the point. If, like thousands of others, Brenda Clarke had simply taken ACAS's answers as the end of the matter, a serious injustice would have resulted. But she did not. An AUEW shop steward to whom she spoke thought that she had a case because she was employed for over 16 hours a week, and suggested that she should look at Jeremy McMullen's book on employment rights.[2] She did so and read this:

"Discriminatory sacking and selection for redundancy are outlawed . . . and a dismissal on grounds of race, sex or marital status is also unfair . . ." For further information the book suggested, among others, the National Council for Civil Liberties. Brenda Clarke phoned the NCCL and asked if they had anything on part-time workers. They did have,[3] and a copy was sent to her by return.

NCCL's Women's Rights Unit had taken a decision in 1979 to initiate a campaign on the disadvantaged position of part-time workers, more than 80 per cent of whom in Britain are women. The booklet, *Part-time Workers need Full-time Rights* was published in 1980 as a first major step in the campaign, . At about the same time other groups were starting to highlight this area of discrimination,[4] and the EEC had issued a draft Directive[5] aiming to equalise the rights of part-timers and full-timers. The resolution passed at the 1980 TUC was a significant statement of principle, but it had shown few signs of filtering through the trade union movement into industrial practice. The next vital step for the NCCL was to demonstrate that although the law deliberately denied part-time workers many of the rights it accorded to full-timers, there were some areas where the law could be made to protect them. In particular the booklet contained this advice: "No redundancy agreement that allows for part-time workers to be first in line for redundancy should be concluded by a union. As most part-timers are women, this would be unlawful indirect sex discrimination. Last in first out should apply to all workers, regardless of hours worked." It also stressed the need for workers to deal with these issues through their trade unions, and for trade unions to ensure that part-time workers were properly protected in local and national collective agreements.

When Brenda Clarke, having looked at the booklet, got back in touch with NCCL there was hope that this would be the right case to test the crucial issue of whether sacking part-timers first amounted to unlawful sex discrimination. But there was no question of simply issuing proceedings. The first need was to see if by co-operation with the union the process of discrimination could be reversed.

Brenda Clarke had been upset from the beginning that the union of which she was a member had actually been responsible for making the arrangement under which she was to lose her job. She took it up with the stewards and the convenor, and getting no satisfaction there she went on to regional level. Two weeks before her notice of dismissal took effect, she received a letter from the Regional

Officer, saying that he had corresponded with the legal department of the union and continuing:

The agreement relating to selection for redundancy at IMI Witton [i.e. Eley Kynoch] does not appear to be sexually discriminatory in the opinion of our legal advisers . . . The union's policy is, that where a member goes to an outside body to pursue their case the union does not become involved. I am therefore informing you that the union will not be joining the NCCL (National Council of Civil Liberties) in representing you at the tribunal.

I am sorry that you will lose your employment as a result of these redundancies. It is a great pity that so many jobs are being lost within the West Midlands and the country in general at the present time.

The NCCL continued to correspond with the TGWU at both regional and national level during the summer of 1981 when their legal officer had taken over the conduct of the cases, but with no further result. In contrast with the earlier case of *Price* v *Civil Service Commission*,[6] which the NCCL had successfully conducted with union support, the union was not prepared to enter the proceedings in order to question the lawfulness of a collective agreement to which it was a party. Both the local Trades Council and the TUC nationally said they had no power to intervene.

It was one of the local MPs, Jeff Rooker, who came to the women's aid, giving them much-needed support and encouragement when none was coming from the union side. Hidden or indirect discrimination is not an easy concept. The Sex Discrimination Act 1975 contains a practical means of identifying it by a series of tests,[7] but in real life the problem remains of recognising that some of the injustices which seem simply to be facts of life are in fact ways in which women are silently but systematically disadvantaged.

It was therefore only when Brenda Clarke found her own way to the handful of "non-official" publications which were attempting to push out the frontiers of the employment and discrimination legislation that the relevance of sex discrimination began to be apparent. The fact that the operation of the collective agreement might be sexually discriminatory now provided a means of establishing in law the unfairness of her dismissal and perhaps getting redress for it. Perhaps the chief reason why the issue did not readily fall into place as one of sex discrimination was that there were women on both sides of the dividing line between part-time and full-time workers. The situation was certainly not on its face a typical favouring of men as against women. It took the company and the union much longer than it took Brenda Clarke to see the point. The company, for example, continued both at the Industrial Tribunal and at the Employment Appeal Tribunal to put the "women-against-women" argument at the forefront of its case. The reason why the argument did not afford an answer to an accusation of indirect sex discrimination is that it failed to dovetail with the statutory test. The statutory question was whether the proportion of women in the redundancy pool at Eley Kynoch who could comply with the requirement to be full-time was considerably smaller than the proportion of men able to comply with it. Of the 86 women dismissed, only 26, about one-third, could comply with the requirement to be full-time. Of the 20 men dismissed, all could comply. Viewed in that light, the fact that over 80 per cent of all the dismissals were of women loses any significance: the statutory test picks out the real issue, which is that women as a class of employees are disadvantaged when benefits of any kind are tied to full-time work.

Initially 19 of the sacked part-timers came to NCCL for help. Four of them dropped out, leaving 15, who stuck loyally together and saw the whole battle through. That in itself was unusual: the pressures to give up are enormous in situations like this, and although they had worked under the same roof, some of the women in the group hardly knew any of the others to start with. But a local law centre, the Saltley Action Centre, made its offices available, and at considerable cost in working and travelling time the 15 women came to a series of meetings with NCCL's legal officer and women's rights officer. There was an enormous amount to discuss and ascertain. The women were interested in the whole legal position; NCCL had to determine the factual position of each of them. Then by discussion and agreement the right test cases had to be found.

Sandra Powell was an obvious choice in the sense that her position was not only a typical one but was the least open to attack on the ground that she need not have been working part-time. With a young dependent child, part-time work was clearly all that she could manage. Brenda Clarke also wanted her case to be used as a test case, principally because she was determined to see the issue through and was prepared to pay the price of unwelcome publicity and criticism which it would probably involve. She also represented in her personal circumstances a still larger group of part-time workers: women who did not have children or whose children were now off their hands, but who for a variety of reasons connected with the work done by women and the social expectations with which they lived were nevertheless working part-time. It was important to ensure that any favourable decision included women like Brenda Clarke, who was by now her family's breadwinner, and the decision was taken to use her as the second test case. The solidarity which these meetings created was probably the single most powerful factor which kept the women together to the end. Without it, it is possible that most, perhaps all, of them would have given up.

One of the most vexed issues which came up at the meetings was the union. Brenda Clarke was firm in her view: their job was not to turn their backs on the union but to stay in it, support it and get it to stand up for them. It was not plain sailing for their helpers either. Both within NCCL and within the Equal Opportunities Commission doubts were raised as to whether the cases were viable. But the two test cases looked and felt right, and the pressure to go ahead carried the day.

The support of the Equal Opportunities Commission was necessary because legal aid is unavailable in industrial tribunals and NCCL could not have afforded to conduct a case of this size out of its own resources. The EOC, as well as being careful of its expenditure, was restricted by the Sex Discrimination Act itself to giving assistance for claims under the Act[8] – it could not finance the element of the claims which was going to proceed from sex discrimination to unfair dismissal and thence to reinstatement.

An originating application was issued for Brenda Clarke in May 1981. On 12th June, a fortnight before the dismissals were due to take effect, all the redundancy notices were withdrawn. It was likely that the respite was only temporary, and it was also undesirable to get involved in a cat and mouse game. Brenda Clarke's originating application was therefore amended, and a second one was put in for Sandra Powell, each of them now making the allegation that the continued existence of the collective agreement was itself a detriment within the meaning of the Sex Discrimination Act because it reduced their job security. Early in July the EOC decided to give limited financial assistance for the claims; and less than a fortnight later, as had been anticipated, a new set of redundancy notices was issued by the company with effect from 23rd October 1981. What had not been anticipated was that these notices of dismissal affected the entire unit at the works. Everybody was to lose their job regardless, and there was no longer any question of discrimination in the dismissals. Brenda Clarke, no longer eligible for EOC assistance, consulted a local firm of solicitors about pursuing her own claim of unfair selection for redundancy. It was rumoured that some or all of the redundancy notices were again going to be withdrawn before they took effect, but by the end of September there was no sign of it and the date for the hearings on 12th October, set as a matter of urgency so that the justifiability of the dismissals could be tested before they took effect, had to be abandoned. On 20th October, 3 days before the notices expired, the company withdrew a number of them.

The situation was now back to what it had been in April: a selective dismissal was taking place, and full-timers with relatively short periods of service were again reaping the benefit of the collective agreement at the expense of long serving part-timers, all of them women. The legal officer wrote immediately to the employers asking them to hold off the dismissals on the 23rd until an industrial tribunal could adjudicate. The company refused, but the fact that the request had been promptly made became crucially important later on. In mid-November the EOC gave full financial assistance to the two claims, and on 25th and 26th November 1981, they were heard before an Industrial Tribunal in Birmingham.

Not every Industrial Tribunal is a particularly good advertisement for the system, but the Birmingham tribunal was exemplary. A dense assembly of fact and law was sifted through and argued out in the course of two days. Brenda Clarke and Sandra Powell both gave evidence about their own circumstances. Brenda Clarke, despite her command of the history and the issues, was very nervous and was later angry with herself because of the things she had omitted to say. She would have liked to explain, for example, how other workers had used their authority to tell some part-timers they could and others that they could not go full-time. She wished that she had taken her husband's advice to go and watch an Industrial Tribunal sitting first.

The Industrial Tribunal's written decision, which arrived just before Christmas, was both a triumph and a shock. Sandra Powell had won and Brenda Clarke had lost. The Powell victory was of great importance. The Industrial Tribunal had found that to be full-time in order to avoid prior selection for redundancy was a condition or requirement within the meaning of the Sex Discrimination Act. They had gone on to find that a considerably smaller proportion of the women than of the men in the redundancy pool could comply with that requirement. They found that the requirement was not justified, even applying the low standard of justifiability which recent decisions of the appellate courts were setting. In particular they noted that both the personnel manager and the convenor had disclaimed any desire to stand by a sexually discriminatory agreement; that this addition to the ordinary last in–first out principle was unnecessary; that a majority vote which denied a minority its legal rights could not amount to justification; that the women-against-women argument missed the point that the Act was trying to deal with; that it was no longer correct or fair to assume that part-time workers were not breadwinners; and that the organisational and economic arguments for getting rid of part-timers first did not stand up. They also went out of their way to point out that the fact that sacking part-timers first was quite prevalent in industry was absolutely no justification for breaching an Act which had been on the statute book since 1975. But they went on to find that whereas Sandra Powell had in practical terms no option but to work part-time, Brenda Clarke for a few years past had been in a position to work full-time but had not made more than one attempt to transfer – in other words, they reasoned, she *could* have complied with the relevant requirement at an earlier date.

So far as Sandra Powell was concerned the Industrial Tribunal went on to reject the argument that the discrimination against her was intentional. It had been argued that by the time the second round of dismissals occurred in the summer of 1981, the company had been given the clearest possible warning by the NCCL that what they were doing amounted to sex discrimination, that by going on to repeat the procedure they were doing a deliberate act.[9] The Industrial Tribunal held that "intention" in the Act involved a desire to discriminate, and that that was absent in this instance, so that damages could not be awarded for the bare act of discrimination. That left the all-important question of redress. The Sex Discrimination Act is relatively toothless: if damages cannot be awarded, it is only possible for the tribunal to make a recommendation for remedial action or a declaration of rights, neither of which will solve any practical problems for the victim. But if it can be said, as this tribunal was prepared to say, that any dismissal which is discriminatory must automatically also be unfair, then all the forms of redress provided by the Employment Protection (Consolidation) Act 1978 become available, including orders for reinstatement in the same job or re-engagement in an analogous job, and full monetary compensation for the losses that have been caused. Sandra Powell was held to have been unfairly dismissed and was ordered to be reinstated in her job, with liberty to apply for any compensation which could not be agreed with the employers. The victory in her case was full and dramatic.

An appeal to the Employment Appeal Tribunal was immediately lodged against the dismissal of Brenda Clarke's claim. The employers shortly afterwards cross-appealed against the allowance of Sandra Powell's claim. But without waiting for their appeal to be heard the company reinstated Sandra Powell in her job. When she returned to work the full-time women with whom she was working sent her to Coventry. Then as 1982 wore on, with the appeals still pending, Brenda Clarke was offered temporary employment with the company and accepted it. She too was ostracised: ironically, such encouragement as there was came from the male workers. The full-time women thought that some of them were going to lose their jobs to make way for returning part-timers. In the event, the company found room for all of them and personal relations went back to normal.

In July 1982, again with financial support from the EOC, the appeal and cross-appeal came on for hearing before the Employment Appeal Tribunal under its President, Mr Justice Browne-Wilkinson. By this stage the live questions were these:

(1) Did the implementation of the "part-time workers first" clause apply a requirement or condition to either applicant within Section 1(1)(*b*)?
(2) Do the words "can comply" in section 1(1)(*b*)(i) and "cannot comply" in section 1(1)(*b*)(iii) include past opportunities to comply with the relevant requirement or condition?
(3) If sex discrimination is found, what is the standard of justification needed to establish a defence to it?
(4) Had the industrial tribunal erred in law in finding justification not established?

(5) Is an unlawfully discriminatory dismissal necessarily unfair?

There was no appeal against the industrial tribunal's finding that the discrimination was not intentional.

The translation of real events into evidence and of evidence into legal arguments is an unconvincing and artificial process. For the lawyer it brings tidiness and rationality to an otherwise incoherent mass of material, expelling emotion and introducing reason. For the applicant, listening in silence once she has given her evidence, it turns tragedy into farce, reality into fiction, deeds into words.

At the Industrial Tribunal there had been some sense of contact with reality. The evidence and the argument were dealing with concrete factual matters. Even there, however, some of the argument had been abstract and unreal, for example the debate about what amounted to a requirement or condition. At the Employment Appeal Tribunal the entire proceedings seemed remote to Brenda Clarke. It was like a dream, difficult to grasp or to keep track of. Somebody else was fighting her entire case for her and she felt a helpless spectator. The hearing took two more days in July 1982, and the Employment Appeal Tribunal reserved its decision, promising if possible to give it before the end of the month. But it was not until late September, when fears had developed that there was going to be a split decision, that the judgment was given.

The EAT found that the "part-time workers first" clause was a requirement or condition to which the indirect discrimination provisions applied. It found that whether a woman can or cannot comply with the condition related to the moment of time at which she had to comply with the condition or be dismissed: it had nothing to do with how she might have organised her life in the past. Brenda Clarke had won.

Next the Employment Appeal Tribunal held that although the standard of justification was the evasive standard of "reasons acceptable to right-thinking people" which the Court of Appeal had developed in relation to race discrimination, the industrial tribunal had found that the employers failed to surmount even that modest hurdle. They went out of their way to assuage the fear that this would mean that the ordinary principle of "last in first out" would also be struck down as discriminatory, since women typically have shorter periods of service than men for all the familiar social reasons: that, they pointed out, would undoubtedly be held to be a justifiable form of discrimination, whereas picking on part-time workers, over 80 per cent of whom nationally were women, was grossly discriminatory and unable to be justified on the evidence.

Then came the key issue of unfair dismissal, carrying the case from the largely cosmetic remedies of the Sex Discrimination Act into the harsher world of the employment protection legislation. The Industrial Tribunal had accepted the argument that it could never as a matter of law be fair to dismiss somebody in circumstances amounting to unlawful discrimination. On appeal it was clear that this argument had been put too high, shutting out the possibility of a freak factual situation intervening. Instead the EAT accepted that it would take very special circumstances to make a discriminatory dismissal fair, and that the evidence in this case showed no such circumstances. Once again the preparation of the case told: the painstaking correspondence which NCCL had conducted with the employers in the early stages of the dispute had put them clearly on notice that what they were proposing to do was unlawfully discriminatory; they had gone ahead in the knowledge that this was being alleged against them; and they could not now take refuge either in ignorance or in their own legal advice.

The victory was complete. Brenda Clarke's appeal was allowed, the company's appeal against Sandra Powell's successful claim was dismissed. Leave to appeal to the Court of Appeal was given, but the company took the cases no further. Instead the two test cases, together with the 13 others awaiting the decision, were remitted to the Industrial Tribunal for a decision on the appropriate remedies. It was by no means the end of the road: a substantial series of arguments on the complicated interlocking provisions for redress still lay ahead.

Shortly before the 15 cases came up for the last time before the Industrial Tribunal, the EAT without opposition gave the only two forms of relief available under the Sex Discrimination Act: a declaration that each complainant had the right not to be selected for dismissal for redundancy on the ground only that she was a part-time worker; and a recommendation that the employers forthwith renegotiate and within two months conclude a revision of the collective agreement on redundancy procedure made with the TGWU on 16th January 1981 so as to remove from it any provision which unlawfully discriminates against women. The agreement was finally revised by the agreed removal from it of clause 5.

Two more days in February 1983 were taken up in the Industrial Tribunal with the arguments about redress. All 15 applicants now had the benefit of a finding that they had been unfairly dismissed and unlawfully discriminated against at the time of their dismissals for redundancy in October 1981. Sandra Powell needed no further remedies. Cash settlements were agreed for four more. Three others had resumed work with the company the month before with continuity of service established. The company argued that some of the women had failed to reduce their losses by resuming work as general labourers when it was offered by the company in January 1983. Four of them had declined to go back because they were afraid of the working conditions to which they might be assigned. The chemical powder was known to turn the hair and skin green; there were flash fires, and one of the women had previously been injured in one; another of the women had developed a trigger finger condition. The Tribunal decided that the refusal was reasonable in the two graver cases, but unjustified in the cases of the two women whose reasons were fear rather than experience!

But the major argument was still to come. Two of the women, Brenda Clarke and Joan Clarke, wanted their jobs as gatekeepers back. Two more, Sheila Standley and Beryl Parry, wanted to be reinstated in their jobs in the centre fire production area. The company was only prepared to offer the four of them jobs as general labourers, and claimed that this was all that they had ever been, with an option in the company to assign them to specific tasks at will. The Industrial Tribunal rejected this contention: it found that it was only since the dismissals in October 1981 that the company had begun employing people on a "mobility clause" basis. So far as concerned Sheila Standley and Beryl Parry, their old jobs had gone; the only re-engagement which was practicable was as general labourers; and neither woman wanted to take the physical risks involved. For Sheila Standley, who had a heart condition, the Tribunal accepted that heavy work was not realistic, and made a recommendation under the Sex Discrimination Act that the company during the next 12 months should seriously consider her for re-engagement as a general labourer in any job that became available and which did not involve heavy lifting and moving of materials. For Beryl Parry, who was one of those whose objections to the cap priming work were thought to arise from fear rather than experience, it was held that she was not justified in picking and choosing. Her case, and that of Winifred

Burgess who was also frightened of the powder work, had the saddest results, although neither went wholly uncompensated.

Brenda Clarke's and Joan Clarke's jobs as gatekeepers, said the company, no longer existed and that was an end of the matter: they could not be reinstated. The jobs had been merged with those of the firemen, following the 1981 dismissals, when the site fire brigade had been disbanded. The full-time women who had initially been put on to the gates in the "bumping" redundancy had in turn been moved to make way for two ex-firemen. Brenda Clarke argued that there was no obvious need for the firemen to be put on gatekeeping duties in order to be available if fires occurred: indeed, it was arguable that they would be less use there than if they were on production work. The description given by the personnel manager of how the gatekeepers and the rest of the workforce would now be responding to a fire had a Keystone Cops air about it and the company failed to convince the tribunal that there was no reasonable alternative to the system which they had adopted.

What was even more remarkable was that the third of the newly created posts of fireman/security man had remained unfilled for most of the intervening period, and in January 1983 had been internally advertised – but as open only to permanent employees. Brenda Clarke was by then working for the company again, but only as a temporary employee. One of the reasons she had come back to temporary work in March 1982 had been an indication that she would then be better placed to apply if a gatekeeper's job came up; but when it did come up she was unable to apply. At the time of the internal advertisement there were 19 temporary employees on the payroll, 16 of them women, and 290 permanent employees, half of them women. It did not seem to have occurred to the company, after all that they had gone through, that they might be committing a fresh act of sex discrimination by limiting applicants to permanent employees.

The Industrial Tribunal concluded that there was no good reason why Brenda Clarke and Joan Clarke should not go back, as they were now willing and able to go back, as full-time gatekeepers under an order for reinstatement. Once again, careful correspondence came to the applicants' aid. After the EAT victory the company had again been urged not to reorganise the workforce so as to prejudice possible reinstatement.

Even if difficulties of practicability legitimately arise for our consideration [said the Industrial Tribunal], we unhesitatingly exercise our discretion in favour of the applicants. We recognise that almost certainly it would cause a considerable dislocation and inconvenience to the Respondents to replace the firemen/security men by a fireman/service man so leaving the gatehouse free. That, however, is something which is entirely of the Respondents' own making, having wilfully disregarded the requests of the applicants' representatives not to take the precipitate steps which might prevent reinstatement or re-engagement.

So, using their powers under the Employment Protection (Consolidation) Act 1978 in pursuance of the finding of unfair dismissal, the Industrial Tribunal ordered that Brenda Clarke and Joan Clarke be re-engaged as full-time gatekeepers within 14 days of the decision, having all the rights and privileges which they previously enjoyed. They added a recommendation to the same effect under the Sex Discrimination Act, silently pointing up the difference in real effectiveness between the two statutes.

Her second appearance in the witness box had been a much better experience for Brenda Clarke. She felt more self-confident, gave her evidence better, and said what was relevant and necessary. Beryl Parry, by contrast, called the experience the worst few minutes of her life. For Brenda Clarke too the case had been a heavy burden. Perhaps the greatest deterrent to embarking on a claim at all had been the fear of being cross-examined and of being the subject of publicity. To an extent her fears were realised. People ridiculed her for taking the case on, saying that victimisation of part-timers went on everywhere in Birmingham and that she was not going to be able to stop it. The case became overwhelming, even though she had lawyers conducting it for her. For whole nights she could not sleep; she likened it to being ill. She would have felt isolated were it not for her husband, her fellow claimants and the NCCL staff who were supporting her. But in turn she felt a sense of responsibility for all of them, and also for Sandra Powell who without Brenda's encouragement would probably not have gone ahead by herself. The others were all more afraid than Brenda, and she had to try to keep their morale up as well as her own.

Something which lawyers constantly overlook, and which other advisers and campaigners need to have in mind, is how frightening the average person finds the prospect and the experience of giving evidence. For many women, given the image and expectations which they learn to have of themselves, this is especially so. That is why the support which these fifteen women gave each other, and the support which NCCL was able to give them, was probably decisive in enabling the cases to be fought through to a conclusion.

Looking back, Brenda Clarke felt that perhaps the worst thing of all was that it took two years to establish her right to keep her job. For her advisers, by contrast, the two years were time relatively well spent: it is not in many cases that law and justice can be brought into a satisfactory constellation.

Brenda Clarke, Sandra Powell and the others are now not only accepted but respected in the workforce. Throughout the period of the claims, newspaper publicity brought part-time women workers in other factories in the Midlands into contact with Brenda Clarke, making the creation of a Part Time Workers Campaign possible. Other firms in the Midlands have been persuaded by the results of the case to revise their own collective agreements so that they do not discriminate against part-timers. It is known that hundreds of jobs have already been saved in this way.

Much later the union's national officer with responsibility for women, Marie Patterson, went to explain the result to the full-time women shop stewards. They resented legal interference with what they felt was a democratic decision, and they argued that full-timers also brought up children without the "privileges" of part-timers. Ms Patterson herself thought it a misfortune that a workplace had been chosen where women did most of the full-time as well as the part-time jobs: a straightforward male/female divide would have provided a more suitable test case. As to collective redundancy agreements with a "part-timers first" clause in other works and areas, local officials had been notified about the case. But, she says, "We can't monitor them. We're not a research unit. We move on to the next job."

For all the women who have returned to work for Eley Kynoch morale has greatly improved. They have won back an hour which the company docked from part-time workers' standard hours, something that they would never have done before. For both Brenda Clarke and Sandra Powell there has also been a lift in their own self-confidence. Brenda Clarke in her restored job is undertaking new functions traditionally reserved for men.

Looking back, there were several indispensable elements: first and foremost the initiative and determination of the women who fought the test cases and those who supported them; then the existence of a campaigning organisation with whom they could make contact and which was in a position to help and support them and to take their case up; an imaginative approach to the unexciting letter of the law; and, it has to be said by good fortune, tribunals at both levels which wanted to do justice and to make the equality legislation work. Looking forward, Brenda Clarke and Sandra Powell and their 13 fellow workers are not the only ones who have learned from the experience that people can fight back and influence their own fate and that the law can sometimes provide the means of doing so. Both women remain loyal members of their union; but for the union, as well as for the employers, it may be that there is a lesson still to be learned.

NOTES

1. *Clarke and Powell* v *Eley (IMI) Kynoch Ltd.* [1983] Industrial Cases Reports p. 165.
2. Jeremy McMullen, *Rights at Work* (Pluto Press, 1979).
3. Ann Sedley, *Part-time Workers Need Full-time Rights* (NCCL Rights for Women Unit, 1980).
4. For example *Mrs. Hobson's Choice* (Welsh Women's Aid, 1980); Jennifer Hurstfield, *Part-time Pittance* (Low Pay Unit Review No. 1, 1980).
5. COM (81) 775.
6. [1978] Industrial Cases Reports, p. 27 (Employment Appeal Tribunal); [1978] Industrial Relations Reports, p. 3 (Industrial Tribunal).
7. Section 1(1)(*b*): "A person discriminates against a woman . . . if . . . he applies to her a requirement or condition which he applies or would apply equally to a man but (i) which is such that the proportion of women who can comply with it is considerably smaller than the proportion of men who can comply with it, and (ii) which he cannot show to be justifiable irrespective of the sex of the person to whom it is applied, and (iii) which is to her detriment because she cannot comply with it."
8. Section 75.
9. Section 66(3) of the Act provides: ". . . no award of damages shall be made if the respondent proves that the requirement or condition in question was not applied with the intention of treating the claimant unfavourably on the ground of his [*sic*] sex . . .".

PART II

The Classic Issues

4

FREEDOM OF SPEECH

PETER WALLINGTON

Give me the liberty to know, to utter, and to argue freely, according
 to conscience, above all liberty.

(Milton, *Areopagitica* (1644).)

Members of the jury, would you let your servants read this book?
(Mervyn Griffiths Jones QC, Counsel for the Prosecution, in the
Lady Chatterley's Lover case, 1961.)[1]

It seems that arguments and attitudes to freedom of speech have
changed little over the centuries, even though the capacity of
mankind to communicate has continually developed and latterly
been revolutionised. The case for freedom of expression is indeed the
same as in Milton's day. Its strength, however, is even greater in an
age in which the capacity to communicate and the state's ability to
conceal are both so much enhanced. In this essay I shall attempt to
paint an overall picture of the extent to which freedom of expression
is a reality in Britain today. To anticipate my conclusion, I believe
we have significantly less freedom of expression either in law or in
practice than is generally believed, that on balance that freedom is
declining and that the threats to its preservation are real and
imminent.

It is as well to begin with a reminder of the justifications of
freedom of speech. It might be thought that the issues have been well
enough articulated over the years, both before and since Milton's
celebrated (but unsuccessful) attack on press censorship in 1644, that
an attempt to reformulate the case for free speech would be

redundant as well as arrogant. It was certainly well enough understood by the men and women who came together in 1934 to found the NCCL in response to police attacks on the hunger marchers. Nor do I pretend to have anything new to say here. Nevertheless if we are to understand how far law and practice fail to protect freedom of expression, it is important to remind ourselves first of *what* it is, then of *why* it is of value to society and to individuals, and hence finally of *what criteria* can legitimately be used to set its limits where it collides with other rights and freedoms.

ABOVE ALL LIBERTY?

The liberty to speak and write is a necessary part, but not necessarily the most important part, of the concept of freedom of expression. To protect *only* the freedom of the author or speaker could be to engage in little more than self indulgence. The state need not prosecute playwrights if it can close theatres, or censor journalists if it can control official information. Control over the extent of dissemination of ideas and information may be a more effective, and is certainly a much easier, form of suppression of freedom. Freedom of expression is in essence two freedoms acting in tandem: the freedom of those who have ideas and information and opinions to voice them publicly, and the freedom of the public to have access to information, and to the ideas and opinions of others. Real freedom of speech must involve an *opportunity* to speak, and an *opportunity* to hear.

The need for freedom of speech tends to be taken for granted by those who are able to partake of it. I suspect it is for this reason that many such people advocate restrictions on forms of expression they happen to find alien or offensive, without realising the hypocrisy that this involves. That part of freedom of speech that we take for granted is in some ways the least important, because it is least under threat – and that is because it is not seen as a threat in itself. The freedom that *is* worth something is the freedom of the unknown, the innovatory, the eccentric, the hateful or obnoxious idea. The paradox of freedom of expression is that it is both a precondition of democratic government and not susceptible to normal principles of majoritarian regulation: it serves democracy but is not subservient to it. This was put by Mill in the following well-known proposition: "If all mankind minus one, were of one opinion, and only one person were of the contrary opinion, mankind would be no more justified in silencing that one person, than he, if he had the power, would be in silencing mankind."[2] This may sound like the libertarian rhetoric of a comfortable middle class intellectual, but to dismiss it is to dismiss the lessons of history. It may be true that there is nothing so powerful as an idea whose time has come, yet from Copernicus to the Suffragettes there is ample evidence that fear and violent hostility are common responses to ideas whose time is just over the horizon. Issues of current controversy, such as the long-term genetic effects of radiation from nuclear waste, should serve to remind us to preserve a due sense of humility over the rightness of "received opinion" on any issue.

Just as it is unpalatable ideas that most need protection, so it is society's attitude to unconventional channels of communication that is a yardstick of the extent of freedom of expression. Limitations on opportunities to communicate ideas leave the streets as the last – in some cases the only – channel of communication for those with deeply felt grievances beyond the mainstream of "acceptable" views. I shall not be dealing with freedom of assembly in much detail in this essay, because it is fully covered by Patricia Hewitt, but its place in the overall picture should not be overlooked.

Many people see freedom of speech primarily in terms of intellectual and artistic freedom, the liberty of the creative author or playwright to explore new dimensions in human thought and emotions. This is then contrasted to the philistine responses of those who seek to suppress anything which undermines contemporary social taboos. There is, indeed, often a patronising elitism in the responses of the aspirant censors, nowhere better illustrated than in the gaffe of prosecuting counsel in the *Lady Chatterley* case quoted at the beginning of this chapter. It is an attitude apparently shared by many of those who struggle to maintain a degree of control over the disclosure of information about the processes and decision-taking of government. The attitude was candidly displayed in this revealing remark by the eminent and respected judge Lord Reid, ironically in the course of a judgment significantly curtailing the state's power to suppress information relevant to litigation: "The business of government is difficult enough as it is and no government could contemplate with equanimity the inner workings of the government machine being exposed to those ready to criticise . . ."[3]

Those who adopt these attitudes usually mean well, but the

attitudes serve to perpetuate a system which denies the reality of democracy by concealing the wherewithal of informed criticism and choice, and the reality of freedom by constraining the free evolution of thought.

Of course freedom of expression cannot override all other interests, and the need for some limitation in the interests of, for instance, the protection of an individual's reputation from malicious and untrue allegations would be generally accepted. The line between generally accepted limits and majoritarian dictatorship is a thin and uneasy one, as is the line between paternalist interference and the protection of legitimate interests. The question how far there should be freedom of expression for racialist views is a particularly clear example. A yardstick, though in itself a question-begging one, can be taken from the European Convention on Human Rights. Article 10 of the Convention sets out in forthright terms the basic premise of freedom of expression: "Everyone has the right to freedom of expression. This right shall include freedom to hold opinions and to receive and impart information and ideas without interference by public authority and regardless of frontiers." The Article then sets out extensive grounds on which interference with these rights is permitted, but qualifies them all with the critical words that they must be both "prescribed by law" and "necessary in a democratic society". How far our own law and practice can match these conditions is a good starting point for an evaluation of freedom of expression in the UK.

THE COMMUNICATIONS REVOLUTION

Public television services did not exist fifty years ago, radio was a precociously conservative infant, and sound tracks had just started to appear in the cinema. The speed of change in the technical capacity of the various media of communication has continued to accelerate to an almost bewildering extent, with the advent in turn of computer typesetting of books and newspapers, electronic transmission of business data, home video recorders and CB radio, and with satellite and cable television services poised in the wings. At the same time as there has been a revolution in the technology of telecommunications, the wider technological changes of which it is a part have created a massive extension of the capacity to gather data, with all the implications for privacy this involves[4] There has also been a steady decline in support for and participation in more traditional methods of communication, most notably the political meeting.

Some of the particular consequences, problems and opportunities created by technological developments will be discussed later. Here I wish to pinpoint three: the internationalisation of channels of communication, the concentration of control and the growth of opportunities for selective disinformation.

The development of our capacity both to circumnavigate the globe and to destroy it has made both possible and necessary a much closer economic and cultural relationship between states and between peoples. We no longer have a government which can act independently of its neighbours and allies. Corporate capital transactions now operate across national boundaries with almost the same freedom, across perhaps two thirds of the world, as they might have been expected fifty years ago to operate across the state boundaries in the USA. Inevitably this phenomenon has its counterpart in the communication of information. News from virtually anywhere in the world may be of direct relevance to us, and its instantaneous transmission to our living-rooms excites no surprise in itself. But the availability of the information may be entirely dependent on the political attitude to the dissemination of news of the authorities of the state concerned. Access to information is no longer the prerogative of our own government to delineate.

This may also be true of information possessed by the British government. Military information in particular may be the "property" of an alliance, and collaboration in areas such as the development of nuclear power is likely to involve a shared responsibility for the disclosure or suppression of information. To the extent that governments' own access to information about the corporate planning of multinational corporations is curtailed, so too is the right of public access through government.

The sophistication of technology has of course contributed to the trend towards the concentration of capital resources into fewer, larger units that is apparent in most aspects of life. This is mirrored in areas such as the press and publishing, where a steady flow of mergers and takeovers has created a worrying concentration of ownership (often as a subsidiary to other commercial enterprises). This has had the effect of sharply reducing the range of choice of publications, at least as far as newspapers are concerned.

This process is apparent also in other areas of mass communication. While the arrival of the home video industry might look like a small businessman's dream, the technology of cable and satellite television transmission necessitates large financial consortia to provide the services. However diverse the range of programme making companies, for each town within a franchise area, cable TV will be a monopoly product. The effect of growing monopoly in the ownership of the various channels of communication is increased by often close links between companies and consortia working in different fields of communications. We have also seen since the war the establishment of a virtual duopoly in the commercial cinema in Britain.

The most worrying feature of these trends is that at the same time the great majority of the population has no effective access to sources of information, and particularly political information, except through the media of TV and radio and the mass circulation newspapers. As their ownership or control is concentrated and becomes decreasingly accountable, so the danger of the kind of programmed disinformation about which Orwell wrote in *1984* becomes, albeit in more subtle forms, a real risk of the real 1984.

THE MEDIA TODAY

The Press The British press is, by international standards, relatively free from formal censorship and external interference. Formal censorship has not operated, in peacetime, since the seventeeth century. But this is not necessarily an accurate indicator of how "free" our press is. As I shall explain, the existence of laws of uncertain dimensions in the fields of defamation and contempt of court can have an inhibiting effect that may be less definable but is nonetheless as real as a system of formal censorship. In one particular area, that of government information, the inhibiting effect of the law has been institutionalised through the Services, Press and Broadcasting Committee, and the D-notices it issues, into a semi-formal system of joint self-censorship and imposed controls.

The Official Secrets Act 1911 makes it an offence for any officer of the Crown to disclose *any* unauthorised information, and also makes the knowing receipt and reporting of the information by journalists an offence.[5] In the field of security-sensitive information,

D-notices replace the uncertainty of possible prosecution with a certain system of agreed restrictions on reporting. However the Official Secrets Act has proved to be a dangerous weapon for the Government to use against the press, and in a number of instances the more radical sections of the press have flouted D-notices without being prosecuted. The system is a collaborative one which probably reflects the wishes of the editors and proprietors of the mainstream media to err on the side of caution in protecting military secrets. Imposed regulation, in this and in other areas, is made unnecessary by compliance.

The fact that the press is relatively free of external constraints does not mean that it is properly performing its function of providing a forum for the dissemination of a broad range of information and opinion. To the extent that the press, along with radio and television, fails in this task, the prospect of an informed, democratic political process is diminished. The charges levelled against the press in these respects are familiar: right-wing bias, selective reporting and trivialisation of complex issues, and in the other direction a failure to control excessive intrusions into the privacy of individuals in the quest for "news" of dubious public interest. This is not the place to re-examine in detail the arguments on these issues.[6] Important aspects of civil liberties conflict in this area – the freedom of proprietors and editors to express opinions and select news against the freedom of others to gain access to the press to correct misinformation, and the freedom of the public to have access to information against the freedom of public figures to preserve a degree of personal privacy are examples. It is also disingenuous to imagine that a free press will be free of any bias towards the existing distribution of power and privilege, so long as in practical terms only those in positions of power and privilege can sustain the operation of a mass circulation newspaper. However there are trends, evident in the recent history of *The Times* and *The Sunday Times*, which give pause for thought.

In 1981 both *The Times* and *The Sunday Times* were taken over by Mr Rupert Murdoch's News International Ltd. Mr Harold Evans, then editor of *The Sunday Times*, was appointed editor of *The Times* shortly afterwards. Considerable concern over the takeover was expressed in Parliament, not least because of the standing of *The Times* as a national newspaper of record. Mr Murdoch's company already owned the *Sun* and the *News of the World*, and the increased concentration of ownership was such that it would normally have been necessary to refer the takeover to the Monopolies Commission for its independent assessment of the public interest in the matter. The takeover was not referred because of the supposedly parlous financial state of both papers.[7] Instead, safeguards of editorial independence, including the appointment of independent Directors with a veto on the dismissal of the editor, were formally accepted by News International.

Since the takeover, both *The Times* and *The Sunday Times* have moved from an independent, if right of centre, editorial position to join the *Telegraph, Mail* and *Express* stables, as well as Murdoch's other British newspapers, as committed supporters of the present Government, particularly on economic matters. Mr Evans soon left his editorial chair, and has since documented several instances of personal interference by Rupert Murdoch in the paper's editorial line and the selection of feature articles.[8]

It may be that the choice was between ownership by Mr Murdoch or closure for *The Times* at least; nevertheless this is only part of a trend towards clear domination of the British press by Conservative Party ideology. Thus the Liberal-supporting *News Chronicle* was merged in 1961 with the *Daily Mail*, which now bears no discernible trace of liberalism; and the *Sun*, which was *founded* as a successor to the Labour-supporting *Daily Herald* in 1963, has since moved almost as far to the right politically as it has slid down-market in quality. These trends are of concern not just to the political left, but to anyone who values diversity in the press, both of editorial comment and of the range of information and the manner of reporting it.

Another serious worry to civil libertarians is the simple failure of an important and widely-read section of the press to report serious news in a credible fashion at all. Whatever accoutrements may be necessary to sell newspapers, it is difficult to believe that the virtual omission of serious news coverage from newspapers with perhaps a third of the national daily readership is necessary to their economic health. It is certainly not a contribution to an informed democracy.

Television and Radio Broadcasting in Britain is effectively a duopoly. Two television channels, all national and some local radio are under the control of the BBC, while the other two TV channels and the other local radio stations are operated by commercial enterprises licensed by the IBA, a statutory corporation whose members (like the Board of Governors of the BBC) are appointed by the Government of the day. Programme schedules of the independent companies must be approved by the IBA, which also has important duties under the Broadcasting Act to regulate to enforce restrictions on advertising and maintain standards of taste, decency and impartiality.

We are fortunate in two respects in the history of British broadcasting. The first broadcasting organisation, the British Broadcasting Company, was granted a Royal Charter in 1926, after only four years of broadcasting, and became a public corporation with a duty of impartiality as one of the conditions of its monopoly. This tradition of public accountability and impartiality was reaffirmed in the statutory framework for independent broadcasting when the Independent Television Authority (later the IBA) was created in 1955. Secondly the early direction of the BBC under Lord Reith was towards broadcasting as an agent of enlightenment rather than just entertainment. The straight-laced image of the BBC produced by this policy may have been a long time fading away; but there has been a more successful resistance here to the pandering to the lowest common denominator of audiences associated with much American television than in many other countries, and as a result British broadcasting deserves its reputation for (relatively) high standards.

Nevertheless there are several reasons for concern over the ability and willingness of the broadcasting authorities to avoid unjustifiable restrictions on freedom of expression. It is only fair to acknowledge the difficulties under which they must operate. There is a necessarily finite amount of air time, and a very large number and range of interested groups seeking to ensure either as full a representation of their point of view as possible or the suppression of information unfavourable to their interests. As an almost universal medium of entertainment, television in particular has the capacity to intrude into the privacy of individuals' homes in a way which makes the avoidance of undue offence, or of harmful impact on the immature, a particularly sensitive and highly public subject. But there are causes for concern over the concept of impartiality as it operates in practice, the range of views that are given a hearing, and an excessive subservience to government and to the views of particular interest groups.

The concept of impartiality is a notoriously slippery and subjective one. Clearly it cannot simply consist in adopting a neutral position between opposing points of view on any given issue. A position of neutrality between the burglar and the burgled would not command much public support. Nor would neutrality as between the British and Argentine Governments' position during the Falklands war have been called for. Impartiality does however involve an abstention from preselecting *information* about the other point of view. Interviews with burglars, as a source of general public understanding of why burglaries occur, might make a valuable contribution to public appreciation of what should be done to prevent them, or how burglars should be dealt with by the courts. Why should a similar argument not be applied to the presentation of the Argentine case in 1982, or the IRA case today?

On political issues, a superficial concept of impartiality might be that the broadcasting authorities should maintain a position at the centre of the political spectrum. On this basis, politicians of the right and of the left complaining of bias by turns would be a source of reassurance not criticism. But support for a centre position is quite distinct from impartiality, first because centrism is itself a political ideology, but secondly because on many issues the centre shares the viewpoint of either the right or the left and is associated accordingly with one or other side of a controversy. Impartiality requires a detachment from the centre or consensus view as much as from any other, and a willingness to allow the advocacy of a range of opinions. Unfortunately the impression which television particularly creates is of support for consensus rather than impartiality, with insufficient acknowledgement of the diversity of opinions outside the consensus.

An illustration of this point is the treatment of the Common Market. It is now part of a broad political consensus that the Common Market is seriously defective in many of its policies and practices, and it is not uncommon for radio or television to carry news items or documentaries illustrating some eccentricity, wastefulness or counter-productive policy. But it is quite exceptional for the issue to be broadened to a practical examination of the implications of a British withdrawal from the Community. It is almost as if there is an unspoken consensus that such a policy would be so absurd – for all the imperfections of the system – as to be beyond the pale of a range of credible opinions: notwithstanding that it has been for some years, and still is, the official policy of the Labour Party and has been supported in opinion polls by between

30% and a small *majority* of the electorate. No doubt many of those involved in the direction of TV and radio *do* think the idea of withdrawal is dotty. Impartiality is only achieved if such attitudes are not deployed to predigest ideas before they are exposed to the public.

The relationship between the broadcasting authorities and the government of the day is inevitably delicate. Governments are sensitive about criticism, especially when they are performing badly, and there is a perfectly human temptation to overreact. The government appoints the members of the IBA and advises the Queen on the appointment of the Governors of the BBC. The government fixes the BBC licence fee – of especial importance at times of rapid inflation. The government has extensive residual powers of direction over the broadcasting authorities, extending even to a complete takeover in an emergency[9] – a power never used to date, but seriously considered by the Cabinet at the time of Suez. The government also has effective control over access to much information on important matters, and can give and withhold favours and facilities.

All of this leaves the broadcasting authorities vulnerable to pressure and influence on matters ranging from the making of senior appointments to the handling of particular news issues or the choice of politicians to appear on particular programmes. Necessarily, the general public cannot know how much pressure there is, or how well it is withstood when it does occur. The extent of the possibility alone is cause for concern.

Occasionally matters do come to the surface. The management of news by the Ministry of Defence during the Falklands war is an example, admittedly in extreme circumstances. Another recent example occurred in the aftermath of the shooting down of the South Korean airliner in September 1983. The BBC World Service, true to the tradition of impartiality which has secured it a high reputation around the world, referred only to the "disappearance" of the airliner until the USSR conceded the shooting down. Shortly afterwards, Mrs Thatcher, in a public speech in Canada, implicitly criticised the World Service for a lack of patriotism. At a time when the Service, which is directly financed through the Foreign Office, had been under threat of major financial cuts, the implications were obvious.

Vulnerability to government influence is not the same thing as public accountability. Public accountability is no panacea; it can very easily slide into undue manipulation by sectional interests and pressure groups. Nevertheless there is a worrying lack of public accountability in broadcasting. Meetings of the governing institutions are not open to the public, and the all-important process of allocation of independent TV and radio franchises is largely conducted behind closed doors. But the degree of accountability, such as it is, of the present system, is likely to be undermined substantially by the arrival of cable television.

The government has accepted the approach of the Hunt Committee that regulation of cable TV should be kept to a minimum once franchises have been let out by the proposed Cable Television Authority. We can expect a further weakening of concepts of balance and public service which is bound to put a strain on the established services, and if American experience is emulated freedom of expression will be eroded just as much as programme quality. Franchises will probably be awarded to consortia including local press, radio and television interests, so that diversity may be constricted even more tightly in many parts of the country. Attempts to prevent too close a link between press interests and the independent TV and radio companies have not been very successful as it is. The effort seems unlikely to be made for cable.

Cinema and video The cinema has had a short but powerful heyday. The public cinema in Britain is in serious and continuing decline, but the dramatic growth of home video is re-establishing film as an important medium of art and entertainment. Those with access to video recorders have a much wider choice of films than the commercial cinema can offer, especially in areas of the country away from the larger cities, where there may only be one cinema left open, offering a limited range of films chosen by one of the two major cinema chains for their box office attraction. There are also a small number of specialist cinemas and numerous film clubs, but collectively these do not provide a viable financial return for films that are not accepted for general release.

The cinema is the only medium in the UK currently subject to a formal system of censorship. It is a rather strange system, born of a twist of history. The local authorities, given powers to license cinemas in 1909 in the interests of fire safety (after several disastrous fires) used their powers to impose conditions on the content of films, and their claims to do so were upheld by the courts in a series of decisions which more accurately reflected the letter of the statute than the original intention of Parliament.[10] Faced with the anarchy of censorship by each of the many hundreds of local authorities, the film industry itself set up the British Board of Film Censors, and persuaded most local authorities to accept the Board's judgments in place of their own. This system still operates, with legal recognition but without formal legal status, and although the Court of Appeal has ruled that there is no obligation on local authorities to censor[11] (or to apply the Board's censorship) except for children, no authority has yet abandoned the system of censorship.

The present film censorship system is as good as we are likely to get. The BBFC has displayed a reasonably enlightened approach (with occasional controversial exceptions, and in contrast to a fairly conservative approach in its earlier days). The Board offers guidance to film makers without which the commercial risks involved would almost certainly restrict creative initiative. The Board's certificate is in practice (though not in law) more or less a guarantee against prosecution, since the right to bring private prosecutions for obscenity against the commercial cinema was removed in 1977. The occasional eccentricities of local authorities in banning particular films are objectionable in principle but probably counter-productive in practice (people are simply stimulated to travel to the next town by the publicity for the ban), and serve as a salutory reminder of how much worse a system of censorship under more direct political control might be. Cinema clubs are to a limited extent exempt from any form of prior control by either local authorities or the BBFC. The real deadening censorship is the private making and breaking of films by the commercial organisations which own the great majority of the commercial cinemas.

The Williams Committee on Obscenity and Film Censorship, a generally enlightened body, whose report recommended significant restrictions on the scope of the obscenity laws, nevertheless concluded that film censorship should be retained, and put on a formal statutory basis. The Committee reached this conclusion in part because of the sheer horrifying violence they saw in some of the films which had been refused a certificate.[12]

Any system of formal prior censorship is open to fundamental objections of lack of accountability of the censors, lack of ascertained criteria for censorship and lack of any judicial or other independent scrutiny of decisions. In theory it should be opposed for the cinema as for other media. In reality the present system probably protects freedom of expression more than any likely alternatives. Simple exposure to the criminal law, unpredictable as it would inevitably be, would be a blow to the jugular for artistic freedom because of its effects on the financial backers of controversial proposals. A statutory system of censorship, with statutory criteria, would play into the hands of self-appointed censors who could seek judicial review of the censorship authority's decisions to pass films to which they took exception. As previous judicial intervention shows, they would get a sympathetic hearing. This would soon stymie any creative liberalism to which the censorship body might be tempted. The thought of censors appointed by the Home Office is quite terrifying enough without adding a posse of judges to keep an eye on them! Curious as it may seem, an extra-legal system of cinema censorship is on balance in the interests of civil liberties.

Things are about to change, and for the worse. For several years there were no moves to implement the Williams Report. But the current epidemic of concern about "video nasties" and their availability to children has led to a Private Member's Bill in Parliament, which with government support will certainly become law in 1984,[13] under which a statutory system of censorship will apply to most video recordings. It is probable that the BBFC will become the agency of the censorship. It is also probable, whether or not statutory criteria of censorship are included in the Bill in its final form, that the activities of the BBFC will be exposed to litigation from which their unofficial position has hitherto largely protected them. It is reasonable that there should be some control over video tapes, especially in the interests of children; but it is also inevitable that the criteria which will come to be applied to video will be tighter than for the cinema, because it is impossible to prevent children seeing "restricted" video recordings. The cost of certificates alone will prevent some low budget and experimental video packs from being made. Further pressure on the television companies is also likely. 1984 may well mark the start of the establishment of a much more close control of materials available on film, with restrictions on freedom of choice well beyond those necessitated by the problems that have led to the new Bill. Is it just coincidence that the authorities have made no attempt to use the obscenity laws against video nasties before resorting to the extreme of the introduction of statutory censorship?

The Theatre Formal theatre censorship was abolished in 1968 and since then the British theatre has been little troubled by the criminal law which took its place. The Theatres Act 1968 introduced special offences of producing obscene plays or plays likely to incite racial hatred, but with the all-important public good defence available in the former instance, on the lines of the Obscene Publications Act. No prosecutions of the serious theatre have been brought under the Act. Unfortunately however the theatre is not immune from prosecutions under other provisions of the criminal law which afford no defence of public good. This was made clear in 1981 when Mrs Whitehouse initiated a prosecution against the Director of a National Theatre production, *The Romans in Britain*, for procuring an act of gross indecency in connection with a scene involving the simulated homosexual rape of a druid on stage. The case was dropped after an Old Bailey judge had ruled that such a charge was not precluded by the Theatres Act. That such a charge can be brought against a serious play must have a dampening influence on the theatre. In an obscenity production the defence would undoubtedly have raised the issue of public good, in relation to a play that was decribed as an allegory of the British rape of Northern Ireland, and it is unsatisfactory that the law permits prosecutors to select a charge which excludes the issue, as well as reprehensible that any should take advantage of the opportunity.

The more significant threat to artistic freedom in the theatre is of course financial. Popular West End musicals and comedies may make a comfortable profit, but most professional theatre has to be heavily subsidised to survive. Most of the subsidy is public money, a commodity under increasing pressure – the abolition of the GLC and the Metropolitan County Councils, for instance, would take away one significant source of public subsidy. Government policy is likely to accelerate a trend towards seeking private patronage for the arts, a policy with clear dangers for artistic freedom. It may be easy enough to persuade a major company with some concern for its public image to sponsor the odd Shakespeare cycle, but there will be no money for a contemporary anti-war play or an attack on corporate interference in the political system. Radicalism, without which the theatre would be greatly impoverished, will suffer, discreetly but inevitably, from a shift to private financing.

Nor are public authorities immune from the paymaster's temptations, although it is rare for them to go as far as the last Conservative leadership of the GLC, which threatened to withdraw its grant to the National Theatre over the *Romans in Britain* affair.

The printed word The diversity of book publishing houses, while declining, is still enough to ensure a reasonable range of literary publishing, and financial constraints rarely prevent the publication of books for which there would be a significant readership. Indeed technological developments in printing have made it easier to produce short print-runs of specialist works.

That is not to say that all is well. We are not a nation of book buyers, and our books are, by international standards and in absolute terms, exorbitantly expensive: which is the chicken and which the egg is a matter of speculation. Our public library system, remarkably comprehensive and heavily used as it is by international standards, has been seriously damaged by cuts in real budgets and rises in real levels of book prices. In consequence, the financial rewards and support given to serious authors are insufficient. The recently-introduced Public Lending Right scheme makes a welcome but token gesture of acknowledgment to what is probably the single greatest restriction on freedom of literary expression.

As with the theatre, the shadow of the criminal law over books has faded, but not disappeared. The kind of intolerance of 50 years ago that could convict books like *The Well of Loneliness* has gone (to be replaced by other kinds of intolerance). *Causes célèbres* of the run-up to the Obscene Publications Act in 1959 now have a dated ring, and it is difficult to remember in 1984 the climate that was demolished by the acquittal of *Lady Chatterley's Lover*. The office of the Director of Public Prosecutions was made to look foolish by repeated acquittals of publishers tried for obscenity in the late 1960s and early 1970s, and by the extraordinary boost to sales that the free publicity gave to the offending books. The final straw was the not guilty verdict in the *Inside Linda Lovelace* case in 1976, since when no major trial under the Act has been attempted. Magistrates do occasionally order the forfeiture of books freely on sale elsewhere in the country, and importations are still subject to the more puritanical regime of the Customs authorities; but the Williams Committee probably regarded their recommendation that obscenity laws should no longer apply to the printed word as little more than a formalisation of existing practice. (The Obscene Publications Act has never been extended to Scotland, but the potential for anomaly has largely been avoided by the practice of successive Lord Advocates not using the common law equivalent offences against serious literature where a prosecution has failed in England.)[14]

Magazines are of course still very much subject to the Obscene Publications Act. Prosecutors have learned to avoid recourse to juries – and in practice albeit not in law to the defence of public good – by using the procedure under section 3 of the Act of applying to the magistrates for an order for the forfeiture of the offending magazines. This involves no criminal penalty but a substantial financial loss, at least when large stocks are seized.[15] Manchester police in particular have been pursuing pornography of all strengths with the almost crusading fervour demanded by their Chief Constable. Unfortunately the overall effect of the law looks very much like the effect of prohibition in the USA in the 1920s. Pornography is not publicly displayed, though this is the result more of the recent Indecent Displays legislation[16] than the obscenity law, but it is available at a price which doubtless correlates closely with the risk of successful forfeiture proceedings. The latter are little more than a tax on the suppliers. Regrettably, but predictably too, both corruption in the police "dirty books" squads and the involvement of organised crime in the chain of supply have become evident.

Obscenity laws as such probably do not conflict with the requirements of the European Convention – that at least was the view of the European Court of Human Rights in the *Little Red School Book* case. Nevertheless, there is an overwhelming practical case for scrapping the obscenity laws altogether, and replacing them (if at all) with very narrowly defined laws for the protection of those most vulnerable to exploitation in the making of pornographic material. The case was cogently argued by the Williams Committee.[17] It is however scarcely conceivable that anything of the kind will be done in the foreseeable future, if only because the prevailing attitudes of the rest of the media virtually preclude sensible public discussion of what the law *can* do, as distinct from what it *ought to* be able to do.

Fortunately, however unsatisfactory the obscenity laws may be, they impinge only marginally on freedom of expression via the printed word. But as with the theatre, the protection given by the law to literature can be circumvented. The establishment[18] and subsequent confirmation[19] of the offence of conspiracy to corrupt public morals is an instructive example. This offence neatly circumvents the statutory ban on common law obscenity prosecutions[20] by the use of conspiracy, and thereby avoids the defence of public good. The activities complained of in the cases concerned were, respectively, the publication of a *Ladies Directory* of the addresses of prostitutes and of gay "lonely hearts" advertisements in *International Times*. The use of charges of conspiracy here has all the finesse of the howitzer, and the judicial categorisation of activities at worst legally marginal as corrupting betrayed a disdain for Parliament that provoked concern over a wider front as to the role of the judiciary. Nevertheless the offence of conspiracy to corrupt public morals was expressly preserved by Parliament in 1977 when the rest of the law of conspiracy was reformed; the excuse for not acting (despite a recommendation from the Law Commission) was the forthcoming review of the law by the Williams Committee – whose recommendations, predictably, have been ignored.

An even more disturbing example of the circumvention of safeguards for freedom of expression occurred when Mrs Whitehouse brought a private prosecution against the magazine *Gay News* and its editor, Denis Lemon, for blasphemy, in the shape of a poem about the Crucifixion, by a Canadian Professor of English Literature. Quite apart from the incongruity today of an offence which gives special legal protection to the susceptibilities of the Christian religion (an incongruity keenly felt by many Christians), again the choice of charge had the effect of denying the defence the opportunity to give evidence that the publication of the poem was for the public good. The defence claimed that so far from vilifying Christianity the poem (a fantasy of the love of a Roman centurion for the crucified body of Christ) was an affirmation that Christ's love extended even to homosexuals.[21] Nevertheless the defendants' convictions were upheld by the House of Lords,[22] which took the opportunity to redefine the offence in broad terms eliminating any need to prove an intention to vilify Christianity. Lord Scarman even suggested that the law should be extended to give protection to all religious beliefs. A Bill to abolish the offence of blasphemy was subsequently rejected by the House of Lords despite support from some Bishops.

Neither of these offences does credit to the legal system or to the safeguarding of civil liberties, and it is difficult to believe that either is, in the words of the European Convention, "necessary in a democratic society".

LEGAL RESTRAINTS

I have so far considered some of the formal restraints, such as film censorship and obscenity, which impinge on particular sections of the media. There are other restraints of more general importance, two of which require further consideration here: defamation and contempt of court.

Defamation The proposition that individuals' reputations should be safeguarded against unjustified and damaging published statements would command general support. It is acknowledged as one of the grounds on which freedom of expression may be restricted in Article 10 of the European Convention; indeed personal privacy is expressly protected by Article 8. But it is important that in protecting these interests the law does not restrict the free flow of information and comment more than is necessary. The English libel laws manage to fail on both counts. Significant reforms of the law were recommended in the Report of the Faulks Committee in 1975[23] but the proposals have largely been ignored by successive governments.

There are two main ways in which individuals' reputations are often left unprotected by the present law: privileged statements and the unconscionable expense of legal proceedings. For very good reasons, statements made in certain situations are given "qualified privilege", which means that they are not actionable unless it can be shown that they were made in the knowledge that they were false. In a more limited range of situations – statements made during judicial proceedings or in Parliament – even deliberately false accusations are protected, as are fair and accurate reports of them in the media. When a former General Secretary of the NCCL was falsely accused in the House of Commons of supporting the IRA, he had no legal remedy even though the MP concerned refused either to substantiate or retract his allegation. No doubt the accusation was made in good faith, but even if it had been made out of sheer malice there would still have been no remedy.

The enormous cost of litigation, and the risk of paying both sides' costs if you lose, deters all but the very rich, the very determined and those supported by Legal Aid or insurance, from embarking on litigation. Libel actions are a peculiarly expensive form of litigation. Legal Aid was of course introduced to redress some of the imbalance in the accessibility of the law. It is a serious defect in the Legal Aid scheme that it does not apply to actions for libel or slander. Most ordinary people cannot take the financial risk of suing a wealthy institution such as a national newspaper for libel, even if their case is a racing certainty (the metaphor is not inapt for this kind of proceeding). In the result reputation is a preserve of wealth and power. The converse is equally true – a journalist or author may not be able to afford to defend an action brought by a wealthy plaintiff, however convincing the defence.

The libel laws also constrain freedom of information. In the USA, the emphasis placed by the courts on the importance of freedom of the press has led to the exclusion of libel actions by public figures for false accusations that were made in good faith. Investigation of the improprieties of those in positions of public authority is clearly much easier if damaging but unprovable statements are not automatically actionable. Because such a freedom to report is too easily abused (and it *is* abused in the USA), safeguards would be needed, but some move away from the present position would be of public benefit.

Because defamation actions (unlike nearly all other civil actions) are tried by jury, awards of damages are unpredictable, and often very large. (It has been pointed out more than once that this may be the only time in their lives that the jury can fill in the figures on a blank cheque to be drawn on someone else's bank account.) In a famous case in the 1930s the plaintiff was awarded £30,000 for an implication in a film that she had been raped by Rasputin, and more recently in 1963 a jury awarded over £200,000 to a company and its managing director for truthful reports in the *Daily Telegraph* and the *Daily Mail* that the company's affairs were being investigated by the Fraud Squad. The jury had found that the articles implied that the plaintiffs were guilty of fraud, but the House of Lords held that the words used were incapable of bearing that meaning.[24] Cases like these make the libel laws a gold-digger's charter for those rich enough to use them.

It is in the field of criminal libel that the law is most unsatisfactory of all. When Sir James Goldsmith mounted a frontal attack on *Private Eye* for falsely accusing him of helping to hide Lord Lucan, he turned to criminal libel. The case was eventually dropped after a settlement of the whole dispute, but by then the High Court had given a ruling reaffirming the astonishing breadth of this offence.[25] It is a crime to publish a written statement defamatory of another, even if the only publication is to the other person, and *even if the statement is true*, unless the *defendant* can prove that publication was for the public benefit. The suppression of truth unless the defendant could prove it was of public benefit could perhaps be justified by the other element once thought to be required for this crime – that the libel was likely to provoke a breach of the peace – but the *Goldsmith* case settled that this is not necessary. Criminal libel seems now to have faded from its brief limelight, but the breadth of the offence, uncertainty as to when it might again be disinterred, and the history of its use as an instrument of oppression in the nineteenth century and the early years of the twentieth,[26] all point to an urgent need for it to be scrapped.

Contempt of Court. Fifty years ago, overly robust criticism of judges could land you in jail. The editor of the *New Statesman* narrowly escaped this fate in 1928 for suggesting that Mr Justice Avory had been biased in his conduct of a libel action brought by Dr Marie Stopes.[27] But 40 years later Lord Denning pronounced the last rites on this form of contempt of court, when an unsuccessful attempt was made to commit Mr Quintin Hogg (later to be Lord Chancellor) for an uncomplimentary article in *Punch*.[28] It is now quite commonplace for articles savagely critical of the judiciary to be published. In one area of the law freedom has progressed.

In other areas progress is less certain. Press reporting or discussion of public affairs that incidentally impinges on the conduct of legal proceedings has been an uncertain area of the law for a long time. In the famous *Sunday Times* case, in which an article detailing allegations of negligence against the makers of the drug Thalidomide was banned because of its possible prejudicial effect on the Distillers Company's defence in the Thalidomide children's pending claims for compensation, the House of Lords placed the protection of pending proceedings from prejudgment at the top of the hierarchy of interests protected by the law.[29] The case was taken to the European Court of Human Rights, which ruled that *The Sunday Times*' freedom of expression had been infringed, and such solicitude for the sanctity of pending proceedings could not be justified as "necessary in a democratic society". The Court's ruling finally forced the Government to legislate, and the Contempt of Court Act 1981 has introduced three major reforms. First, comment is no longer restricted by pending civil proceedings as soon as a writ is issued; there is no restriction on comment until the case is set down for trial. (In criminal cases, restrictions begin as soon as a suspect has been arrested or a warrant or summons issued.) Secondly, there is a new and clearer test of what constitutes contempt; it is now necessary to establish a "substantial risk" that the proceedings will be "seriously prejudiced" to the proceedings (section 2 of the Act). Thirdly, a new defence has been formulated, that any prejudice was "incidental to" a bona fide discussion of a matter of general public interest. This defence was generously interpreted by the House of Lords in the first case under the new Act.[30]

The *Daily Mail* had published an article by Malcolm Muggeridge in support of an anti-abortion candidate in a Parliamentary by-election, in which it was asserted that babies born with deformities were often left to die. The article appeared during the trial of a doctor accused of murdering a new-born Down's syndrome baby by leaving it to die (he was later acquitted). The House of Lords held that this was not contempt; the new defence was applicable because, said Lord Diplock, however much the article might affect the trial, it would have been impractical to argue the case of the by-election candidate without asserting that babies were left to die; it would have been "tilting at imaginary windmills". This important ruling that public discussion of issues of public interest is not automatically suppressed for the duration of any relevant litigation it might influence is the most positive result of the 1981 Act.[31]

But the changes have not all been in one direction. Lord Diplock's judgment had a sting in its tail: the present case was quite unlike the *Sunday Times* case, where the article had been specifically about the pending Thalidomide claim (never mind that the case was itself a matter of major public interest), and by implication the 1981 Act would not protect *The Sunday Times* in an equivalent situation today. If that is correct then Britain is still in breach of the European Convention.

The Act has also extended the powers of the courts to conceal information. A series of cases in the 1970s about the disclosure of the identity of witnesses had left the law in disarray. The 1981 Act made two amendments. Courts were given a specific authority to punish for contempt those who published the names of witnesses contrary to a valid instruction from the court (but the Act gives no clear guidance as to when an instruction would be valid), and a general power to postpone the publication of reports of proceedings where this was necessary to avoid prejudice to those or later proceedings.[32] It is easy to envisage cases where press reports could prejudice a following trial, but it soon became clear that courts were taking to the new power with undue gusto. A case brought by the National Union of Journalists, backed by the NCCL, produced a confirmation by the Court of Appeal that the sensational nature of evidence to be given in committal proceedings is no reason for a blanket ban on reporting even the identity of the accused until the trial proper begins; only a real risk of prejudice could justify a ban.[33] That did not stop an Old Bailey judge in October 1983 from banning any reporting of an allegation made against Mr Edward Heath in the course of a rape trial, when the reporting of it could hardly have had any effect on the course of the trial itself.

The right to an unbiased trial is of course an important civil liberty in itself; when it conflicts with other civil liberties, a balance must be struck. We should all lose some freedom if the American approach of giving almost total precedence to freedom of the press were to be adopted in Britain, and newspapers were free to publish interviews with witnesses or reconstructions of cases on the eve of the trial. But in striking a balance it is important to remember that even if the openness of proceedings sometimes conflicts with the interests of justice to the parties, openness is itself a part of the fabric of a fair trial. The public has a right to know what is done in its name. Moreover, it is the knowledge of the possibility of public scrutiny, when justice is not dispensed behind closed doors, that imposes a discipline on the standards of conduct of judges, advocates and witnesses.

These aspects of judicial procedure got short shrift from the House of Lords in the *Harman* case. Harriet Harman, at the time NCCL Legal Officer, had acted as solicitor for Michael Williams, who had sued the Home Office over the conditions of his detention in the Control Unit in Wakefield Prison. The High Court had ordered the Home Office to disclose, for the purposes of the trial, substantial quantities of documents including notes of discussions between officials and ministers over the planning of the Control Units. Ms Harman gave the usual undertaking not to use the documents for purposes other than the litigation. However, many of the documents were read out by counsel at the trial (which was of course open to the public) and reasonably enough she saw no objection subsequently to letting a *Guardian* journalist check through the papers that had been read out, for the purpose of a feature article on the background to the case. The article, which was highly critical of the Home Office, used some of the documentary material to sustain its arguments. No doubt the Home Office found this upsetting and embarrassing. Their response was to cite Ms Harman for contempt of court. Astonishingly, she was convicted.[34]

If the journalist had been present in court, he could have taken notes as the documents were read out; or he could (at some cost, but without needing any special permission) have bought a transcript from the shorthand writers. Nevertheless the High Court, the Court of Appeal and a majority of the House of Lords considered that she had broken an undertaking, which apparently still bound her alone. A near-contempt for the importance of openness comes out in the judgments. Lord Denning was particularly angry that the information was used to *criticise* the Home Office, while Lord Diplock felt it would not have been contempt if she had shown the documents to a law reporter preparing a report of the case for the Law Reports, instead of a journalist intending to comment on the case. It was left to Lords Scarman and Simon, in an eloquent dissent, to suggest that we might adopt the American rule that all documents tendered in evidence in a public trial become matters of public record (it may surprise many that they are not), and even they failed to puncture the ultimate absurdity of the case, that a Department of State, in its capacity as a private litigant, sought the protection of the court to safeguard "its" private property, in the shape of documentary evidence of the implementation of policy on behalf of the public.

The government refused to amend the Contempt of Court Bill to overrule this decision, but instead set up a Committee to examine the issue. In the meantime NCCL has pursued Harriet Harman's case to the European Commission on Human Rights. The facts of the case are unlikely to be repeated, but the principles it raises about open justice are fundamental.

ASSEMBLY AND ORATORY

Patricia Hewitt has discussed in her contribution some of the increasing restraints on freedom of assembly, and I need not re-cover the ground. In an increasingly polarised society, access to the opportunity for peaceful protest, and to the streets as a platform for the expression of opinion, becomes more important; at the same time protest becomes more apparently threatening to those in authority, and freedom itself then comes more under threat. In a whole variety of often individually minor ways, freedom of expression through demonstrations, picketing and the distribution of propaganda on the streets is under pressure.

The technical legal position was exposed with an almost embarrassing clarity in 1975, when Mr Justice Forbes ruled that a line of six pickets standing on the pavement outside an estate agent's office were committing a public nuisance.[35] An injunction was granted against them, but public nuisance is also a crime, with a theoretical maximum punishment of life imprisonment. In the view of the judge the offence covered *any* stationary gathering which was not incidental to using the highway for passage and might potentially obstruct other highway users. The judgment is open to doubt,[36] and public nuisance is seldom prosecuted, but its statutory sibling, wilful obstruction of the highway, is undoubtedly available in almost any case where the police choose to use it, against stationary demonstrators and leafletters at least. Notwithstanding that freedom of peaceful assembly is guaranteed by the European Convention on Human Rights, its exercise is dependent on the goodwill of, and even-handed exercise of discretion by, the police.

Some examples (there are many others) of the institutional pressures on freedom of assembly can be mentioned. In most large towns now important parts of the shopping centres are privately-owned precincts the owners of which have the right to prevent demonstrations, pickets and leafletters. Public buildings are often hired for political meetings, but local authorities have no duty to let their premises (except for public election meetings), and increasingly some are refusing to let to particular organisations for political reasons. (It is of course understandable that fears of a riot should inhibit lettings, but to ban the National Front from public buildings as a policy, however outrageous its views, is the start of a slippery slope.) The control of important centres for demonstrations has increased too; the Department of the Environment, whose permission is needed for rallies in Trafalgar Square, has maintained an indiscriminate ban on demonstrations related to Northern Ireland, while for security reasons the police routinely cordon off Downing

Street from demonstrators and tourists alike.

Judges too have contributed to the process of erosion. Magistrates' willingness to use binding-over powers against peaceful demonstrators (with a sanction of imprisonment for those who refuse to give an undertaking) has been too evident. Binding over has on many occasions been used against those whose only threat to the peace was the reaction of others to the views they were putting forward; the Greenham Common women are only the latest victims. And in one recent case, where the Central Electricity Generating Board was trying to force John Alderson, then Chief Constable of Devon and Cornwall, to evict demonstrators from a site the Board wished to survey for a possible nuclear power station, Lord Denning tried to extend the definition of unlawful assembly (a serious criminal offence) to cover demonstrators engaging in passive resistance to authority. [37]

There have also been legislative changes for the worse. In Scotland, a general statutory requirement to obtain permission from the local authority for a procession has been introduced, [38] and many local authorities in England and Wales have obtained or are seeking (with Home Office backing) statutory powers to require the advance notification of demonstrations. New powers for the police to attend meetings on private premises are contained in the 1983 Police and Criminal Evidence Bill. The legal immunity given to peaceful trade union picketing, without which virtually all pickets are potentially liable to arrest, has been twice limited by recent legislation. The 1980 Employment Act removed legal immunity for peaceful picketing except at the pickets' place of work, while the 1982 Act, by redefining what is a trade dispute, removed protection altogether from pickets acting in a "political" dispute. Picketing is an important aspect of freedom of speech, an opportunity to draw attention to the strikers' claims and to canvas the support of other workers and the public. (If disputes were not so tendentiously reported in most of the press, this would be of less moment.) The reason for the changes was to curtail strikers' economic power, but its effect has also, and largely unnoticed, been to diminish strikers' freedom of expression – and that of supporters, whose presence on the picket line is likely to be actively discouraged by the police.

Together these and other points, including the growing recourse to banning orders under the Public Order Act described by Patricia

Hewitt, add up to a steady undermining of a vital element in the fabric of a democratic society.

CONCLUSION

One matter I have so far dealt with only incidentally is access to information. This is more fully covered in John Griffith's chapter, which follows this, and some of the general points are mentioned in my Introduction to the book. The position can be summarised as one of piecemeal and largely superficial gains that have been overshadowed by increasingly sophisticated governmental management and manipulation of information about public affairs. We have not yet so far departed from democracy as to be subjected to Orwell's Thought Police. But I believe we are experiencing the more insidious erosion of democracy which occurs when people believe that they are exercising a free choice of government, unaware that accountability is managed and manipulated by those in power.[39]

We may or may not have more freedom of speech than in 1934. So much has changed that the comparison would be largely meaningless. We probably have less freedom of speech than is generally assumed and we almost certainly have less than we are entitled to by our national commitment to the European Convention on Human Rights. As I have explained in the Introduction, this is a period of eroding liberty, and in this chapter I have pointed to many examples of recent provenance, in the particular field of freedom of expression, which accentuate the erosion. If over the next 50 years freedom of expression dies the death of a thousand cuts, most will have been inflicted by government, but we will all share the guilt of the bystander who watches the crime without any attempt at intervention or protest.

NOTES

1. *R v Penguin Books* (1961), reported in C H Rolph, *The Trial of Lady Chatterley* (Penguin, 1961).
2. *On Liberty* (1859), ch. 2.
3. *Conway v Rimmer* [1968] Appeal Cases, p. 910, at p. 952.
4. See James Michael's essay (chapter 8) for a full discussion.

5. Section 2. This was the charge against the editor of the *Sunday Telegraph* and Mr Jonathan Aitken in 1971 (*R v Aitken*, unreported. See J Aitken, *Officially Secret* (1971) for a full account), and one of the charges in the "ABC" secrets trial in 1978.

6. A comprehensive review is contained in the *Final Report of the Royal Commission on the Press* (Cmnd. 6810, HMSO, 1977).

7. Mr Evans has subsequently alleged that the figures presented to the Secretary of State for Trade were deliberately misleading: see his book *Good Times, Bad Times* (Weidenfeld and Nicholson,1983).

8. See note 7, above.

9. See the BBC's Licence and Agreement, clause 21. The Broadcasting Act 1981, s. 29 confers more limited powers of control in relation to the IBA.

10. The leading case was *London County Council v Bermondsey Bioscope Co.* [1911] 1 King's Bench Reports, p. 445. For a full general account see N March Hunnings, *Film Censors and the Law* (London, Allen & Unwin, 1967).

11. *R v Greater London Council, ex parte Blackburn* [1976] 3 All England Law Reports, p. 184.

12. See the *Report of the Committee on Obscenity and Film Censorship* (Cmnd. 7772, HMSO, 1979), ch. 12.

13. The Video Recordings Bill 1983, which received an unopposed Second Reading in the Commons on 11th November 1983.

14. This does not mean that there is no cause for concern in Scotland. Procurator Fiscals (the Scottish public prosecutors) have recently been resorting increasingly to using the very broad common law offence of "shameless indecency" against sellers of allegedly pornographic materials. The Civic Government (Scotland) Act 1982 has also created (in section 51) a new offence of publishing obscene articles that provides no defence of public good.

15. There appears to be no equivalent procedure in Scotland.

16. Indecent Displays (Control) Act 1981.

17. Cmnd. 7772, chs. 9 and 10: The Protection of Children Act 1978 already makes the possession of most such material illegal.

18. *Shaw v DPP* [1962] Appeal Cases, p. 220.

19. *R v Knuller* [1973] Appeal Cases, p. 435.

20. Obscene Publications Act 1959, section 2(4).

21. I have seen the original poem. This interpretation of it is, in my view, a perfectly credible alternative.

22. *R v Lemon* [1979] 1 All England Law Reports, p. 98.

23. *Report of the Committee on Defamation* (Cmnd. 5909, HMSO, 1975).

24. *Youssoupoff v MGM* [1934] 50 Times Law Reports, p. 581; *Lewis v Daily Telegraph* [1964] Appeal Cases, p. 234. The latter case is the basis on

which newspapers can report that someone is "helping the police with their enquiries" without attracting a writ if the suspect is later cleared.

25. *Goldsmith* v *Pressdram Ltd* [1976] 3 Weekly Law Reports, p. 191.

26. See the absorbing review of the history of criminal libel in J R Spencer, *Criminal Libel – a Skeleton in the Cupboard* [1977] Criminal Law Review, pp. 383 and 465.

27. *R* v *New Statesman* [1928] 44 Times Law Reports, p. 301.

28. *R* v *Metropolitan Police Commissioner, ex parte Blackburn (No. 2)* [1968] 2 Queen's Bench Reports, p. 150.

29. *Attorney-General* v *Times Newspapers Ltd* [1974] Appeal Cases, p.273; *Times Newspapers Ltd* v *UK* [1979] 2 European Human Rights Reports, p. 245.

30. *Attorney-General* v *English* [1982] 2 All England Law Reports, p. 903.

31. However the position would probably have been different if there had been a direct reference to the trial – compare the Scottish case of *Atkins* v *London Weekend Television* 1978, Scots Law Times p. 76.

32. Sections 11 and 4(2) respectively.

33. *R* v *Horsham Justices, ex parte Farquharson* [1982] 2 All England Law Reports, p. 269.

34. *Home Office* v *Harman* [1982] 1 All England Law Reports, p. 532.

35. *Hubbard* v *Pitt* [1976] Queen's Bench Reports, p. 142.

36. The case went to the Court of Appeal, where it was decided on a different point; Lord Denning, who thought the different point irrelevant, dissented strongly from the view that the picketing was unlawful. (*Ibid.*).

37. *R* v *Chief Constable of Devon and Cornwall, ex parte CEGB* [1981] 3 All England Law Reports, p. 826.

38. Civic Government (Scotland) Act 1982, section 62. For the position before this, see *Loyal Orange Lodge No. 493, Hawick 1st Purple* v *Roxburgh District Council*, 1981 Scots Law Times, p. 33.

39. I do not mean this just as a synonym for "the Government".

5

THE DEMOCRATIC PROCESS

JOHN GRIFFITH

In this chapter, an attempt is made, by selecting a few examples, to show how civil liberties and the democratic process relate to each other.

We live in a highly regulated society, managed by public and private institutions able to determine the terms and conditions of our existence. Within these institutions are hierarchies of authoritarian groups with varying degrees of manipulative power, direct and indirect. Civil liberties are the diminishing residues of uncontrolled action that can lawfully be taken despite these institutions and these hierarchies.

This society is pluralist in that power is distributed amongst many institutions including some, like the press and broadcasting, which actively from time to time promote civil liberty of one kind or another. But, at the highest levels of the state, power becomes concentrated in the hands of a few. The oligarchy then spreads its influence widely and deeply over subordinate institutions, private as well as public. Being based on class, it is able to engage the self-interest also of that great number who depend on the preservation and continuance of its considerable power. It becomes highly manipulative and can rely not only on persuasion and propaganda but also on that self-interest. Its hegemony is all the easier to maintain because its dependants cannot see any alternative structure that will obviously give them more of the better things in life.

State regulation may enhance civil liberties when it provides social and financial benefits without which freedom becomes the freedom to sleep under bridges. But the power of state institutions is always liable to be exercised in a way which is excessive or arbitrary or for the advancement of private or personal interests. Inevitably the preservation or extension of civil liberties then conflicts with those who manage state institutions.

The democratic process is one means whereby the power of state institutions may be contained, or made responsive. The process commonly but not necessarily relies on elections both to give legitimacy to those put in authority and to provide a way of dismissing them. Parliamentary government is often criticised because, it is said, the exchange of one group of Ministers for another group makes little practical difference to the ordinary citizen as it leaves untouched the fundamentals of the economic and political systems, the institutions remaining essentially the same. Election is itself a highly unusual means of achieving high office. Judges and magistrates, army and police officers, members of boards of nationalised industries, university professors, archbishops and bishops, all and many more are appointed not elected. Only at the top of the political tree are jobs reserved for elected persons. Even there, the elections are not to the offices themselves but only to a body – the House of Commons – from which the appointment of Ministers will be made. Although constitutional writers insist that we do not have a presidential system, in practice the Prime Minister is the only person who can be said to be directly elected to high office. Moreover, Ministers – even Foreign Secretaries – may be drawn from the House of Lords and so hold high office without being tainted in any way by the democratic process.

Despite all this, the possibility, ever-present in the mind of Ministers, that power may, at a General Election, be wholly removed and vested in political opponents, has hitherto been a very real restraint on its exercise. And the same applies, though much less importantly, to the only other group of elective institutions: the local authorities.

THE ATTITUDE OF THE PUBLIC AND OF THE POLITICAL PARTIES
TO CIVIL LIBERTIES

It cannot be said that civil liberties are a general concern in this country. Positive promotion of the cause is limited to a small number of people. Nor is it easy to arouse support for any but the most flagrant examples of infringement of civil liberties.

There is not, and never has been, a civil liberties movement.

Instead there have been many civil liberties movements, promoting the merits and values of this cause and of that. A particular cause may catch the imagination of a wider public but typically it is only the particular event that is seen as significant and only those particularly affected who are concerned.

The public at large has a high level of acceptance of occurrences which, on their face, appear alarming enough. Reports of the death or serious injury of persons in police custody seemed to grow in frequency in the 1970s. If the police were in any way to blame for any of these occurrences, this was surely a matter of the utmost seriousness, showing that practices in this country could not be easily distinguished from those in such countries as South Africa. One MP – Michael Meacher – raised questions in the House of Commons and outside. It could not be said that either the Home Office or the general public appeared to react with very great concern. Over recent years, very large numbers of police officers of all ranks, from chief constables downwards, have been convicted of or dismissed for serious offences and many more have resigned. Investigations in the Metropolitan Police, initiated by Sir Robert Mark as Commissioner and by others, have shown how considerable was the corruption in that and other forces. There were of course very many honest and conscientious policemen and policewomen, and to say that the corruption was considerable no doubt reflects a high expectancy of proper conduct. But until the disclosures were made, most people had been led to believe in that standard. So the general reputation of the police suffered greatly during the last decade. But nothing happened that could be called a public outcry.

Again, prosecutions brought by the police are remarkably unsuccessful, more than half of those who plead not guilty in the Crown Court being acquitted. There are many reasons for this but one seems to be a willingness on the part of the police to charge individual suspects on inadequate evidence. Again, a scandal of great dimensions has arisen by keeping in custody on remand for several months before trial accused persons, many of whom do not eventually receive custodial sentences. This is not the fault of the police but of the system which the Home Office permits to continue and is the consequence, in part, of inefficient and underworked court arrangements. But it cannot be said to have become a matter of general concern.

For it must be recognised that, in politics, taking a stand on matters of liberal principle wherever that may lead is not common. This is not meant as cynicism. It is extraordinarily difficult to persuade others, whatever their intelligence or education, to support a particular cause on the basis of some general liberal proposition if the application of that proposition strikes them as unattractive. Campaigns on behalf of convicted prisoners, of homosexuals or of prostitutes are obvious examples. One result has been that civil libertarians in this country have been reluctant to develop statements of general principle. Should the NCCL fight for the right of the National Front to march through areas of our cities where the population is predominantly or significantly black? On what grounds should the use of troops in Northern Ireland be supported or condemned? Where are the lines of accountability of the police to be drawn? How do we decide what should be the limits of official phone-tapping or interception of other communications? What should be the rules governing obscene publications? By what standards is the protection of government secrets to be considered legitimate in the public interest?

It is not difficult for each of us to provide pragmatic answers to these problems in particular cases, but it is not easy to construct sets of coherent principles which will guide us to coherent applications in similar cases. Nor is it popular. The appeal to principle is often seen as weakness, not strength, and the dangers of entrusting discretionary or even arbitrary powers to established authorities are regarded as less serious than the failure to deal strongly and immediately with what may become an explosive situation. When it is pointed out that to allow the authorities a special latitude in a special case will almost certainly result in the creation of a precedent of behaviour which will be applied in other cases where the immediate justification is not obvious at all, the response is often a shrug of the shoulders and a decision to deal with that future situation when it arises.

Civil libertarians are to be found in all except the most authoritarian of political parties. And all political parties have some members so authoritarian that they would reject any conceivable ground of principle.

It is worth considering what are seen as civil liberties causes by the supporters of the two principal Parliamentary parties. Members of all parties, when they speak of civil liberties, see themselves as opposing particular manifestations of authoritarianism. Civil liberties are the converse of those manifestations.

By tradition and history, Conservatives are associated with law and order, resistance to change in the established ways, though not averse to reform so long as its foundations are well laid and it is shown to be a reasonable and not unnatural development. Conservatives are the party of authority, of property, wealth, capital and free enterprise. They stand on a position which regards the existing order as by no means ideal, certainly capable of improvement, but as good as can be expected at this time. And they see the injustices in society, or many of them, as unfortunate but inevitable concomitants of fundamental and necessary goods. So free enterprise, competition and individual profit-seeking are instruments for the creation of a common wealth in which everyone can share. If the result of the use of those economic means is inequality and unemployment that is unfortunate but the market is not an egalitarian institution.

Economic laisser-fairism coupled with political authoritarianism (especially shown in its attitude to law and order issues) leads inevitably to ambivalence in the attitude of the Conservative Party to civil liberties. Perhaps this is why Conservatives do not much use the phrase. Instead they tend to speak of "rights". Anything that interferes with free enterprise can be seen as a curtailment of rights. Public ownership can be so condemned, though with exceptions where it can be shown that nationalisation (for example, of coal, gas and electricity) brings positive economic gains to the private industries it serves. Similarly they speak of the right to choose private education and private medicine. Police powers of arrest, search and questioning provide a test and demonstrate the ambivalence. The Conservative Party gives strong support to the police, as it does to the armed forces. It seeks to strengthen the position of the police but may be forced to give way, as over the Police and Criminal Evidence Bill when first introduced in the last Parliament, if its policy is strongly opposed by affected interest groups (in that example, of professionals) which normally support its policies. That the opposition to the search provisions of that Bill could be made in the cause of professional rights gave public strength to the professional interests. But the provisions allowing, in effect, detention for questioning for many days before the accused need be brought to court, did not arouse general widespread concern. No professional or similar interests were affected. So the civil libertarians had to fight that cause almost alone.

Nor is the Conservative Party much concerned about minority

groups or immigrants, as the debates on the Nationality Bill showed. On the other hand it is concerned about the rights of individual workers vis-a-vis trade unions. The authoritarianism of the trade unions – as the Conservatives see it – arouses their strongest feelings and the closed shop becomes a monstrous invasion of rights.

Labour supporters at first sight present a natural antithesis, being highly suspicious of increased police powers, sympathetic to the disadvantages suffered by minority groups, sceptical of the press, against official secrecy, disapproving of independent schools and of private medicine. Their attitude stems from a belief that society is unjust both in its concentration of wealth in the hands of a few and in the economic system that ensures the continuation of gross inequalities. An official aim of the Labour Party is to bring about "a fundamental and irreversible shift in the balance of power and wealth in favour of working people and their families".

Whether or not Labour's policies were or are "extreme", as the Conservative politicians claim, they are certainly designed to make radical changes and certainly envisage considerably more direct governmental intervention in the management of the economy than do the policies of the Conservative Party. This has always been so. If the Conservative position on authority and freedom is ambivalent, the Labour position is seemingly paradoxical. It strongly espouses civil liberties but its political and economic programmes require a powerful government and a powerful bureaucracy.

The views of party supporters of whichever party about civil liberties, significant or insignificant, seem not greatly to be reflected in the policies of governments. The Home Office, the Lord Chancellor's Department, and others more marginally involved, remain largely unmoved by representations or protests. Recent examples are easy to find. Lord Hailsham's "little ewe lamb", which became the Contempt of Court Act 1981, was drafted in response to the requirements of the European Convention on Human Rights after the finding of the European Court against the United Kingdom in the Thalidomide case. It was indeed very little, very lamblike, and did not fulfil the obligation under the Convention to bring UK law into conformity with the Court's decision. The prosecution by the Attorney General of Harriet Harman, the NCCL solicitor, aroused general derision in the legal profession. No attempt has been made to legislate on the official reports on obscenity or blasphemy. Supervision of phone tapping was left to the mercies of Lord Diplock.

Invasion of privacy by computers in government service is not likely to be much restricted by future legislation. And, again, the Home Office view of the importance of civil liberties is best reflected in the Police and Criminal Evidence Bill, whose most serious extensions of police powers are unlikely to be affected by earlier protests.

The Home Office, as ever, stands firm and foursquare, conscious of what it seems to believe is its constitutional function of protecting sovereigns from the curiosity of subjects and of resisting liberalising proposals until the pressure becomes overwhelming – which it rarely does. There have been 13 different Home Secretaries since 1945, eight of whom have been Conservative and five Labour. Of these only two could remotely be said to regard civil liberties as worthy of serious political consideration. These were R A Butler (1957-62) and Roy Jenkins (1965-7 and 1974-6). Certainly it cannot be said that Labour Home Secretaries were more liberalising than their Conservative equivalents. The cold dead hand of the Home Office lay as firmly on the neck of Merlyn Rees as it did on the neck of William Whitelaw, neither of whom could be said to be oppressors by nature.

THE POWER OF GOVERNMENT

Many of the constitutional issues of the last decade are most unlikely to be of any importance during the next five years.

In 1978, Lord Hailsham published his book (*The Dilemma of Democracy*) about the need for a written constitution, for limitations on the power of our system of what he called elective dictatorship, for a Bill of Rights, for devolution. Within a few months, by the flick of a feminine wrist, he became, for the second time, Lord Chancellor. It is not often given to a politician to be so quickly given a dominant position from which to urge the execution of his mature reflections on the constitution. No-one expected immediate results. But even those of us who regarded Lord Hailsham, on his record, as an opportunist and little else, did not expect that he would say absolutely nothing, in public, about what had seemed to be deeply held convictions, during the period of his Lord Chancellorship in Mrs Thatcher's administrations.

The movement for a Bill of Rights is very dead. And today civil libertarians would need to look very carefully indeed at any such proposals that might at any time be resurrected by the present Conservative Government. It is most unlikely that the power of the Executive will be fettered before the next general election, by devolution or any other constitutional change. On the contrary, the considerable diminution of the powers of local authorities through financial control and the abolition of the Greater London Council and the Metropolitan County Councils will strengthen the central government.

Nor has Mrs Thatcher shown any liberalising interest in the reform of the law relating to official secrets or in promoting open government. The highly critical reception given to the Conservative Government's Protection of Official Information Bill was aided by the Blunt affair, and prevented re-statement of the Executive's very tight control over the flow of information. We still operate under the Official Secrets Acts which, some suspect, the more autocratic and authoritarian Ministers and senior civil servants are happy to retain.

Early in 1983, the Labour Party published a discussion paper on Freedom and the Security Services which, if ever implemented, would be considerable in its effects. The paper proposes two new statutes: a Security Act and an Information and Privacy Act.

The Security Act would provide a statutory basis for each of the security and intelligence agencies, Parliamentary approval being required for the appointment of the directors, the objectives of the agencies being detailed. Espionage would be clearly defined. The controls over surveillance through all manner of interception devices would be tightened and the power of the Home Secretary to issue warrants for their use defined and limited. Ministerial accountability would be made much clearer than it is at present, with annual reports from the agencies. The Official Secrets Act would be repealed.

The Information and Privacy Act would make all government documents publicly available unless specifically exempted. Individuals would have a general right of access to information on data banks. Bugging, tapping and other unauthorised access to personal information would be made illegal.

The Labour Party paper, especially when read against the background of the well-known events of recent years, would provide the basis for reform. The paper also considered how Parliamentary accountability might be strengthened. This raises wider questions which are dealt with below.

The relationship between the police and the public is dealt with in detail in another chapter. But that between the Attorney General, the Director of Public Prosecutions and the police has continued to cause concern and alarm and will do so until radical reforms are introduced. What follows can be no more than a summary of some of the problems.

THE ATTORNEY GENERAL, THE DIRECTOR OF PUBLIC PROSECUTIONS AND THE POLICE

Serious criminal offences are reported by the police to the DPP who, sometimes after consultation with the Attorney General, and usually after taking the advice of barristers in private practice, decides whether or not to prosecute. The decision obviously may be of the greatest importance and have political significance, not least when the allegations are of police wrong-doing. Criticism of the DPP is common.

The DPP is a public official appointed by the Home Secretary on the advice of the Attorney General who is himself, as principal Law Officer, a Minister of the Crown. The DPP must be a barrister or solicitor of not less than ten years standing. He acts "under the superintendence" of the Attorney General and, in addition to his prosecuting functions, he is required to give advice and assistance to chief officers of police who are under a statutory duty to inform the DPP with respect to serious offences. The present Attorney told the House of Commons on 19th December 1979 that he was responsible for the DPP's actions "in the sense that I am responsible in the House for what he does".

In deciding whether or not to prosecute, the DPP considers whether a jury, properly directed, would be likely to convict. This is sometimes called the 50 per cent rule. In the view of the DPP, it is often difficult to obtain sufficient evidence against policemen to justify prosecution. So the prima facie evidence against a policeman has to be higher than against others to satisfy the 50 per cent test. Beyond this the DPP has to satisfy himself that it would be in the public interest to prosecute. Whenever he decides not to prosecute on this ground and the matter is at all political, the DPP is likely to be accused of failing to act objectively.

The most controversial of recent decisions not to prosecute have arisen in cases involving the police. Liddle Towers and James Kelly both appeared to have died from injuries received while in police custody but no charges were brought. Then on 23rd April 1979, during the general election campaign, Blair Peach died as the result of a deliberate blow from a handheld implement aimed at the head. He had an unusually thin skull but the injury could not have been accidental. The blow was struck during a clash between the police and demonstrators in Southall. The NCCL committee (chairman: Professor Michael Dummett)[1] reported that the inescapable conclusion which followed from the medical and eye witness evidence was that Blair Peach was killed by a blow deliberately inflicted by a member of Unit 1 or Unit 3 of the Special Patrol Group of the Metropolitan Police.

Commander Cass, head of the Metropolitan Police Complaints Investigation Bureau, was appointed by the Commissioner for the Metropolitan Police to investigate Blair Peach's death. He submitted his report, which has not been published, to the DPP who decided there was insufficient evidence to prosecute any police officer or anyone else. The number of police officers who could have been involved was small and it was known who they were. It is not clear why conspiracy charges were not brought against them.

Operation Countryman was a police exercise set up in 1978 to investigate allegations of widespread corruption among officers of the police in London. Very soon reports began to circulate that the investigation was being obstructed by senior and junior police officers and by the DPP. On 25th February 1980 the Attorney General told the House of Commons that there was no truth in the allegation that the DPP was blocking the investigation·or that senior police officers were doing so. He said he did not know whether junior officers were exercising their right not to answer questions. On 7th July 1980 it was alleged in the House that Chief Constable Hambleton from Dorset, who had been in titular charge of the investigation, had said that there had been considerable obstruction by junior officers and some obstruction by one senior officer. The Attorney General replied that Hambleton had not given him or the DPP details of any obstruction of the type reported in the newspapers. Allegations and counter-allegations continued to be made about the investigation and its progress or lack of progress; and about the DPP's attitude to some of the methods adopted by some of the investigators.

Some idea of the confusion that seems to have existed is perhaps exemplified by an incident in which Operation Countryman officers arrested a senior police officer on what is thought to have been a holding charge. Apparently this angered the DPP. On 25th October 1982, the Attorney General told the House of Commons:

The Director of Public Prosecutions did everything that he could to keep closely in touch, but, unfortunately, from time to time Countryman officers did things that could not be justified. Without telling the Director that they had done so they arrested a senior officer on a charge that had nothing to do with Countryman. He did not learn about it for some weeks. There was found to be no evidence when the facts were analysed, and the officer had to be discharged.

Three days later, on 28th October, the Attorney General was asked whether any charges were subsequently brought against that senior officer. He replied:

The senior officer concerned was subsequently prosecuted for two offences of conspiracy to contravene the provisions of the Prevention of Corruption Acts; was convicted on both counts at the Central Criminal Court; and was sentenced to a total of three years' imprisonment.

By many, Operation Countryman was seen at its inception as a major inquiry which, supported by senior people in Government and the police, would expose as truth or falsity the serious allegations of police corruption in London which were circulating at that time. It was realised that this would not be an easy task for the team of police investigators drawn from the provincial forces. In the event, Operation Countryman was a failure and left truth and falsity no better determined than before. The ambiguous and ambivalent position of the office of the DPP was exposed.

The Attorney General and the DPP, and the DPP alone, frequently assert that their decisions whether or not to prosecute are not political (just as judges say their decisions are not political) but, on any reasonably broad interpretation of that slippery word, politics must often be an element. The decision in 1979 not to prosecute the oil companies for infringing sanctions against Rhodesia may not have been political in the sense that the Government wished to protect the companies or to be lenient in its attitude to the Smith regime, but it was political in the sense that the whole context was directly political. The allegations were political, the setting up of the Bingham inquiry was political. In these circumstances, the decision whether or not to pursue legal remedies cannot avoid being political or having political consequences. Once "the public interest" is invoked as a reason for non-prosecution, the decision is political.

After the Bristol riots in 1980, twelve defendants were charged with riotous assembly. Eight were acquitted. The decision to prosecute for that most serious offence seems in retrospect to have been an error of judgment. In the case of four other defendants the jury failed to reach a verdict and the DPP decided to drop the charges. Some argued that this was a mistake, but the DPP was reported as saying that good race relations was one of the factors that decided him against ordering a retrial. That also is a political decision.

On the other hand, the reported decision in 1983 of the DPP not to prosecute anyone concerned with housing associations in which three Conservative members of the Greater London Council were involved, was certainly explicable on grounds relating solely to the likelihood of obtaining convictions.

Geoffrey Robertson has argued[2] that the legal conventions binding the DPP are constitutionally incapable of combatting successfully abuses of power, amounting to systematic corruption, in the police or elsewhere; that what is needed is something like the special prosecutor in the USA – which has parallels with Board of Trade inquiries into company frauds. This means investigation by a team, headed by lawyers, which is completely independent of the system under investigation. On this argument, inquiries by police officers into the activities of other police officers, using police methods, are doomed to failure not because the investigators will seek to cover the faults of their colleagues, but because presenting suspected officers with statements of complaint (some of which may have come from persons with criminal records) and inviting their replies, is a wholly inadequate way of proceeding and is unlikely to produce evidence that would stand up in court.

In the present system, only police officers make the necessary investigations when what is needed is the independence that only an outside team can enjoy.

All this may be seen as part of the present discussion about the reform of the prosecuting system which was examined by the Royal

Commission on Criminal Procedure and which may result in some form of regional organisation of prosecuting officers.[3] Some reform for ordinary cases is no doubt necessary but such proposals will not solve the problem of police corruption or malpractice.

The need for an independent team of investigators is strongest in major cases of police corruption or serious malpractice. The DPP himself is in an ambiguous position, his relationship with the police being close and strong. He may issue written instructions to chief constables in respect of offences which he requires to be reported to him and his advisory functions enable him even more to influence police activity and policy. In the public disputes about enlarging police powers or reforming the system of complaints against the police, the DPP supports the police.

Because of the inevitable closeness of the DPP's relations with the police, and his support of greater police powers, it is not surprising that his objectivity is questioned when investigations into police behaviour, with which he is connected – one of his staff, for example, was seconded to Operation Countryman – fail to result in expected prosecutions. Moreover, many of his decisions are about cases which have their own strong political overtones. Blair Peach was a schoolteacher in East London and an active member of the Anti-Nazi League and the Socialist Workers Party. The demonstrations in which he took part on the day he died were against the National Front's decision to hold a meeting in Southall Town Hall, in an area with a large Asian population. In these circumstances it was unfortunate that, under the existing system, the inquiry was conducted by the police. No-one, so far as I know, has suggested that Commander Cass, within the limits imposed on him by the system, carried out anything other than a very thorough examination. Yet it would seem that he was unable to produce evidence strong enough to satisfy the DPP. To the decision not to prosecute any single police officer or any group of officers, the Attorney General must surely have been privy. Only two conclusions seem possible: either the means of investigation open to Commander Cass were inadequate or the decision was political and based on considerations other than the likelihood of obtaining a conviction. It is no secret that many senior police officers were dismayed at the failure to prosecute some members of the Special Patrol Group.

For the large-scale cases like Operation Countryman, a special team of truly independent investigators is no doubt necessary. The suspicions of direct police involvement in crime could hardly have been more serious. This is also necessary for cases of public corruption not involving the police, such as the Poulson affair or the busting of oil sanctions against Rhodesia. For individual acts of police malpractice, a single independent investigator armed with the necessary powers of examination is more likely to succeed than a police officer with limited powers. Here the parallel is with the French *juge d'instruction* or investigating magistrate. The French system has its weaknesses but the separation of the *juge d'instruction* from both the police and the prosecutor is its key strength.

The *independence* of the team or the single investigator is absolutely crucial. They must be, and be manifestly seen to be, wholly disconnected from the political machine. A small powerful group of such investigators, some full-time and some part-time, protected from dismissal during their term of office, drawn from the legal and other professions, beholden to no-one other than themselves, would do much to restore public confidence.

Two separate problems thus emerge from the relationship of Attorney General, the DPP and the police. The first concerns the efficiency of large-scale investigations, especially (but not only) where police corruption may be involved. The second is that of accountability. In local police authorities outside London much disagreement has arisen because of the failure to distinguish the limits of the decision-making power of the chief constable, on the one hand, and his accountability on the other. There are many areas of action where the decision should rest with the chief constable, not with the police committee. These include decisions to prosecute and not to prosecute. So also it is right that, in serious cases, the DPP or the Attorney General should decide whether or not to prosecute. But both the chief constable and the DPP or Attorney General should be fully accountable to the local police committee and the House of Commons, respectively, for their decisions. And this includes explaining and justifying those decisions.

THE POWER OF PARLIAMENT

Since the sixteenth century, the liberties of the individual and the rights of the subject against established authority have been closely connected with the powers and privileges of the House of

Commons and its Members.

Members of the House of Commons have been trying since before 1914 to reform the committee system in the House, seeing this (rightly in my view) as the only way in which true accountability of the Government to Parliament is likely to be improved. The physical presence of Ministers in the House of Commons makes them appear exposed and vulnerable. But the practical working of the party system protects them. It is right that elected Governments should be able to put their policies into effect by virtue of their majority. But non-Ministerial members of the House have the constitutional responsibility of ensuring Ministerial accountability. In an ideal world, Government backbenchers should distinguish support for Government policies from scrutiny of Government activities and should be ready to join Opposition members in insisting on that accountability. But such ideal conduct is not to be expected especially when Opposition members do not hesitate to use administrative shortcomings of Ministers as sticks to beat policy as much as administration.

But the unfortunate consequence is that Ministers have managed to get control over the means by which the Commons is supposed to fulfil its critical role of holding Ministers accountable for their actions. So when, for example, the reforms of Select Committees came about, while it was greatly to the credit of the Leader of the House, Norman St John-Stevas, MP, that he introduced them and persuaded his Ministerial colleagues and backbenchers to support him, the Government was able to put limitations on their work, such as determining that certain governmental functions should be excluded from their scrutiny and that each Select Committee should be enabled to appoint only a certain number of sub-committees. Here it is surely the principle that is wrong. The Commons should be able, without governmental interference, to decide what means it should adopt to carry out its constitutional responsibilities of scrutiny and criticism.

For this to happen, it would be necessary for backbenchers on both sides of the House to come together sufficiently to reach a limited agreement on what was desirable. One obvious forum would be the Liaison Committee which presently seeks to provide modest co-ordination of the activities of the Select Committees. Given the strength of the party system and the differences in policy which separate Members, it would be unrealistic to expect radical reforms.

But wresting from the Executive the power to determine the limits of the powers of those Committees would be an advance. If the will were there, the change would be effected.

Another recent reform, also associated with Mr St John-Stevas, is the National Audit Act 1983. It strengthens Parliamentary control and supervision of the expenditure of public money by making new provision for the appointment and status of the Comptroller and Auditor General, establishing a Public Accounts Commission and making new provision for promoting economy, efficiency and effectiveness in the use of such money by Government Departments and other authorities and bodies. The Act requires that the agreement of the Chairman and of the Public Accounts Committee shall be obtained to the appointment of the C & AG and that he shall be an officer of the House. It is unfortunate that the Public Accounts Committee is not given power to direct the C & AG to undertake specific examinations. But perhaps his duty to take into account any proposals from that Committee will suffice. The new Public Accounts Commission consists of the Chairman of that Committee, the Leader of the House, and seven other MPs, none being Ministers. After much debate, the nationalised industries were kept free of the C & AG's jurisdiction. Commons control of expenditure will be further enlarged if the recommendations of the Select Committee on Procedure (Finance) of May 1983 are implemented.

Does the democratic process as executed in the House of Commons do anything to protect or promote civil liberties? Directly and in individual cases, the answer is very little. But the House is seldom of much use in its traditional role for the redress of grievances. Indirectly, the individual can often be helped by his Member in his dealings with Government Departments. This is particularly shown in immigration cases where the intervention of MPs will result in the staying of Home Office action on deportation while the individual's case is further examined. When a Member champions an individual case of whatever kind, he has the opportunity to give publicity to the case and so possibly to embarrass the Department involved, as well as perhaps being able to raise the matter on the floor of the House. This makes ignoring him difficult and politically damaging. None of this, of course, can work in cases where Ministers disclaim responsibility: for example, for actions taken by the police outside London.

So also, the legislative process in Parliament provides many opportunities for the raising of civil liberties issues and for focusing campaigns on those issues. Readers of this book will be well aware of such cases, of which some of the most important arose over the Police and Criminal Evidence Bill which fell on the dissolution of Parliament in May 1983 and was reintroduced in the new Parliament. Indeed, much of the history of the NCCL is written around the campaigns against legislative proposals put forward by Governments and Private Members.

The matter is worth emphasis. It is not always appreciated that proceedings in Standing Committee on a Government Bill do subject the Minister in charge to considerable examination, even though he is supported by a majority on the Committee. His reputation as a Minister is put under challenge, and his competence as a defender of Government policy is tested. If he has not mastered his brief or if he is unable to present that brief well, his party colleagues on the Committee will also be critical although they may not voice this criticism openly. Certainly there are many examples, known to those who follow such proceedings, of Ministers who have failed this test. Nor is it unknown for Government backbenchers to vote against their Minister, or to abstain on crucial issues, with results that can, at the least, be embarrassing to Governments.

To use the Parliamentary machinery successfully either in individual cases or more generally requires skilled expertise and long experience. Only a few organisations are effective and much depends on a very few persons. In this the NCCL has been outstandingly successful, taking into account the relative unpopularity of many civil liberty causes.

The Labour Party paper on the security services[4] proposes the setting up of a Legal Affairs Select Committee to monitor the functions of the Attorney General, the Lord Chancellor and the DPP. This would be an excellent extension to the existing Select Committee system. Amongst its less obvious functions would be to oversee the Lord Chancellor's responsibilities in relation to the Public Record Office. The Labour Party paper also proposes the setting up of a select committee on the security services. This might be better subsumed as a sub-committee under the Select Committee on the Home Office. Of course these select committees would cause problems but experience would enable a system of scrutiny to be evolved which would incorporate the necessary safeguards for confidential and secret matters.

While all such Parliamentary developments are desirable – and, since the sixteenth century have been part of the campaign for the rights of the subject against the great powers of established authority – they must not be mistaken in the late twentieth century for the substance of civil liberties. Parliamentarism, as Ralph Miliband has long emphasised, is also an organ for containment and management of public opinion while seeming to present a way of achieving radical reform.[5] Whether it will prove to be the means of achieving that liberation from authoritarianism that is envisaged by those who look forward to the flowering of the democratic process is a crucial question for tomorrow.

NOTES

1. *Southall: 23 April 1979* (NCCL, 1980).
2. *The Guardian*, 26th July 1982.
3. This was written before the Government White Paper of October 1983, announcing the Government's intention to set up a national prosecution service based on the office of the DPP [Ed].
4. See above.
5. Most recently, see his *Capitalist Democracy in Britain* (1982).

6

POLICE POWERS:
A QUESTION OF BALANCE?

LARRY GRANT

The liberty of the subject and the convenience of the police . . .
are not to be weighed in the scales against each other.
(Lord Simonds in the House of Lords case of *Christie* v
Leachinsky[1])

The two years preceding 1984 saw a vigorous public debate on police
powers, spearheaded by the NCCL. This followed the introduction
by the Government of the Police and Criminal Evidence Bill of 1982
and, after the fall of that Bill because of the 1983 General Election, of
another Bill of the same name later in that year. What was at stake
was a criminal justice system which was both fair and just. No-one
appeared to dispute that any such system not only has to provide for
the detection and conviction of the guilty but also has to ensure that
those suspected of criminal offences are protected so that the
innocent are not pursued to arrest, detention and subsequently
conviction. There was also general agreement that the law relating
to the powers of the police had developed piecemeal and that the
time had come for codification.

There the agreement ended. There were those who believed that
police powers were adequate, if not over-extensive, and that a
greater emphasis should be placed on the protection of the
individual. The Government and its supporters argued for an
increase in powers which was said to be necessary for the proper
detection and conviction of those committing criminal acts. The
philosophy behind this latter view was that a balance had to be
struck between the "interests of the community" in preventing
crime and catching criminals, on the one hand, and the rights and
liberties of the individual on the other. It will be argued that this

notion of balance is fallacious, but first it is necessary to explain the background to the debate.

In February 1978 the then Home Secretary, Merlyn Rees, set up a Royal Commission on Criminal Procedure. That the Commission was established was due in no small part to the *Confait* case, in which three youths were convicted of murder and arson. Their conviction was based largely on their own "confession statements". A campaign initiated with evidence obtained by the NCCL and led by their MP, Christopher Price, resulted in the Court of Appeal quashing their convictions, and much later in the Home Office offering £65,000 compensation between them for their 3 years' imprisonment. The circumstances leading to their conviction were subsequently investigated by Sir Henry Fisher, a former High Court Judge, at the request of the Home Secretary.[2] He reported serious failings by the police and those responsible for the conduct of the prosecution. In particular he found that Colin Lattimore, a mentally handicapped youth, had been questioned in an "unfair and oppressive" manner and that the police throughout the investigation did not follow the Judges Rules and the Administrative Directions annexed to the Rules, which together form the ground rules upon which the police may question and detain an individual for questioning. One particular direction which was ignored was that which instructs the police to allow a suspect, subject to certain exceptions, to consult with his lawyer. The report revealed serious failings by prosecuting counsel, the Office of the Director of Public Prosecutions and a Home Office pathologist.

Emphasis has been placed on the *Confait* case because it vividly illustrates how the system can go seriously wrong and that when it does so, there is more at stake than the nebulous concept of injustice: individual lives are affected. Moreover, a proven case of injustice threatens the public's confidence in the whole of the system, a factor which those involved in the prosecuting process sometimes appear to forget.

The Home Secretary avoided dealing with the questions raised by the *Confait* case by referring it to the Royal Commission, which was directed by its terms of reference to strike a balance between community interest and detection of crime. The Commission never questioned the correctness of the requirement of "balance" and indeed developed the concept in its Report.[3] The weighing of the scales condemned by Lord Simonds proved the central theme of its

Report. That the guilty may go free in order to ensure that the innocent are not wrongly convicted is itself a general principle worthy of developing. However, the fallacy in the Royal Commission theme is that there is a "community interest" in dealing with crime, which conflicts with the "individual interest" in justice. The Commission failed to recognise that there are two community interests: firstly, the interest in being effectively protected from crime and in the detection and conviction of those who commit it; and secondly, the interest in protecting the innocent from the injustice of wrongful detention and conviction. It should not be forgotten that for each innocent person convicted, a guilty person goes free. Community interest requires that there should be an effective system of criminal detection, but that effectiveness can only be enhanced if there is an improvement in the justice of the system so that the innocent are protected from wrongful conviction.

Even if one were to accept the Commission's reasoning on balance, a further problem arose when it came to the drafting of legislation. The Government ignored many of the Commission's recommendations but retained those which increased the powers of the police. Whilst the Government continued to pay lip service to balance, the Bill was introduced to satisfy the law and order brigade at the expense of civil liberties. Indeed the 1982 Bill did not provide for a system of prosecution independent of the police, which was the centre of the Commission's reasoning. The Commission had recommended that a proper balance of interests could only be achieved if the power to prosecute was removed from the police.

The difficulties which have arisen since the publication of the Report can be seen when three specific areas of police powers are analysed.

ARREST

Arrest is a very serious matter. As it involves the deprivation of liberty it is important that the law is both certain and clear. The existing law is however hopelessly confused. A police officer may arrest without a warrant someone whom he reasonably suspects of committing or having committed (1) an "arrestable offence" – usually one punishable by at least five years' imprisonment – or (2) a lesser offence, where Parliament has given a power of arrest. He may also arrest someone causing a breach of the peace. These powers are extensive but often unclear to a person being arrested, so that he is not at the time of arrest in a position to challenge the arrest as unlawful.

The approach adopted by the NCCL was that far greater use should be made of the procedure for summonsing an individual rather than making an arrest, and that arrest should be confined to those offences punishable by more than five years imprisonment.[4] The NCCL also proposed that the power to arrest for breach of the peace should be retained. The Commission rejected these proposals and recommended that there should be a single statutory power of arrest for all imprisonable offences. The Commission accepted that the power of arrest should be used less frequently but also made a recommendation that a person should be liable to arrest for all offences, including non-imprisonable offences where an officer saw an offence being committed and the suspect "positively" refused to give his name and address.

These recommendations were largely rejected by the Government, which produced a Bill providing for no substantial changes in the existing law except in one crucial area. The Government adopted and extended the recommendations concerning the power to arrest for failure to give a name and address. It extended the power to circumstances where a police officer merely suspected an offence had been committed, and was not satisfied that the name and address given was correct. The end result is that the law of arrest will remain as uncertain as ever and there is a strong likelihood that there will be an increased number of arrests for minor offences.

DETENTION

The length of time that a suspect can be held in a police station before he is charged and brought to court is an important issue, as detention is a form of punishment in itself. As in the area of arrest, existing law is vague and unsatisfactory. There is no overall limit to the period during which a person may be held without charge. The law simply states that where the offence is not serious a person should be brought before a court or bailed from the police station within 24 hours and in other cases he must be before a court as soon as is "practicable".[5] The law does not provide for any definition of "serious". The only remedy available to a suspect in detention who is held for a lengthy period is to apply for a writ of *habeas corpus*, but this is no easy matter for a person held in custody and the courts have not been vigilant in ordering releases.

There is little disagreement that the present system requires to be changed so that there is a statutory limit to the period in which a person may be kept in police custody. The period itself is however a subject of considerable dispute. NCCL's proposals to the Royal Commission were that the normal maximum period for detention be four hours, with the possibility of two further extensions each of twelve hours on application by the police to a court. One of the more extreme proposals put to the Commission was that of the then Metropolitan Police Commissioner, Sir David McNee, who advocated that the police should be entitled to hold a suspect for 72 hours before charges and thereafter obtain further extensions of 72 hours at a time for an unlimited period. No doubt this proposal and others of a similar nature from senior police officers were designed to provide the police with maximum powers unfettered by considerations relating to the protection of the individual. It should be noted in this context that the Australian Law Reform Commission proposed a maximum period of four hours from the commencement of custody, with power to grant extensions, having heard evidence that the majority of investigations after arrest were investigated and concluded within this time.[6] American research produced similar findings, and police officers told the Commission that four hours was realistic.

The Royal Commission rejected the NCCL and other similar proposals, apparently on the ground that the research on which they were based was not a study of police work in the United Kingdom. Yet its own research showed that detention beyond six hours occurred only in a quarter of cases and for beyond three days only in a tiny percentage. It might be thought that this would be sufficient to justify a relatively short period in detention before charge or release. The Commission however recommended a scheme whereby a suspect may be detained for up to 24 hours and for a further period of 24 hours on application to a magistrate if he is suspected of a "grave offence". The Commission declined to provide a definition of "grave".

The Government's approach was to double the detention period proposed by the Commission. The 1982 Bill enabled the police to detain for "a serious arrestable offence" (defined only as one which a police officer regards as serious),[7] for 24 hours and then by application to a magistrate for a further 24 hours without legal representation. After that period the Bill proposed further periods of detention of 48 hours with the approval of a magistrates' court, at which time the suspect could be represented. In short the proposal was an upper limit of 96 hours, 48 hours of which might be without access to a lawyer. In the 1983 Bill, although the definition of "serious arrestable offence" has been tightened up somewhat, the detention periods proposed are the same as in the 1982 Bill.

SEARCH AND SEIZURE

The 1982 Bill contained provisions to codify the existing powers of the police to enter and search private premises in order to make an arrest or prevent a breach of the peace. It contained provisions however for a wholly new power to be granted by a Magistrate (and in some cases by a Circuit Judge) authorising the police to enter the premises of an owner or an occupier who was not suspected of any criminal offence in order to search for evidence and to seize any items found there. This power undoubtedly caused the greatest controversy of any of the clauses in the Bill. That the power was limited to "serious arrestable offences" was not a consideration which carried much weight to those who opposed the proposals for reasons which should now be clear. Opposition was not confined to the NCCL and like-minded groups traditionally concerned with the encroachment on individual liberty by the increase of powers given to those who administer justice. Concern was expressed by the Law Society, the Bar Council, the British Medical Association, and many church groups and organisations of all denominations. That concern was expressed in terms of action and extensive lobbying, spearheaded by the NCCL, which resulted in the Home Secretary announcing extensive changes in the 1982 Bill which are now reflected in the current Bill.

The Government's proposals represented a fundamental departure from the existing principles concerning the power to enter and search private premises and seize possessions. Hitherto such power was limited to circumstances where the owner/occupier was suspected of an offence: the new powers enabled the police to search the premises of an entirely innocent person in the hope of finding evidence against another person. The right under attack was the entitlement to privacy in one's home, a right never codified but recognised by the law in that, on each occasion the right has been encroached, those seeking change have been required to justify their actions. The justification has always been that the particular material which had been removed was evidence of a crime so repugnant that an infringement of individual liberty was a necessary price to pay. Yet no such justification was offered by the police, who originally sought the powers, nor, as will be seen, by the Royal Commission which, in a narrower form, endorsed it. Perhaps this is not surprising: it is difficult enough to justify a power to search and seize the property of an innocent individual in "exceptional" circumstances, let alone as a general principle. Not long before the Government introduced its Bill the House of Lords criticised a similar but narrower power of search conferred on the Inland Revenue and *limited* to tax fraud investigation. It was decribed as "an altogether unnecessary power which ... dangerously encroaches an individual liberty" and as "a breathtaking inroad on the individual's right of privacy and the right of property".[8]

The greatest criticism of the provisions in the 1982 Bill arose because of the implications of the denial of the right of innocent individuals to be free from having their homes forcibly entered into and their possessions searched and seized by the police. The police were now free to search the premises and papers of those holding information in confidence: doctors, lawyers, priests, journalists, social workers, all of whom were at risk because the Bill intended to destroy the duty of confidentiality which they owed to those who confided in them.

Why were these provisions introduced by the Government? It is difficult to come to any conclusion other than that they would assist in appeasing the "law and order" brigade. It also provides a further example of the dangers in believing that criminal procedure "packages" will be accepted by a Government. In evidence before the Royal Commission the police bemoaned their lack of powers but did not press heavily for extended powers of search and seizure. They clearly recognised that it would have been very difficult to have provided justification for a *general* search power for the police. The Commission, partially accepting this difficulty, concluded that "a compulsory power of search for evidence should be available only as a last resort" and stated that rigorous safeguards should be provided. The Government had no difficulty in ignoring this stricture and produced legislation which extended police powers of search generally without any of the safeguards.

The pressure on the Government required it to think again. Major changes were made to the 1982 Bill, now reflected in the current legislation, so that the police are not permitted to search for and seize "excluded material". Such material includes items covered by legal privilege (e.g. correspondence between solicitors and their clients); medical records and confidential personal records held by the police, social workers, and voluntary agencies; samples of human tissues and tissue fluids; and confidential journalistic records.

An important battle was therefore won. But the Government remains secure in having introduced legislation which extends police powers far beyond those traditionally recognised. By no stretch of the imagination can it be said that the new powers have been made available "only as a last resort".

The Government has adopted other recommendations of the Royal Commission, including the codification and extension of police powers to stop and search in the streets for stolen and prohibited articles, the searching of individuals and searching of premises and vehicles including the power to set up and operate road blocks.

CONCLUSIONS

The recommendation by the Commission for the introduction of Codes of Practice to replace the present Judges' Rules and Administrative Directions was also adopted. It is here however that the fundamental weakness of the Commission's recommendations can be seen most clearly, giving rise to the allegation that the Commission has failed to protect the suspect from abuse or misuse of police powers. The real value of a code of this nature would be if evidence obtained from the suspect in breach of the code were to be excluded at trial. The Commission rejected this proposal and sought to rely on such breaches being prevented by two traditional methods: a complaint against an individual police officer or a civil action for damages, both of which have proved unsatisfactory in the past. Indeed the Commission itself recognised the serious defects in the present police complaints machinery. The most serious criticism of the present Judges' Rules is not their contents but that the judges can choose to ignore them by admitting evidence obtained in breach of the rules. The new Codes of Practice and other measures proposed in the Bill, such as improved reporting procedures in police stations, are undoubtedly a marked improvement on existing procedures. But their effectiveness remains open to question if there is no adequate means of enforcement. The proposed new powers which are to be given to the police are real; they are there to be used and will be used. The safeguards for the suspect exist in theory but will in practice exist only if police officers follow the code. The greatest incentive to police officers to act in accordance with the code would be the certain knowledge that any illegal act would result in exclusion of evidence. Without such incentive the suspect remains at risk.

Reference has already been made to the failure by the Government in the 1982 Bill to provide for a Public Prosecutor, a central recommendation of the Commission's Report. This is likely to be remedied, along the lines of a White Paper published together with the 1983 Bill, in separate legislation in the near future. There were however two other important recommendations made by the Commission which have been ignored. Firstly, there is no statutory provision for the introduction of tape-recordings in police stations. The Government has chosen instead to introduce a further experiment notwithstanding that the Commission itself carried out extensive testing. Secondly there are to be no statutory controls over police telephone-tapping and the use of other surveillance methods. The Royal Commission recommended controls on surveillance similar to controls on police entry and search of private premises.

The tragedy of the Royal Commission's approach is that not only did it misunderstand the concept of balance but it was also naive in believing that having produced what it considered to be a carefully balanced package, such a package would be adopted by the Government in its entirety. As has been seen, the Commission's recommendations have been used to introduce legislation which increases police powers and provides inadequate safeguards for the suspect. The Commission has done nothing to prevent another *Confait* case tomorrow, for all the uncertainties which may give rise to a wrongful arrest and conviction still remain. One point however is certain: when the next case does arise no Home Secretary for the remainder of this century will set up a Royal Commission on Criminal Procedure.

NOTES

1. [1947] Appeal Cases, p.573.
2. *Report of an Inquiry by the Hon. Sir Henry Fisher into the circumstances leading to the trial of three persons on charges arising out of the death of Maxwell Confait and the fire at 27 Doggett Road, London SE6* (HC Paper 90, HMSO, 1977).
3. *Report of the Royal Commission on Criminal Procedure* (Cmnd. 8092, HMSO, 1981), ch. 1.
4. See generally the Submission of the NCCL to the Royal Commission on Criminal Procedure (NCCL, 1979).
5. Magistrates' Courts Act 1980, section 43.
6. *Criminal Investigation Report No 2 (Interim)* (Law Reform Commission of Australia, 1975).
7. Police and Criminal Evidence Bill 1982, clause 74.
8. *IRC* v *Rossminster* [1980]] 1 All England Law Reports, p.80.

7

PROSECUTION AND TRIAL
IN THE CRIMINAL PROCESS

PETER THORNTON

In such circumstances the Defence was naturally in a very
ticklish and difficult position. Yet that, too, was intentional.
For the Defence was not actually countenanced by the Law,
but only tolerated, and there were differences of opinion even
on that point, whether the Law could be interpreted to admit
such tolerance at all.

(F Kafka, *The Trial*)

INTRODUCTION

Changes in the law relating to the prosecution and trial of suspects
are rarely dramatic. Although crime is of continual public interest
the criminal law receives much less attention. Changes are normally
made piecemeal through fragments of legislation, isolated judicial
decisions and reactive administrative directions. Constructive analysis and self-criticism tend to give way to complacency.

As a consequence the underlying direction of change in the
criminal process is not always easily discernible. Regrettably,
examination of certain significant changes and proposals for reform
in recent years reveals a disturbing trend towards the extension of
authority at the expense of the rights of suspects. The threat to civil
liberties posed by this trend is not of concern just to the individual; it
affects the whole society. If the wrongful arrest, detention and
conviction of the innocent is a gross injustice to the individual, it is
also an injustice to us all in letting the guilty go free. A just and
efficient system is in everybody's interests.

Fresh hopes for new, progressive changes had been placed in the Royal Commission on Criminal Procedure, the first complete review of the criminal process in England and Wales this century. It was established in 1977 partly because of public anxiety about the *Confait* case, in which three youths, one mentally handicapped, had been wrongly convicted of murder, manslaughter and arson on their own "confession" evidence. But these hopes were misplaced. The Report of the Royal Commission on Criminal Procedure, published in January 1981[1] (and draft legislation that followed it) completely failed to strike a satisfactory balance between "the interests of the community in bringing offenders to justice" and "the rights and liberties of persons suspected or accused of crime" as the Royal Warrant demanded. It merely confirmed the trend which had been exhibited in many aspects of the criminal process – for example, in the arbitrary decision to prosecute, in the unnecessary refusal of bail, in the persistent attacks upon trial by jury, and in the inadequate system of appeals.

Whether the disregard for civil liberties has emerged from the growing crime rate and the decreasing detection rate, or from the financial restraints imposed by politicians on an issue of low priority, or from an essentially weak and conservative legislature and judiciary, or for other reasons is uncertain. The effect for the future, however, is undeniable: decreasing confidence in a traditionally cherished system of justice and a hardening of official attitudes to the rights of suspects. These are the areas of concern which will be examined in this chapter.

THE DECISION TO PROSECUTE

A brief analysis of the present arrangements for the prosecution of criminal offences in England and Wales would be impossible. The difficulty lies in the startling variety and apparent haphazardness of the present system. But the main feature is that the police have the primary responsibility for the decision to prosecute. The obvious and substantial defect of this aspect of the system is that it confuses the vigorous investigation of crime with the quite separate functions of objective assessment of evidence and of the need for prosecution. It follows that it offends against the principle that prosecution should be independent, impartial and fair, concerned with the pursuit of

truth rather than winning or losing. It is a strong-minded investigating officer in charge of a case who, instead of seeking to fit the
evidence to the arrested suspect, sets off to search for evidence
which may point to the suspect's innocence, and who will disclose
that evidence to the defence if it becomes available.

There is also the danger of widely varying prosecution policies
produced by the hotch-potch of prosecution authorities throughout
the country. There are prosecutions initiated by the Director of
Public Prosecutions (sometimes with the consent of the Attorney
General, sometimes without), prosecutions by government departments such as the Department of Trade and Industry, and there are
police prosecutions, brought by and on behalf of the local Chief
Constable, who is assisted in some forces by a Prosecuting Solicitors'
Department and in others by advice and representation from local
solicitors. This variety of prosecution authorities is equalled by the
widely differing attitudes of individual Chief Constables in the
development and execution of prosecution policy at a local level, an
aspect seen most vividly in the prosecution of controversial offences
and in the use of cautions to avoid prosecution. And there is the
"private prosecution", the right of anyone, whether individually or
as a group, to begin criminal proceedings.

Both practice and procedure differ so greatly, without any
coherent plan of policy or accountability for individual decisions,
that the official figure[2] that more than 40% of all acquittals at the
Crown Court are ordered or directed by the judge is hardly
surprising. It means that a substantial number of cases should never
have been brought in the first place.

In the light of this chaos the Royal Commission's proposal for an
independent prosecutor service was one of its more welcome
recommendations. Three options were subsequently put forward by
the Home Office for consideration. The first option was an integrated
national system with a chain of locally based prosecutors controlled
and appointed by a central department. The second option (favoured
by the Royal Commission) was a decentralised national system with
regional prosecutors having a degree of autonomy as independent
office holders under the Crown. The third was a local system with
each area having a prosecution department, independent of the police
and accountable to a local supervising body. The case for an integrated
national service headed by the Director of Public Prosecutions and
under the superintendence of the Attorney-General was argued in a

White Paper published in October 1983, *An Independent Prosecution Service for England and Wales*. But the Government, recognising "the complexity and wide-ranging nature", let alone the cost, of its proposals, has taken no final decision. The opportunity to legislate in tandem with the Police and Criminal Evidence Bill has been passed over.

Whichever option, if any, is eventually chosen there is an overwhelming case for separating investigation from prosecution. The police should certainly take the case to the point of charge. Thereafter, the prosecutor should be able to withdraw or modify the charges, take any necessary pre-trial decisions and be responsible for the conduct of the prosecution at all hearings. The police would be freed from pre-trial and Court work so as to be able to get on with their main task of preventing, detecting and investigating crime.

But there is need for considerable caution. Just as an effective police complaints machinery requires a truly independent element throughout its system, so too must the prosecutor be truly independent from the police and capable of overriding police demands. As the White Paper rightly states: "Decisions on prosecution must not be susceptible to improper influence either in individual cases or in categories of cases". This is not just a question of formal arrangements. A recent study of the independent prosecution system in Scotland has shown just how easily the role of the Procurator Fiscal (public prosecutor) in taking the effective decision whether to prosecute can be undermined by an excessive case load and the unhelpful way in which the police present their reports to the Procurator Fiscal.[3]

Furthermore, in order to work effectively the system must be both uniform and accountable. In a fully comprehensive and coherent system the right of private prosecution which has been much abused in recent years would have to be abolished and the public prosecutor would gradually take over the prosecuting role of the government agencies. Accountability would be achieved first through Parliament and secondly through a Review Tribunal.[4] Parliament would lay down guidelines on the decision to prosecute, covering areas such as the youth or old age or mental condition of the alleged offender, the triviality or the staleness of the offence, and the possibility of harm or suffering caused to a victim such as a child. A Review Tribunal, consisting of lay members appointed for fixed periods, would need to be established in order to monitor the operation of prosecution policy and the independence of prosecutors from the police, and to receive complaints from police and public on the operation of the system.

At the same time the introduction of the public prosecutor should be marked by a new criterion for the decision to prosecute. The present minimum standard is the existence of a "prima facie case", the existence of evidence which, if believed by a magistrates court or a jury, would justify a conviction. The Royal Commission rightly felt that the more stringent test applied by the DPP, namely whether there is more than a 50% chance of conviction, was more appropriate.[5]

BAIL

Once the decision to prosecute is made the next critical function of the police and courts is the grant or refusal of bail. A proper bail system strikes a fair balance between the protection of the public and the freedom of the suspect. Refusal of bail is "the solitary exception to Magna Carta",[6] and improper refusal is a violation of the Habeas Corpus Act 1679 and of the Bill of Rights 1688. But constitutional theory is far removed from daily practice. Official statistics show that nearly 50% of those refused bail are either acquitted or receive non-custodial sentences.[7] Denial of bail may cause severe hardship. Preparation for trial is more difficult in custody, and home and livelihood may be jeopardised. Present remand conditions are unacceptable. Remand prisons are overcrowded and police stations and court cells are used as emergency accommodation with cramped, unsuitable living conditions. Lawyers have complained of difficulty in gaining access to their clients. And unlike the systems in many other countries, including West Germany, Japan and the United States, the acquitted defendant has no right to compensation for loss suffered during a remand in custody.

After many years of discussion judicial control over bail was codified by Parliament for the first time in the Bail Act 1976. The Act was designed to reflect the presumption of innocence in a statutory presumption of bail. It was introduced specifically as "a means of enabling courts to release more persons on bail ... without diminishing the protection of the public". The Act was seen as a liberal move and predictably faced heavy criticism, not least from the then Lord Chief Justice and Director of Public Prosecutions, even before its effect could be seen. Sir David McNee described it as "an engine for the release of hardened criminals". Another senior police officer described it as "the logic of the madhouse and a betrayal of the public".[8] Some magistrates' courts deliberately log-jammed the business of their courts by spending excessive time on the new paper work as a means of protest.

The critics of the Act were not disappointed for long. The presumption of bail was fettered with discretionary powers which were soon used extensively in the refusal of bail. The practice of Nottingham justices of refusing to hear a second application for bail unless there had been a change in the defendant's circumstances was sanctioned on appeal.[9] The decision seriously undermined the working of the Bail Act throughout the country. Bail applications were made less often and defence lawyers found themselves arguing not for bail but that a change in circumstances had occurred. A subsequent appeal decision[10] restricted the established right of the accused to apply for bail in committal proceedings. Even the grant of bail became fettered by the growing use of conditions, such as the imposition of a curfew.

One long-sought improvement in bail procedures has been made: the introduction in May 1983 of the right of appeal to the Crown Court against the refusal of bail by magistrates.[11] This change is intended to supplement, if not eventually replace, the awkward "judge in chambers" appeal procedure in the High Court, for which legal aid remains unavailable. It is too soon to see the results of the new procedure, although some magistrates' courts are already using the existence of the new right of appeal as a reason, in addition to the reason in the *Nottingham Justices* case, for refusing to hear second applications for bail.

But there is still considerable scope for improvement in the bail system. The operation of the Bail Act has shown that amending legislation is now necessary – to place a heavier burden on those opposing bail, to reverse the *Nottingham Justices* case, to ensure that legal aid is granted for representation for all cases where bail is opposed or refused, to restrict remands in custody for medical and welfare reports after conviction, and to compensate acquitted defendants for loss suffered during detention. The few but much-publicised cases of offenders committing further offences after release on bail should be seen not as an argument for less bail but as powerful evidence that greater care should be taken by magistrates on all applications for bail.

DELAY

The question of bail is closely connected with the question of delay in bringing proceedings to a conclusion. The old maxim "Justice delayed is justice denied" reflects the problems of cases becoming stale and of the distress and inconvenience caused to witnesses, victims and suspects. In Scotland the "110 day rule" operates in cases where the accused is kept in custody. It provides that unless the case is brought to trial and concluded within 110 days from committal for trial the accused must be released from custody and freed for all time from the charge. In England and Wales, with one minor and ineffective exception, there are no time limits, and therefore no punitive sanctions for lengthy delays before trial.

While favouring a greater element of discipline in the system the Royal Commission complacently rejected the use of time limits during the bringing of proceedings.[12] But the practice in Scotland and the proposals of the Thomson Committee on Criminal Procedure in Scotland[13] suggest that a scheme of fixed time limits, rigidly applied, can have the effect of preventing unnecessary delays in criminal proceedings. In custody cases the 110 day rule, or a shorter period, should apply for indictable cases, with a reduced 40 day period from the first appearance in summary cases. In non-custody cases the periods should be 12 months for indictable cases and six months for summary cases. Extensions should only be granted because of the illness of the defendant or witnesses or at the defendant's request.

Apart from the use of time limits, delays would be further reduced by a more efficient use of the courts' time in the listing and hearing of cases and by a measure frequently encouraged by senior judges, namely the reduction in the scale of some cases. This can be achieved by avoiding an excessive number of charges, by the more frequent use of separate trials and by restricting the quantity of evidence upon which the prosecution relies.

MODE OF TRIAL

All criminal cases go through the magistrates' courts and about 90% of them are concluded there. Particularly serious cases go automatically to the Crown Court, but some cases fall into the category of "triable either way". The choice of forum for this category between summary trial in the magistrates' court and trial on indictment before a jury in the Crown Court rests first with the nature of the offence and second with the decision of the accused. Many defendants choose trial by jury, not because the chances of acquittal are higher (official statistics indicate that the acquittal rate in the Crown Court is slightly lower than the 50% acquittal rate for those who plead not guilty in the magistrates' courts), but in the belief that the quality of justice is better and the care and attention given by lawyers, judge and jury, are generally greater than can be expected in the lower courts.

Not surprisingly, this view is not one which is appreciated by the authorities who have to manage the system. Trial by jury is considerably more expensive than summary trial.[14] The cost of a full-time Crown Court judge sitting with a jury obviously outweighs the minimal cost of lay magistrates. Furthermore the sheer volume of work in the courts and the growing cost of litigation has put intense strain on the whole administration of justice. Not only has the crime rate increased but recent years have also seen a rapid growth of legislation and subordinate legislation, creating additional offences. The legal aid bill has rapidly increased to a politically unacceptable level. In the absence of a complete overhaul or change of direction severe cutbacks can be expected.

These are not encouraging signs for the development of fairness and efficieny in the administration of justice. And one of the obvious and most controversial areas of cutback has come in the distribution of business between the Crown Court and magistrates' courts. In 1975 a committee chaired by Lord Justice James[15] recommended abolition of the right to jury trial in a number of selected categories of offence, chief of these being some 20,000 cases a year of theft of property under the value of £20. This proposal was met by strong public opposition on the ground that a conviction for dishonesty remains a serious stigma with potentially severe consequences, and the Labour Lord Chancellor of the day, Lord Elwyn-Jones, was forced to withdraw it in order "to maintain public confidence in the Courts".[16] Nevertheless, certain offences were demoted as a result of the James Committee's report, and none were promoted to the "triable either way" category despite the report's excellent recommendation that offences of assaulting a police officer, an offence which frequently attracts a prison sentence on the evidence of police officers alone, should be triable by a jury.

The James Committee made a quite separate proposal which did receive widespread support but still awaits statutory implementation, namely the provision for advance disclosure of the prosecution case in magistrates' courts. Disclosure is given as a matter of right in the Crown Court. It ensures full notice in advance of the case against the accused and gives an opportunity to obtain evidence to rebut it. In the experience of lawyers it also ensures that a large number of defendants quite properly plead guilty when they see the strength of the case against them.

In magistrates' courts the practice of disclosure is variable. Some police officers will disclose the case in advance, others do so minutes before trial, others refuse altogether. There may be material helpful to the defence or contradictory of prosecution witnesses that will be kept secret from the defence and the court throughout the proceedings. In other cases after waiting months for trial defendants have to ask for an adjournment to counter an allegation which had not been previously disclosed.

The spirit of the James Committee's proposal for disclosure is embodied in Section 48 Criminal Law Act 1977 which provides the power to make rules "for the purpose of securing that the accused is furnished with advance information concerning the facts and matters of which the prosecutor proposes to adduce evidence". But it remains on the statute book with a commencement date "to be appointed". The James Committee declared that it was "most desirable in the interests of justice that defendants should be fully acquainted with the case against them".[17] The Royal Commission agreed and said that Section 48 should now "receive priority".[18] The absence of advance disclosure is a continuing injustice in the lower courts.

TRIAL BY JURY

The traditional and established role of the jury is to safeguard the liberty of the subject. "Trial by jury is more than an instrument of justice and more than one wheel of the constitution: it is the lamp that shows that freedom lives".[19]

Introduced by the Normans into England from the procedure of the Carlovingian Kings of France, the jury in origin was a body of neighbours summoned by a public officer to give upon oath a true answer to some question. Henry II turned the jury into an instrument for doing justice, and Blackstone described it as "the principal criterion of truth in the law of England".

Juries were formerly a common feature of civil proceedings, but now they are normally limited to actions for defamation, false imprisonment and malicious prosecution. Under the criminal law trial by jury embodies the everyday practical experience of laymen; it gives protection against tyranny and unfairness; it helps to ensure the independence of judges; and it gives protection against laws which the ordinary person may regard as harsh and oppressive.

Our system of trial by jury has survived and is likely to continue to survive. But in recent years it has been the subject of serious and repeated attacks by those who seek to undermine its value as "the grand bulwark" of our liberties.

First came the assaults upon the right of silence. Under the English accusatorial system of trial it is not enough to say merely "I accuse"; it is for the prosecution to prove the defendant's guilt. From this stems the privilege against self-incrimination, the right at all times, from being suspected of crime to the conclusion of trial, to remain silent in the face of accusation and the corresponding right to have no adverse inference drawn from that silence. It is enough to say "You make the accusation, you must prove it". Abolition of the right of silence would be inconsistent with the onus of proof and with the very essence of the accusatorial system. Yet there has been strong support for its abolition. The proposal was adopted by the Criminal Law Revision Committee in 1972[20] and endorsed by Sir Robert Mark in his notorious Dimbleby Lecture in 1973,[21] but it was temporarily buried by powerful public opposition, particularly from the legal professions. And despite renewed calls for abolition, primarily from the police, the Royal Commission proposed the retention of the right.[22]

Second, there are the various attempts to remove the right to trial by jury in serious cases. The James Committee's proposals to redistribute the business of the courts were only partly implemented.

But attacks upon the collective intelligence of juries are frequently made. Calls for the abolition of juries in fraud cases have so far failed despite recent support from Lord Hailsham, the Lord Chancellor, and Sir Ralph Gibson, Chairman of the Law Commission. But we are forewarned. The absence of juries for the last ten years in the "Diplock Courts" in Northern Ireland has been a major factor in the lack of confidence in the special courts. Despite the results of a public opinion survey carried out in 1980 for the Standing Advisory Commission on Human Rights, which revealed that a majority within both communities were in favour of the restoration of jury trial, there is no serious move towards the return of trial by jury in Northern Ireland.

Third, there have been a number of specific changes in jury practice and procedure. These changes include the introduction of majority verdicts, abolition of disclosure of the occupation of jurors, reduction of the defence right of peremptory challenge of jurors from seven to three challenges, and the forthcoming extension of categories of disqualified juries. Some of these changes may have more effect than others. But individually and cumulatively these mostly unchallenged changes show how easily significant practical alterations in the system can be made.

Fourth, there is the call for greater disclosure of the defence case. The presumption of innocence places the burden of proof upon the prosecution. The defence does not have to give any information to the prosecution in advance of the trial. The use of surprise defence, or surprise witness, is a rare, but sometimes an important, feature of a defendant's case. It prevents the prosecution from forewarning its own witnesses or seeking to fudge or even cover up its own position. The first major exception to the rule of non-disclosure by the defence came in 1967 with the requirement of advance notice of an alibi defence. The James Committee did not consider that the principle of advance disclosure by the defence should be extended beyond the alibi notice:

We only observe that there is considerable strength in the argument that it is wrong in principle, in a system which presumes innocence until guilt is proved, to require disclosure of the defence before the details of the evidence for the prosecution are disclosed; and we believe that such a change might be generally unacceptable.[23]

The change was however considered acceptable by the Royal

Commission, who wanted to extend the alibi exception "to other defences which by taking the prosecution by surprise can cause the trial to be adjourned while investigation is carried out to confirm or disprove them".[24] Their proposal took form in the draft legislation of the Police and Criminal Evidence Bill which provides the power to make rules for the advance disclosure of expert evidence. The inconsistency of principle will no doubt continue.

Fifth, the defendant's right to make an unsworn statement from the dock was abolished in May 1983. The statement from the dock dates from the reign of Queen Anne. It was specifically preserved by the Criminal Evidence Act 1898 as a valid third option to the defendant's remaining silent or giving evidence under oath. The Crown was protected by being allowed to call evidence in rebuttal. The statement could not be drafted by counsel; it had to be the accused's words alone. It was particularly important in jury trials where earlier the defendant was unrepresented or feared cross-examination on his criminal record because he had mounted an attack on prosecution witnesses – for example in attempting to show that a confession had been improperly obtained. This "very age-old and respectable institution"[25] has now gone.

These five areas are of considerable importance in considering the future of trial by jury. It is no coincidence that the impetus of most of these attacks has come since the passing of the Juries Act 1974, which removed the stringent property qualification for jurors and widened the social basis of the jury's composition. With certain exceptions anyone on the electoral roll between the ages of 18 and 65 can now qualify. If we hold up the system of trial by jury as the standard bearer of democracy in the criminal process we should be warned for the future. We should also remember Blackstone's warnings in the eighteenth century,

that these inroads upon this sacred bulwark of the nation are fundamentally opposite to the spirit of our constitution; and that, though begun in trifles, the precedent may gradually increase and spread, to the utter disuse of juries in questions of the most momentous concern.

EVIDENCE

The exclusion of inadequate or unfair or oppressive evidence from the trial of an accused is no less an important function of the criminal process. But the dangerous use of illegally obtained evidence and confessions, and the use of identification evidence, continue to cause widespread anxiety over the inadequacy of the laws of evidence to provide safeguards against wrongful convictions.

Despite a draft code of evidence put forward in 1873 by Sir James Fitzjames Stephen, who had drafted the India Evidence Act, this area of the law remains largely uncodified. The development of the laws which govern the principles of evidence, such as relevancy, proof, opinions, presumptions and hearsay, rest mainly in the hands of the judiciary. Most striking of recent judicial decisions was the ruling by the House of Lords in 1979 that illegally obtained evidence could be used at trial even if its use would be unfair or oppressive to the accused.[26] If, for example, the evidence was obtained by an "agent provocateur" (defined as "a person who entices another to commit an express breach of the law which he would not otherwise commit and then proceeds to inform against him"),[27] it would afford the accused no defence (contrary to the law in the United States). Prior to this decision there was some constraint on police officers tempted to act illegally or to obtain evidence by deception or by a trick. Now there is none.

The law relating to the evidence of confessions or admissions made during police interrogation is no less unsatisfactory. The ultimate safeguard for improperly obtained evidence is its exclusion at trial. But the operation of this essential safeguard is rare. Under the proposals in the Police and Criminal Evidence Bill it will be even rarer.

The dangers of confession evidence have been demonstrated by independent research commissioned by the Royal Commission into the effect of police questioning of a suspect in custody; by the rule of Scottish law which forbids the use of a confession without supporting evidence; and above all by the overturning of convictions in cases such as the *Confait* case, which led to condemnation of the present practice by the Fisher Report.[28]

But the Bill proposes a new "unreliability" test for confession evidence. In so doing it rejects recommendations made by the Royal Commission and in the Fisher Report and falls back on a proposal of the heavily criticised Criminal Law Revision Committee Report in 1972.[29] This proposal is more likely to increase the risk of wrongful convictions based on false confessions. It fails to replace the uncertainty of the present "voluntary" test with a clear and precise formulation which would provide for rigorous exclusion of confessions when the rules on the treatment and questioning of suspects are broken. It introduces the admission of evidence as to the truth or falsity of a confession in considering how it was obtained. And it reinforces a disturbing trend in police investigation of crime: namely, undue reliance on the process of questioning suspects in detention with a view to obtaining a confession as opposed to the search for independent evidence of guilt or innocence.

There is only one formulation that provides clarity, certainty and fairness. It requires automatic exclusion of evidence obtained in breach of the rules on the treatment and questioning of suspects and the hard-and-fast rule that no conviction can stand on confession evidence alone.

The dangers of wrongful conviction on identification evidence are no less great. It was public disquiet about the possibility of miscarriages of justice in a number of individual cases which led in 1976 to the Devlin Report on identification in criminal cases,[30] to guidelines from the Attorney-General[31] and to a decision by a five judge Court of Appeal in the *Turnbull* Case.[32] As a result of this exceptional attention special procedures were built into identification cases. Warnings had to be given to juries of the need for caution. The circumstances of identification had to be examined closely. Judges were told to stop cases when the only evidence was identification evidence of a poor quality which depended, for example, solely on a fleeting glance or on a longer observation made in difficult conditions.

But, as with other progressive steps forward, this admirable enthusiasm for rigour and caution was shortlived. A series of appellate decisions whittled away the hard-won principles:[33] it was wrong to apply or interpret the *Turnbull* decision too inflexibly, it was only intended to deal with the ghastly risk run in cases of fleeting encounters. Then the Attorney-General followed suit. He modified his guidelines, drawing back from "rigid adherence" to the new safeguards.[34] As practising lawyers observed, the fuss was over, back to the pre-*Turnbull* position. Once again it is commonplace to have direct confrontation between witness and suspect, even in London to use escalators as a substitute for identification parades, and to found a conviction on uncorroborated identification evidence. The central proposal of the Devlin Report, that the codes of conduct governing identification procedures should be made statutory and that failure to observe them would permit the trial judge to exclude the relevant evidence, remain unimplemented.

APPEALS

The Court of Criminal Appeal, now known as the Court of Appeal (Criminal Division), was created in 1907 after considerable public concern had been generated over a number of wrongful conviction cases. But the Court has always taken a narrow view of the scope of its statutory powers, preferring to deal with mistakes of law or defects of process rather than with the assertion of an appellant that he was wrongly convicted because he was innocent. In particular the Court of Appeal has been reluctant to review convictions with the assistance of new information. The concept of "fresh evidence" has been narrowly interpreted and the development of the "lurking doubt" approach to the correctness of a conviction extremely muted.

At the same time successive Home Secretaries have shown a marked unwillingness to exercise their power to refer cases back to the Court of Appeal, and those cases which have been referred back have proved the Court of Appeal to be a reluctant instrument for providing redress for the victims of injustice.

Two important changes are necessary. First, the Criminal Appeal Act 1968 must be amended to provide a new framework for considering miscarriages of justice. Second, an independent review body must be set up to consider the cases that slip through the net of the formal appeal system, and it must have the power to refer them back to the Court of Appeal. This second proposal, which has been put forward by Justice, the British Section of the International Commission of Jurists,[35] and endorsed by the House of Commons Select Committee on Home Affairs, has been rejected recently by the Home Office. All that is offered instead is that the Home Secretary will "more readily" invite the Court of Appeal to reconsider a case and the Court will "more readily" consider it. It is not anticipated that this will make a significant contribution to the redress of wrongful convictions.

Meanwhile, recognition of the injustice suffered by those wrongly convicted who may have served years in prison before their release, should be marked by the introduction of a statutory system of full compensation to replace the present seemingly random system of ex gratia payments.

CONCLUSION

This review of certain areas of the process of prosecution and trial should not be seen as comprehensive. It does not include, for example, the practice of plea bargaining or the grant to informers of immunity from prosecution. Nor does it include the growing use of the Contempt of Court Act 1981 to restrict the freedom of the press in reporting criminal proceedings. It omits the subjects of sentencing and the representation of suspects in the courts. It seeks only to demonstrate the clear, if gradual, development of principle and practice in the criminal process running contrary to the interests of society and the individual.

The view that the protection of the suspect against injustice should give way to the protection of society against crime is growing. It involves the increase of police powers, tighter control over the courts and tougher penalties for offenders. It also involves fewer safeguards for suspects. Two leading authorities on crime and penal policy concluded:

The natural response to rising crime, declining standards of justice, failing hopes, is to hit out and demand change. The tough authoritarian approach to the control of crime has its own ideological vitality. It aims to support a regime, to preserve a set of values, to hold a community together and maintain order within it. Yet it exacts a very high price of the whole society as well as of those suspected or convicted of crime.[36]

If the course of development is clear, the way to its reversal is less clear. It may not be enough to fall back on established liberal traditions. A fresh approach to the codification of the criminal law, the rationalisation of the courts and the practice within them may be necessary. Whichever approach is adopted, the solution to the problem will require the expression of public opinion, the persistence of pressure groups and the force of reason. The first step is to recognise that the problem exists.

NOTES

1. *Report of the Royal Commission on Criminal Procedure* (Cmnd. 8092, HMSO, 1981).
2. *Report of the Royal Commission*, para. 6.18.
3. S R Moody and J Toombs, *Prosecution in the Public Interest* (Scottish Academic Press, 1982).
4. Submission by NCCL to the Royal Commission (NCCL, 1979).
5. *Report of the Royal Commission*, paras. 8.6-8.11.
6. Lord Hailsham, speaking to the Gloucester Branch of the Magistrates' Association, 11th September 1971.
7. See the figures quoted in Patricia Hewitt, *The Abuse of Power* (Martin Robertson, 1982), p. 23.
8. Mr David Powis, reported in the *Daily Telegraph*, 15th June 1978.
9. *R v Nottingham Justices, ex parte Davies* [1980] 3 Weekly Law Reports, p. 15.
10. *R v Slough Justices, ex parte Duncan* [1982] 75 Criminal Appeal Reports, p. 384.
11. Supreme Court Act 1981, section 81.
12. Paras. 8.32 – 8.35.
13. *Criminal Procedure in Scotland (Second Report)* (Cmnd. 6218, HMSO, 1975), ch. 15.
14. Despite continuing "financial management initiative" at the Lord Chancellor's Department, no official figures for the cost are available, although the figure of £1,000 per day for an average Crown Court trial is often quoted.
15. *The Distribution of Criminal Business between the Crown Court and Magistrates' Courts* (Cmnd. 6323, HMSO, 1975).
16. Reported in *The Times*, 28th January 1977.
17. Para. 212.
18. Para. 8.17.
19. Lord Devlin, *Trial by Jury* (Hamlyn Lectures, Stevens, 1956).
20. *Eleventh Report of the Criminal Law Revision Committee: Evidence (General)* (Cmnd. 4991, HMSO, 1972).
21. "Minority Verdict", reprinted in R Mark, *Policing a Perplexed Society* (Allen and Unwin, 1977), ch. 5.
22. *Report of the Royal Commission on Criminal Procedure*, ch. 4.
23. Para. 229.
24. Para. 8.22.
25. Lord Widgery, the Lord Chief Justice, in *R v George* [1979] 68 Criminal Appeal Reports, p. 210.

26. *R* v *Sang* [1979] 2 All England Law Reports, p. 1222.
27. *Report of the Royal Commission on Police Powers and Procedure* (Cmd. 3297, HMSO, 1929).
28. *Report of an Inquiry by the Rt Hon Sir Henry Fisher into the circumstances leading to the trial of three persons on charges arising out of the death of Maxwell Confait and the fire at 27 Doggett Road, London SE6* (HC Paper 90, HMSO, 1977).
29. See note 19.
30. *Report of the Departmental Committee on Identification in Criminal Cases* (HC Paper 338, HMSO, 1976).
31. House of Commons Debates, 27th May 1976, cols. *287-289.*
32. *R* v *Turnbull and Others* [1976] 63 Criminal Appeal Reports, p. 132.
33. *R* v *Keane* [1977] 65 Criminal Appeal Reports, p. 248; *R* v *Oakwell* [1978] 1 All England Law Reports, p. 1223; and also *R* v *Curvey*; *R* v *Keeble, The Times,* 23rd July 1983.
34. House of Commons Debates, 25th July 1979, cols. *2236-7.*
35. See *The Law Society's Guardian Gazette,* vol. 80, no. 31, p. 2029.
36. Radzinowicz and King, *The Growth of Crime* (Hamish Hamilton, 1977) p. 325.

8

PRIVACY

JAMES MICHAEL

Winston Smith smiles as he drops the copy of George Orwell's *1984* into the library return slot, gets into his car, and begins driving toward Heathrow for what he thinks is a well-earned holiday. His eccentric parents named him after the character in the book when he was born in 1949, and he thought that he would read it again around 1984 just to reassure himself that Orwell wasn't much good at predicting the future. Winston's television set doesn't watch him, there are no Thought Police to be afraid of, and there is nothing at all like pictures of Big Brother staring at him.

True, he is a little puzzled as to why he was selected for redundancy instead of someone else. But he is drawing supplementary benefit, and gets an occasional cheque for some part-time work. He still has his credit cards and his health, thanks to the new pills that the doctor gave him for that awkward genital infection. And he has plenty of time to read widely and watch whatever films he likes, when he likes, on the new cable television system. All in all, he is content, and is reassured that he is not living in the nightmare predicted for his namesake.

Somewhere in central London a light flashes on a television screen. A man in shirt-sleeves presses a key, and the screen displays the registration number of Winston's car, which has just entered the Heathrow car park. There are other numbers below it, and the man touches the keyboard a few more times. The screen shows that Winston Smith has reported his car stolen three times, only to find it later, that he is a member of a group called Against Cruelty to Animals, and that he was once suspected of damaging the house of an eminent research scientist because his car was seen parked nearby. His flat has also been burgled twice.

More keys are pressed. Winston's bank balance does not quite square with the benefits he is claiming, nor do they match his income tax return. More key-pressing shows that he has travelled abroad quite a bit for someone on the dole, and to some rather peculiar places. There have been some international telephone calls, too. His taste in films summoned up on cable tends towards soft porn.

The man then taps out a special code, and sees that Winston complained to his doctor about headaches after taking the new pills. Another code reveals not only the genital infection, but the partners named by Smith, along with his medical history. He has flat feet and piles, and is allergic to antibiotics.

Another display shows that Winston's library reading has tended toward military history and technical manuals, which are often overdue when he finally returns them. Is he a terrorist with a home-made bomb, bent on hi-jacking the plane? The man at the desk signals his superior at another terminal, where the information is flashed again. Should Mr Smith be picked up at passport control?

No, says the superior. He's only a work-shy scrounger with some dubious morals and politics. The morals were what the security firm hired to check on Smith and other employees were interested in. It was really against the rules to pass the information on, but a mention of the Old Pals Act and a drink was enough to persuade the officer that a respectable company would really be better off without someone like Smith. As for the fiddles, those can be taken care of when Smith returns, if they think he's worth the trouble. Another line appears on the screen. *1984*, and not even overdue. The two men make the connection, and smile at each other. It takes all sorts, but this is an odd one.

It is not yet possible for such instant and thorough surveillance of the hypothetical Winston Smith, at least not so far as we know. Or at least it is not quite possible, and those parts which are would be more difficult and time-consuming. But the potential is there, and concern about it is not limited to paranoids.

There is a pilot scheme for automatic screening of automobile registration numbers. This uses the Police National Computer, which also has entries for reported thefts, suspicious affiliations, and information about crimes committed by the automobile's keeper. Both the Thames Valley and Scotland Yard criminal intelligence systems have space for much more detail, although the Lindop

Committee on Data Protection was not able to learn much about the Metropolitan Police system in 1978, and complained about it in a diplomatic way.[1] Banking has been automated for some time, and both the income tax and social security systems are following suit. Airlines could not function without computers, although the information is assumed to be erased after flights. The recorded information about telephone calls under System X should end disputes about telephone bills, and the computerisation of reported side-effects of new drugs should lead to better safety precautions. The new machine-readable passports will help in crime and immigration control.

All of these systems of automated information handling have their benefits, but there are dangers as well. There have been documented cases of people denied employment because of wholly unfounded suspicions of terrorism (such as Jan Martin, who was only able to set the record straight because her father was a retired police officer), of private security firms compiling dossiers (for the *Sun*, on Michael Meacher MP, in 1982), and of police officers prepared to pass on Police National Computer information.

To their credit, professional bodies such as the British Medical Association have been quite vocal in demanding safeguards for new systems of computerised medical records. Presumably, librarians and cable television operators would be reluctant to allow the use of their automated records for purposes other than recording books borrowed or billing for services. But in view of the *Malone* case now before the European Court of Human Rights,[2] it is not really possible to say that British Telecom will take the same attitude towards System X telephone records.

And in any case, wasn't this Winston Smith in the wrong in fiddling his social security? Yes, but what about the other information, which did not reveal any wrongdoing, but which he perhaps would not like to have circulated? At any rate, he probably would like to decide for himself who knows these things about him. He just feels that way, perhaps because he is English. After all, as George Orwell wrote (in *Inside the Whale and Other Essays*) in 1941:

The liberty of the individual is still believed in, almost as in the nineteenth century. But this has nothing to do with economic liberty, the right to exploit others for profit. It is the liberty to have a home of your own, to do what you like in your spare time, to choose your own amusements instead

of having them chosen for you from above. The most hateful of all names in
an English ear is Nosey Parker.

Orwell was expressing a common belief that the English (and
perhaps even the British) place a peculiarly high value on privacy. At
a 1976 Council of Europe conference in Austria one delegate
remarked that signs in the United Kingdom rarely "prohibited" one
activity or another, but instead simply said "private". Yet there is no
general right to privacy in this country, and in 1972 the Younger
Committee recommended against such a right, largely because of
problems in defining exactly what was to be protected.[3] Instead, the
Committee proposed a number of specific legal measures, almost
none of which has since been adopted.

The literature on privacy in English alone is enough for a small
library, far too great to be surveyed in this chapter. But the
development of the literature and law of privacy is a useful way of
considering how different legal systems affect each other generally,
as well as providing some indication of how the law to protect
privacy may still develop in this country.

WHAT IS PRIVACY, AND WHY?

The very idea of privacy, the definition of which gave the Younger
Committee so much trouble, requires consideration, as well as the
reasons why it is thought important enough to require laws and
codes of ethics. In essence, privacy is but a particular aspect of the
legal and moral rules about information. The title of a book on ethics
and the social sciences, *Who Should Know What?*[4] expresses part of the
general problem. It is only a partial formulation, however, as
nothing is ever completely known or unknown by everyone, and the
methods by which information is obtained and communicated
further are very important. A more complete expression might be
who should know what, and how, and when?

Narrowing the formulation somewhat, it is important to remember that privacy concerns information about natural persons, as
distinct from artificial legal persons such as companies. This is not as
obvious as it might seem, and various reports and statutes, such as the
Franks Committee on the Official Secrets Act,[5] and the Memorandum of the Scottish Law Commission on the Law of Confidence[6]

have treated information about living individuals and companies as being the same.

Asserting a rough definition of privacy as being the control of information about natural living persons by those persons, the threshold question is why there should be any concern about who knows what (and how and when) about other natural living persons. It is clear that there are significant variations between cultures, many of which are expressed in law. To take a single example, one's annual income is generally regarded in the United Kingdom as highly confidential between the taxpayer and the Inland Revenue, while in Sweden it is a matter of public record.

Why should individuals feel strongly about who knows their income, or their medical histories? Obviously, disclosure of such information in some circumstances could have detrimental commercial or personal consequences. But the desire to control such information seems to go deeper, and is not limited to controlling information which is false, or unfavourable true information. The desire for privacy can also include controlling true information which could generally be regarded as favourable.

One of the more perceptive analyses of the reasons for keeping secrets is in Sisella Bok's book *Secrets*.[7] Drawing on anthropology and developmental psychology, she argues that "to realise that one has the power to remain silent is linked to the understanding that one can exert some control over events – that one need not be entirely transparent, entirely predictable, or . . . at the mercy of parents who have seemed all-seeing and all-powerful".[8]

The ability to withhold or disclose information, especially information about oneself, is thus seen as a part of the process of individuation, following from the infant's discovery of itself as an observing and acting being, existing apart from the swirl of perception and able to influence those things which are perceived. The extent to which personal reticence, or at least the ability to be reticent or open, is indulged or restricted varies greatly between societies, of course. The emphasis of liberal individualism on personal autonomy leads naturally to a value placed on personal privacy.

It is not at all clear, and perhaps may never be, whether there is a minimum degree of personal privacy necessary for psychological and social well-being among all human beings, or whether it is simply a strongly-held value in certain kinds of societies, which may be important to the functioning of such societies. This chapter is not about intuitive or revelatory theories of human rights. It is enough to assert that a right to some personal privacy is felt to be important in modern society, and is expressed in provisions such as Article 8 of the European Convention on Human Rights.

AMERICAN AND EUROPEAN PRIVACY

There have been two general sources of influence on the development of privacy law in the United Kingdom, both of which are still very much in the preliminary stages of development: the first is the evolution of obligations in common law and equity; the second the more civil law approach of broad statements of principle developed by application in particular cases. The two are not so sharply divided as is sometimes thought, and the development of privacy law in the United States offers a convenient illustration.

The Bill of Rights attached to the US Constitution derives historically from the British Bill of Rights and philosophically from natural rights theorists. A right to privacy is nowhere mentioned in it, but it has been developed gradually through a combination of case law and statute and a re-interpretation of specific rights to freedom of religion, speech, and rights against unreasonable searches and seizures. The common law development was largely based on academic and judicial interpretation of the English law of confidence, and in particular of the expression of that equitable doctrine in *Prince Albert* v *Strange*.[9]

That case involved a set of etchings executed by Queen Victoria and her consort, which had found their way into the hands of a publisher who intended to publish them with a descriptive catalogue. The Prince might well have got an injunction to stop sales of the prints alone on grounds of copyright or even property, but it would have been difficult to restrain communication of the information in the catalogue on those grounds. The law of confidence was used instead by the Solicitor-General to persuade the Vice-Chancellor to enjoin both exhibition of the etchings and publication of the catalogue. It was not, as is often thought, an entirely novel use of the doctrine, but its use by the Royal Family drew attention.

The law of confidence was to be used by Royalty to protect their privacy again over a century later, although this has not yet led to further judicial interpretation. But its application following Prince Albert's case was largely limited to commercially valuable information. Across the Atlantic the words of the Vice-Chancellor decrying the "sordid spying into the privacy of domestic life" were to lead to rather different applications than he probably intended. The wedding of the daughter of Samuel Warren, a Boston attorney, is a familiar one in privacy literature, and perhaps illustrates the role that serendipity can play in the development of the law. The publicity given to it by the press was unwanted, and the result was not a lawsuit, but an article in the *Harvard Law Review* by Warren and his partner Louis Brandeis, later to become a Supreme Court Justice. Drawing heavily on *Prince Albert* v *Strange*, they argued that there was a general common law right to privacy.[10]

The influence of such an article on legal decisions is illustrative of the more civilian aspects of the US legal system. Within a few years courts had taken up the argument almost simultaneously with state legislatures. By 1960 the right to privacy had become firmly established, albeit with many variations, in case and statute law, and was the subject of another landmark law review article by Dean Prosser of California.[11] He found four distinct torts as aspects of privacy: intrusion, disclosure of embarrassing private facts, presenting an individual in a "false light", and appropriation of a name or likeness.

None of these was a tort in English law (or is now), but the Americans were to go much further just five years later. In 1965 the US Supreme Court elevated the right to privacy from a mere matter of tort to a Constitutional right.[12] Taking together enumerated rights such as freedom of speech, rights against unreasonable searches and seizures, and the right to silence, the Court found a right to privacy which was violated by a Connecticut state statute limiting the sale of contraceptives, and declared the statute void. Since then the Court has applied this constitutional right in ways which would have seemed curious to the Vice-Chancellor in Prince Albert's case, including upholding the right to watch pornographic films in one's home[13] and striking down state laws limiting abortions in the first three months of pregnancy.[14]

In England the right to privacy remained firmly limited to the law of confidence, which itself was hardly used outside intellectual and industrial property. The first real excursion of confidence into matters personal again was, according to counsel in *Argyll* v *Argyll*,[15] the result of his reading the original Warren and Brandeis article. The action to restrain the Duke of Argyll from writing about his ex-wife, which would have fitted neatly into Prosser's "disclosure of embarrassing private facts", was successful under the law of confidence. Since then the English courts have not exactly been flooded with similar cases involving personal rather than commercial information, although there have been occasional developments, and the Law Commission has produced a comprehensive proposal for a statutory tort.

Quite apart from the Duchess of Argyll's concerns, the late 1960s saw an increased interest in privacy by the public, press, and Parliament. As is too often the case in matters of civil liberties, the Parliamentary concern was almost entirely on the part of backbenchers, expressed in various Private Members' Bills. These were directed at a variety of activities, not all of which would fit even Prosser's four torts. In particular, some of them, including one introduced by the now Minister of Information Technology, Mr Kenneth Baker, were to control the processing of personal information by computers.

These would now be called, as is the Bill being considered by Parliament as this is written, "data protection" measures. It is worth considering why this aspect of privacy, out of all the others, is the first to become law in the United Kingdom. The reasons are largely Continental and commercial.

What is almost certainly to be the Data Protection Act 1984 began with the determination by post-war European countries that the depredations of fascism would not happen again. One of the first acts of the Council of Europe, and probably still its most important, was the formulation of the European Convention on Human Rights, Article 8 of which proclaimed a right to personal privacy. Development of jurisprudence under the Article through the procedures of the Commission and the Court was slow, and was outstripped during the 1970s by national legislation to regulate the handling of personal information by computers.

The first of these was a statute in the German *Land* of Hessen in 1973, followed the same year by a national law in Sweden. These were followed with alacrity, first by other Scandinavian countries, and then by many other members of the Council of Europe. These were not, and are not, entirely consistent. To mention just a few issues, there is considerable divergence in the treatment of natural and legal persons, public and private sector data banks, and manual or automated records. Although there are still few concrete examples of it, the possibility that such inconsistent statutes might impede international data processing (rather inelegantly known as transborder data flows) began to worry data processors in several countries.

This concern was translated into efforts at harmonising the national statutes. In this the EEC largely deferred to the older, larger, and looser Council of Europe, which in turn co-operated with the Organisation for Economic Co-operation and Development. The result was the Convention for the Protection of Individuals with Regard to Automatic Processing of Personal Data, commonly known as the Data Protection Convention, which was opened for signature and ratification in January 1981. The OECD guidelines were produced at the same time, to almost exactly the same effect.

Meanwhile, there had been movements towards privacy law in the United Kingdom, although there were few of them in the courts or in Parliament. The various expressions of concern about privacy in the late 1960s, together with some unease over the 1971 census, led to the appointment of the Younger Committee on Privacy in 1970. The Committee's brief was limited to the private sector, and representations to both the Labour Home Secretary and his Conservative successor failed to get authorisation to consider threats to privacy from government. Despite this, the Committee produced an authoritative report in July 1972,[16] rejecting a general statutory right to privacy in favour of a number of specific measures. Perhaps the most significant of these, apart from proposals relating to computers and personal information which were developed further by the Lindop Committee in 1978, was a suggestion that the Lord Chancellor make a reference to the Law Commissions to examine the law of confidence as a means of protecting personal privacy. The references were duly made, and the Commissions produced discussion papers, in 1974 by the English Commission,[17] and in 1977 by the Scottish Commission.[18] The English Commission produced a final Report in the autumn of 1981,[19] considering the law of confidence in exhaustive detail and including a draft Bill to define it as a statutory tort. In effect, the Commission balanced the interests of the press against those of individuals in protecting confidential information.

The law of confidence had moved considerably even as the Commissions deliberated. It had hardly been used before to restrict the press, and, apart from the success in *Argyll* v *Argyll*, other attempts had been unsuccessful.[20]

But in 1975 it was relied upon, along with a less precise argument that the courts should enforce conventions such as Cabinet confidentiality, by the Attorney-General in an effort to stop publication of the Crossman Diaries. The attempt was unsuccessful, and the then Lord Chief Justice, Lord Widgery, apparently reformulated the doctrine in refusing to stop publication. No longer would it be sufficient that the information was confidential (i.e. not generally known) and communicated under an obligation of confidentiality which was about to be broken, to obtain an injunction. In addition the plaintiffs would have to persuade the court that the public interest required publication to be stopped, which the Attorney-General had failed to do.[21] Formerly such a public interest could only be raised as a defence, and one which could only be used to justify breaching confidence to disclose "iniquity", usually limited to crime or fraud.

The Law Commission took up Lord Widgery's reformulation, which had been neither widely noticed nor followed. Under the Commission's Bill, the defendants would only have to assert that the breach of confidence was justified in the public interest, and the burden of arguing that the public interest justified restraining publication (or damages for a past breach) would shift to those seeking an injunction or damages. It was, in effect, something for the press, already concerned by the use of the doctrine together with pre-trial discovery to force Granada Television to disclose the identity of the "mole" who had leaked British Steel papers in *British Steel* v *Granada Television*[22] (although the informant later came forward voluntarily).

On the other hand, the Commission significantly expanded the definition of a breach of confidence to include information disclosed through an interception rather than by a breach on the part of someone who had accepted the obligation of confidence. Among other things, this would make it a breach of confidence to tap telephones or to open letters. Coincidentally, that very question had come before the Vice-Chancellor in *Malone* v *Metropolitan Police Commissioner*.[23] Breach of confidence did not apply to telephone-tapping, he said, commenting that the subject was one which "cried out" for legislation. As promptly as Strasbourg procedures allowed,

Malone invoked Article 8 of the European Convention on Human Rights. In 1982 the Commission of Human Rights found that his rights had been violated by telephone interceptions under administrative warrants, and referred the case to the Court of Human Rights.[24] A decision is unlikely before 1984, but it seems very likely that the Court will also find a violation, particularly in view of their description of what safeguards were required in the West German case of *Klass* in 1978.[25]

The rule in Prince Albert's case came to the aid of the Royal Family again during this same period, although, unfortunately for purposes of clarifying the law, none of the efforts led to a clear legal decision. In the spring of 1980 a journalist produced what purported to be transcripts of intercepted telephone conversations between the Prince of Wales in Australia and his then-fiancée, Lady Diana Spencer. A writ seeking an injunction was issued by them, but lapsed when the journalist retracted his story amid allegations that the transcripts were bogus. There was a somewhat similar incident about a year later (although on this occasion no writs were issued) when surreptitiously-taken photographs of the bikini-clad pregnant Princess were published. Both of the incidents involved information obtained by interception or intrusion, and it would have taken a significant change in the law of confidence to justify an injunction or damages. And it was just such a change that the Law Commission had proposed.

A more orthodox breach of confidence action involving the Royal Household was brought in early 1983 to restrain Royal servants and the *Sun* from disclosing information about the Royal Family and to recover profits made by such breaches of confidence. Once again the action was settled out of court, to the satisfaction of the Royal Family. It involved a fairly clear breach of confidence, and the main unresolved question was whether the obligation of confidentiality was owed to the treasurer of the Household (who brought the action) or to the Queen, and, if it was owed to the Queen, whether she could or should sue in her own courts.

PRIVACY, AND SECRECY, NOW

Thus far this chapter has been an attempt at an historical introduction to the law of privacy. Inevitably, much has been left out, but two general lines of development have been selected. The first is the reception of the English law of confidence into the law of the United States and its expansion into a constitutional right of privacy. The second has been the more European emphasis on data protection, culminating in the Council of Europe's Data Protection Convention. 1984 is peculiarly appropriate for considering just how well law in the United Kingdom now protects rights of individual privacy, and what the prospects are for developments in future.

It is for others to argue over precisely what George Orwell sought to achieve with his novel, but it is difficult to dispute the proposition that the world which he described was one in which the state knew nearly everything about individuals, while they knew very little about the state. When Winston Smith began to write his journal he had no idea that he was being observed. It would seem to be a maxim for the late twentieth century (if it has not always been so) that those who exercise power inevitably seek maximum secrecy for themselves together with minimum privacy for those who are subjected to that power.

This chapter is not primarily about the first part of that maxim, except to argue that privacy for human beings is something quite different from the institutional secrecy of government and other institutions. There are legitimate reasons for some degree of such institutional secrecy, but they are largely derived from considerations of efficiency and the protection of legitimate commercial interests. These are fairly easily distinguishable from what is widely felt to be a fundamental human need for some area of life which is protected from intrusion and disclosure. The issues presented by open government have been considered elsewhere,[26] but it is worth remembering that there have been parallel developments in the United States, Europe, and the Commonwealth for both privacy protection and open government legislation.

The immediate prospects for changes in British law to require greater openness in government and other institutions of power are slim, although such proposals have more political legitimacy than they had just ten or fifteen years ago. The prospects for changes to protect personal privacy are slightly better, but only just. A convenient method of considering those prospects is to measure British law, as it now is and is likely to be in the near future, against expressions of law protecting privacy in other countries.

Prosser's four torts are very much in the common law tradition, but the home of the common law has hardly taken them up at all. Rights against intrusion are still very much tied to property rights, and almost entirely aimed against physical intrusion. At the very least these fail to deal with developments in technology. In the case of *Bernstein* v *Skyviews*[27] it was held that the taking of aerial photographs (and only of property at that) did not amount to a trespass. The only prospect for change was a suggestion in the case that such intrusions might, under other circumstances, amount to a legal nuisance.

Less obvious intrusion by technology is now possible through the use of various photographic and listening devices. The very unobtrusiveness of such intrusions makes it quite possible for them to be unknown to the individual whose privacy is invaded (and one thinks again of Winston Smith, writing without knowing he was observed). A reduction in secrecy surrounding surveillance in itself would be a significant step towards protecting against it. But once again British law is tied to the notion of physical trespass to property. There is some legal protection against such a trespass if it occurs in planting microphones on private property, but that is all. The only other legal protection is that if the microphone includes a wireless transmitter it could be in contravention of the Wireless Telegraphy Act 1949.

Visual surveillance is even less protected against. This is less likely to require physical trespass, and the law provides almost no remedy against photographs from aeroplanes or with telephoto or infra-red lenses. Both types of intrusion by device were considered by the Younger Committee and the Law Commission, and the latter proposed legislation to deal with the problem in its draft Breach of Confidence Bill. Essentially, this would provide a civil remedy against such intrusions based in part on the nature of the device and the reasonable expectations of privacy on the part of the person subject to surveillance. As I have argued elsewhere, such legislation would almost certainly have provided the Princess of Wales with a remedy against the surreptitious photographs taken of her in 1982.[28]

But there would remain one defect in this remedy. The Law Commission proposed that information obtained by such surveillance would be subject to an obligation of confidentiality, and that any further communication of it would amount to a breach of confidence. So the publication of surreptitiously-taken photographs or transcripts of "bugged" conversations would be a civil wrong, but there would be no remedy if they were not published, or perhaps if they were only circulated within a small circle. Thus there would be a remedy against such surveillance by the press (at least if the results were published), but less of a remedy against surveillance by private or government investigators.

The related threat of surveillance by interception of telephone conversations and the post seems most likely to be dealt with in the near future. The reason is the *Malone* case already mentioned, which is likely to be decided by the European Court of Human Rights in 1984. If the United Kingdom continues in its pattern of introducing the absolute minimum of legislation to comply with decisions of the Court (as in the Contempt of Court Act 1981 and the administrative changes responding to the Court's decisions regarding prisoners' correspondence), the likely result would be a statute approving the existing system of ministerial warrants for interceptions of telephone conversations and post.

A far better solution would be legislation to deal both with the difficult problems of interception in the interests of crime detection and the broader issues involved in surveillance generally. For the first, Parliament would look both to the requirements of the European Convention and the examples of other common law countries such as Canada. A system of judicial warrants for such intrusions could actually benefit the police, and aid in law enforcement. Under such a law it would be possible for the police to use information obtained by lawful interceptions in court, and they could abandon the existing practice of using only such information as leads to other evidence.

To deal with other intrusions, the Law Commission's draft Bill would be a considerable improvement. That would provide a civil remedy not only against unlawful interceptions, but also against intrusions by surveillance devices generally. For investigative journalists resorting to devices such as carrying concealed tape recorders there would be a public interest defence extending well beyond that of disclosing "iniquity" under the existing law of confidence.

The Law Commission's Bill would also provide a remedy for what Prosser called disclosure of embarrassing private facts. There is now almost no such remedy in English law. The civil law of defamation only gives a remedy against publication of defamatory information which is substantially untrue. The unsatisfactory alternative is a prosecution for criminal libel, under which the defence must be both that the information was true and that it was in the public interest for it to be published. Although there may perhaps be a case for retaining this in modified form, a changed law of confidence would be far better, allowing damages for emotional distress caused by a breach of confidence together with a public interest defence.

It is commonly thought that the law of defamation in the United Kingdom is far more strict than that in the United States. This is generally true, but Prosser's third tort, of publication portraying an individual in a "false light", is an exception. This is an easier test of harm than that of "hatred, ridicule and contempt" under English law, and one which might usefully be considered. In effect, this is an American method of balancing the rights of most people under defamation law against the wider degree of allowable defamatory criticism of "public figures" under the constitutional case of *New York Times* v *Sullivan*,[29] and its successors. The exception, which only allows damages for such figures if the defamation was malicious or reckless, was expressly rejected for Britain in 1975 by the Faulks Committee,[30] but it might at least be considered, together with a change to allow legal aid in defamation actions. Under existing law defamation is a remedy only for those "public figures" and others who have the very substantial amount of money needed to afford it.

The tort of appropriating the likeness of an individual for commercial gain would probably not be a major change in the protection of privacy if it were introduced into English law. It mostly compensates those whose pictures are used without their consent in advertisements, and is primarily (although not exclusively) used by those who already make their living from their faces. Its use by less well-known people in news photographs is still the subject of legal dispute in the United States (and it is largely a matter of New York State law), but such an application might restrain the more intrusive photographers who flock to the scene of every fatal accident.

As it is, the only remedy under English law for the use of a person's picture in commercial advertising is if the picture contains a defamatory innuendo (as in the implication that an amateur golfer was professional by the use of his picture in an advertisement for chocolate).[31]

Developments in the civil law of privacy, that is, rights which individuals would have to sue others (including government officials) for damages or to restrain further invasions of privacy, are unlikely to be influenced greatly or quickly by legal developments from across the Atlantic. Even the moderate proposals of British Committees such as Younger and Faulks have been gathering dust for several years now. The Law Commission's proposals on the law of confidence have not been mentioned in any Queen's Speech since they were published in 1981, but they do have the advantage of being formulated in a draft Bill. It would be an important step towards effective legal protection of personal privacy if back-bench MPs of all parties succeeded in securing its passage as the Law of Confidence Act 1984.

But that would not be nearly enough. Other legislative measures affecting personal privacy are now on the way to becoming law, and strenuous efforts are required to prevent them from becoming charters for further invasions of privacy. The Police and Criminal Evidence Bill came under its most severe criticism in 1983 for the provisions allowing the seizure of confidential personal information by police. Even privacy advocates can conceive of cases in which a serious and specific threat might justify breaches of professional confidentiality. But the Bill must be carefully amended to ensure that medical and pastoral confidentiality may be breached only in such cases.

The Police and Criminal Evidence Bill will authorise invasions of privacy, and the task is to ensure that these are kept to a defensible minimum, with appropriate procedural safeguards. The Telecommunications Bill is unlikely to authorise interceptions of telephone calls, but should be amended to establish a system of judicial warrants (as has been tried before, unsuccessfully). A close look at the *Klass* decision and the Canadian Act would allow the United Kingdom, for once, to put its house in order before being told to by the European Court of Human Rights. On a more specific, but important point, the Telecommunications Bill should provide that the detailed information to be provided by the new System X about what calls are made to what numbers, and when, should be used only for billing purposes unless sought under a specific warrant. The Commission on Human Rights report in *Malone* was uncertain about such monitoring, and System X offers an opportunity to do what should be done, rather than a grudging acceptance of what must be done.

It is, however, the Data Protection Bill which offers the opportunity to legislate for privacy protection most relevant to 1984. The commonplace observation by Home Office Ministers that there is little public concern and few recorded instances of abuse ignores, perhaps wilfully, the fundamental problem. It is the chilling effect on political and other human activity that is at the bottom of civil libertarians' concern. Incidents of lost jobs or harassing surveillance are dramatic when they do come to light, but we are already uncomfortably close to a transparent society in which those in power view us all through a one-way glass. One need not have more than a general idea of what records are kept on what individuals in order to feel an almost subconscious inhibition about all but the most innocuous activity. The petition not signed, the vocal colleague shunned, the trip not taken, even the purchase not made, all of these are not entirely fanciful results of the vague knowledge that it is all recorded, and that it can all be retrieved by those in authority who may then use it in making important decisions about us.

It is the ability to retrieve and connect such information through information technology that has led to the emphasis on computers in proposed legislation. But the basic problems are presented by paper files as much as by disk memories, and most of the recorded abuses in countries such as the United States are of information in manual files. The Council of Europe Convention on Data Protection only requires legislation to deal with the automatic handling of personal information, it is true, but it also allows and even encourages the same standards of conduct for the manual processing of the same kind of information.

There are two basic and related principles of data protection to be insisted upon. One is called "subject access": the right of "data subjects" (as we all are known) to inspect and correct information recorded about them, and also to challenge its compliance with the other principles that it should only be used for the purpose for which it was collected, and that it should be both accurate for and relevant to that purpose. Exceptions to the rule of subject access to detect crime and for limited purposes of national security are both allowable under the Convention and understandable. But these must be restricted to just those purposes. In particular. the exceptions should not allow, as the Government Bill does, for any system certified by a Cabinet Minister as being for national security purposes to be completely exempt from any supervision by the Data

Protection Registrar. Sweden manages with supervision by a data protection official, and the United Kingdom could well do the same.

The other principle is that information should not be used for purposes other than those for which it is collected. A very limited exception for the detection of serious crime is allowable under the Convention and justifiable. But it should be limited to just that, which would not include the proposed use of personal information to prevent evasion of tax laws.

BEYOND 1984

Parliament is likely to be considering all of these issues as this is published, and may already have decided some of them. But further efforts in Parliament and the courts will still be necessary. Legislation on breach of confidence is very unlikely to be brought forward without considerable pressure. The government will almost certainly wait for the *Malone* decision before legislating on telephone-tapping (and is likely to continue waiting as long as possible). If the deficiencies in the Data Protection Bill are not made good, discrepancies between the resulting Act and what the Data Protection Convention requires must be brought to the attention of the European authorities. And the lack of other laws to protect personal privacy should be measured against the requirements of the Human Rights Convention by taking individual cases to Strasbourg.

Law is not everything, of course, even when it provides remedies which are effective in protecting rights such as those to privacy. Although the Press Council is hardly an advertisement for self-regulation, there is still a place for voluntary efforts by those who handle personal information to establish their own standards for respecting personal privacy. Local authorities, educational institutions, employers and others need not wait for legal rules and sanctions to introduce new practices such as giving tenants, students and employees rights to see the files kept on them. Most "data users" are also "data subjects", and their basic rule of conduct should be to accord the privacy of others the same respect that they would want.

Such an even-handed approach is difficult for many to accept. It is a cliché that information is power, and control over information about people is not given up easily. Nevertheless, the goal should be a combination of law and practice in which government secrecy is kept to a necessary minimum, and personal privacy is given more effective protection. The National Council for Civil Liberties has a history of campaigning on both of these related issues. In 1938 NCCL organised a meeting opposing the Official Secrets Act after its use against a journalist was upheld by the Court of Appeal.[32] Since 1970 NCCL has been active in drafting Bills and lobbying both for reform of the Official Secrets Act (including a public right of access to government records) and for personal privacy, particularly in data protection. One way of ensuring that the Winston Smiths of the future do not live in Orwell's *1984* is to continue that effort.

NOTES

1. *Report of the Committee on Data Protection* (Cmnd. 7341, HMSO, 1978).
2. *Malone* v *Metropolitan Police Commissioner* [1979] 3 All England Law Reports, p.620; *Malone* v *United Kingdom* [1982] 4 European Human Rights Reports, p.330.
3. *Report of the Committee on Privacy* (Cmnd. 5012, HMSO, 1972).
4. J A Barnes, *Who Should Know What?* (London, Penguin, 1979).
5. *Report of the Departmental Committee on Section 2 of the Official Secrets Act 1911* (Cmnd. 5104, HMSO, 1972).
6. Scottish Law Commission Memorandum No. 40 (HMSO, 1977).
7. Pantheon Books, New York, 1982.
8. *Ibid.* p.38.
9. (1849) 41 English Reports, p.1171.
10. Warren and Brandeis, *The Right to Privacy*, (1890) 4 Harvard Law Review, p.193.
11. 48 California Law Review, p.383.
12. *Griswold* v *Connecticut* [1965] 381 US Reports, p.479.
13. *Stanley* v *Georgia* [1969] 394 US Reports, p.557.
14. *Roe* v *Wade* [1973] 410 US Reports, p.113.
15. [1967] Chancery Reports p.302.
16. *Report of the Committee on Privacy* (Cmnd. 5012, HMSO, 1972).
17. Law Commission Working Paper No. 58 (HMSO, 1974).
18. Scottish Law Commission Memorandum No. 40 (HMSO, 1977).
19. Law Commission Report No. 110, *Breach of Confidence* (Cmnd. 8388, HMSO, 1981).
20. See, e.g., *Fraser* v *Evans* [1969] 1 Queen's Bench Reports, p.349; *Hubbard* v *Vosper* [1972] 2 Queen's Bench Reports, p.84.
21. *Attorney-General* v *Jonathan Cape Ltd.* [1975] 3 All England Law Reports, p.484.

22. [1981] 1 All England Law Reports, p.417.
23. [1979] 3 All England Law Reports p.620.
24. See note 2, above.
25. 2 European Human Rights Reports, p.214.
26. See, e.g. *The Politics of Secrecy* (London, Penguin, 1982) and Delbridge and Smith, *Consuming Secrets* (National Consumer Council, 1982).
27. [1978] 1 Queen's Bench Reports, p.479.
28. New Law Journal, 4th March 1982.
29. 376 U.S. Reports, p.254 (1964).
30. *Report of the Committee on Defamation* (Cmnd. 5909, HMSO, 1975).
31. *Tolley* v *Fry* [1930] 1 King's Bench Reports, p.467.
32. *Lewis* v *Cattle* [1938] 2 All England Law Reports, p.368.

PART III

Some Critical Issues Today
(1) The Framework of Civil Liberties

9

THE POLICE AND THE PUBLIC

MARTIN ENNALS*

The group of journalists and others who met with Ronald Kidd (the first General Secretary of the NCCL) in the crypt of St Martin-in-the-Fields in February 1934 to set up a national council for civil liberties were predominantly concerned with police handling of the fascist marches in London. Police violence and political prejudices and preferences have continued to be one of the central concerns of the NCCL ever since.

The police then were noted for protecting the fascists marching under the banner of Oswald Mosley but for being less conscious of the rights of the poor, the unemployed and of minorities.

It could be said that nothing much has changed, but this would be an over-simplification. An essay on the police must take account of the conflicts and contradictions shown by most people in their attitudes to the police. Ben Whittaker draws attention to some of these differences when he points out that a member of the public expects the police to administer the law yet to waive it with discretion; to be members of society without reflecting society's prejudices and postures; to seek information without mixing with informers, to eradicate crime but only by "sporting" means, to be rigid in enforcing the law on others but understanding in cases where the person concerned is affected. The policeman should be representative of the community which he polices, yet very few members of any community want to become policemen. The result is that,

---

* The views expressed in this chapter are the author's personal views, and do not necessarily represent those of the Greater London Council. This essay does not deal with the question of complaints against the police, which is extensively discussed in John Griffith's contribution on the Democratic Process (chapter 5).

particularly in London but also elsewhere in the "difficult" inner city and urban areas, the police are not recruited from within their own community – 80% of London recruits come from elsewhere in the UK. Members of minorities do not join the police, for such mistrust has developed that to become a policeman is to "join the enemy". Police recruits are trained for an initial period of 16 weeks before being allocated to station sergeants who quickly tell them to forget all they "learnt at Hendon". If society wants police who are isolated, defensive, prejudiced and inefficient then the present techniques of recruitment and training are succeeding.

Successive governments, and all the political parties, have failed to come to grips with the fact that good policing of any community is linked to, and as important as, educational and other social welfare services. There have been two Royal Commissions on the Police in comparatively recent history; one in 1929 and another in 1960–62.[1] In 1959, writing about the *1929* Royal Commission Report, the *Guardian* said:

There is obviously something radically wrong in the relations between the police and the public; it is a problem which has existed for a long time . . . it is surprising that this [the 1929 Report] covers every aspect of present relations between the police and the public; it might have been written yesterday.

The 1962 Report did little to change the situation and now, 20 years later, the same problems exist with the same complaints and the same resistance to fundamental change.

The "law and order" lobby, including the police, constantly and successfully presses for greater police powers over the public, and Conservative and Labour administrations provide new legislation accordingly. Civil liberty elements which are strong within the Liberal and Labour Parties have still not succeeded in persuading their colleagues of the need for a "Liberal" or a "Socialist" policy for law and order. Thus law and order has become identified with the hangers and floggers. Civil libertarians are dismissed as being soft on crime, anarchistic in tendency and anti-police.

In practice, if the purpose of policing is to reduce crime, the roles should be reversed. The saturation policing techniques adopted in Brixton and elsewhere, which were blamed for the riots or uprisings against the police in 1981, and criticised by Lord Scarman, were significantly inefficient at catching criminals. The efficiency rate of the Metropolitan Police in London has declined alongside every increase in police powers granted by Parliament. The clear-up rate for crime is down in London from 20 per cent in 1980 to only 16 per cent of reported crime in 1982. Only 8 per cent of burglaries are cleared up and only 7 per cent of auto crimes. Yet it is precisely these types of powers which the police have been calling for and are being granted by the government through the 1983 Police and Criminal Evidence Bill: random powers to stop and search vehicles, set up road blocks, take fingerprints compulsorily, detain suspects in police stations for four days without preferring charges, and for up to 36 hours without access to lawyers. Such powers are acquired by the police in more totalitarian states than the UK.

In England the notion of policing is bedevilled with one particular myth which crops up whenever the subject is discussed. The myth was well expressed by the 1929 Royal Commission on the police which stated that

The police in this country have never been recognised either in law or in tradition as a force distinct from the general body of citizens . . . the principle remains that a policeman, in the view of the common law, is only a person paid to perform, as a matter of duty, acts which, if he were so minded, he might have done voluntarily.[2]

The 1983 Police and Criminal Evidence Bill would confer powers on the police which no individual member of the public would ever dream of exercising without running the risk of immediate arrest. It would be a brave person who decided to set up a road block to stop traffic in an area where he had reason to believe that a serious crime had been committed. . . . The myth however is particularly absurd when consideration is given to the powers which the police have acquired over the individual, not only on the street and in the police station but also through a highly technical and totally inaccessible national computer system capable of storing information on all citizens. This information starts with all those who have cars and moves on not only into the area of hard information such as criminal records, but also into soft and speculative "information" about political, trade union and other pressure group activities collected by the Special Branch, and into the whole range of gossip and hearsay which is fed into the local police computer by the officer who acts as "collator" in each station. The neighbourhood watch scheme introduced in 1983 is a further extension of intelligence gathering without any verification or right of access by the individual affected.

With modern technology and national information systems at present installed or being extended through the police computers, the police anywhere in the country can have access to information about each one of us. Yet none of us has the right to know what is stored, on what basis, by whom, or to whom it is made available. No "ordinary member of the public" would be entrusted with such knowledge or such powers. There have been a number of committees looking at information handling and controls, most recently the Lindop Committee, which reported in 1978.[3] The Lindop Report, in so far as it concerns its experiences with the Metropolitan Police, was particularly disturbing in that the Committee complained forcefully of the lack of co-operation it had received from the Metropolitan Police in the course of its enquiries. If this is the experience of a formally constituted government committee, what hope is there for the ordinary citizen confronted with police power based on a multiplicity of information available to the central data base and accessible only to those who are within the system? The 1983 data protection legislation does little to protect the public and in fact falls short even of the international standards being set in other countries.[4]

If the policeman or woman can therefore no longer be seen as a public-spirited member of the public undertaking professionally "acts which he might have undertaken voluntarily", who is he/she? The answer is not easy to find.

It is argued that the individual constable is constitutionally an officer of the Crown. He acts on his own responsibility and is liable for his actions before the courts. He must act legally and is also accountable in some complex fashion to the public.

In practice police officers are part of a disciplined service. Hierarchical ranks and uniforms are indicative of paramilitary organisation. The police receive specialised weapons training ranging from batons and shields to water cannon, plastic bullets and guns. (In 1981, 4,274 Metropolitan Police officers were authorised to use firearms and guns were issued on 2,164 occasions.) They are also highly mechanised both on the ground and in the air.

The police, in addition, not only conduct enquiries and take effective decisions as to whether and what charges are to be brought, they also conduct the prosecution (based on their enquiries) in magistrates' courts. In the past the Judges' Rules were meant to circumscribe the police's investigative rights. Under the Police and Criminal Evidence Bill there are to be "guidelines" issued by the Home Office, but none of them will be binding on the individual constable who, theoretically, is responsible in his own right. In practice, he is surrounded and protected by his colleagues who form a phalanx of solidarity which it is very difficult to break. The Policy Studies Institute, which undertook a survey of the Metropolitan Police at their request, stated in its Report (published after deliberate leaks and public pressure in November 1983) that "we believe that police officers will normally tell lies to prevent another officer from being disciplined or prosecuted, and this is the belief of senior officers who handle complaints and discipline cases".[5]

The police are not therefore simply civilians in blue doing what could be done by the man on the Clapham omnibus. They are a "special" group of people with special powers, special training, special arms and special discipline. Certain questions must therefore be answered. To whom are this "special" group answerable? Who tells them which powers to exercise, what weapons they need, what training they require, and for what offences they should be disciplined? The whole issue of the police being accountable to the people who pay them and whom they serve is the core of the problem.

LOCAL GOVERNMENT AND ACCOUNTABILITY

"Accountability" is in fact a euphemism for "control". There is no national police force but there is a highly co-ordinated police service composed of 42 police forces each based on a geographical region. Apart from the special case of the Metropolitan Police, the police have always been seen as a local responsibility, and local government, through elected councillors, has been responsible in varying degrees for the police in its area. In the last 50 years the number of police forces has decreased and the regions covered have grown larger. Local borough council control has been eroded (nominated magistrates were added to the police authority in 1964). Now that it is proposed to abolish the large Metropolitan authorities, the role of elected councillors and local government in controlling the police becomes even more obscure.

The local authorities through the rates pay for 50% of the costs of the police and have a statutory duty to provide an adequate and an efficient police force. How "adequacy" or "efficiency" are evaluated or controlled has never been defined, though the Home Office, through the Inspectors of Constabulary (themselves ex-policemen), has an important role in establishing minimum standards. The Data Protection Bill treats the Chief Constable as being the employer of his constables and as an integral part of the Home Office for purposes of data protection. However, the Chief Constable was also described by Lord Denning in 1968 as being "not the servant of anyone save of the law itself. . . . The responsibility for law enforcement lies on him."[6] This position would seem to be a confirmation of the report of the 1962 Royal Commission on the police which stated that

The Chief Constable is accountable to no-one and subject to no-one's orders for the way in which for example he settles his general policies in regard to law enforcement . . . the disposition of his forces . . . the manner in which he handles political demonstrations . . . and instructs his men when preventing breaches of the peace arising from industrial disputes.[7]

With this power in the hands of the Chief Constable or Commissioner, it is not easy to feel confident that police accountability to the public is a reality. It sounds more like a fiction created by a politician and marketed by a public relations officer.

Paranoia however is not necessarily all on one side. With the continuing decline in confidence between large sections of the community and the police themselves, it is important also to recognise that the police force is not completely monolithic. There are differences between the 42 police forces. Chief Constables can make a difference and the powers of the Police Authorities if used with vigour and direction can be more effective than in the past. During the 1981 riots police were drafted from all over the country to the trouble spots. Indeed the experience was a salutary one for a number of police forces when they encountered the aggressive style of other forces such as the Met or Merseyside. There are serious professional police officers, good beat policemen, incorruptible men and women, highly specialised and skilled persons working in areas of acute sensitivity. Not all policemen are racially prejudiced bully boys. But many are, and they survive and indeed flourish in the heady atmosphere of the police station.

This strong racist element within the police was confirmed dramatically in the Policy Studies Institute Report of November 1983. There are pages of evidence devoted to this subject, which is summarised in the conclusions by saying that "racial prejudice and racialist talk between officers are pervasive ... expected, accepted and even fashionable".

The issue of police powers and the protection of the citizen from their arbitrary use or abuse, is one of the key questions to be resolved and on which a political policy is needed. I emphasise and repeat the word *political*, because it is the word which the police use whenever these issues are raised. It is part of the police credo that the police are not like other services in society, in that they should not be subject to political control. This ignores the fact that the Home Secretary, by definition a powerful party politician, effectively controls the budgets, the appointment of Chief Constables and the legislation which administers the police. He is the Police Authority for the largest and most influential police force in the country. Thus he carries considerable political responsibility for how Britain is policed. At local government level where the police forces are subject to the supervision of a Police Authority made up of local government elected councillors and nominated magistrates, the Chief Constable in practice decides what equipment is needed, what priorities to adopt in policy and operations, how to deploy personnel and how to recruit and train them. It is the Chief Constable who takes the political decision about how to police industrial disputes or political demonstrations and whether to lean heavily on gays or to clean up pornography or concentrate on prostitution or parking, burglary, speeding, street assault, drunken driving. . . .

Many police apparently fear that if the force really became subject to political control from local government structures then pressures would be brought in individual cases, that the worst of the American experience of local corruption would be imported, and elected councillors would nominate their own favourite stooges as chief police officers. Thus nepotism would replace benevolent despotism. Ironically this attitude shows a lack of faith in the very democratic system which all police officers are convinced they believe in, and which they argue that they defend. The police are willing, if reluctant, to talk to Consultative Committees which have no power of decision-making but only as equal partners not as public servants. They accept the need to maintain relations with the Police Authorities even if the relationship is occasionally uneasy or even querulous. But they defend every inch of the independence which they have achieved and support any extensions of their power, as under the Police and Criminal Evidence Bill. They have effectively prevented the implementation of Lord Scarman's recommendation that racially prejudiced conduct should be a disciplinary offence justifying dismissal from the force. The Police Federation campaigns openly and vigorously for the return of capital punishment. They have until recently resisted any outside or independent involvement in the investigation of complaints against police officers.

In fact, the police represent the most powerful political lobby in the field of civil liberties; they conduct their campaigns with public funds and in high places. They have their Parliamentary spokesmen – formerly James Callaghan and latterly Eldon Griffiths. They have the ear and cameras of the media and protest earnestly when one or other programme is critical of their methods. In short, the police, although divided into separate forces, exist as an entity in political life in a way which recalls the Conservative Party of the past when Tories were "independents" in local government.

RECRUITMENT AND TRAINING

Recruitment of police officers is the responsibility of the Chief Constable and in London the Commissioner. The Chief Constables themselves are appointed by the Police Authority on the basis of an approved shortlist of candidates, and in cases of dispute the Home Secretary becomes involved. While overall guidelines exist about minimum standards for recruitment of police officers, discretion is left to police forces to handle matters in their own way.

This has produced a police force which is largely white and male. (The PSI Report states: "From the selection of statistics it is difficult to escape the conclusion that the Force discriminates unlawfully against women applicants under the Sex Discrimination Act 1975 . . . We have reason to believe that it is unofficially Force policy to keep the proportion of women to about 10 per cent.") In this, it is not unlike most other British institutions and the recruitment process undertaken by existing policemen tends to perpetuate the situation rather than change it. In times of full employment, the number of women recruits goes up. But as soon as salaries rise and more men become available for the police, the proportion of women decreases. Few women make careers in the police, and few are promoted to inspector or higher levels. There is in fact no feeling within the force that women are real police-persons. They are a necessary adjunct for searches of women and other situations where a woman is involved. Their duties have expanded alongside their fellow officers but by and large the police regard policing as a man's profession.

The "white" police force is a somewhat different issue but contains similar elements. At the time of the 1962 Royal Commission there were no "coloured" policemen and it was not considered appropriate to start recruitment among ethnic minorities. When the issue was raised in the early 1960s the answer from senior police and others was that "it is too soon". Even the NCCL evidence to the Commission was more tentative on the issue than would be the case today or indeed during the later 1960s and the 1970s. But there were complaints of racism against the police, and the police themselves were not willing to open their doors to "outsiders". In 1983, despite advertising campaigns for black police, there were only 183 police officers drawn from all the minority ethnic communities out of a total Metropolitan Force of 26,000 officers. The result is the perpetuation of a monocultured police force where conformity is respected and non-conformity discouraged. In a country renowned for its clubs, the police force is probably the largest and most self-protective.

The dangers are obvious. Not only are the "like-minded" responsible for recruitment, they are also in charge of the training. Thus any hope of an "original" slipping through the recruitment net is dashed by the initial training and probationary period when those who do not fit into the discipline, the saluting, the uniforms "at all times", the heavy initial workload and the regulation haircuts, are soon weeded out. After 16 weeks of training those who fit the official mould are then turned over to policemen in the police stations to see what happens in real life.

Advertising campaigns have been undertaken to persuade the young members of ethnic minorities to join the force. The results however have been minimal. Not only do the peer groups of young blacks resent police behaviour and the overt racism encountered on the streets, particularly, but not exclusively in the inner city areas, the actual recruitment process is undertaken with a different stereotype in mind. The club analogy is particularly valid.

In a recent TV interview the President of the Police Federation was asked whether a police officer should be dismissed for calling a black a "nigger". He answered

No, no, indeed not. It's like everything else. Why should he be dismissed for calling him "nigger"? I mean what about the colours – "nigger-brown" – are we going to change those sort of things? No, it's a word, it depends on intent. But if somebody, all his life, has used the phrase "nigger" and he does not use it detrimentally, he recognises a black man by that particular phrase, the same as I recognise "cockney" by that particular phrase or any other walk of life, then it's a matter of how the recipient receives it.

The *Economist* reported that exchange under the heading "Not Alabama 1963: England 1983".[8] When such an attitude is rewarded by the police with election to national presidency what welcome is a black to expect within the police station should he survive the recruitment procedures and the initial training periods? Is the President of the Police Federation not aware that police use of language reflecting their sexist and racist attitudes is often as instrumental in creating tension as are the thousands of stops and searches which are carried out with little justification and even fewer results in terms of crimes cleared up or criminals caught?

The police at the senior level appreciate the problem, but have done little about it. In the Hendon Police Training College, the recruits are subjected to a period of training in "human awareness". One course is hardly likely to overcome the prejudices of a post-colonial life-time. Colonial attitudes are deeply ingrained in the British life style, in our educational system, in our attitude to immigration and people of different backgrounds and in our policing and other practices. Discrimination exists. Laws have had to be passed to protect the rights of everyone to be treated equally. But prejudice and racism continue within our society and therefore within our police force. Furthermore they are perpetuated by recruitment procedures which automatically select the same type of person.

Isolation from the community starts with recruitment. From that time onward the individual is systematically inducted into a police culture. Although outsiders and "civilians" are brought in at the higher levels of training such as courses at Bramshill and the many

regional inspector and other training courses, during the first
formative period in the service, isolation is encouraged, the team
spirit is inculcated and the process of creating a mutual protection
group begun.

THE FUTURE

All political parties have failed to consider these three issues of
control, recruitment and training in any depth. The Conservative
administration in the mid-1980s will continue its policy of increasing
police powers without increasing the powers of local authorities or
protecting the rights of the individual citizen. The other parties have
made statements and passed resolutions but have not framed their
own clear policies on what could be called the "law and order" issue.

What is needed is a comprehensive policy on police accountability, recruitment and training, worked out in detail by any party
which considers that it offers a possible alternative government. The
NCCL can offer its considerable expertise and experience to assist in
formulating such policy. It should also be remembered that the
problems of policing and democracy are not unique to Britain and
that within the Council of Europe and even the United Nations a
body of standards relating to police practices and police training is
being developed. The political parties in the UK might well prepare
their policies in the light of the experiences – both good and bad – of
their friends and neighbours. There are no final solutions but
concern over these issues and experimental research is now
widespread, particularly in North America and countries of
Western Europe.

There are other long-term problems which require examination
and negotiation, such as the command structure of the police, the
rights of police personnel and the effective control of information
technology available to the police. But in terms of the police and the
public the central areas remain control, recruitment and training.

The following suggestions and approaches could provide a basis
for discussion of any reassessment of the relations between the police
and the public.

Control The concept of policing as a local government responsibility
should be strengthened. The present electoral system does not
however provide local councils which are necessarily representative

of the many minorities in their midst. Proportional representation is a vexed political issue in terms of national and local elections but perhaps the possibility could be envisaged of having a Police Authority composed in part of elected councillors and in part of members directly elected using some form of proportional representation. There are many difficulties to such an approach, which would for instance require the registration of voters in a chosen category for purposes of calculating representation. It is a system which would require much research and discussion. In the meantime, however, the principle of one third of the local Police Authority being composed of community representatives, chosen by whatever means, would ensure a better balance of new ideas, broad participation and wider representation than at present. Magistrates should in any case be excluded from the Police Authorities as they are part of the judiciary and as such should be seen to be quite independent of the police, and vice versa.

A Police Authority for London – and possibly for other Metropolitan areas – could be on a two-tier basis, providing regional responsibility for common services, recruitment, training, administration, personnel management, data protection, regional crime problems and specialised services. Individual boroughs could each have their own police committee working with the regional Police Authority but responsible for personnel levels, priorities in policing policies and local appointments at the higher level of the police service within their boroughs.

The national functions of the police should be under the responsibility of a National Police Authority composed of either the Chairs of the Police Authorities or of a Parliamentary Select Committee, with provision for the involvement of the Police Authorities themselves in the process of policy and decision making. The Home Secretary should retain his overall responsibility as the Minister of the Crown responsible to Parliament for policing issues, national funding, preparation of policy guidelines, and involvement in senior appointments.

A new Police Council should be established to be responsible for research into policing policy, and legislation affecting the police and police powers, and to handle the investigation of individual complaints against the police. It should be assisted by an independent team of investigators and should have the right to subpoena witnesses, to call for information from the police and to make recommendations to the Police Authorities with regard to substantiated complaints in their areas. Disciplinary actions resulting from the complaints procedures would be the responsibility of the Chief Constables, and be reported to the Police Authority. A series of disciplinary offences and substantiated complaints would be cause for dismissal from the police service. Racist attitudes and action should, as Lord Scarman recommended, be a cause for dismissal from the police service.

The Chief Constables would participate in the work of the Police Authorities as at present, but would serve as officers of the Authority. Police Authorities would not be involved in individual cases of policing, investigation or prosecution but would, as now, have the right and the duty to call for reports from the Chief Constable on issues of both policy and operations.

Recruitment This would become the responsibility of the Police Authority using central guidelines issued by the National Police Authority or the Home Secretary as at present. There would be no sex or race discrimination in the recruitment process. Chief Constables and their officers would participate in the recruitment process under the guidance of the Police Authority, which would also involve local education authorities, careers services and employment agencies. Local recruitment priorities would be established by the Police Authorities in accordance with local circumstances. The entire process of recruitment should involve lay as well as police personnel.

Similarly, there should be involvement of the Police Authority in the career structure and promotions procedures within the police service. The "civilianisation" of the maximum number of police services should be considered as a priority and be the subject of a national review. The police themselves may wish to review their structure in the light of the demand for wider local government involvement in the services currently provided by the police. This however is a separate issue.

A national system of promotion and training should be considered under the aegis of the National Police Authority in conjunction with the local equivalents.

Training Here again, the whole programme of police training should become a local and national issue and not be left exclusively in the hands of the police themselves. There is no need for police training to be undertaken in isolation from the community to be served, or from the educational facilities which already exist. The integration of police training into Colleges of Further Education, Polytechnics and Universities would remove the mystique of police training as being for special groups of persons abstracted from the rest of the community for purposes which arouse suspicion. It would enable teaching staff from many disciplines to be involved, and would involve students working alongside each other whether they were in training as police officers, social workers, teachers, etc. There is presumably nothing to hide about police training, and there is no reason to assume that once recruited a member of the police only has to be put into uniform and taught to salute and move at the double.

Policing is an essential social service like any other. Specialist training and discipline are required at certain stages of police training, but the basic need is to give the police-person a training in the skills of policing a community. Specialist training such as crowd control and the handling of shields and batons is part of the training for a specialist job just as a social worker learns to implement laws in relation to children in care. The demystification of the police is long overdue and can best be handled through recruitment and, above all, through training.

The Police Authority should therefore have overall responsibility for training their police service. Police should be trained to standards set (as in other professions) by the National Authority in the light of relevant local and national expertise. Promotion would be through training and the training staff would in general be part of the civilian element mentioned above.

The new legislation required with regard to control over the police would not obviate the need to change the powers which the police currently have and use. Effective public control however over the police and their recruitment and training would be a strong element in strengthening police relations with the public and so stimulating further public co-operation and police efficiency.

What emerges constantly from any discussion of police in the UK is that no government has yet been willing to take the matter seriously. Salaries have been raised to encourage recruitment. Laws have been changed to increase powers. But funds have never been made available to train professionals to do their job within the community which they are supposed to represent and serve.

Successive governments have made their policy decisions in a series of reactive measures to counteract public outcry at crimes and violence. No evaluation of the long-term effects of these laws and these powers has taken place and no attempt has been made to root the police in the community as part of a normal and necessary public service.

The next political change of government is the first and maybe the last time when the matter can be tackled effectively. The police lobby is unfortunately stronger and more cohesive at present than that represented by organisations like the NCCL. The next 50 years will be infinitely worse unless something drastic is done soon.

NOTES

1. *Report of the Royal Commission on Police Powers and Procedure* (Cmd. 3297, HMSO, 1929) and *Report of the Royal Commission on the Police* (Cmnd. 1728, HMSO, 1962).
2. Cmd. 3297, quoted in the *Report of the Royal Commission on the Police* (Cmnd. 1728, 1962), p. 10.
3. *Report of the Committee on Data Protection* (Cmnd. 7341, HMSO, 1978).
4. See James Michael's essay (chapter 8) for a detailed discussion of the legislation now proceeding through Parliament: [Ed.]
5. *Police and People in London* (London, Policy Studies Institute, 1983). (This report was published after the draft of this chapter had been completed, and references to it have been added to underline the points I sought to make.)
6. *R v Metropolitan Police Commissioner, ex parte Blackburn (No. 1)* [1968] 2 Queen's Bench Reports, p. 118.
7. Cmnd. 1728.
8. *The Economist*, 23rd July, 1983.

10

THE POLICE
AND THE EUROPEAN CONVENTION

JOHN ALDERSON

The European Convention on Human Rights was signed by the Government of the United Kingdom on 4th November 1950 and came into force on 3rd September 1953. It is remarkable how in the intervening thirty years so little of this great charter of human rights has percolated into the training and management of our police forces (the same is true in most, if not all, member countries). It was for this reason that the Committee of Ministers of the Council of Europe adopted Resolution (78)41 in 1978 which, amongst other things, recommended the governments of Member States to take whatever measures are appropriate to teach the subject of human rights at all levels of education. In particular, it requires Member States "to promote the teaching of the safeguard of human rights and the relevant protection machinery in an appropriate manner as part of the training for members of the civil and military services". Although this recommendation is not legally binding on governments, it places a heavy moral duty upon them to promote training of police officials in this subject. In the United Kingdom that burden falls primarily on the Home Office and the Scottish and Northern Ireland Offices, together with their professional and academic advisers.

Police awareness of the European Convention, the work and role of the European Commission on Human Rights, and the status and role of European Court of Human Rights is of considerable importance if the object of the Convention is to be achieved, and if the United Kingdom Government is to avoid undue embarrassment caused by excessive recourse to the European Commission and Court by complainants in cases of breaches of the European Convention by police officials.

This essay aims first of all to deal with the ethical framework within which the police in the United Kingdom might see their role in relation to human rights, secondly to deal with the purport of particular Articles of the European Convention as they relate to police practice, and thirdly to suggest approaches for the training of police.

POLICE POWER AND HUMAN RIGHTS

Free people expect much of their police. In such societies the police stand at the point of balance, on the one hand securing human rights, and on the other exercising their lawful powers given to them by governments in the name of the people, to protect the people and their institutions.

Societies which are not free, or which are despotic, acquire omnipotent police who serve only those in power. Laws are promulgated which give police wide powers to deny human rights, in some cases even the most basic civil liberties. Police in such corrupt systems are themselves corrupted and through degeneration are permitted to indulge in arbitrary conduct including torture, and inhuman or degrading treatment. But the police of the world are not divided neatly into two distinctive forms, for there are degrees of both.

Police authority can be abused even in democracies. It can become more the master and less the servant. It can snuff out more freedom than it protects. The main problem lies in control. This is particularly so in the growth and practice of secret police. It is important to remember that abuses can flourish not only because of official negligence or acquiescence but because, rightly or wrongly, broad sections of the people identify with such practices and consider that in spite of their excesses the police are carrying out a task that is unpleasant but necessary if both state and society are to be preserved and protected. Such conditions, great or small, place considerable moral burdens on decent police officials whose actions to check drifts of this kind are of paramount importance to the preservation of human rights.

In an ideal world there would be no need for police. Society would achieve order through agreement, mutual tolerance and the leadership of true authority. There would be no call for physical coercion and its threat. But human experience indicates that noble sentiments alone are too weak to control those whose ambitions, greed, aggression and anger, give way to threatening and damaging activity on either a small or on a grand scale. From rebellion to simple theft there are requirements for laws and for some form of enforcement of those laws. The great instrument of enforcement in most states is police and the judicial processes.

In creating such instruments free societies have to take great care on two counts. Firstly, they have to ensure that the system created to protect them does not become the instrument of their bondage; that the manner of its control and the nature of its work ensures that in containing crime and disorder it does not take away those basic freedoms enshrined in the best of domestic laws, the United Nations Declaration and other instruments, and in the European Convention and its extensions. The police have to be seen to be carrying out their function within the law to which they themselves are subject.

Secondly, nations have to ensure that those who are chosen to exercise the power and authority of police officials are carefully selected for their human qualities, properly trained to perform their difficult duties in an ethically correct manner, and, very important-ly, to be led and directed by persons with high qualities of human excellence. Nothing less than this will help to secure the balancing of human rights with adequate control of excessive human misbehaviour.

Even in the best regulated of democratic police systems, aberrations will emerge from time to time in which groups and individuals will fail to maintain the high criteria which are sought. In such cases measures have to be available to maintain correct standards by the imposition of disciplinary regulations, having regard to the human rights of the malefactors, to be followed by such internal reforms as may be necessary to reduce repetition.

It has been said that power corrupts and that "absolute power corrupts absolutely". Police officials have to be on guard to avoid the potential and insidious corrupting influence of power if it is to be neutralised in them as individuals and in the groups to which they belong. Power for the police is not to be seen as an end in itself but as a means towards a free social order. It is therefore in the proper use of their considerable powers that one test of police at the service of human rights will be made.

One police ideal would be in circumstances where all the many parties would so respect and trust the police that they would offer maximum assistance to them in their functions of law enforcement, investigation of crimes, maintenance of public tranquillity and the prosecution of offenders. Where the police are seen to be at the service of human rights in particular and humanitarian acts in general it might be expected that such public support will be forthcoming to a greater or lesser degree. It is important therefore that police officials under training should be enabled to address their minds to this phenomenon.

Since it is an important principle of the police function that crimes should not only be investigated and detected but should also be prevented by other means, it follows that social actions and influences of police could be brought to bear in this connection. Thus for example where individuals or groups are exposed to great inequality of treatment or rendered victims to denial of human rights and civil liberties generally they may resort to anti-social or criminal behaviour. If the police therefore have a highly developed social awareness they will often be presented with opportunities for the prevention of crimes and the maintenance of social order through bringing their influences to bear against such injustices. In this way police will enhance their own stature and function and in so doing will improve their position as law enforcement officials. It is important therefore that through an understanding of the subject of human rights police officials will see their relationships with the many differing sections of the public as positive.

As a society becomes more civilised, free, educated and informed at all levels, its expectations of police along with other public servants are raised. Amongst other things it requires not only that the police carry out their primary functions but that they do so with greater sensitivity, and understanding.

As peoples become more aware of the dignity of the individual and of human rights they are likely to criticise and complain about police behaviour which in another age would not have been regarded as wrong. This phenomenon may lead to the false impression that police have deteriorated in behavioural matters but close consideration may often reveal that it is the higher demands being made upon them. This should not be seen as an attack upon police officials and organisations but as a recognition of their civic importance and of the high standards of conduct which are manifest in the best of police practice.

The general demeanour required of the police is not necessarily constant. In the plural multi-racial society, particular care has to be taken in this regard. A society which is homogeneous, mono-cultured, and classless would require less adaptability from police officials than one in which there are ethnic, religious, cultural and other differences.

Police at the service of human rights will develop a demeanour which embodies an instinct or a perception for human dignity. Being witness to human beings, as they sometimes are, in degrading and degraded situations, police are exposed to the influence of cynicism. They have to avoid becoming indifferent, however difficult that may be, if they are to develop and retain proper judgment of and appreciation for the rights and dignities of all.

The foundations of good police practice will therefore be based on an understanding and acceptance of ethical principles of duty to the enforcement of laws not as an end in themselves but as a means of securing fairness and justice to all manner of persons irrespective of their race, creed, religion or social standing. The provisions of human rights legislation seek no lower standard of police behaviour and practice.

THE EUROPEAN CONVENTION AND POLICE PRACTICE

The overriding importance of Article 14 of the Convention requires to be emphasised throughout since it conditions all police decisions in their relations with the public, not only in the exercise of their powers but in the provision of their many services:

The enjoyment of the rights and freedoms set forth in this Convention shall be secured without discrimination on any grounds such as sex, race, colour, language, religion, political or other opinion, national or social origin, association with a national minority, property, birth or status.

"Discrimination" may not be unlawful however where it has a beneficial purpose and may for example be exercised for the benefit of juveniles, the mentally retarded, and the sick in the way they are dealt with by the police – what has been described in other contexts as "reverse discrimination".

Articles of the European Convention which have a bearing on

police practice are many and varied but the following examples of arrest, detention, and interrogation will serve to illustrate the way in which police practice and the Convention may interact.

Arrest

Although the proper administration of justice and the prevention of more serious crimes require that police officials have adequate powers of arrest, depriving a person of liberty in democratic countries is regarded as a most grave step even where it is necessary. The liberty of the individual person is central to all the advantages of a civilised society. It is not surprising therefore that international laws and conventions on human rights have much to say on the subject which is of primary importance to police and public alike.

Article 5 of the European Convention provides the key element towards an understanding of the limitations placed upon police officials when seeking to carry out the arrest of persons.

So far as arrest is concerned, Article 5 declares:

1. Everyone has the right to liberty and security of person. No-one shall be deprived of his liberty save in the following cases and in accordance with a procedure prescribed by law.

This provision makes the arrest of a person by a police official a contravention if such an arrest is not in accordance with domestic laws or if those laws themselves are in contravention of the Convention.

This Article permits *inter alia*:

(b) the lawful or detention of a person for non-compliance with the lawful order of a court or in order to secure the fulfilment of any obligation prescribed by law;

(c) the lawful arrest or detention of a person effected for the purpose of bringing him before the competent legal authority on reasonable suspicion of having committed an offence or when it is reasonably considered necessary to prevent his committing an offence or fleeing after having done so;

(f) the lawful arrest or detention of a person to prevent his effecting an unauthorised entry into the country of a person against whom action is being taken with a view to deportation or extraction.

Article 5 seeks to make provision for procedures both on and following arrest which guarantee human rights:

2. Everyone who is arrested shall be informed promptly in a language which he understands of the reasons for his arrest and of any charge against him.

3. Everyone arrested or detained in accordance with the provision of paragraph 1(*c*) of this article shall be brought promptly before a judge or other officer authorised by law to exercise judicial power and shall be entitled to trial within a reasonable time or to release pending trial. Release may be conditioned by guarantees to appear for trial.

4. Everyone who is deprived of his liberty by arrest or detention shall be entitled to take proceedings by which the lawfulness of his detention shall be decided speedily by a court and his release ordered if his detention is not lawful.

5. Everyone who has been the victim of arrest and detention in contravention of this provision of this article shall have an enforceable right to compensation.

Case Law (Examples)

The European Court has stressed the importance of the rights to liberty in a "democratic society" within the meaning of the Convention: in a question involving "*ordre public*" within the Council of Europe, the organs of the Convention should in every case exercise a scrupulous supervision of all measures capable of violating the freedoms which it guarantees.[1]

The "right to security of person" under Article 5(1) provides protection against arbitrary interference by a public authority with an individual's personal "liberty" and implies that any decision taken by the latter in the field of Article 5 must conform to the procedural and substantive requirements laid down by an already existing law.[2]

It should be noted also that the words "liberty" and "security of person" should be read as a whole.[3]

As Article 5 is contemplating the physical liberty of a person, restrictions upon liberty of movement (Article 2, Fourth Protocol) have to be judged upon the facts of each case to determine whether Article 5 has been violated.[4]

When Article 5 says that deprivation of liberty must be effected "in accordance with a procedure prescribed by law" this means domestic law, but such domestic law must be in conformity with the Convention.[5]

It has been held by the European Commission on Human Rights under Article 5(1)(*c*) that "Good reasons to believe that the person concerned has committed an offence are sufficient to justify his arrest or detention, there being no need at this stage to definitely specify the character of the offence".[6] Thus it seems that where reasonable suspicion exists for the arrest this would not necessarily be in contravention of the Article, although good police practice would require every effort to be made to be as definitive as possible under the circumstances.

Under Article 5(2) the Commission has held that "In the case of a person arrested as being suspected of having committed a crime (Article 5(1)(*c*)) the purposes of Article 5(2) are to enable him to challenge the reasonableness of the suspicion against him and to state whether he admits or denies the offence".

Article 5(2) "neither requires that the necessary information be given in particular form, nor that it consists of a complete list of the charges held against the arrested person".[7]

The general provisions of Article 5 are exhaustive and any arrest which does not satisfy any of the six conditions laid down would violate the Convention.[8]

Furthermore, a person cannot be deprived of his liberty (i.e. arrested) *solely* for the purpose of bringing him before the competent legal authority. His arrest (and detention) has to comply with *two* conditions: (a) the existence of legal provisions under domestic law and (b) the absence of any arbitrary measure on the part of the authorities. In a case where a person suspected of belonging to a terrorist organisation was detained under administrative law without trial it was held that Articles 5 and 6 provided no legal foundation for detention without trial. Therefore the arrest and detention were in breach of the Convention.[9]

Detention Following Arrest   Once a person has been arrested his detention begins until release from custody has been brought about. In this sense detention is a continuance of arrest, but since human rights law is concerned that detained persons should receive proper and humanitarian treatment there are particular provisions to be carefully regarded.

So far as police officials are concerned, they will mainly be concerned with the detention of persons before trial. Such persons are in the eyes of the law innocent, which means their detention is usually an administrative requirement and convenience rather than a punishment. The provisions of human rights law begin to operate as detention begins.

The European Convention Article 5 deals with the need for legality of detention, but not the conditions. Article 3 is a most important provision so far as treatment of detained persons is concerned and Resolution 73(5) of the Committee of Ministers seeks to govern conditions of detention.

Where a police official is party to the detention of persons it must be (1) legal under domestic law and (2) not outside the provisions of Article 5. Furthermore, the provisions of Article 3 require that "No-one shall be subjected to torture, inhuman or degrading treatment or punishment." Police officials are required to maintain the strictest observance of these fundamental rights.

Under Resolution 73(5) of the Council of Europe Committee of Ministers the "Standard Rules for the Treatment of Prisoners" have considerable force and are governed by two principles: (1) the conditions of detention must ensure respect for human dignity and (2) detention must be enforced in an impartial manner and without discrimination. These rules apply with equal force to prisoners awaiting trial, e.g. in police custody, as well as to those sentenced. Although this Resolution is not part of the Convention or its Protocols, it has the weight of Member States' Government Ministers behind it.

Since detention takes place outside of general public scrutiny, there are occasions when the treatment and conditions of prisoners falls below humanitarian standards and such cases have given rise to case law of considerable importance.

Case Law

The general provisions of Article 5 are exhaustive and any detention which does not satisfy its provisions is in violation of the Convention.[10] Furthermore, where a person is deprived of his liberty, i.e. detained *solely* for the purpose of bringing him before a competent legal authority, this violates the Convention. Detention has to comply with *two* conditions: (a) the existence of legal provisions (for detention) under domestic law and (b) the absence of any arbitrary measure on the part of the authorities.

Thus where a person suspected of belonging to a proscribed terrorist organisation was detained under administrative law *without trial*, it was held that Article 5 and Article 6 provided no legal foundation for such detention. Therefore the detention was in breach of the Convention.[11]

The legality of detention is therefore of primary importance but once that hurdle has been overcome there are other important provisions to be considered. By requiring that a person shall be brought promptly before a judge, Article 5 restricts the length of police custody. The Commission has accepted a maximum delay of four days and a delay of five days in an exceptional case where the prisoner had to undergo medical treatment.[12]

An air journey under police escort of a person being deported amounted to a deprivation of liberty, i.e. detention.[13]

(Police officials have to be particularly cautious and understanding where juveniles, persons of unsound mind and those speaking foreign languages are concerned, particularly as they may not fully understand the nature and intention of detention. Every effort should be made to ensure that parents or guardians of juveniles, and friends of persons of unsound mind, are informed and that aliens are informed in a language which they understand.)

Attention is also drawn to the important principle of not detaining innocent persons (i.e. persons not found guilty) for too lengthy a time on remand. The European Court of Human Rights has held that each case has to be decided on its merits.[14] (The principle of reducing detention before trial to a minimum provides good grounds for appeal to the organs of the Convention.)

As would be expected, there is a large body of case law (too large to be comprehensively dealt with here) on the subject of Conditions of Detention and the European Convention. Much of it concerns the detention of convicted persons but it follows that persons in police custody who have not been convicted stand at least as high (or even more so) in the concern of the organs of the Convention. In as much as

Article 5 itself does not provide for conditions of detention, however, it should be noted that conditions which are in breach of other Articles, e.g. Articles 3, 4, 6, 8, 9, 10 and 11, provide grounds for the jurisdiction of the organs of the Convention.

The "Standard Minimum Rules for the Treatment of Prisoners" have already been referred to and these should be studied in full if police officials are to play their own part in the guaranteeing of prisoners' human rights. "The Convention prohibits in absolute terms torture and inhuman or degrading treatment or punishment irrespective of the victim's conduct" and "Article 3 makes no provision for exception . . . and . . . under Article 15, para. 2, there can be no derogation therefrom, even in the event of a public emergency threatening the life of a nation."[15]

Isolation of prisoners of itself has not been regarded as in violation of the Convention but the Commission has stated that prolonged solitary confinement is undesirable, especially when the person is detained on remand.[16]

Failure to provide adequate medical care and treatment may possibly amount to "inhuman" treatment under Article 3.[17]

The case law concerning the rights of prisoners covers many of the issues raised under Article 8, i.e. the right to respect for a person's private and family life, home and correspondence. Most cases concern prisoners sentenced for crimes but the general principles apply in some cases to persons in police custody and careful attention to this Article by police officials performing or supervising custodial duties is essential.

Rights to family visits can be interfered with under para. 2 of Article 8, in the interests of national security, public safety, the prevention of disorder and crime.[18] The right to freedom of correspondence applies to prisoners in police custody as it does to prisoners generally and unless interference is in accordance with the limitations in para. 2 of Article 8, e.g. prevention of crime, it violates the Convention.[19]

Interrogation It is within the everyday function of police to seek information concerning the prevention and detection of crime, the maintenance of public order, and the prosecution of persons against whom allegations of crime are made.

When it comes to carrying out the duty of questioning or interrogating persons in police custody, domestic laws on the subject may vary, and different legal and police officials may be required to carry out this function. Again, however, it is emphasised that whatever domestic rules, regulations and laws are involved, they must not be in violation of the European Convention.

The Articles of the Convention do not specifically refer to this police function but there are provisions which govern the limitations placed upon police officials as well as important case law to be borne in mind.

Allegations of the violation of Article 3 of the Convention have been the prime source of complaint. Article 3 provides: "No-one shall be subjected to torture or to inhuman or degrading treatment or punishment." This is a fundamental and immutable provision. Although Article 15 permits derogation of some obligations in time of war or other public emergency, Article 3 along with Articles 2 (right to life etc.), 4(1) (slavery etc.), and 7 (no guilt without illegality) permits no such derogation then or at any time. There can be no excuses for a police official contravening Article 3.

Case Law

The European Commission on Human Rights has analysed the meaning of the provisions of Article 3 in the following terms:

It is plain that there may be treatment to which all these descriptions apply, for all torture must be inhuman or degrading, and inhuman treatment also degrading. The notion of inhuman treatment covers at least such treatment as deliberately causes severe suffering, mental or physical, which, in the particular situation, is unjustifiable. The word "torture" is often used to describe inhuman treatment, which has a purpose, such as obtaining information or confessions, or the infliction of punishment, and it is generally an aggravated form of inhuman treatment. Treatment or punishment of an individual may be said to be degrading if it grossly humiliates him before others or drives him to act against his will or conscience.[20]

(This passage should be impressed on police officials concerned with interrogation at crucial stages of their training).

It cannot be stressed too strongly that even in a "tragic and lasting crisis" the "longest and most violent terrorist campaign witnessed" in the circumstances of the case that there can be no diminution of the provisions of Article 3.[21] In this case amongst other issues the Court was considering methods used by police officials to obtain information and confessions during the currency of a most violent and protracted terrorist campaign involving the murder of police officials, other members of security forces, and innocent members of the public.

Methods used by police officials included:

(a) *Wall-standing*: forcing the detainees to remain for periods of hours in a "stress position", described by those who underwent it as being "spreadeagled against the wall, with their fingers put high above the head against the wall, the legs spread apart and the feet back, causing them to stand on their toes with the weight of the body mainly on the fingers".

(b) *Hooding*: putting a black or many-coloured bag over the detainees' heads and, at least initially, keeping it there all the time excepting during interrogation.

(c) *Subjection to noise*: pending their interrogations holding the detainees in a room where there was a continuous and loud hissing noise.

(d) *Deprivation of sleep*: pending their interrogation depriving the detainees of sleep.

(e) *Deprivation of food and drink*: subjecting the detainees to a reduced diet during their stay at the centre and pending interrogations.

These techniques, whilst approved at a "high level" were not committed to written instructions. Many detainees were subjected to these techniques and large amounts of information of value to the authorities were thereby obtained. These techniques were agreed in the main to be against the domestic law. The question for the Court, amongst other things, therefore, was to what degree did they violate Article 3? Amongst its findings were unanimous decisions that a practice of inhuman treatment took place and by sixteen votes to one that during the relevant period the five techniques constituted inhuman and degrading treatment in contravention of Article 3, and by thirteen votes to four that such treatment did not amount to torture.

TRAINING IMPLICATIONS

From the three examples of police practice set out above, it will be seen that the European Convention on Human Rights is gradually creating an important body of international law which should now find its place in the training of police officials. At the early stages of training the young official should be made aware of the existence of the Convention and its aims. As training and experience progress, more detailed attention requires to be given to the provisions of the Convention and the impact of its case law. To allow police officials to enter into their profession in ignorance of the European Convention on Human Rights should no longer be acceptable or tolerated.

The responsibility for devising and implementing education and training in human rights in police duty falls to the Home Office and to Chief Constables. The Police Training Council, made up of police, Home Office officials, representatives of local police authorities, and academic advisers, has until recently shown little awareness of the importance and implications of the European Convention on Human Rights so far as it affects the police. Since Lord Scarman's inquiry on the Brixton and other disorders in 1981,[22] however, there appears to be a growing awareness of the problem and some changes are being considered. It is a matter for considerable regret that Lord Scarman's important recommendation on racist behaviour amongst police officers has not been implemented. He believed, and I fully support him on this issue, that there should be a formal disciplinary offence where an officer manifests racial prejudice and discrimination in the performance of his duty. This would obviously be in accord with Article 14 of the Convention.

Nothing less than a sense of urgency and drive towards education in this subject of all police officers, of whatever rank, will bring about desirable changes in both attitudes and in action.

BASIC TRAINING

In the beginning it would be important to instil into the minds of all junior police officials in their basic training the importance of the subject alongside those provisions of domestic laws, and that the British Government is a Member State of the Council of Europe and party to the content and spirit of the European Convention. At this early stage of training, junior police officials will be faced with the considerable task of assimilating a great deal of domestic law and procedure. Nevertheless, it is important that they are made aware that in the performance of those duties, e.g. arrest and detention, which impinge upon the fundamental human rights as set out in the European Convention, the Convention should be borne in mind at all times.

In these early stages, the short handbook published by the Directorate of Press and Information, Strasbourg, entitled *The European Convention on Human Rights* should be taken into use. The handbook sets out the basic text of the Convention. The subject might first of all be introduced in general terms (stressing in particular Article 14 – which forbids discrimination at all times) and as training progresses the trainee should be made aware of the particular Article of the Convention which touches upon the subject being dealt with. Thus where a trainee is being taught domestic laws and procedures of arrest, Article 5 should be drawn to his attention. In these early stages the simple text of the Article should be set out but later on it would be appropriate to include questions in elementary tests and examinations. The aim would be to ensure that at the end of their basic training all junior police officials should not only be aware of the existence of human rights provisions but of their relevance to the daily police function. The Declaration on the Police of the Parliamentary Assembly of the Council of Europe should therefore be studied in detail, as should the United Nations Code of Conduct for Law Enforcement Officials.

Ideally, such officials should be able to regard themselves not only as enforcers of laws but, in their own function, as guardians of the great cause of human rights and freedoms.

INTERMEDIATE TRAINING

As training and experience progress to intermediate levels, the work and role of the Commission, the European Court and the Committee of Ministers should be introduced in detail. The trainee should be aware of procedures involved in taking a submission or complaint to the Commission and of the various stages such a case may take. This would also be the appropriate stage to introduce the topic of Case

Law and the nature of its effect for the Government of the Member State concerned. Where trainees are being prepared for promotion and leadership, the importance of their own example and the supervision of their subordinates in maintaining the provisions of the European Convention and its extensions should be highlighted.

Where examinations are being conducted it would be important to include questions on human rights, the provisions for securing them, and the constitutional implications upon domestic affairs of international human rights legislation.

At this stage of training, useful texts published by the Secretariat of the European Commission on Human Rights should be taken into use. That entitled *Stock-taking on the European Convention on Human Rights* would be particularly useful.

HIGHER TRAINING

When training reaches the higher echelons of police, the implications of human rights law and procedure will require to focus both on responsibilities of governments and on the entire range of the function of the Council of Europe. The senior police official not only requires the knowledge and ability to ensure that his organisation is functioning in accordance with the intention of the Council of Europe and his own Government, but should be in a position to advise those higher officials whose work takes them into the Committee of Ministers, Parliamentary Assembly, Court of Human Rights and the Commission of Human Rights. He should be well aware of the relevant case law and of its implications for the Government of his own country. He should be capable of giving talks on the subject and of writing erudite reports on aspects of it.

If police education and training in the obligations for the upholding of human rights are made effective so that they pervade the attitudes and daily work of the police, a considerable step forward towards the attainment of the ideals of the European Convention will have been taken.

NOTES

1. *Vagrancy Cases*, European Court of Human Rights (1971) 1 European Human Rights Reports, p.373.
2. European Commission on Human Rights, Case No. 7729/76.
3. European Commission on Human Rights, Cases Nos 5573/72 and 5670/72.
4. See the cases of *Engel* (1976) 1 European Human Rights Reports, p.647, and *Guzzardi* (1980) 3 European Human Rights Reports, p.333, in the European Court of Human Rights.
5. *Winterwerp*, European Court of Human Rights (1979) 2 European Human Rights Reports, p.387.
6. Case B8224/74 – 15/211.
7. Case D8098/77 – 16/111.
8. *Engel* (1976) 1 European Human Rights Reports, p.647.
9. *Lawless* (1961) 1 European Human Rights Reports, p.1.
10. *Engel*, above, note 8.
11. *Lawless*, above, note 9.
12. Cases Nos 2394/66 (Yearbook of the European Convention of Human Rights, vol. 9) and 4960/71 (Collection of Decisions of the European Commission, No. 42).
13. *Engel*, above, note 8.
14. *Wemhoff* (1968) 1 European Human Rights Reports, p.55.
15. *Ireland* v *United Kingdom*, European Court of Human Rights [1978] 2 European Human Rights Reports, p.25.
16. Cases Nos 6038/73 and 7586-7/76.
17. Case No. 4340/69.
18. *Vagrancy Cases*, above, note 1, and *Golder* (1975) 1 European Human Rights Reports, p.524, European Court of Human Rights.
19. *Golder* case, above, note 18.
20. *Yearbook of the European Convention on Human Rights*, vol. 12, p.186.
21. *Ireland* v *United Kingdom* [1978], above, note 15.
22. *The Brixton Disorders 10-12 April 1981* (Cmnd. 8427, HMSO, 1981).

11

ACCESS TO THE LAW

WALTER MERRICKS

Civil libertarians have always been conscious of the need for procedural as well as substantive justice, and have been in the forefront of demands for easier access to the law and to legal services. Even if the substantive law guarantees fewer rights for the citizen than we would like to see, at least we would claim the right to know in some detail exactly how limited our rights are, and to enforce those rights we have. Some have argued that this demand merely deflects attention from more fundamental injustices, and that the state can in reality hold just as tight a grip on its citizens while giving the appearance of concessions on the right to legal services. Yet this has, by and large, not been the NCCL view over the years. Rightly or wrongly lawyers and the legal professions have been allies of civil libertarians in the struggle for increased access to the law. And while much remains to be done, the history of the struggle is largely a success story. Never before have individuals had greater access to independent legal services; indeed it may be that we are now witnessing the high water mark and that the future will see a struggle not so much to expand as to retain those rights so far won.

The point should first be made that access to the law should not be equated with access to lawyers. Individuals should be able to find and understand legal provisions which affect them. The law should be stated in comprehensible language and its provisions should not be so complex that it is rendered unusable. In this sense progress has been slower than in some other areas. The statute book is longer and larger than ever, and the corpus of legal decisions deemed by experts to be relevant to an understanding of the law grows inexorably. The work of the Law Commissions in consolidating and codifying statute law has really made very little impact on public awareness. The legal language of Acts of Parliament is as convoluted and unnatural as ever. There is a sense in which the law is simply not designed for public consumption – only for the consumption of lawyers.

Yet if source materials have remained obscure the past decades have seen considerable improvements in secondary outlets of legal information to the public. There has for instance been a great improvement in both the quantity and quality of official leaflets from Government departments. Consumers' guides to legal rights now sell in large quantities and are better written and presented than ever. Even legal text-books are now more accessible to the lay reader, their range and style having expanded greatly in recent years. Public libraries have increased stocks of legal materials for the ordinary citizen to consult. This demand-led rights awareness seems likely to continue to grow, and may finally make an impact on legislators and judges.

Information and advice services have expanded but still lack any sensible co-ordination. Citizens' Advice Bureaux, housing advice centres, law centres and welfare rights centres all find themselves offering overlapping services to much the same clientèle, while in the statutory sector social workers still seem to spend much time arguing with social security officials. The provision of information and advice services is still seen as a residual rather than a front-line responsibility of the state.

There is still some hope that external factors may bring about progress in this area. First, paradoxically, the pressure for public sector cuts may bring about a rationalisation which could in the end result in an improvement in the quality of services. The other factor which may yet bring about progress is the great leap in information technology. Computer-based legal information retrieval schemes are currently designed as tools for the legal profession rather than for the lay person, but the development of home computers, teletext, cable and video may soon provide a channel through which individuals will be able to obtain relevant information about their legal rights. Initially this will probably be simply a regurgitation of the content of existing materials, but increasing accessibility and awareness of the law may spur changes both in format and even in some areas in substance.

But for most people, access to law will continue to mean access to lawyers, to solicitors and occasionally to barristers. There are a few important areas where the citizen still does not have a clear right to see a lawyer – notably in the police station and in prison. These apart, however, there remain the more general problems of accessibility: mistrust, money, ignorance and geography. The problem of the quality of the services eventually provided has also recently come under scrutiny, but this may be regarded as a separate issue: nonetheless important, but one which this chapter will not attempt to address.

It has long been recognised that the distribution of solicitors' offices throughout the country is related to the distribution of property and wealth rather than to the population at large. Given the large amount of property-related work that is the staple of most solicitors' practices, this should not be surprising, but it was this among other considerations that gave rise to the concern in the late sixties about equal access to the law and resulted in the law centre movement. The two tracts from the Conservative and the Labour lawyers (*Rough Justice* and *Justice for All* respectively) published in 1968 both drew attention to the problem, but their remedies were different. The Labour lawyers advocated the establishment of neighbourhood law firms on the American model, while the Conservatives recommended subsidising solicitors' firms by means of capital grants so that they would be encouraged to open in poor areas. Neither of these two proposals gained easy acceptance. First, it seems that the state has never accepted that the distribution of lawyers' offices is its responsibility in the same way that the National Health Service saw a duty to provide hospitals and doctors' surgeries on a consistent basis throughout the country. Lawyers have always been part of the private sector, independent, professional, profit-making businesses. As such, although the distribution was a little uneven, the over-provision in Bournemouth and the City produced no injustice while the under-provision in the inner cities and some rural areas was not so glaring that state intervention could not be avoided.

The difficulty with the Conservative lawyers' proposal is and always has been that merely establishing a solicitors' office in a poor district will not ensure that it meets the needs of the local inhabitants. A branch office of a big firm established with a grant could be used simply as a typing pool. There is no way, short of an elaborate and expensive monitoring system, that solicitors could be prevented from misusing the grants. More recently, however, the idea has been revived with modifications; it is now suggested that initial loans could be made to encourage the establishment of new firms, but the loans would be repayable either on attractive terms by being off-set against legal aid payments, or at less attractive interest rates if repaid in cash. Although this scheme would be less open to abuse, there is still no sign that the Government regards itself as under a positive duty to ensure that legal services are actually provided to people in need, as opposed to being theoretically made available.

The establishment of law centres in London and other cities began in 1970. North Kensington, the first, was soon followed by Camden, Islington and Paddington – the latter funded by individual London Boroughs. It says something for patterns of mobility that these districts, none more than three miles from the West End, could be said to have been under-solicitored. The truth perhaps was that the establishment of law centres was not simply a response to a paucity of solicitors' offices, but more a combined assault on all the perceived accessibility problems at once. Law centres were to provide services free (thus overcoming the financial barrier), they were to be able to advertise themselves (thus people would know about them), and they would specialise in those areas of law relevant to the problems of poor people (which other solicitors were rarely interested in). At one blow they struck at all the defects in the traditional model of the solicitors' office.

The growth of the law centre movement has been well documented elsewhere – they now number about forty, with the majority still in London. From an initial surge in the mid-seventies, the number of law centres now seems to have steadied, and large scale further growth is not expected even by the optimists. The fourteen-year history of the movement has however demonstrated a number of difficulties. The full frontal attack on the private professional model for delivering legal services was abandoned fairly early on when the centres agreed not to undertake certain sorts of work (including matrimonial work and criminal defence) which the profession regarded as reasonably lucrative and as being its own preserve. The centres agreed to supply different non-competing services on different terms to a different clientele. Private practitioners were assured of holding on to their position as virtual monopoly suppliers of legal services, except for a tiny proportion of the market for which they did not wish to compete anyway. The centres no longer expect to cover the entire country or to take over the supply of legal aid services to the majority of the population.

To a certain extent the centres became victims of their own success. For it was not surprising that, having provided such an attractive and accessible service, they were inundated by clients, and had to find ways of cutting down on the amount of work. Some centres decided to concentrate on community work and test-case strategies; others which wanted to continue with a volume of casework found themselves obliged to refer away a high proportion of those who ask for help. The centres showed the existence of demand which they had no hope of being able to fulfil. It had been hoped that the mere demonstration of this "unmet need" would of itself be enough to embarrass the Government into providing more funds for a massively expanded service, but governments proved to be singularly resistant to such lessons.

Meanwhile private practice had not remained totally static. The number of firms continued to increase as the number of qualified solicitors rose, and a considerable number decided to orient their practices to legal aid work. By 1982 there were nearly 7,000 solicitors' offices receiving legal aid payments. Ironically a number of these new firms had started up in business near to law centres, cashing in on the spin-off referrals from the centres. At the same time the private profession was gradually trying to change its image. Legal aid referral lists, detailing by region the specialities of each firm, were introduced by the Law Society and were widely distributed. Yet the Law Society remained steadily resistant to the change which might have permitted the biggest improvement in the profession's image – individual advertising. Although this was recommended by the Royal Commission on Legal Services in 1979, the Law Society did nothing but prevaricate on the issue. Even modest efforts by individual firms to promote their services to the public were prohibited. The only move came in 1983 when the Solicitor's Directory was expanded to replace the legal aid referral lists by including all firms and giving their range of specialisations. Even this however had provoked controversy within the Law Society, some seeing this as the thin end of the advertising wedge. It is true that advertising, if it were used on a large scale, could put up the price of legal services to the consumer. But the opposition was not based on this ground, and the public interest in having a competitive, forward-looking profession, offering and promoting its services openly, was largely ignored.

For most people the biggest single hurdle to easy access to the law is of course a financial one. With most solicitors having to charge upwards of £25 per hour in order to cover their overheads and make a modest profit, legal services for all but the most modest contentious matters are beyond the reach of the majority of the population. Even those who could afford to pay something might feel that the service represented poor value for money.

Before considering the impact of legal aid, it is worth emphasising that the basic cost of legal services still remains very high. This is of course partly due to the way the profession structures itself. Much of a solicitor's time is still spent dictating routine correspondence to shorthand typists. Many practices are burdened by the need to provide substantial incomes to retired or semi-retired partners. Elaborate court procedure, much of which seems designed to prolong rather than resolve disputes, requires the employment of clerical and out-door staff. And of course the division of the two branches of the legal profession, solicitors and barristers, adds immensely to the cost of the higher forms of litigation. Computers and word processors are now beginning to be installed in solicitors' offices and have the potential to cut costs substantially. Whether these cost reductions will be matched by price reductions to the consumer remains to be seen.

But when allowances for all these factors have been made, legal services mean in essence the time of trained middle-class professionals, and whether these individuals are found in the accountancy, architecture, medical or legal professions, they still aspire to and receive a level of remuneration which ensures that the basic cost of their time is not cheap. Accordingly the legal aid scheme, enabling free or subsidised access to lawyers, must be considered the primary means for the state to discharge its duty to ensure that people are not deprived of justice as a result of lack of funds.

The Legal Aid and Advice Act 1949 is regarded as the foundation of the scheme which exists today, although there were schemes for both civil and criminal legal aid in existence before the war. The schemes established under the 1949 Act have been broadened considerably and the present governing legislation is the 1974 Legal Aid Act, itself amended by the 1979 Act.

As a public service, legal aid is remarkable for the number of different functions it is perceived to perform. For the Treasury it appears to be a demand-led welfare benefit; for lawyers it is a source, for some the main source, of their remuneration; for the courts it is an aid to the smooth administration of justice; for the citizen it is, or ought to be, a civil right. Few seem to regard it as a social service, perhaps since so many of its personnel are in fact in the private sector. How far can it properly be seen as a civil right? Each of the three schemes, the civil, the criminal and the advice and assistance scheme must be considered separately.

CIVIL CASES AND ADVICE

Civil legal aid is available to persons whose means are below fixed income and capital limits either free or, if their means are within a further range, on payment of a contribution towards the cost of their case. The maximum contribution is calculated exactly to the nearest pound for each applicant by officers of the DHSS (formerly the National Assistance Board and then their successors the Supplementary Benefits Commission did the task). If however the cost of the case does not look like exceeding the maximum calculated, the applicant will be asked to pay a sum which it is thought will approximate to the cost of the case, with a liability to pay up to the maximum should this become necessary. If at the end of the case costs are recovered from the opposing party, the contribution may be returned. But if the costs recovered are not enough to cover the outlay paid to the applicant's solicitor, the contribution and any money or property recovered in the action will be retained. The aim is said to be to put the legally aided person in the same position, no better, no worse, as the paying litigant.

Clearly the levels at which the financial limits for eligibility and for free assistance are set are of crucial importance in judging the scheme. These levels are adjusted each year by regulations made by the Lord Chancellor's Department. Also the proportion of the applicant's annual income over the free limit which is demanded by way of contribution, presently one quarter, is critical in determining the real availability of assistance. The Legal Aid Advisory Committee has recently been asked to conduct an enquiry into the principles which govern the financial conditions – an admission that there are presently none. The limits last underwent a major revision in 1979 after a Lord Chancellor's Department survey showed how coverage of the population had dropped during the seventies because of the failure to up-rate the limits in line with inflation. The exercise then carried out involved the withdrawal of legal aid from undefended divorce and the use of the funds so saved to increase the eligibility limits and to reduce the contribution fraction. As a result it was said that the coverage of the scheme was increased to some two thirds of the population. However these estimates are not easy to arrive at, since up-to-date figures on average income are not available, nor are there any reliable figures on the distribution of capital among families of different size and income.

The civil legal aid scheme is then available to finance those individuals who come within the financial limits to litigate in the High Court and the County Courts. The scheme however does not cover all proceedings. It does not cover representation in undefended divorce cases which are now dealt with through the advice scheme. Nor does it cover representation at a tribunal. Nor does it cover cases where the legal issue is not in dispute – i.e. rent arrears or debt cases where the defendant simply needs time to pay. The result is that civil legal aid is used predominantly for custody and financial disputes arising from family breakdown, and for compensation claims for personal injury. These may be important, but it is arguable that the range of cases decided before tribunals represent an equally important field for the citizen, and their omission is an undeniably serious blot on the scheme.

The advice and assistance scheme has seen a massive growth in the past few years. Introduced in 1973, the scheme has taken off in a spectacular way – helped by the removal of civil aid from undefended divorces. The numbers of individuals helped has doubled over the past five years and the value of the bills submitted by solicitors has quadrupled. Some of these increases represent work which was previously paid for, or work which is now paid for in a different way. But there is no doubt about the underlying trend. More people than ever before are receiving legal help from solicitors at public expense. The paradox however remains that the demand seems always to outstrip the supply, and the more people are helped the louder is the clamour pointing to the unmet need of those who have not sought advice. The significant fact is that the advice scheme is here to stay, and that it would now be extremely difficult for any government to cut it. The civil right of individuals to approach a lawyer and to receive independent legal advice either free or with a limited contribution to the cost is an important one and must be jealously guarded.

CRIMINAL CASES

It is the criminal legal aid scheme however that civil libertarians are likely to identify as the more significant. It is of course widely accepted that those accused of serious criminal charges should be entitled to be represented. If the state is represented by legal counsel the defendant should also be. This, it can be said, is the more important in a criminal justice system which is adversarial in nature, and where the court relies on the advocates to cross-examine the witnesses in order to tease out the truth. In civil law jurisidictions on the Continent, the defence advocate plays a much less important role in criminal proceedings, but this is said to be not unjust given the judicially supervised inquisitorial nature of the earlier investigative stage. In fact the recognition of the need for representation for the defence in this country has been relatively recent. In historical terms, although the right to counsel predates the right of the defendant to give evidence, the widespread representation of defendants in routine as opposed to state trials really dates from the 1960s. Even in murder trials in the early part of this century advocates such as Marshall Hall and Patrick Hastings depended on being paid by newspapers who had bought the defendant's story. The provision of legal aid at the state's expense was virtually nonexistent.

The crucial issue in the development of criminal legal aid has been the question of whether the defendant should have to disclose the nature of his defence to the granting authorities. At first this was taken to be a natural requirement both to curb abuse of legal aid and to stop unscrupulous lawyers from dreaming up defences for guilty people. This requirement was however removed by the Poor Prisoners Defence Act of 1930 as far as trials in the higher courts were concerned. Since then there have been a number of occasions when the authorities have attempted to question whether a defendant should not be obliged to disclose his story before legal aid is granted. In the late 1970s a move by the Justices' Clerks nearly produced this effect by the simple device of placing a question on the legal aid application form. More recently the Lord Chancellor's Department began to see possibilities in an arrangement under which criminal defendants would be entitled only to advice until either it was clear that it was a very serious or complex case, or they produced a defence. Happily both moves were defeated. But it would not be surprising if in an attempt to cut back on legal aid expenditure a further move in this direction were made.

It is now the case that in the higher courts almost all accused persons are represented – over 90% on legal aid. Applications in the Crown Court for legal aid are virtually never refused except on financial grounds. The judiciary now find it difficult to conduct trials with unrepresented defendants, and it may be thought that the offer of legal aid owes as much to concern for the smooth administration of the courts as it does for defendants' civil liberties. The other unwitting allies of defendants' rights are of course the barristers and solicitors who now receive over £100 million of public money from criminal legal aid cases. Any attempt by the Government to limit or cut back criminal legal aid is sure to encounter stiff opposition from this powerful vested interest.

The area where civil libertarians' concern has been strongest in the criminal legal aid field has been the inconsistencies in the grant rate by magistrates' courts for proceedings in those courts. While nationally nearly 70% of adults tried for indictable offences in magistrates' courts are granted legal aid, this figure conceals wild variations from court to court. The Lord Chancellor was finally persuaded that some form of appeal would be necessary and he bowed to pressure during the passing of the 1982 Legal Aid Act. The right takes the form of a reapplication to a committee of practising lawyers under the aegis of the Law Society – it is not called a right of appeal so as to avoid giving magistrates the impression that their opinions were being overruled. At the same time the Lord Chancellor commissioned a survey of 60 magistrates' courts and concluded that inconsistencies indeed existed and were not attributable to external factors such as the different class of business dealt with. New guidelines are to be drawn up to assist courts in deciding whether to grant legal aid.

Until the 1982 Legal Aid Act the financial conditions relevant to criminal legal aid were relatively uncontroversial. Sometimes a down-payment of a small sum was requested before aid would be granted, but this was the exception rather than the rule. Otherwise contributions were assessed at the end of the case by the court on those who appeared to have the means to make them. There was said to be some inconsistency in the way contribution orders were made, but generally these were often nominal or even forgotten about. The total sum raised by way of contributions was only £2 million in 1980 and has indeed declined since then. The aim of the provisions in the 1982 Act was said by the Government to be to end the variations in contribution order practice by the courts by imposing a standard scheme obliging courts to make orders on all who came within the financial limits before the case started rather than at the end. The Government admitted that an important goal of the new scheme was also to increase the number and amount of contribution orders; the estimate given was that it might increase the sum raised by a further £2m, giving a total revenue of £4m in a full year. There was strong opposition to this measure from the civil liberty lobby. These new contribution provisions would work just as arbitrarily as the old system, and moreover the levels of contribution to be demanded might deter accused persons from seeking help when they needed it. The new contribution scheme was modelled by the Lord Chancellor's Department on that which applied in civil legal aid and the eligibility and free limits were to be exactly the same. This made it less easy to oppose on the grounds of hardship, but it also exposed the paucity of the Government's thinking on the issue. Criminal legal aid is not the same as civil legal aid, and the principles which should be applied should surely differ. It was a symptomatic product of the transfer of responsibility of criminal legal aid from the Home Office to the Lord Chancellor (which took place in 1980) that a change in the arrangements for legal aid in criminal cases should be brought about without a consideration of the impact that the changes would have on the criminal process as a whole. The new contribution scheme will no doubt be watched with much cautious attention.

Nevertheless the criminal legal aid scheme is in large measure a success story. Ten years ago the proportion of adults represented in magistrates' court trials of indictable offences was only 32%. Only 9% of juveniles were represented in criminal proceedings and the total amount spent by the state was under £15 million a year. These bare statistics indicate the vast change not just in the numbers who have been represented (and there has of course been a large increase in the numbers coming before the criminal courts), but in attitudes towards legal aid. For a start the numbers applying for legal aid have climbed on virtually the same path as those who received it. Thus knowledge and expectations of the entitlement have risen – though it has to be admitted that the Lord Chancellor's survey still gives cause for concern about variations in application rates in different court areas, the reasons for which remain largely unknown.

Now the focus of interest is moving away from the provision of legal representation at trial to legal advice at the earlier stages – at the police station and at the first remand hearing. For it has at last been officially recognised that the outcome of a case may be critically dependent on what happens at these early moments. A person who can demonstrate to the police his lack of involvement may avoid charge altogether, while an accused who is granted bail at an early stage will probably stay out of custody and may have a better chance of being acquitted. Duty solicitor schemes at magistrates' courts began as volunteers' experiments and for some time remained unco-ordinated. The Law Society then took an interest in their development, and finally the Lord Chancellor was persuaded to include a statutory scheme in the 1982 legislation. This will come into force gradually, but the eventual result should be that all courts will be covered by duty solicitors ready to advise and represent those appearing in court for the first time. The solicitors will be paid a proper rate for their attendance, and the schemes will be properly monitored by local committees.

The crucial problem of legal advice at the police station has always been the refusal by the police to permit access to a lawyer. The Home Office Administrative Directions to the police (which have no legal status) effectively give the police a discretion on whether access should be allowed. But relatively small numbers of those arrested actually ask for the presence of a solicitor. Perhaps they do not know one, or they do not wish to appear unco-operative to the police, or they anticipate a refusal, or they envisage an unacceptable delay. The other main problem is simply lack of rights awareness at this stage. Most of those in custody simply assume they have no real rights and fail to ask. The Government is now, as part of the package of measures under the Police and Criminal Evidence Bill, providing in a police code of conduct that every arrested person must be told of his right to legal advice. The Bill provides for an arrested person the right to see a solicitor in private, except that in certain cases of serious offences the right may be delayed. The restriction on the rights of those suspected of the serious offences proposed must cause concern for civil libertarians. But the general statutory provision for the majority of suspects must be welcome.

Much in this field remains to be seen. At the time of writing the Bill has not completed its passage and may be amended. But the Government has had to announce a financial provision of £6 million to pay for the costs of a police station duty solicitor scheme. The solicitors' profession has yet to gear itself to this potential major demand on its services. It is questionable whether solicitors will be willing to turn out of their offices at short notice or out of their beds at night to visit police stations. Even more worrying is the quality of the advice that many of them can be expected to give. For few solicitors, even those who regularly engage in criminal advocacy, have much experience of advising at the police station. Without the framework of procedural rules and the protection of a court, solicitors and police officers will find themselves in confrontation at a crucial stage of the process. Police officers know their role at the interview and charging stage well; solicitors who are more used to defending charges already laid will have to learn new tactics and find a clear role for themselves. Brought in as defenders of a person's rights, they may find it tempting to engage in bargaining at too early a stage over the suspect's future.

CONCLUSION

In a time of financial cut-backs and restraints in public services it is surprising to see a civil liberty such as subsidised legal aid enjoying such an apparent boom. This arises partly from the inclusion of legal aid within the untouched "law and order" programme, partly from the increase in criminal cases before the courts, and partly from the strong position of lawyers as a vested interest.

The future may not be so rosy. There are signs that the lawyers are losing their importance as an interest group, and that real cuts may have to be made. Civil libertarians will need to identify the key areas where cuts would hurt individuals (as opposed to lawyers' incomes) and where long usage can be said to have given rise to prescriptive rights. Some new areas (such as police station attendances) need to be watched and monitored carefully. Rights have been won over the past twenty years with little struggle; they will need jealous preservation.

12

THE EUROPEAN CONVENTION ON HUMAN RIGHTS AND THE PROTECTION OF CIVIL LIBERTIES IN THE UK

JEREMY McBRIDE

INTRODUCTION

Despite its enduring antipathy to declarations of rights and freedoms, the United Kingdom was actually the first member of the Council of Europe to accept as binding the provisions of the European Convention on Human Rights.[1] However, the government did not seem to envisage that this first regional effort to give legal force to some of the principles of the 1948 Universal Declaration of Human Rights would really be of any relevance to the protection of civil liberties in this country. At most the Convention was an opportunity, amidst hesitant moves towards European unity, to affirm respect for principles supposedly guaranteed by our law and to establish the enforcement machinery to ensure that in future they would also be respected by other states in Europe. The United Kingdom did not, therefore, accept the most significant feature of the Convention's enforcement machinery, namely the possibility of complaints being brought against it by individuals, until 1966,[2] and governmental ambivalence to the Convention still continues to be manifested in a number of other ways. Nevertheless, the Convention has come to play a valuable part in securing and extending our civil liberties.

As a statement of principles the Convention enshrines many, although not all, of the civil liberties that are valued (if not always respected) in the UK. In particular, it amounts to an expression of commitment to the right to life, freedom from torture and inhuman and degrading treatment and punishment, freedom from slavery and arbitrary arrest, the right to a fair trial, freedom from retrospective penalties, the right to privacy, freedom of religion, conscience, expression, assembly and association and the right to marry.[3] Of course, such a declaration cannot in itself be a sufficient guarantee that the rights and freedoms it proclaims will not be violated, or that violations will be remedied, but the Convention is more than an expression of good intentions. Its contribution to the protection of civil liberties is real, and with respect to the UK it can be seen in three discrete ways.

In the first place, it affords a forum for challenging governmental actions in a way that is at present impossible within the UK. Petitions to the European Commission of Human Rights in Strasbourg, if declared admissible, can lead to a "friendly settlement"; or failing settlement to a binding determination by the European Court of Human Rights or the Committee of Ministers.[4] In either case this should ultimately ensure that the rights and freedoms proclaimed by the Convention are respected. In this way it acts as a hybrid Bill of Rights; the methods of adjudication are similar to those of a constitutional court but the ruling, although binding in international law, does not actually have any legal force within the United Kingdom and its implementation thus requires further action by government or Parliament.

Secondly, the Convention provides a set of minimum standards which can be invoked in the context of struggles within this country's own institutions to secure and extend civil liberties. The formulation of the rights, together with our international undertaking to respect them, gives this catalogue a legitimacy which is probably only exceeded by the much more symbolic Magna Carta. These standards are capable of influencing reform, deterring encroachment on civil liberties and shaping judicial decisions without having to resort to the Strasbourg machinery.

Thirdly, and potentially most importantly, so long as the Convention continues to be binding on the UK, there is an international commitment which should deter governments from a wholesale abandonment of those nebulous but vital prerequisites of civil liberty, democracy and the rule of law. Western European solidarity is increasingly tied to the principles enshrined in the Convention and it is to be hoped that this has the effect of safeguarding them for the future.

It would be wrong, however, to regard the Convention as a

panacea for the protection and development of civil liberties. The Convention is certainly not the centrepiece of the machinery protecting civil liberties in the UK; the principal responsibility still rests with our own legal system. Nor do the Convention's provisions cover the whole field of civil liberties (a notable omission is an "equal protection" clause, guaranteeing the equal protection of the law without discrimination), and resort to the Strasbourg machinery does not always produce the result hoped for. Furthermore, despite its increasing legitimacy as a yardstick within this country, the Convention still does not have sufficient status to ensure that respect for its provisions has a conclusive influence on law reform.

The Convention is not, therefore, without its shortcomings. These, however, limit rather than negate the contribution that it has made, and can continue to make, as will be seen from a more detailed evaluation of the ways it has helped to protect civil liberties. It ought, therefore, to be well-regarded by civil libertarians, and efforts should be made to ensure that its contribution becomes still greater.

THE VALUE OF GOING TO STRASBOURG

Since the acceptance of the right of individual petition in 1966 resort to Strasbourg has gradually become more and more popular as an avenue of redress. There may be some surprise at this development as the public and the legal profession still only have a limited understanding of the Convention system (it is common to assume that one can go straight to the Court of Human Rights, and there is an abiding confusion with the legal order of the European Communities). Awareness and understanding have not been improved by the fact that the cases considered in Strasbourg tend to be shrouded in secrecy for several years until the Commission stage of the proceedings is complete. Nevertheless the attraction of the Convention system is readily apparent; interferences with, or limitations on, civil liberties are often expressly authorised or required by statute or the common law, and the Strasbourg machinery may be the only hope of a remedy in such cases, since the courts of this country are powerless to provide redress and the government and Parliament may be unwilling to do so.

As more and more petitions are successful, so it seems others are eager to try the system. In recent years the number of petitions registered against the United Kingdom has always exceeded a hundred and at least as many again may have been provisionally filed.[5] Indeed more often than not the UK is the object of the largest number of petitions against a member state in a given year, though this is probably more an indication of the level of confidence in the system than a suitable basis for a comparative analysis of the state of liberty in European countries. Britain is also one of the few signatories to the Convention that has not made the Convention enforceable in its domestic courts.[6] Nevertheless, it is apparent that consideration of civil liberties problems in the UK figures prominently in the operation of the Convention system, and this becomes even clearer when it is realised that cases involving this country have accounted for well over a quarter of all the petitions declared admissible so far.[7] These are the cases in which a *prima facie* case of a violation of the Convention is established and on which most of the Commission's energy is expended.

The main value of such figures, however, is merely as a guide to the breakdown of the Commission's workload, and as a confirmation of people's increasing expectations that the Convention will afford them a remedy where their own constitutional system has failed them. Only an examination of the cases themselves and the governmental reaction to them will indicate the extent of the Convention's contribution to the protection of civil liberties in the UK. Nor is it enough to consider only the cases in which a violation was established or a settlement reached; the cases which have failed or were never brought are also an important measure of the limits of that contribution. Moreover, since decisions by the Convention organs are only binding in international law, the manner of their implementation is clearly crucial to any assessment of the Convention's impact.

The cases in which there has been an express finding that the Convention has been breached, as well as those in which this is tacitly admitted by the government's undertaking in a friendly settlement to introduce changes in the law or administrative practices, cover a wide range of civil liberty issues. Nor are these cases concerned simply with the particular problems of individual applicants. The vast majority of them have a bearing on the civil liberties of many other people similarly placed. This class interest will generally be apparent even if the petition is the only one on a given subject, but it is emphasised where several petitions on the same issue are joined together by the Commission. The general applicability of the cases determined by the Strasbourg machinery needs especially to be borne in mind as the length of the proceedings may actually result in the outcome losing its importance for the individual applicant.

Amongst the areas in which UK law and practice have been expressly or implicitly held to have fallen below Convention standards are: restrictions on the publication of comment relating to the Thalidomide affair;[8] the use of judicial corporal punishment in the Isle of Man, and of corporal punishment in schools in England and Scotland without parental consent;[9] the use of techniques of interrogation such as hooding and wall-standing in Northern Ireland;[10] the absence of a system of immigration appeals and the breaking up of families through immigration control;[11] the restrictions imposed on prisoners with respect to their access to courts and legal advice, freedom of correspondence and the right to marry;[12] the fact that homosexual relations between consenting adults were unlawful in Northern Ireland;[13] the conditions in which mental patients were held and the limitations imposed on challenges to the legality of their detention;[14] and the circumstances in which an employee was obliged to join a trade union or be dismissed.[15]

In all these situations the Convention requires a greater degree of freedom than the government or Parliament had been able or willing to grant in the absence of external compulsion. On a results basis, therefore (and before considering the details of their implementation), it would be hard to deny that the resolution of these cases has, by extending a wide range of civil liberties, made a contribution to the cause of freedom in this country. However, in such a survey of the cases as the present one, it is impossible to detail the nuances or explain the reasoning behind the individual decisions. There might, therefore, be grounds for dissatisfaction even though the result could be described as favouring greater freedom – either because it is felt that the extensions of civil liberties achieved are limited or because the reasoning employed by the Court of Human Rights allows little scope for further development of civil liberties. This reaction, however, is hardly an appropriate response to decisions which require restrictions on freedom of expression in the interests of the administration of justice to be strictly scrutinised,[16] or condemn as unacceptable the control that the Home Secretary enjoyed over civil litigation by prisoners.[17] Nor is it a valid criticism of some of the decisions involving other countries which have laid the foundations for an assault on inadequacies in our own law, such as the decision assessing the compatibility of Germany's law on telephone tapping with the Convention.[18]

Nevertheless in some areas it might be thought that such comments are justifiable. For example, in the case concerning interrogation practices in Northern Ireland a requirement that detainees perform irksome and painful exercises was not held to be degrading treatment;[19] the Court's condemnation of corporal punishment in schools was based only on the right of parents to control their children's education, and not the children's right not to be subjected to degrading treatment;[20] and in deciding that a blanket prohibition of consensual homosexual relationships in Northern Ireland was in breach of the Convention, the Court accepted that some criminal restrictions would be permissible.[21] Other shortcomings of the Convention, are evidenced by the cases in which the Strasbourg organs failed to find any violation of its provisions. For example, the use of the Obscene Publications Acts to suppress the distribution of the *Little Red Schoolbook* and the limits on the lobbying of soldiers imposed by the Incitement to Disaffection Act 1934 were not regarded as unacceptable limitations on freedom of expression;[22] detention for an examination lasting 45 hours under the Prevention of Terrorism legislation was acceptable;[23] and the due process requirements of the Convention were held to have no application to the deportation of an alien on alleged security grounds.[24] Moreover, disappointment is the most likely reaction to the Convention's role in relation to the situation in Northern Ireland. The widespread discrimination on religious and political grounds was the subject of petitions in 1968, but these proved abortive; internment without trial was upheld as compatible with the lower standards permitted by the Convention in emergency situations; and the denial of political status for prisoners and the resulting "dirty protest" did not result in any violations of the Convention being established. Although certain interrogation methods have been held to be inhuman and degrading and a case concerning the use of plastic bullets as a means of crowd control is now under way, the general impression is that the Convention has had little impact on the special civil liberties problems of Northern Ireland.[25]

It would be unfortunate, however, if, these limitations on what the Covention system can do for civil liberties were to lead potential claimants to ignore it as a waste of effort. There are in fact several reasons for the limited effectiveness of the Convention, and not all of them are attributable to the working of the Strasbourg machinery. In the first place, no court system should be blamed for the short-comings of the cases introduced into it. Not all the cases sent to Strasbourg have been clear or even arguable violations of the Convention. Some have had a weak factual basis, others have had only the most tenuous connection with any of the rights or freedoms guaranteed by its provisions and still others have failed because they did not meet the admissibility requirements (such as the 6 months' time limited and the requirement to exhaust domestic remedies before complaining to the Commission).[26] Some petitions have been presented more in hope than in confidence and others point to the need for better legal advice, the absence of which may be seen to be a governmental failing.

Secondly, the Convention does not guarantee everything that one might consider to be a civil liberty. There is, for example, no right not to be discriminated against other than in relation to the enjoyment of the other rights and freedoms included in the Convention. Many areas of discrimination, such as in employment, housing and the provision of services, are outside the scope of the Convention and cannot, therefore, be the subject of successful petitions. Also the due process clause (Article 6) is drafted in such a way as to impose serious restrictions on its applicability to administrative decision-making on issues such as the detention and deportation of immigrants. Moreover, not all the provisions of the Convention are binding on this country; the United Kingdom has yet to ratify two Protocols, the Fourth (concerning freedom of movement) and the Sixth (requiring the abolition of the death penalty in peace-time). It is not surprising, therefore, that cases concerning freedom of movement have a lowish rate of success and it is impressive that the Strasbourg machinery has still been able to afford some protection by finding that aspects of our immigration control amount to inhuman and degrading treatment and a violation of the right to family life.[27] Thirdly, and related to the previous point, the Court and the Commission in applying the Convention have to interpret its provisions, and it would be amazing if they were always in agreement with the petitioner. There is certainly no one view of civil liberties or even the detailed requirements of any particular freedom. In interpreting the broad provisions of the Convention, there is undoubtedly scope for policy-making by the Commission and the Court. In some instances this is favourable to government, as in the development of the doctrine of the margin of appreciation by which a respondent government may be given the benefit of the doubt in considering whether its measures comply with the Convention. In many others it is favourable to the petitioner; for example, the interpretation of the Convention that revealed a right of access to domestic courts for which there was no express provision.[28] The opportunity afforded by the Convention for such judicial law-making is what some find most objectionable in the idea of a Bill of Rights, considering as they do that political decisions about the ambit of civil liberties should be made only by a democratically elected legislature.[29] Without conceding that that is a fatal objection to a Bill of Rights, this criticism has far less force against a system which is not constitutionally entrenched and which is only designed to protect minimum standards. If one is unsuccessful at the Convention level, that failure does not foreclose the political argument for greater freedom in this country. In any event, although any such assessment must be subjective, there is good reason to consider that the "successes" of the Convention for civil liberties in the United Kingdom still outweigh the "failures".

Finally, on one occasion this country's immigration control over UK citizens and passport holders escaped condemnation simply because of a defect in the Convention's machinery, which has since been effectively remedied. In several cases concerning the exclusion of East African Asians from the United Kingdom, the Commission had found violations of the right to family life and the right not to be subjected to inhuman and degrading treatment, but the case was then referred to the Committee of Ministers (the only body other than the Court competent to make a binding decision), where the Commission failed to secure the two-thirds majority needed to confirm the finding that the Convention had been violated and there was, therefore, no conclusive determination of the petitions. In the event the Asians were admitted to this country, and the practice of the Commission in referring cases to the Court indicates that the Committee of Ministers is unlikely in future to be given a similar opportunity to leave cases in that sort of limbo.

Even though resort to the Convention does not always result in a favourable outcome, it is clear that those cases that have succeeded have had a progressive influence on the civil liberties standards to be observed in this country. Moreover it is likely that that influence will become even more significant as it becomes increasingly apparent that many areas of our law raise Convention issues. As a consequence of this the volume of petitions being registered shows no signs of abatement.

A finding that our standards do not meet those of the Convention does not, however, mean that our law or practice is automatically brought up to scratch. Since the Convention is not part of our law, any change required depends on the government taking the appropriate action, whether it be to initiate legislation in Parliament or to amend its practices under existing powers. The implementation of the necessary changes may not occur for some time, or changes may not even be implemented properly. It is often a year and sometimes two before any action is taken to give effect to judgments of the Court. The delay is usually explained by the need to "study" the judgment and it is understandable that its implications should be considered. Nevertheless, the time taken often seems excessive, particularly since the prior report of the Commission gives a good indication that a violation is likely to be established. This should allow for the necessary measures at least to be drafted in advance; indeed, as the cases concerning the right of prisoners to marry in prison demonstrate, it is possible to act before the final decision.[30] It is not surprising that, having fought a case to the bitter end, the government does not display any enthusiasm for changing what it has defended, but the delay, coming after several years of proceedings, should be minimised.

This problem tends to be obviated where there is a friendly settlement, as the necessary change in law or practice has to be specified so that the Commission can be satisfied that it is "on the basis of respect for Human Rights" as defined in the Convention; that is, that the petitioner is not being bought off and that the general interest is not being ignored.[31] Another advantage of a friendly settlement, as far as implementation of amendments to the law is concerned, is that the Commission generally has the opportunity to assess the adequacy of the purported reforms. This is not possible where the final decision on the existence of a violation is taken by the Court or the Committee of Ministers; it is clear that the United Kingdom did not do enough in at least one case, and in others there are also doubts about whether the measures taken were sufficient. A judgment of the Court will indicate that there has been a violation but, apart from a personal remedy for the petitioner (usually damages and legal costs), it does not make clear what measures are required to ensure conformity with the Convention for the future. The Committee of Ministers is no more helpful, as its findings are based on the reports of the Commission, which again only explain why there is a violation but not what needs to be done. Whether the final determination is by the Court or the Committee, it is for the latter, a body of Foreign Ministers lacking legal expertise or advice, to judge whether adequate steps have been taken to bring the law or practice into line. In fact the Committee tends to accept the respondent government's opinion that the measures it has taken or proposes to implement are satisfactory, and no attempt is made to subject them to scrutiny; for example, it merely "took note" of the reforms implemented after the judgment in the *Golder* case concerning prisoners' correspondence with their legal advisers, even though the change was insubstantial.[32] The UK has always, even if belatedly, taken steps in purported implementation of decisions by the Strasbourg organs but given the lack of supervision at this stage it is quite possible that they will not meet the required standard. As the cases concerning prisoners' correspondence demonstrate, the only option for those whose human rights are still denied is to start the process all over again.[33] Since the need to implement such decisions is likely to increase, it is clear that this is an aspect of the Convention system in urgent need of reform. In the absence of effective scrutiny at this stage, the efforts of the Strasbourg machinery to improve our civil liberties could be frustrated.

It is not only in its attitude to implementation that the government appears ambivalent towards the Convention and thereby undermines the contribution it can make. This attitude is also apparent in several matters relating to the conduct of proceedings at Strasbourg. In the first place, there seems to be an almost overwhelming reluctance to concede a violation in any case, even to the extent that after a change in government, the new administration will still actively defend something which it almost certainly considered indefensible when in opposition: for example, the present government's defence of its predecessor's legislation concerning the closed shop and the compensation to be provided after the nationalisation of the aircraft and shipping industries.[34] Secondly, even though the Convention system is now an accepted addition to the avenues of redress in this country, the legal aid scheme has not been extended to it. Would-be petitioners in need of legal advice must bear their own costs at least until their claim is declared admissible or the government has submitted its written observations on this question, as that is the point when the Convention's own legal aid scheme becomes operative.[35] Yet it is prior to that point that legal advice is often most crucial. At present still less than two-fifths of the petitions going to Strasbourg are introduced through a lawyer, and it is not surprising that so many fail at the admissibility hurdle. If legal advice were made available through the legal aid scheme, the success rate might increase and the government and the Commission would be less likely to be bothered by hopeless petitions.

Thirdly, where the petition concerns the refusal to allow the petitioner to stay in this country, the government will not always permit him to remain until the case has been determined.[36] This does not prevent petitions from being submitted but it could make the conduct of the cases more difficult, particularly as the petitioners may be removed to a country without lawyers able to advise on the Convention.

Finally, although the right of individual petition is now generally renewed for five-year periods, there is always considerable uncertainty whether the government will actually make the necessary declaration. The impression is certainly given that some departments of state find the Convention system irksome and are, therefore, opposed to renewal. If the government were to declare, as the Dutch and Irish governments have done, that it accepts the possibility of individual petitions indefinitely, it would demonstrate that its commitment to the Convention is nothing less than wholehearted.

THE CONVENTION IN THE UNITED KINGDOM

The success of the Strasbourg system in extending civil liberties in this country underlines the failings of our own constitutional system. However effective resort to international machinery may be, its existence enables reform to be further delayed and it is, therefore, only a second best solution. It would certainly be preferable if the minimum standards embodied in the Convention could be vindicated in this country's own institutions, whether in Parliament or the courts. This preference for a domestic remedy has resulted in proposals to incorporate the Convention; that is, give it the force of law in the UK, so that it can be enforced by our own courts. Although incorporation would probably reduce, if not eliminate, the need to go to Strasbourg, it has been opposed on the ground that any kind of Bill of Rights is undesirable; so far this view has prevailed in Parliament.[37]

Nevertheless, the fact that the Convention is binding on the UK in international law still gives it some influence on the development of the law independently of petitions to the Commission. It is increasingly common to find the provisions of the Convention being invoked both in the course of litigation within the UK and in the law reform process, and on occasions this can have some effect on the outcome. However, the Convention is more likely to have been one of several factors taken into account than to have been decisive by itself. Moreover, there are still many situations where the relevance of the Convention has been ignored. Overall, the use of the Convention by UK institutions remains rather unadventurous but this is not entirely a matter for regret, as there are also difficulties and dangers in relying on it in this way, particularly with regard to interpretation. Clearly a cautious approach by legislators and judges is preferable to their giving full effect to a restrictive interpretation of the Convention's provisions which might then deter resort to a more enlightened arbiter in Strasbourg.

The Convention's provisions have been invoked by counsel in many reported cases, with respect either to the interpretation and application of statutes or to the development of common law rights and obligations. As far as statutes are concerned, such invocations have not, save for one truly exceptional case, had any decisive influence on decisions by the courts. The exception was where the case-law of the Commission on the meaning of "torture or inhuman or degrading treatment" was used to interpret the same words in a statute governing the admissibility of confessions in Northern Ireland, on the ground that they had been derived from the Convention.[38] At one point Lord Denning MR seemed willing to give the Convention a more significant role, suggesting that, despite the absence of incorporation, it would prevail over inconsistent provisions in statutes.[39] This view was quickly retracted as an aberration and the courts have not been prepared to go further than to say that since Parliament is to be presumed not to have acted contrary to its international obligations, ambiguous provisions in statutes will be construed so as to conform with the Convention. [40] However, in no case in which the courts have asserted that the Convention could be so used has it led to a result which might not otherwise have been expected. At most, reference to a relevant provision in the Convention has lent further support to a presumption already used in statutory interpretation, such as the presumptions against the imposition of retrospective penalties and against interference with the right of access to the courts.

As a consequence there remains some uncertainty about the actual applicability of the presumption of consistency with the Convention to measures inconsistent with the Convention. Can an apparent inconsistency itself suggest ambiguity or must the ambiguity be established first of all? Can it be used to secure the widest possible freedom or should the courts only adopt an interpretation which prevents the UK being held to be in breach of the Convention? If the courts give an affirmative answer to the second alternative in each question, it is unlikely that the presumption will have more than a marginal influence on statutory interpretation; statutes affecting civil liberties rarely seem to be ambiguous except in the context of an awareness of the standards established by the Convention. On the other hand, an affirmative answer to the first alternatives would give Convention a much more significant influence on the interpretation of statutes; inconsistencies would become more readily apparent and the courts might adopt an interpretation which secures the most extensive degree of freedom possible.

In either case the impact is still in the realms of the potential; and the narrower view seems the more likely one to be adopted in view of the way the courts have rejected the suggestion that the Convention is a factor to be considered by government bodies in the exercise of their administrative powers. At first Lord Denning MR was favourable to this idea, saying that immigration officers should take account of the Convention's provisions (the right to family life is particularly relevant) in deciding whether to grant leave to an immigrant to enter the country. However, he again rapidly changed his mind and concluded that this was far too onerous an obligation for immigration officers, [41] although this seems inconsistent with the Home Secretary's subsequent decision to require them to have regard to treaties concerning refugees. [42] This refusal to consider the Convention to be relevant to the exercise of administrative powers seems somewhat strange, particularly since most such powers are derived from statute. If Parliament is presumed to act consistently with the Convention, then surely it follows that the use of a power in a manner contrary to the Convention should be presumed to be beyond the powers conferred by the statute and therefore invalid? By refusing to take this approach, the courts have imposed a serious limitation on the potential impact of the Convention within the UK.

The impact of the Convention on common law rights and obligations affecting civil liberties has, so far, been almost non-existent. Moreover, insofar as there is any scope for influence on the development of the common law, there are no signs that it is likely to be of any great significance. In a number of cases, one finds little more than a bald statement that the common law relating to, for example, freedom of assembly gives effect to the appropriate provision in the Convention.[43] In such cases the examination of the Convention is little more than cursory and it is rare for the judge to refer to the relevant case-law of the Commission and the Court. It is certainly doubtful whether the courts in these cases were seriously confronted with, or allowed themselves to consider, the possibility that the common law was actually failing to secure the rights and freedoms guaranteed by the Convention.

However, in one case it has actually been held that the common law fell below the Convention standards. This was a case concerning the legality of telephone tapping by the police. Vice-Chancellor Megarry's judgment[44] is remarkable for its full consideration of the Convention and the relevant case-law and for his strong call for the necessary remedial legislation. The case is also important because it seems to accept the idea that the Convention can have a part to play in the development of the common law as well as in the interpretation of statutes. Since there is not an appropriate precedent for every situation that can arise, judges develop the common law to meet the new situation by drawing on the principles laid down in previous cases. Where judges have a choice about how the law is to be developed, it is clearly desirable for consistency with the Convention to be promoted if at all possible. Although Sir Robert Megarry accepted that the Convention could influence the common law in this way, he felt unable to give effect to the appropriate Convention standards, because the detailed regulation required by the Court of Human Rights in the *Klass* case[45] went far beyond what he considered was possible or permissible in the development of our common law.

Individual judges in the Court of Appeal and the House of Lords have, however, invoked the Convention in determining the development of the common law on, for example, the award of punitive damages for libel, blasphemy, the granting of an injunction to restrain a breach of confidence and contempt of court.[46] In none of these cases was the invocation of the Convention actually critical to the outcome, as the majority of the judges in the cases concerned did not resort to it in their reasoning. Nevertheless, they do indicate that, where there is no clear line of authority leading to a particular result, the Convention can be used as a beneficent, if limited, influence on the development of the common law affecting civil liberties.

The government's undertaking to secure the rights and freedoms guaranteed by the Convention might also have some influence on the judges' conception of what is public policy. Certainly one judge, Lord Wilberforce, has accepted its relevance in principle but, as yet, no practical application has been reported. However, if respect for it was a matter of public policy, then this might lead the courts to hold, for example, that a contract requiring one of the parties to surrender rights and freedoms guaranteed by the Convention was invalid.

So far the use of the Convention by the courts, whether in relation to statutes or the common law, has demonstrated potential rather than solid achievement. However, a headlong judicial rush to use the Convention, in the absence of incorporation, could have deleterious as much as beneficial effects on civil liberties in this country. Its provisions are phrased in general terms and their interpretation requires a broader approach than the literalism often adopted in relation to our own statutes. This has not, however, always been demonstrated in the cases in which the Convention has been invoked. Whether it was a case of dismissing a particular freedom as too vague to be applied, or of readily accepting certain limitations on a right as acceptable, or of finding that a guaranteed freedom is secured by the common law, the courts have by and large treated the Convention's provisions in a simplistic fashion.[47] This criticism applies to counsel as well as the judiciary; counsel appear sometimes to have invoked the Convention as an additional argument in a case on the assumption that it must protect their conception of a particular freedom. This is not always the case, and to invoke it without full argument in support of a particular interpretation, especially where there is little or nothing in the way of supporting case-law, may lead the judge to find that the Convention only requires the much lower standard of freedom already guaranteed by our law. The caution of Lord Scarman in refusing to adopt a particular interpretation of freedom of association in the absence of a ruling by the Court of Human Rights is perhaps excessive.[48] Nevertheless, if the Convention is to have any beneficial effect on the interpretation of statutes and the development of the common law, then efforts must be made to ensure that the courts use the appropriate techniques of interpretation.

Although the courts have some leeway to ensure that statutes and the common law meet the Convention's standards, there is nothing that can be done where they clearly require a breach of its provisions. In such cases, a petition to Strasbourg may well be an essential preliminary to bringing the UK's law or practice into line with the Convention. However, such petitions are, by their nature, after the event and in a number of instances it would seem that the law is being changed in such a way as to violate the Convention (or exacerbate existing violations) simply because our obligations under the Convention are not considered or do not have a decisive influence on those responsible for the change. Although it would be impossible to prevent law reform or changes in administrative practice from becoming the vehicle for new violations of the Convention, it does seem desirable that a determined effort should be made to prevent such an event happening. There is, however, little evidence of the Convention's provisions receiving serious consideration by government on a regular basis even though this would do much to safeguard our civil liberties. This is undoubtedly an aspect of our law-making process which needs to be overhauled.

It is difficult to make any assessment of the impact of the Convention other than through the published reports of public bodies recommending reform and of parliamentary proceedings. The Home Office, a major source of law reform proposals, rarely refers to the Convention in its public documents, but it must be aware of the relevance of its provisions given the many cases going to Strasbourg in which it has been involved. On a number of occasions, notably the revisions of the Immigration Rules in recent years, it appears as if it might have been willing to take the risk that reforms which it has promoted would subsequently be challenged. It is regrettable, therefore, that civil service memoranda on such matters are not made available to assist Parliamentary debate on and scrutiny of law-making. The Convention is not invoked by MPs and peers on any systematic basis but a survey of the reports of Royal Commissions, government and Parliamentary committees and the Law Commission on various aspects of civil liberties in recent years shows that there has been some public acknowledgment of the Convention's relevance to law reform.

The consideration of the Convention's provisions in the light of this acknowledgment has, however, been of varying quality. In some instances, particularly where the case-law is or was undeveloped, the reference to the Convention was only cursory: for example, in reports concerned with freedom of assembly and aspects of privacy and data protection. In other cases, the consideration of the relevant provisions has been superficial or incomplete. An instance of the former was Lord Diplock's failure in his review of telephone tapping to discuss the standards set in the *Klass* case with respect to the interception of communications. He contented himself with the simple observation that the obligation to secure the right of everyone to respect for his private and family life, his home and correspondence was not absolute.[49] Examples of incomplete examination of the Convention's provisions can be seen in the Phillimore Report on Contempt of Court,[50] which discussed those relevant to a fair trial but not those relating to freedom of expression, and the Report of the Royal Commission on Criminal Procedure,[51] which considered the right to privacy when discussing the interception of communications but did not refer to the provisions on arrest and detention when it proposed to extend police powers in that area. The Convention's provisions have, however, been treated seriously in some reports, such as Lord Gardiner's decisive dissent in the Compton Report on interrogation practices in Northern Ireland; the Bennett inquiry into the same subject, and the Home Affairs Committee's examination of the 1980 Immigration Rules,[52] even though the Home Affairs Committee failed to make any specific recommendation to the House of Commons.

Taking the Convention into account in making recommendations does not of course guarantee that the new law will comply with its provisions. An individual case may throw up a situation which the reformers could not have imagined in the abstract. Moreover, it may be that the political body responsible for the change will disagree with an assessment that certain changes are necessary to comply with the Convention or that other changes will lead to a violation of its provisions. Nonetheless, this does not gainsay the value of attempting to ensure that the United Kingdom's obligations under the Convention are given proper consideration in the course of law-making.

There are several useful moves which could be made in this direction. First, there could be, as a standing remit for all public bodies making proposals for law reform, a requirement that they include in their report or White Paper an account of the implications of their recommendations for this country's obligations under the Convention. Secondly, parliamentary consideration of this question could be institutionalised in some way, perhaps at the Committee Stage of a Bill. Thirdly, the terms of reference of the Joint Select Committee on Statutory Instruments could be expanded so as to require it to draw Parliament's attention to any legislation made by Ministers under statutory authority which appears to conflict with the Convention.[53] These reforms would mean that the possibility of a breach of the Convention is likely to be more apparent and thus the subject of public discussion. It might, therefore, be a little harder politically for a Minister or Parliament deliberately to flout the UK's international obligations.

A GUARDIAN OF LIBERTY

The part that the Convention plays in securing and extending particular rights and freedoms is a relatively visible contribution to the protection of civil liberties in this country. As the preceding two sections have shown, it is generally possible to see when resort to the Strasbourg machinery leads to a change in law or practice and when the invocation of the Convention influences domestic proposals for reform. However, it would be unfortunate if one then overlooked a contribution which is much less visible but nonetheless valuable. This is that the very fact of the UK's continued commitment to the principles enshrined in the Convention itself amounts to a safeguard against any general or widespread abrogation of civil liberties. It is of the utmost importance, therefore, that this commitment should not be weakened but should instead be strengthened and deepened.

Although the Convention guarantees a number of apparently discrete rights and freedoms, they are not really severable. The Convention system is meant to secure respect for all of them because they are all essential components in the achievement of its overall objective, namely the maintenance of a minimum standard of civil liberty within a system of constitutional democracy. If any one of those rights and freedoms is disregarded to any considerable extent, then it is more than likely that others will soon suffer the same fate. Thus, without freedom from arbitrary arrest, freedom of expression is easily suppressed; without freedom from torture, freedom of thought is readily debased; and without freedom to vote in proper elections there is no hope of freedom from governmental oppression. So long as the UK is committed to all the Convention's provisions and their enforcement machinery, then it will be that much harder for it to start out on the road to tyranny.

Although the UK's commitment to the Convention is not at present in doubt, its continued existence depends on both internal and external pressure and the vitality of the enforcement machinery. As far as internal pressure is concerned, it is important that awareness of the Convention be increased both within Parliament and in the country generally. If the Convention is not systematically considered by Parliament when scrutinising legislation and governmental action, then this will allow the Government to consider that breaches of it may be of little or no political significance. If the Convention is not known about by the public at large, then there may not be petitions to Strasbourg reminding the Government that its standards are important. There is certainly scope for improvement in both these respects.

The Council of Europe, a cooperative body committed to the maintenance of democracy and the rule of law, created the Convention and is the most likely source of external pressure. Whether this body and its members individually can be relied upon to provide effective pressure to accept the Convention standards is still somewhat uncertain. Certainly membership of the Council of Europe and acceptance of the Convention did not prevent the abandonment of democracy in Greece in the 1960s and in Turkey in the 1970s. The situations in both countries gave rise to inter-state cases, the latter of which is still under consideration.[54] Although the Commission found that Greece had broken a number of Convention provisions, Greece chose to leave the Council of Europe instead of having to implement reforms under the threat of expulsion. European pressure to accept the Convention standards might, therefore, be regarded as ineffective, although the fellowship of

European states was sufficiently attractive to Greece for it to rejoin the Council of Europe after the restoration of democracy. On the other hand, it seems more than likely that pressure from European states, including the commencement of an inter-state case, had some influence on the decision by Turkey to hold in 1983 the first elections for several years.

Whatever doubts there may be about the influence that fellow Council of Europe members wield over each other, the pressure to accept the Convention as binding is likely to be much greater for those members, such as the UK, who are also members of the European Communities. This is because a resolution of the European Parliament and a declaration of the Council of Ministers[55] have made it clear that becoming or remaining a party to the Convention is now effectively a qualification for membership of the Communities. Indeed the desire to consolidate the individual obligations of the member states was one of the factors prompting the suggestion that the Communities should actually accede to the Convention.[56] Although that proposal may not actually be implemented for some time, if at all, the intertwining of economic interests and respect for civil liberties could prove to be a valuable restraint against abandoning the Convention standards.

The pressure that states use on each other to ensure respect for the Convention is more political than legal. It is certainly rare for states to bring cases under the Convention system, even though it is open to them to do so. They have generally only done so where the alleged violations have some domestic repercussions[57] or where there has been a widespread disregard of civil liberties, as in Greece and Turkey. It is perhaps significant that in the latter two cases, neither country recognised the right of individual petition. The ability to vindicate individual grievances itself contributes to the maintenance of a minimum standard of civil liberty and is preferable to waiting until the damage done is sufficient to prompt a complaint by another state. There can be little doubt that, if the right of individual petition were to be withdrawn from people living in this country, the influence of the Strasbourg system would be considerably diminished. Although it is technically optional, it is clear that the acceptance of this right is an essential part of the commitment to the Convention standards.

CONCLUSION

The impact of the Convention since ratification, and particularly since the acceptance of the right of individual petition, has undoubtedly been of much benefit to civil liberties in this country. There were many much-needed reforms which were ignored and neglected until resort to the Convention system was seized upon as a last hope. It may be that reform would eventually have come even if the trip to Strasbourg had not been made, but that is no comfort to those whose rights and freedoms are being violated in the meantime. Going to Strasbourg has clearly quickened the pace of reform for a wide range of civil liberties issues and it is reasonable to expect that the Convention systems will continue to contribute to the extension of our freedoms. On the other hand, petitions to Strasbourg may also be used as an excuse for not yielding to political pressure for reform. It might be argued that one should wait for the Court's ruling and that would, of course, delay matters for at least five years. This would make any sense if the Convention standards represented the optimum level of liberty feasible, but they are no more than the minimum acceptable. There is no justification, therefore, for refusing to implement reforms while a case is being considered in Strasbourg. If they are subsequently shown to be more than the Convention requires then so much the better.

Going to Strasbourg is a slow process. This is partly because of insufficient funds and staff for the Commission and partly because the present procedure is time-consuming.[58] Even if changes were implemented, the proceedings are still likely to be fairly lengthy and reform in the UK would be delayed accordingly. This points to the need for action within the UK to ensure that the Convention's standards are being respected. The Strasbourg system is, after all, meant to remedy shortcomings in the domestic system and not to take on almost the whole burden of reform in a particular country. So far the impact of the Convention within the UK's institutions has been fairly limited. Certainly there is scope for taking the Convention into account more often in the course of both judicial decision-making and legislating. There are, however, limits to what can be achieved by this course of action and it is clear from the range of cases going to Strasbourg that there is a need for more substantial action. Whether this is to incorporate the Convention or to undertake an appropriate programme of legislative reform, failure to act without prompting from the Strasbourg machinery amounts to an abdication to them of the government's responsibility for securing our civil liberties.

NOTES

1. It ratified the Convention on 3rd March 1951. For the background to the establishment of the Convention system and accounts of its subsequent operation, see: R Beddard, *Human Rights and Europe* (2nd ed.) (Sweet and Maxwell, 1980); F G Jacobs, *The European Convention on Human Rights* (Oxford University Press, 1975); and A H Robertson, *Human Rights in Europe* (2nd ed.) (Manchester University Press, 1977).

2. States ratifying the Convention are only obliged to accept the possibility of complaints about breaches by other states (Article 24). A separate declaration must be made under Article 25 for individual petitions to be permitted. The UK has made periodic declarations under Article 25 since 1966.

3. Several Protocols to the Convention have also been adopted. The First (which the UK has ratified) and the Fourth and Sixth (which it has not) extend the Convention to include the right to education, freedom of movement and the abolition of the death penalty.

4. The jurisdiction of the Committee of Ministers is compulsory whereas that of the Court is optional (Article 32). The UK has accepted the jurisdiction of the Court but the decision to refer a case to it rather than the Committee is made by the Commission or any state involved in the case (Article 48); the individual petitioner has no right to insist on his case going to the Court.

5. See European Commission of Human Rights, *Statistics 1982* (Council of Europe Document DH (83) 6) and the *Annual Reviews* of the Commission's work.

6. The volume of UK cases is also large because it is more common that several petitions raise the same issue than is the case in other countries.

7. See European Commission on Human Rights, *Stocktaking on the European Convention on Human Rights* (Council of Europe, 1982).

8. *The Sunday Times* case (*Times Newspapers Ltd* v *UK* (1979) 2 European Human Rights Reports, p.245).

9. *Tyrer* v *UK* [1978] 2 European Human Rights Reports, p.1; and *X* v *UK* (Applic. 7907/77) (a friendly settlement) and *Campbell and Cosans* v *UK* (1982) 4 European Human Rights Reports, p.293 (a judgement of the Court).

10. *Ireland* v *UK* [1978] 2 European Human Rights Reports, p.25.

11. *Alam and Khan* v *UK* [1968] Yearbook of the European Convention on Human Rights, p.788 (a friendly settlement).

12. *Golder* v *UK* [1975] 1 Human Rights Reports, p.524, *Reed* v *UK* [1982] 25 Decisions and Reports, p. 5 (a friendly settlement), and *Silver* v *UK* Judgment of the European Court of Human Rights, 25th March 1983 (correspondence and legal advice); and *Hamer* v *UK* [1981] 24 Decisions and Reports, p.5 and *Draper* v *UK* [1981] 24 Decisions and Reports, p.72.

13. *Dudgeon* v *UK* [1981] 4 European Human Rights Reports, p.149.

14. *A* v *UK* [1981] 20 Decisions and Reports, p.5 (a friendly settlement), and *X* v *UK* [1981] 4 European Human Rights Reports, p.188.

15. *Young, James and Webster* v *UK* [1981] 4 European Human Rights Reports, p.38.

16. *The Sunday Times* case (above, note 8).

17. *Golder* v *UK* (above, note 12).

18. *Klass* v *Federal Republic of Germany* [1979] 2 European Human Rights Reports, p.214.

19. *Ireland* v *UK* (above, note 10).

20. *Campbell and Cosans* v *UK* (above, note 9).

21. *Dudgeon* v *UK* (above, note 13).

22. *Handyside* v *UK* [1976] 1 European Human Rights Reports, p.737, and *Arrowsmith* v *UK* [1980] 3 European Human Rights Reports, p.218.

23. *McVeigh, O'Neill and Evans* v *UK* [1982] 25 Decisions and Reports, p.15.

24. *Agee* v *UK* [1977] 7 Decisions and Reports, p.164.

25. See generally *Ireland* v *UK* (above, note 10), and *Stocktaking* 1982 (above, note 7), pp.186 and 189.

26. Over 97% of petitions fail to pass the admissibility hurdle; see *Statistics 1982* (*op. cit.* note 5).

27. See, e.g., *The East African Asians* cases (1973) 3 European Human Rights Reports, p.76.

28. *Golder* v *UK* (above, note 12).

29. See, for example, J A G Griffith, "The Politics of the Judiciary" (1979) 42 Modern Law Review, p.1.

30. Proposals for amending legislation were announced before the Committee of Ministers dealt with the cases; see 24 Decisions and Reports, pp.17 and 83 (1981).

31. Article 28 of the Convention. The *Alam and Khan* case (above, note 11) is an example of a friendly settlement; not only was the petitioner admitted to the UK but an immigration appeals system was established.

32. Resolution 76 (35) of the Committee of Ministers. The inadequacy of the reform, which required the prior ventilation of complaints within the prison system before the institution of legal proceedings, became apparent in the case of *Reed* v *UK* [1981] 25 Decisions and Reports p.5,

and a "simultaneous ventilation" rule was introduced as part of a friendly settlement.

33. The change in the *Reed* case came 11 years after proceedings in *Golder* v *UK* had been commenced.

34. In the *Young, James and Webster* case (above, note 15) and various applications pending on the compensation issue. Article 1 of the First Protocol to the Convention protects the right to property.

35. See Addendum to the Commission's Rules of Procedure in *Collected Texts* (Council of Europe, 1979).

36. See, for example, *R* v *Secretary of State for the Home Department, ex parte Fernandes*, *The Times*, 20th November 1980.

37. Several Bills using the Convention as the text of a Bill of Rights have, however, been introduced in both the House of Commons and the House of Lords, and a House of Lords Select Committee reported in favour (by 6 to 5) of such a proposal: *Report of the Select Committee on a Bill of Rights* (HL Paper 176, HMSO, 1978).

38. *R* v *McCormick* [1977] Northern Ireland Law Reports, p.105.

39. *Birdi* v *Secretary of State for Home Affairs*, *The Times*, 12th February 1975.

40. *R* v *Secretary of State for Home Affairs, ex parte Bhajan Singh* [1976] Queen's Bench Reports, p.198.

41. Ibid. and *R* v *Chief Immigration Officer, ex parte Bibi* [1976] 1 Weekly Law Reports, p.979.

42. *Statement of Changes in Immigration Rules* (HC Paper 169, HMSO, 1983), p.73.

43. *Hubbard* v *Pitt* [1976] Queen's Bench Reports, p.142, at p.156.

44. *Malone* v *Metropolitan Police Commissioner (No. 2)* [1979] Chancery Reports, p.344.

45. *Klass* v *Federal Republic of Germany* (above, note 18).

46. See respectively *Broome* v *Cassell & Co* [1972] Appeal Cases, p.1027, at p.1133 (Lord Kilbrandon); *R* v *Lemon* [1979] Appeal Cases, p.617, at p.665 (Lord Scarman); *Schering Chemicals Ltd* v *Falkman Ltd* [1982] Queen's Bench Reports, p.1, at p.18 (Lord Denning MR); and *Attorney-General* v *BBC* [1981] Appeal Cases, p.303, at p.354 (Lord Scarman) and *Home Office* v *Harman* [1982] 2 Weekly Law Reports, p.338, at p.357 (Lords Simon of Glaisdale and Scarman, dissenting).

47. See respectively *Ahmad* v *ILEA* [1978] Queen's Bench Reports, p.36, at p.41 (Lord Denning MR) on freedom of religion; *R* v *Secretary of State for the Home Department, ex parte Bhajan Singh* [1976] Queen's Bench Reports, p. 198, at p.208, on the refusal to allow an illegal entrant to marry while he was in detention, and *Science Research Council* v *Nasse* [1980] Appeal Cases, p.1028, at p.1068 (Lord Wilberforce), on the right to a fair hearing.

48. *UKAPE* v *ACAS* [1981] Appeal Cases, p.424, at p.445.

49. *The Interception of Communications in Great Britain* (Cmnd. 8191, HMSO, 1981).

50. *Report of the Committee on Contempt of Court* (Cmnd. 5794, HMSO, 1974).

51. Cmnd. 8092 (HMSO, 1981).

52. Respectively the *Report of the Committee of Privy Councillors appointed to consider Authorised Procedures for the Interrogation of Persons Suspected of Terrorism* (Cmnd. 4901, HMSO, 1972); *Report of the Committee of Inquiry into Police Interrogation Procedures in Northern Ireland* (Cmnd. 7497, HMSO, 1979); and *Proposed New Immigration Rules and the European Convention on Human Rights* (HC Paper 434, HMSO, 1980). Although the likelihood of a violation being committed was apparent from the evidence included in the Home Affairs Committee's report, this was not enough to prevent the proposed rules being adopted. Inevitably, they have since been the subject of a number of petitions to Strasbourg.

53. It is already charged with drawing attention to Statutory Instruments which appear to be *ultra vires*.

54. See *The Greek Case*, (1969) Yearbook of the European Convention on Human Rights, volume 12 (*bis*), and Applications nos. 9940-3/82 (against Turkey).

55. Official Journal 1979, C39/47, and (EC) *Bulletin* 3/78, 6.

56. Commission of the European Communities, "Accession of the European Communities to the European Convention on Human Rights", (EC) *Bulletin* Suppl. 2/79. See also J McBride and L N Brown, "The United Kingdom, the European Community and the European Convention on Human Rights", (1981) 1 Yearbook of European Law, p.167.

57. For example, *Ireland* v *UK* [1978] 2 European Human Rights Reports, p.25.

58. For proposals for reform, see G Van Bueren, *An Effective Remedy? A Review of the Procedure of the European Convention on Human Rights* (NCCL, 1981).

13

CIVIL LIBERTIES IN THE NUCLEAR AGE

DUNCAN CAMPBELL

Nuclear energy did not exist in 1934. In the year NCCL was established, no-one would anticipate the political and social effects yet to result from the then still poorly-understood physical equivalence of mass and energy. Two decades on, it would be apparent to all that physics had impacted indelibly on every temporal and spiritual aspect of life in a fashion not even matched by the industrial revolution.

The special qualities of nuclear technology have provided unusual problems both in the exercise and in the protection of civil liberty. Nuclear weapons and nuclear power share a single physical characteristic – the ability to release large quantities of energy from a tiny body of mass. The release may be sudden and destructive, as in a weapon – or slow, over time, as in a nuclear power station. Nuclear weapons and nuclear power also share, as technologies, a social and economic character which includes the need for the intense concentration of capital and manpower resources.

From this concentration of energy and power flow political and social consequences for civil liberties in the nuclear age. It is not accidental that nuclear weaponry and nuclear power tend to go hand-in-hand with autocracy, centralisation and authoritarianism. Nuclear technology was born of, and grew up to reflect, the internal and international goals of organisations and administrations of this type, and we should not be surprised that in many ways, physics and society provide a paradigm for each other.

In the western democracies, nuclear power and nuclear weapons have for two decades generally attracted the greatest, most widespread popular protests of any cause, testing not just the restraints these states may deploy to hinder and contain freedom of expression – but also the democratic mechanisms which should make government responsive to popular causes. Protest has been inspired by the cataclysmic danger inherent in nuclear weaponry, and by the risks of unusually damaging accidents posed by the operation of nuclear power stations. *De facto*, these protests have become – West Germany is a particularly good example – the testing ground for new technologies of repression ranging from electronic surveillance to anti-riot equipment.

Government decisions about nuclear matters have invariably been taken in circumstances of unusually great secrecy. Military affairs are naturally often secret, and decision-taking unaccountable to the public. But information about nuclear weapons, like secret intelligence, invariably enjoys special levels of security protection. These are matters of life and death – but governments and sometimes private institutions have been untrammelled in their pursuit of nuclear technology, to the detriment, often, of public safety and national security.

In nuclear industries, workers and scientists have faced not just the special hazards of radioactivity and toxic chemistry, but considerable restraints on civil liberty. These include vetting to bar entry to persons considered to have undesirable political views or personal character, continuing surveillance to detect unwelcome associations and friendships, constraints on travel and communication, and on the publication of the results of scientific research – and the prohibition of any public comment at all on nuclear matters.

No public hazard is more severe than nuclear war, and there is a common national and international interest in the avoidance of any use of nuclear weapons. Nuclear secrecy has to a degree spurred the arms race, since there can be no public debate or policy discussion about the appropriate level of armaments, when no information at all is available to fuel the debate. In peacetime, accidents and other mishaps with nuclear weapons have been concealed – in the most notorious and serious case in Britain, for 23 years – to avoid public interference with predetermined policies. In anticipation of war, true details of nuclear weaponry are kept secret, and public funds have been devoted to fierce propaganda campaigns waged to win public acceptance of the theorems of nuclear deterrence.

If there was ever a technology – whether of peace or war – that is seductive to the centralist and authoritarian impulses of civil servants and politicians, it is this. The first country with an atomic bomb and a nascent nuclear industry was the United States. Their scientific possession was seen in the 1940s as the key to industrial and military power. The US Congress – and in large measure the whole *psyche* of the American people – seized on atomic energy in 1946 as the lynchpin of postwar American hegemony and surrounded it with special restraints (such as the McMahon Act, which made it illegal to communicate any atomic information) so as to keep atomic secrets secret. The Act reflected the determination of the United States to protect its recently acquired and powerful magic:

The response to this greatest of all triumphs of scientific method and creative intelligence has been in some respects closely akin to the practice of magic among the most primitive of tribes. Having in their possession a fearful image of the god of war, which makes them stronger than all their enemies, the tribe is obsessed with the fear that the image may be stolen or duplicated and their exclusive claim to the deity's favour lost.[1]

The special sanctity that surrounds nuclear information has also been evident in Britain. Right from the start of the British post-war atomic research programme all pretence of accountability to Parliament was thrown aside. On key post-war decisions, not only have neither Parliament nor public been informed about the purpose of substantial sums of expenditure, but most Cabinet Ministers have been unaware that decisions have been reached – or even put on a committee agenda in the first place.

Clement Attlee did this in 1947 on the occasion that it was first decided that Britain should begin manufacturing atomic weapons. A small *ad hoc* committee of six, known only as GEN 163 ("GEN" for "General" Committee) met, considered whether or not Britain should produce the atomic bomb, and if so whether to do so openly or in secrecy. They opted to produce the bomb, and in secret. They did not meet again. Although by this decision, hundreds of millions of pounds were diverted away from social and industrial recon-struction, housing, or other defence needs, neither the Chancellor of the Exchequer nor the Board of Trade were represented, or even aware of the meeting. So secret was the decision that even the man responsible for producing the bomb, Sir William Penney, was unaware that the go-ahead had been given for another four months.[2]

Thus was Britain's Bomb born, and from it later came the nuclear power programme. The first news that Britain was proceeding with atomic bomb development was surreptitiously brought out in a low key Parliamentary answer fifteen months afterwards in May 1948. This was to be the only public report that Britain was developing atomic weapons; ironically, the announcement was made by the Government in order to secure the agreement of the Services' Press Committee (which approved proposed D-notices) to the issue of a new D-notice banning all other reporting of atomic weapons developments.

In the 1970s, key members of another Labour Government (under James Callaghan) again took a critical decision in secret, apart from their Cabinet colleagues. The issue this time was the *Chevaline* programme, a £1,000 million new warhead system for Polaris submarines. Both the existence of the development programme and the decision to go ahead and manufacture the new warheads were kept secret from government MPs and most Ministers throughout the life of the Callaghan Government and only revealed to the public by their Conservative successors. But Mrs Thatcher repeated her predecessors' habit of confining nuclear decisions to a select and compliant handful. She determined that Britain should buy American Trident submarines as a replacement for Polaris, in conclave as Cabinet Committee MISC 3 ("MISC" for Miscellaneous). Most of the Cabinet was excluded from this committee.

In this way, the inadequacies of government accountability to the electorate are exacerbated. Members of Parliament are already weak in their ability to control the executive. Servants rather than watchdogs, their powers of scrutiny are eroded by the government's brushing aside of detailed questions on nuclear weapons matters – in the same way that sensitive security and intelligence subjects such as telephone tapping have been made forbidden topics of Parliamentary debate at government behest.

Atomic power research and development went hand in hand with atomic weaponry. The UK Atomic Energy Authority (UKAEA), a new and independent body responsible for both weapons manufacture and the nuclear power programme, was set up in 1954. Although Britain's first commercial power reactors (opened at Calder Hall two years later) were celebrated as heralding a new age of nuclear power, their purpose was primarily military – producing plutonium for new nuclear weapons.

At first, everyone working in atomic energy for UKAEA was a Crown servant, and automatically bound by the Official Secrets

Act. Over 30 years, the Authority has been divested of most of its assets, some of which have gone to autonomous organisations such as British Nuclear Fuels Ltd (BNFL). But employees of these organisations still remain bound by government security regulations and the constraints of the Official Secrets Acts.

The penalties for foreign espionage in the Official Secrets Acts automatically apply to anyone, government servant or not, who seeks to help an enemy. But by bringing all non-government nuclear industry employees within the scope of the Acts, employees can be punished by up to two years' imprisonment for unauthorised disclosures which do not threaten national security. Indeed they could be prosecuted for making revelations which might enhance public safety (although a government prosecution would be difficult in such circumstances).

Employees of BNFL, for example, are forbidden to travel to Soviet bloc countries, China, and countries such as Yugoslavia or Yemen, without special permission. Many BNFL staff are also positively vetted, a procedure generally only applying to those in the civil service with regular access to Top Secret material. Positive vetting consists of a lengthy background check on an individual, and one or more security interviews. In the late 1970s and 1980s, candidates and their referees began again to be asked whether they were or had ever been members of, or associated with members of, CND. This question reappeared in the security investigators' checklists alongside homosexuality (for men) and Welsh and Scots nationalism (for Celts).

Workers in the nuclear power industry in Britain have not yet been forbidden by law to withdraw their labour – as is the case elsewhere – although threats that strikes would be prosecuted under other laws have been made against workers at BNFL's Windscale plant. However, nuclear and electrical workers have frequently been mentioned as being high on the list of key industrial workers for whom the Conservative Government has considered legislation to prohibit strikes.

In 1976, the Atomic Energy Authority Constabulary, the special police force which guards UKAEA and BNFL nuclear installations, were give the right to carry arms and to engage in hot pursuit of anyone believed to have taken "nuclear material" – and to arrest them and bring them back to be detained at a nuclear installation. Given the extreme dangers to public safety of certain types of nuclear material, it is unreasonable to object (having first protested the prior existence of the material) to the principle of special powers and force being lawful in the recovery of such material. What is objectionable is that these powers are exercised not by an orthodox police force – whose accountability to Parliament and public, if inadequate, is at least clearly understood – but by a *private* police force with no public answerability. Accountability for the actions of the UKAEA Constabulary is remote; they report to the UKAEA which in turn comes under the Secretary of State for Energy.

UKAEA police officials gave evidence in a 1979 criminal trial when anarchists were accused of plotting to bomb nuclear power stations. In the trial, Ronan Bennett, Iris Mills and others were accused of conspiracy to cause explosions (the "Anarchists Anonymous" case). Bennett was accused of having planned to blow up nuclear power stations. The evidence presented in support of this claim was two maps of the United Kingdom, with approximately located dots marking nuclear power stations. This was far less information than is available in many books and magazines, and dozens of government or CEGB publications. The essence of the prosecution case was that anarchist political views, alleged possession of potentially explosive substances, plus a trivial quantity of information on nuclear power, proved such a conspiracy. But the defendants were acquitted.

In the United States, private nuclear power companies have been eager to blur the line between peaceful opposition to nuclear power and potentially violent or terrorist activities. Beside wide FBI surveillance, anti-nuclear groups have been the target for intelligence-gathering activities by a federation of local and state police forces who run the Law Enforcement Intelligence Unit – an intelligence centre which has co-ordinated police information on anti-nuclear activists with intelligence from private investigators working for nuclear power corporations.

The Georgia Power Company, for example, set up a full-scale spying operation in 1973, aimed *inter alia* at their environmentalist opponents, the Georgia Power Project. Some £750,000 a year was being spent in the mid-1970s on a team of nine armed and equipped investigators who spied on and attempted to infiltrate the environmentalist group. The company acknowledged the existence of its "security department", claiming that they investigated "subversives", who were defined as: "Anyone who spoke out against

Georgia Power".[3]

Three anti-nuclear activists in the United States have died, and at least two others have escaped murder attempts – all in circumstances where the motive for the crime pointed to unscrupulous nuclear industry security forces. The best known case is that of Karen Silkwood, a laboratory analyst and union activist who was employed in the plutonium processing plant of the Kerr-McGee Corporation in Oklahoma City. She died in a road accident on 13th November 1974.

At the Oklahoma City plant, 73 workers had been accidentally contaminated with plutonium between 1969 and 1974. The plant was manufacturing plutonium fuel rods for the US experimental fast breeder reactor programme. Karen Silkwood's car appeared to have been forced off the road by an unknown hit-and-run assailant. Papers she carried with her at the time of the accident described her investigation of the lax and unsafe handling of plutonium at the Kerr-McGee plant. At least some of these papers, although missing after the crash, later found their way into the hands of company officials.[4]

In 1975, the US government Nuclear Regulatory Commission explained the dangers to the constitutional rights of Americans posed by an intensified nuclear programme, involving fast breeder reactors[5] and increasing amounts of plutonium in circulation. An NRC consultant, John H Barton, warned that:

The possibility of surveillance is probably the most severe civil liberties effect of a plutonium recycle decision. The surveillance would act at all times; it would not be restricted to emergency situations. It could have significant chilling effects on First Amendment discussion, particularly in the nuclear area.[6]

But a year later, the NRC set up its own "Intelligence Assessment Team", which traded information on protestors' activities between nuclear power companies and intelligence agencies such as the FBI and CIA.

Identical considerations were raised at the same time in Britain by a report on nuclear power from the Royal Commission on Environmental Pollution.[7] Sir Brian (now Lord) Flowers' panel outlined new difficulties and dangers for civil liberties which would result from increasing reliance on nuclear power – and fast breeder reactors in particular. The "plutonium economy" thereby created raised the possibility of "secret surveillance of members of the public and possibly of employees who may make 'undesirable' contacts. The activities might include the use of informers, infiltrators, wiretapping, checking on bank accounts and the opening of mail." These "would be practised on suspected members of extremist or terrorist groups or agents . . . we regard such activities as highly likely and indeed inevitable". Flowers added, correctly, that he supposed that "no doubt" these methods were already in use against "certain small groups that are regarded as dangerous". So their use in relation to the plutonium threat would be "nothing new in principle". "What is most to be feared is an insidious growth in surveillance in response to a growing threat as the amount of plutonium in existence, and familiarity with its properties grows." These "unquantifiable" effects on the shape of future society should, said the Royal Commission, be a "major consideration" in the future of the reactor programme. But there is little evidence that the government or its nuclear and security agencies have paid heed to these remarks.

The most severe danger of civil nuclear power is if a nuclear weapon were to be fabricated from diverted or stolen fissile material. A terrorist threat to disperse nuclear waste by conventional means would be only slightly less terrifying. And such threats are real; between 1975 and 1983 the US Department of Energy's Nuclear Emergency Search Team decided that 20 threats were sufficiently credible to require emergency action. One threat was found to be real; a former nuclear employee had obtained spent reactor fuel rods, which he had threatened to disperse.

The threat of nuclear terrorism is so great that western governments have spoken openly about a possible need to resort to torture to get information. In the UK the Royal Commission anticipated there might have to be: "Restrictions on the rights of movement and assembly, and the suspension of *habeas corpus*, if the threat of plutonium being exploded was serious . . . ." If a threat were thought to be credible, the amount of civilian disturbance involved in a major – perhaps nationwide – search would be considerable. Evacuation could also be required in the event of an accident to a civil power reactor.

"Nuclear terrorism" is almost a redundant phrase; after all, nuclear missiles and bombs are the greatest terror weapons of all, and on that is built their deterrent effect. But the nuclear industry has increasingly sought to criminalise its opponents. A 1978 report by the US RAND Corporation examined the alleged "Attributes of potential criminal adversaries of US nuclear programs" – stressing that physical security measures ultimately had their limitations, and that a more extensive nuclear programme would require considerably more "pre-emptive" intelligence about adversaries, and greater secrecy about plans and procedures.

Right-wing lobbyists in Britain have been ready to brand anti-nuclear protest as serving the interests of the Soviet Union, and see centralised nuclear power as a useful new counter to the traditional bargaining power of trade unions. The main targets are workers in the transport and electrical industry, and above all the industrial muscle of the mineworkers. In 1979, the *Daily Telegraph* expressed a view that:

Our oil supplies are increasingly threatened by subversion and Soviet advances southward and our coal is dependent on the whims of an increasingly Communist-dominated miners' union. Clearly, Britain urgently needs to expand its nuclear-power potential to secure independence from both foreign and domestic blackmail.[8]

In a separate report, the *Telegraph*'s extreme right-wing leader-writer and columnist, Robert Moss, has implied that anti-nuclear protest is inherently criminal, and has claimed that "Moscow . . . in the last resort . . . stands to gain".[9]

The fact that these energy arguments are nonsensical (written, for example, just as Britain began to achieve self-sufficiency in oil) in no way undermines the evident ideological attraction of nuclear power to the authoritarian political right. A further indication of the politically valuable role that Ministers ascribed to nuclear power in curbing the strength of trade unions emerged in 1979 when minutes of Mrs Thatcher's Cabinet Committee on Economic Strategy were leaked. The main item on that committee's agenda on 23rd October 1979 was nuclear power policy. Energy Secretary David Howell told the meeting that: "A nuclear programme would have the advantage of removing a substantial portion of electricity production from the dangers of disruption by industrial action by coal miners or transport workers."

The nuclear industry has become increasingly intolerant of

criticism. "Whistleblowers" inside the industry have been dismissed or otherwise eased out of employment as a direct result of criticisms made of safety standards. The industry's new intolerance of internal dissent partly reflects a taut struggle over reactor design; the government and the current nuclear leadership wish Britain to start building American-designed Pressurised Water Reactors, which are less safe than indigenous designs. (The 1983/1984 Sizewell Inquiry concerns a PWR reactor.) Many scientists and engineers are uneasy at this choice.

Two of four recent victims of the industry's intolerance are scientists who have been critical of radiological safety standards within nuclear establishments. Trevor Brown, a senior industrial chemist at the Aldermaston Atomic Weapons Research Establishment, repeatedly complained of dangers to workers from poorly designed equipment, and warned of the likelihood of radioactive contamination. The warnings he gave over many years were borne out in August 1978, when several Aldermaston workers were found to have been contaminated; work stopped, and many of the processing facilities at Aldermaston were closed pending a special investigation by Sir Edward Pochin. In the end, many key facilities were so contaminated that they will remain closed for the duration, and new facilities have been built.

But Brown was rewarded not with recognition but retribution. His meticulous concern for safety led to constructive dismissal by his superiors – through denial of promotion, criticism of his work, and petty accusations about working practices. Matters reached a head after Brown – who was also a Berkshire Liberal County Councillor – voiced some of his safety criticisms on the BBC programme *Newsnight*. In 1981, he accepted early retirement.

A health physics and safety specialist at Windscale, John Taylor, resigned in 1982 after accusing BNFL managers of "covering up" reports and recommendations he had made which would permit the company to reduce radiation exposure to both workers and the public. He had made proposals for limiting the amount of heavily radioactive effluent discharged into the Irish Sea, and suggested means of improving decontamination techniques inside the plant.

After Taylor had threatened to publicise his allegations in August 1982, he was transferred to a new section; soon after, he resigned. But he lost a case at an Industrial Tribunal that BNFL's action had been an unfair constructive dismissal.

A third nuclear scientist, UKAEA physicist and safety engineer Rodney Fordham, was also forced into resignation after attempting publicly to criticise safety standards in the nuclear industry. Fordham had proposed to give his views to a conference on the PWR, but withdrew after the Authority insisted on vetting his paper before publication. Soon after this, he was accused of producing "ineffectual" work, a charge he strongly refuted; complaining of harassment and mistreatment, he took early retirement in September 1982.

Although it is customary for vetting of publications to be part of normal professional terms of employment, independent evidence has emerged that the Atomic Energy Authority has suppressed its own (internal) official reports – let alone the private views of employees – when they cast doubt on official claims about the safety of the PWR's critical "pressure vessel". A UKAEA report assessing the dangers of a catastrophic crack in the PWR pressure vessel was only offered in evidence to the Sizewell enquiry after industry outsiders had leaked news of its existence to the press.[10]

A fourth nuclear scientist who has suffered for his convictions is research physicist Dr Ross Hesketh, who incurred official displeasure by examining the link between nuclear weapons and civil nuclear power with unwelcome precision. In October 1981, Dr Hesketh wrote to *The Times* from the CEGB laboratories at Berkeley, Gloucestershire, criticising proposals to sell British civil plutonium to the United States. As a supporter of nuclear power, Hesketh was concerned that the sale of plutonium would assist the United States in the production of new nuclear warheads, and in so doing encourage nuclear weapons proliferation elsewhere – as well as playing into the hands of the industry's critics who urged that civil and military nuclear power were inextricably linked.

Subsequently ostracised by his employers, Hesketh soon became one of the most effective such critics himself. After a series of public comments over the next eighteen months, Hesketh was disciplined by the CEGB on a number of pretexts, all peripheral to his public concern about the military use of plutonium. Ordered to a new and demeaning CEGB post in June 1983, he too resigned. After an Industrial Tribunal hearing, he was reinstated to his former job, but put on leave until he became eligible for a pension. A condition of the settlement was that Dr. Hesketh did not speak in public about his case.

Each of these scientists had found that his personal integrity as scientist and citizen was regarded by his employers as subordinate not only to the general interest of the nuclear industry, but in some cases, merely to the prevailing fashion in reactor design.

Dr Hesketh's reports had drawn attention to the barter of nuclear materials which had been conducted between Britain and the United States from the early 1960s on. Under a 1958 UK–US Agreement on the "Use of Atomic Energy for Mutual Defence Purposes", Britain swapped civil plutonium for US enriched uranium. The agreement, as amended to allow for the swap, specified that the transfers should be only *"for military purposes"* (although it was later claimed in Parliament that in fact the United States would not use the material "for weapons purposes"). Hesketh repeatedly and publicly questioned the purposes to which British nuclear material already sent had been put. There was no satisfactory answer. Instead, he was urged out of his job.

Nuclear weapons are distinguished from orthodox military weaponry by the same qualities of concentrated power and extreme effect that distinguish nuclear power stations from their conventional companions. Similarly to civil nuclear power, there are distinct adverse effects on civil liberties in Britain resulting from the possession of nuclear weapons.

The Bomb ultimately threatens not just individual liberty, but all liberty and all existence. No government is keen for its citizens to contemplate the likely effects of nuclear war, so a vocabulary has been formed for discussion and debate in which all offence is defence, terrorism and genocide are deterrence, and the destruction of a civil population is "collateral damage". The lack of true information on nuclear war risks, coupled with desensitising jargon and misdirection from well-funded propaganda campaigns, amount to a substantial attack on free public discussion. Nowhere is this attack more evident than in the civilian preparation for nuclear war – so-called "civil defence".

As I have argued elsewhere,[11] what is called civil defence in the United Kingdom is not merely a travesty of that title; it is its antithesis. In a nuclear-armed state, civil defence has to be a deception – for two reasons.

A state which relies on a posture of nuclear deterrence cannot by reason of that posture engage in real civil defence. The threats and counterthreats that make up nuclear deterrence are only sane if they are believed to work indefinitely. If they fail, both protagonists will be destroyed and either or both would have done better – or at least no worse – to have had no nuclear weapons at all. So for nuclear weapons and nuclear deterrence to be acceptable to the public, it must be believed to work indefinitely. But the more resources that are spent on damage-limiting, on civil defence measures, the more it is apparent to the public that political and military leaders do not have sufficient confidence in nuclear deterrence.

Thus, civil defence has to be a conjuring trick. It must appear to answer, at minimum cost, the fears of citizens who are not as *au fait* with strategic theory as the Generals and Air Marshalls – but it must not have real substance, lest it appear both to potential adversaries and aware citizenry that the nation is too well prepared for a nuclear war.

Secondly, for a nuclear deterrent to be credible, it is necessary for the state to be able to demonstrate to its adversaries that it stands ready, willing and able to use nuclear weaponry, to meet offence with offence, whatever public opinion may have become in the late stages of a crisis. It is at such a critical moment that public opinion, perceiving an imminent holocaust, is most likely to rise against the policy of nuclear deterrence.

The British government is well aware of these difficulties, and anticipates that until the shooting war in Europe begins in earnest, the main enemy is dissent in the home population. The first, key task in British Home Defence plans (which include civil defence) defined in the Home Office's 1975 circular to local authorities on *Home Defence Planning Assumptions* is "to secure the United Kingdom against any internal threat". In such documents as the Home Office's *Training Manual for Scientific Advisers*, the meaning of this phrase is made chillingly clear: "Sabotage, subversion and . . . *adverse public reaction to government policies* [author's emphasis]." The same manual goes on to speak of the threats to the security of the United Kingdom arising from "dissident groups . . . [whose] aim would be to weaken the national will and ability to fight". It identifies the threat as arising from trade unionists and pacifists in particular, and explains the need for fierce measures against them: "Certain dissident extremist groups are . . . known to be in sympathy with our potential enemies and . . . can be expected to react against the national good. The groups are small [but] their significance should not be underestimated." They would engage in: "Fomenting strikes in key industries, promoting anti-war demonstrations to turn the populace against the government and disruptive activities connected with war preparations."

These extracts from official planning documents can leave little doubt that in the early stages of an east–west crisis that might lead to nuclear war, protest would be regarded by the British government as akin to treachery. The right to strike, the right to free speech, or the right to say "no" to war might only be exercised at the gravest risk to life and liberty.

Nevertheless, many who owe no sympathy or allegiance what-soever to the Soviet Union *would* risk life and liberty to stop mobilisation for war. They would reflect that the contingent circumstances and arguments that were deployed in order to jail pacifists in 1939 do not now arise. There would not be the justification of fighting genocide, as such a war would itself be genocide. Even after a nuclear war began, there would be many who on moral grounds would wish to prevent the use of nuclear weapons in retaliation, even if Britain itself had been struck. Nothing of military value could be gained by enlarging the slaughter.

The government knows this, and is – like NATO partners – prepared to counter civil dissent with military force. NATO's regular top-level war games in the "Wintex"/"Cimex" (Winter Exercise/Civil–military exercise) series, held every two years, usually include rehearsals for the suppression of civil unrest, strikes and other disruption to military plans for the transition to war.

Little could be more ironical than these plans; in a defensive alliance whose avowed purpose is the defence of freedom, the first casualty on NATO's side would be the right of its citizens to speak out against war. In the late stages of a pre-war crisis, Britain would be under martial law in all but name. Internment plans have been made to take at least 20,000 political adversaries of the government off the streets. Freedom of movement would be denied, as most major roads would be sealed off as "Essential Service Routes". The telephone system would be shut down for non-essential users, and food and fuel supplies put under government control. Under emergency powers, Parliament would be suspended, and Regional and Sub-Regional Commissioners appointed as shadow direct rulers of 11 individual regions (including Wales, Northern Ireland, and Scotland) after attack. The press would be subject to government direction and censorship.

After a nuclear strike, it goes without saying that there will be neither civilisation nor civil liberty. Democracy and the rule of law will be over for the duration, supplanted for those who do survive by the law of the jungle. There will be death camps for diseased and useless refugees, and ruthless rationing of almost non-existent medical care. Decisions about food supplies and other difficult matters would, say the Home Office circulars, be "harsh and inequitable". Justice would be an expedient and summary matter, with brutal and often capital penalties dispensed without right of appeal or established rules of procedure. Home Office advice to local authority chief executives who would become district "Controllers" in the event of war includes the suggested reintroduction of medieval stocks into the British penal code.[12]

After this, what? According to senior Home Office officials, the government's Regional Commissioners would take over and look forward to "national regeneration", aiming at creating "a stable democratic society inevitably reduced substantially in economic and social terms". "Vital aspects" of this process would include: "The formation of a national government and the restoration of democratic procedures and freedoms." But in a wrecked world where the existence of human life itself might lie in the balance for decades, no time limit is proposed for the slow crawl back to pre-holocaust democracy. The very idea, of course, is fatuous. The point is that there must be no war. Our energies and liberties should be devoted to that cause above all others.

NOTES

1. James R Newman and Byron S Miller, quoted in Margaret Gowing, *Independence and Deterrence*, Vol. 1, *Policy Making* (Macmillan, 1974).
2. *Ibid.*, pp. 181-184.
3. Quoted in Tim Butz, "Nuclear Power vs Civil Liberties", in *Public Eye*, Vol. 1, No. 2 (Repression Information Project, Campaign to Stop Government Spying, Washington DC, 1976).
4. See for example *Rolling Stone*, 27th March 1975 and 13th January 1977.
5. The key feature of a fast breeder reactor is that it manufactures new plutonium fuel during normal operation; the plutonium produced is suitable for use in nuclear weapons, and must therefore be well guarded.
6. Butz, *op. cit.*

7. *Nuclear Power and the Environment: Sixth Report of the Royal Commission on Environmental Pollution* (Chairman Sir Brian Flowers) (Cmnd. 6618, HMSO, 1976).
8. *Daily Telegraph*, 26th November 1979.
9. Institute for the Study of Conflict, *Nuclear Power, Protest and Violence*, by Robert Moss (Report No. 102, December 1978).
10. See reports by Rob Edwards in the *New Statesman*, 4th March 1983, 25th March 1983, and 22nd July 1983.
11. *War Plan UK* (Burnett Books, 1982; Paladin (Granada), 1983).
12. "Exposure to public disapproval" is how it is styled in Home Office Home Defence Circular 3/76, *Briefing Material for Wartime Controllers* [Restricted].

PART IV

Some Critical Issues Today
(2) Protection from Discrimination

14

RACISM IN IMMIGRATION LAW AND PRACTICE*

IAN MARTIN

The Commission finds it established that the 1968 Act had racial motives and that it covered a racial group. . . . It further considers that the discriminatory provisions of the above Act should be seen in the context of two other laws, and of further regulations, in the field of citizenship and immigration which also gave preference to white people. . . . The Commission considers that the racial discrimination, to which the applicants have been publicly subjected by the application of the above immigration legislation, constitutes an interference with their human dignity which, in the special circumstances described above, amounted to "degrading treatment" in the sense of Article 3 of the Convention.

(European Commission of Human Rights, report on the East African Asians Case, quoted in *Proposed New Immigration Rules and the European Convention on Human Rights*, First Report from the House of Commons Home Affairs Committee (HC Paper 434, HMSO, 1980), pp. 52-55.)

Immigration law in this country has developed mainly as a series of responses to, and attempts to regulate, particular pressures, rather than as a positive means of achieving preconceived social or economic aims.

(Home Office evidence printed in *Immigration*, First Report from the Select Committee on Race Relations and Immigration (HC Paper 303, HMSO, 1978) Vol. II, p. 1.)

---

* An earlier version of this chapter appeared as the Conclusion in Lawrence Grant and Ian Martin, *Immigration Law and Practice* (Cobden Trust, 1982).

British immigration law and practice is racially discriminatory in its motivation and in its effect; it is in violation of the UK's international human rights obligations and of standards of natural justice and civil liberties generally claimed to be respected in Britain.

Racialism operates in the present system of immigration control in two ways. The first is the drawing of the definition of those subject to immigration control and those eligible for admission under the immigration rules in such a way as to favour white entrants while restricting as far as possible those who are not white. The second is the provision of arbitrary and oppressive powers and wide ranging administrative discretion, which apply in theory to all those subject to control but which in practice are levelled in their full severity at black entrants.

The most careful yet damning analysis of the way in which immigration legislation has been racially motivated in the definition of those subject to control is contained in the report of the European Commission of Human Rights on the East African Asian cases.[1] The Commission found it established that the Commonwealth Immigrants Act 1968 – rushed through Parliament in the panic to exclude British Asians from Kenya, by confining the right of abode in Britain to those with at least a grandparent who had acquired citizenship in the UK itself – had racial motives and that it covered a racial group. The Report referred to statements made in both Houses of Parliament during the debate on the Bill in February 1968: the Government, while claiming that the Act was based on geography, nevertheless admitted it had racial motives. The Commission noted that even before the 1968 Act, the British Nationality Act 1964 had introduced, as a condition for an entitlement to resume citizenship of the UK and Colonies, a "qualifying connection" of ancestry which would normally be fulfilled by white settlers but not by members of the Asian communities in East Africa.[2]

By the time the Commission made its report, Parliament had replaced the Commonwealth Immigrants Act 1968 and its predecessor with the Immigration Act 1971. While the 1971 Act is generally referred to as a highly restrictive piece of legislation (as indeed it is in the powers of deportation and removal and the criminal sanctions it provides), its effect on the definition of those subject to immigration control was to restore free entry to millions of Commonwealth citizens, overwhelmingly white. It did this by defining as "patrials" with a right of abode all Commonwealth citizens with a UK-born parent. At the same time it maintained the exclusion of "non-patrial" East African Asian citizens of the UK and Colonies. The original Bill would have extended the right of abode to any Commonwealth citizen with a UK-born grandparent; this was defeated in Committee by an alliance of Enoch Powell and the Labour opposition, but draft immigration rules which would have left these white Commonwealth citizens subject to the new work permit requirement were rejected by a revolt of Conservative MPs. The immigration rules have therefore since 1973 provided for the admission for settlement of any Commonwealth citizen with a UK-born grandparent, and this provision survived unscathed (and almost without comment) the latest Conservative Government's supposed assault on the remaining loopholes for primary immigration in their 1980 rules. The Commission took account of both the 1971 Act and the 1973 rules in reaching its conclusion on the racially discriminatory nature of UK immigration control.

Although the 1981 British Nationality Act has now abolished the term "patrial", it has done so by founding its division of citizenship of the UK and Colonies into three new citizenships firmly upon patriality. Only patrial citizens of the UK and Colonies have become British citizens, non-patrials being renamed British Dependent Territories citizens or British Overseas citizens, with the effective statelessness of the latter being thus still more clearly advertised. Commonwealth citizen patrials, while not becoming British citizens, retain their right of abode for their lifetimes; only when the generations that existed on 1st January 1983 die out will the right of abode attach to British citizenship alone.

The immigration rules are prefaced with the injunction that immigration officers will carry out their duties without regard to the race, colour or religion of people seeking to enter the UK.[3] The Conservatives' 1980 rules, however, incorporated the most overtly racially discriminatory provision yet to feature in UK immigration control. The right of British women and other women settled in the UK to have their husbands or fiancés admitted to live with them here, qualified as it already was by supposed safeguards against marriages arranged for immigration purposes, was denied to women who were not citizens of the UK and Colonies born or with one parent born in the UK. The Government thus divided patrial women into two categories in order to deny even women who were patrial

UK and Colonies citizens, by registration or naturalisation (or by citizenship acquired overseas but followed by five years' residence and settlement here), the right to live with a non-patrial husband in this country. It refused to offer any serious answer to the powerful case that the rules were thus in breach of Article 3 (degrading treatment), and Article 14 (discrimination) linked with Articles 8 (respect for family life) and 12 (right to marry and found a family) of the European Convention on Human Rights.[4] Complaints made by the Joint Council for the Welfare of Immigrants and the NCCL to the European Commission of Human Rights on behalf of couples affected were held admissible in May 1982. The Government, after a rare House of Commons defeat brought about by the uglier elements in the Conservative ranks, revised the rules to give all women who are British citizens under the 1981 Act some possibility of the admission of their husbands, while further undermining the qualified entitlement by placing the burden of proof that the marriage was not "entered into primarily to obtain admission" on the applicant. This change falls well short of remedying the discrimination produced by the rules, and appears not to have impressed the European Commission which in its May 1983 report concluded that the UK was in breach of the Convention and in October 1983 sent its report to the European Court for a ruling. It seems that the Government's tactics of delay are unlikely to be able to stave off much longer the predictable and predicted international condemnation.

In addition to the discriminatory "exception on grounds of UK ancestry", the rules for husbands and fiancés, and the (now somewhat less generous) provision for working holidays for young Commonwealth citizens under which thousands of almost exclusively white Commonwealth citizens have in the past found Britain hospitable to their entry and employment, there is widespread racial discrimination barely hinted at in the rules. Other rules are so tightly drawn as to impede the family life of those already settled here or the reasonable expectations of would-be entrants, and leave wide areas for the operation of highly subjective discretion.

There are now two definitions of the family contained in the immigration rules. For EEC workers, protected by EEC regulations, the family includes the spouse, children under 21, other children and grandchildren if dependent, and dependent parents and grandparents. Although the rules omit to reflect it, EEC regulations also require member States to facilitate the admission of any other family member if dependent on the member or living under his roof in the country from which he comes. For others, the admission of a husband is subject to the discriminatory restrictions already discussed, and only children under 18 are readily admitted: the 1980 rules rendered the criteria for the admission of children over 18 and of parents so stringent that very few now qualify.

The wide areas left to the subjective discretion of very junior officials (a Chief Immigration Officer, who must authorise a refusal, is only a Higher Executive Officer) are best seen in the deceptively simple provisions for students and visitors. A student must satisfy the immigration officer that he intends to leave the country on completion of his course of study; a visitor must satisfy the immigration officer that he is genuinely seeking entry for the period of the visit as stated by him. The Act requires that a person refused entry must be given written notice including a statement of the reasons for the decision: the most common statement among the set formulae provided to immigration officers for this purpose must surely be the statement without amplification that "I am not satisfied that you intend to stay only for this limited period". Immigration officers are trained to draft their explanatory statements for appeals in the form "I was not satisfied", and to avoid assertions which would bring upon them an onus of proof that they lack the evidence to discharge.

It is these areas of subjective discretion into which racial discrimination can so easily enter. Although the instructions to immigration officers are secret,[5] it is not to be supposed that they prescribe overt racial discrimination. They do, however, make reference to a would-be entrant being subject to suspicion "because he belongs to a class of immigrant which has strong economic or other incentives to obtain entry to this country and because of the frequency with which other immigrants of that class have evaded or have attempted to evade immigration controls". Immigration officers are instructed that "references to the tendency of immigrants of particular national origins to evade immigration control should be avoided" and that "gratuitous opinions, generalisations, and expressions which might be construed as biased or prejudiced . . . can have a very damaging effect on our case at an appeal and must on no account be included in a report". These injunctions seem aimed more at inhibiting the acknowledgment of prejudice in circumstances where it might result in a successful appeal than at preventing it from influencing decisions: a proper view of the public interest would surely prefer prejudice, it if operates, to be admitted and open to rectification.

Table 1   *Passengers refused by nationality 1980*

		Refused	Admitted
Old Commonwealth	1 in 4,100	174	714,000
USA	1 in 2,780	649	1,800,000
New Commonwealth and Pakistan	1 in 140	6.252	869,000
India	1 in 150	1,239	190,000
Bangladesh	1 in 125	192	24,000
Pakistan	1 in 80	1,040	83,000

(*Source:* derived from tables 1 (a) and (b), Control of Immigration Statistics 1980, Cmnd. 8199)

There is consequently an enormous variation in the proportion of refusals to passengers admitted, as shown in Table 1. The refusal rate for India is nearly 30 times greater than that for Old Commonwealth countries. This variation would be still greater if refusal of entry clearance overseas to would-be visitors were added in. Almost no visitors from the Old Commonwealth or the USA seek entry clearance. No comprehensive figures for the Indian sub-continent are available, but the figures shown in Table 2 have been given for 1977.

Table 2   *Refusal of entry clearance as visitors and port refusals 1977*

	EC Applications	% refused F.C	Number refused EC	Port refusals
India	14,300	6.4	915	676
Bangladesh	1,600	2.1	34	268
Pakistan	3,500	16.0	560	817

(*Source:* written answer, House of Commons 22nd March 1977: Control of Immigration Statistics 1977, Cmnd. 7160)

The rules provide that a period of entry of 6 months "will normally be appropriate" for a visitor, and "the period should not be restricted to less than six months unless this is justified for special reasons – for example . . . if the case ought to be subject to early review by the Home Office". Immigration officers are instructed to use the power to admit for a shorter period where there are doubts about a visitor's real intentions but there is insufficient evidence to justify refusal. It is therefore of some interest to see the analysis by nationality of the periods for which visitors are in fact admitted.

Table 3   Visitors admitted for periods other than 6 months,
1st October 1980–31st March 1981

		Other than 6 months	6 months
USA	1 in 165	3,390	560,310
Old Commonwealth	1 in 100	2,040	197,020
New Commonwealth and Pakistan	1 in 8	38,700	304,860
India	1 in 10	6,850	67,330
Bangladesh	1 in 9	750	6,800
Pakistan	1 in 6	4,660	26,970

(*Source:* derived from Home Office figures provided with letter from Mr Raison to Lord Avebury, undated, October 1981)

Table 3 shows the proportion of visitors not admitted for six months – overwhelmingly those regarded as doubtful visitors and admitted for shorter periods. Put another way, more Indian visitors were treated as doubtful visitors than visitors from the USA and the three white Commonwealth countries combined, although there were 10 times as many visitors in total from the latter. Those who were admitted for less than six months will also include those who have experienced extensive interrogation at the port of entry and may have been delayed or detained overnight or longer.

Passengers from the Indian sub-continent also represent a disproportionate number of those detained at Harmondsworth Detention Centre, as shown for 1979 in Table 4. Thus while a passenger from India is nearly 30 times more likely to be refused entry at the port than an Old Commonwealth passenger, he/she is nearly 160 times more likely to be detained at Harmondsworth Detention Centre.

The only evidence that would give any indication of how far differential refusal rates are justified would be statistics on the proportion of nationals of particular countries admitted who overstay. Even then it would be necessary to allow for different treatment in immigration control and to distinguish between minor

Table 4   *Passengers admitted, refused and detained–1979*

	% all passengers admitted	% all passengers refused	% all passengers detained*	No. detained*
USA	16.4	3.2	1.4	90
Old Commonwealth	7.1	0.9	0.5	33
India	1.6	6.0	16.8	1,074
Bangladesh	0.2	1.2	3.9	247
Pakistan	0.8	5.6	15.7	1,004

*(*Harmondsworth Detention Centre only*)

(*Source:* derived from written answers, House of Commons, 25th July 1979–31st January 1980; Control of Immigration Statistics – 1979, Cmnd. 7875)

infringements and serious attempted evasion of control: an Australian admitted for six months is not going to overstay in order to complete a four month visit, whereas an Indian admitted for three months in equivalent circumstances may do so even if he or she has no more intention of attempting to settle here. No such evidence is available, and the Home Office has never published any figures compiled in the course of its survey of overstaying (1977–79), the findings of which were never made public because it "ran into serious difficulties". It is understood however that it did not support generalisations about the tendency of people of particular nationalities to evade control, and if evidence of attempted evasion were available it would not justify the degree of discrimination against would-be visitors from the Indian sub-continent which is clearly revealed by the statistics cited.

The greatest single source of distress to the immigrant community has been the entry clearance queue allowed to develop in the Indian sub-continent, in clear contravention of assurances, when entry clearance was made mandatory for dependants in 1969, that it would not delay their admission. The length of the waiting period is the product of three factors: the rate of application, the time devoted to interview and consideration of each application, and the number of entry clearance officers in post. The growth of the queue in the early 1970s was not due to any increase in applications but to the increasing time devoted to each application as a result of the priority accorded to preventing the admission of non-entitled applicants. While staff were increased, especially in 1975–6, it is impossible to believe that the separation of white families for such periods of times as still exist for wives, children and husbands in Bangladesh and Pakistan and for husbands in India, or the extension to white applicants of the treatment inflicted on the latter, would be tolerated.[6]

For years an equivalent distress was inflicted on the families of citizens of the UK and Colonies in East Africa, as a limited quota of special vouchers required heads of household to undergo periods of unemployment in East Africa before they received their vouchers. In 1975, the annual quota was increased to 5,000 and the queues in Africa were therefore soon eliminated. The announced quota subsequently became an official deception, since the only remaining queue is of those who went temporarily to India from East Africa when vouchers were not promptly available there. Successive governments refused to increase the allocation to India within the quota,[7] even though vouchers allocated to Africa are not being taken up: thus applicants in India have now waited over six years, while only 1,290 special voucher holders were admitted in 1982 against a theoretical quota of 5,000.[8] (3,390 mainly white Commonwealth citizens with a UK-born grandparent were admitted or accepted for settlement in 1982, in addition to an unrecorded number of white patrial UK and Colonies and Commonwealth citizens).[9]

Some of the worst treatment of black people and the most blatant disregard for their civil liberties results from the powers of detention, deportation and removal, and the criminal provisions of the Immigration Act 1971. An immigration officer at a port of entry can search a passenger and his baggage and detain documents, can require him to be examined by a medical inspector (with no restriction on the nature and purpose of the medical examination, so that the internal vaginal examinations formerly carried out on women seeking entry as fiancées supposedly to determine virginity were not precluded by law); and can detain him for further examination for up to 7 days before he can even apply for bail. An illegal entrant can be detained for any length of time without an opportunity to apply for bail, and irrespective of length of residence can be removed without prior right of appeal. Anyone in either of these categories detained on the authority of an immigration officer can be moved around in the custody of a private security company, and his custodian "may take all such steps as may be reasonably necessary for photographing, measuring and otherwise identifying him"[10] These powers substantially exceed those of the police. A police officer, however, as well as an immigration officer, may arrest without warrant anyone he has reasonable cause to suspect is an illegal entrant or overstayer, and this power is easily abused to allow small and sometimes large fishing expeditions in which the suspects are almost invariably black.

The Home Secretary has unlimited power to deport or exclude most people who are not British citizens when he deems this "conducive to the public good", with no right of appeal where he personally orders an exclusion or a deportation as being "in the interests of national security or of the relations between the UK and any other country or for other reasons of a political nature". This power of deportation is now used to terminate the right to settlement of people alleged to have obtained it by marriages of convenience. Most deportations, however, continue to be of overstayers or those convicted of criminal offences. Those recommended for deportation by a court are automatically detained unless the courts direct release, and only deportees with a pending appeal have an opportunity to apply for bail. Between 1st January and 22nd November 1983, 2,350 persons including 48 children under 17 were detained at the immigration service's Harmondsworth Detention Centre;[11] and in 1982 1,963 non-criminal prisoners were received into prison department establishments under Immigration Act powers,[12] 1,986 deportation orders were made, 540 persons were imprisoned and 430 removed as alleged illegal entrants.[13]

In addition to its racism and general disregard for civil liberties, the existing immigration system often discriminates on grounds of sex. The Immigration Act 1971 followed the sex discrimination in the British Nationality Act 1948 by providing for a Commonwealth citizen to be patrial by marriage to a UK and Colonies citizen husband but not wife; under the 1981 British Nationality Act, the right of abode is preserved for the lifetime of women who were patrial immediately before it came into effect, but not acquired by those marrying after 1st January 1983. The new Act observes formal sex equality in its provisions, but so far as spouses of British citizens are concerned achieves it by ending the automatic and immediate entitlement of wives to register: wives and husbands of citizens now benefit only from a two year reduction in the residence qualification before they can apply, like any resident, for naturalisation at the Home Secretary's discretion, and from exemption from the language qualification. (The right under the new Act of a British citizen mother to pass on her citizenship to her child on the same terms as a British citizen father is however a significant, if long overdue, advance.) The immigration rules for husbands and fiancés are discriminatory on grounds of sex as well as race, and even fiancés eligible for admission, unlike fiancées, require entry clearance. Married women who are British overseas citizens are virtually excluded by reason of their sex from being regarded as heads of household eligible for special vouchers. Men working in approved employment or here as students may have their wives admitted: women are denied the equivalent rights.

Some remedies for this situation might be thought to exist in the immigration appeals system and the supervisory role of the courts. From the start, however, the immigration appeals system has appeared more concerned at providing the appearance of an independent review of administrative decisions than a recognition of the necessity of an effective appeal; as the Wilson Committee put it:

It is one thing for us, after a protracted inquiry, to express our confidence that the power of final decision entrusted to officers of the Immigration Service is being exercised fairly: it is another thing to expect a newly arrived immigrant and his relatives and friends at the other side of the barrier, to feel the same confidence. They are not aware of the safeguards provided by the immigration officer's responsibility through his superiors to the Home Secretary, and the Home Secretary's responsibility to Parliament: all that seems evident to them is that an immediate and summary power to refuse admission rests with one or two officials at the port. In this situation it is understandable that an immigrant and his relatives or friends should feel themselves from the outset to be under a disadvantage, and so should be less willing than they might otherwise be to accept the eventual decision.[14]

The majority of appeals take place in the absence of the appellant, who remains or has been removed overseas. Adjudicators place great weight on the explanatory statements prepared by entry clearance officers, immigration officers or the Home Office, with no facilities for cross-examining the interviewing official even when he is accessible in the UK. Home Office presenting officers adopt a highly adversarial approach. Adjudicators are appointed by the Home Office itself. The Act gives the Adjudicators and the Tribunal no discretion to make favourable decisions outside the rules, and the approach of the appellate authorities has been to interpret the rules in a narrow fashion: an example of this which has caused particular distress to the Caribbean communities is the interpretation of rules for the admission of the children of single parents.[15] The success rate in appeals is not suprisingly low: 12 per cent in 1982.[16] The Immigration Appeal Tribunal is now the only major tribunal from which there is no right of appeal to the courts on a point of law. It is not, however, to be supposed that such a right of appeal would have been of much avail to immigrants given the attitudes the courts have displayed when immigration matters have come before them. There are few more glaring examples of judicial double standards than the contrast between recent attitudes of the House of Lords in the extension of administrative law and its destruction of *habeas corpus* in *Zamir.*[17] It took an outcry against this to bring about a rare change of mind less than three years later in *Khajawa* and *Khera.*[18]

Ministers, immigration officials, the appellate authorities and the courts have all been acting in response to a climate of hostility to black immigration. The immigration system they have thus created is sometimes justified by the proposition that strict immigration control is the necessary pre-requisite for good race relations. The opposite cannot be too strongly asserted: that the racism of the existing immigration system undermines any attempts to create an equal multi-racial society in Britain. At a time when the new British Nationality Act entrenches injustices already done by immigration legislation, and when the political supervision of immigration control has never been less sensitive to justice and compassion, it is hard to be optimistic about achieving the necessary reform. Compelling this reform is, however, a duty incumbent on all those with a commitment to civil liberties.

NOTES

1. European Commission of Human Rights, *op. cit.*
2. *Ibid.* pp. 52–54.
3. The current Immigration Rules, incorporating revisions up to February 1983, are printed as HC Paper 169 (1983). The 1980 rules were published as HC Paper 394 (1980). For references to the 1973 rules, which were amended on a number of occasions, see Grant and Martin, *op. cit.*, pp. 8–9.
4. Compare Home Office evidence with the evidence of Lord Scarman

and Anthony Lester QC, printed in *Proposed New Immigration Rules and the European Convention on Human Rights, op. cit.*.

5. *Secretary of State's Instructions to Immigration Officers.* Successive governments have refused to publish these instructions, but their nature and scope can be understood by consulting the out-of-date copy available by arrangement at the office of the Joint Council for the Welfare of Immigrants, 44 Theobalds Road, London WC1.

6. See *Immigration from the Indian Sub-Continent*, Fifth Report from the Home Affairs Committee (HC Paper 90, HMSO, 1982), Vol. II, *Evidence*, especially the JCWI's evidence, pp. 49–49.

7. See *ibid.*, Vol. I *Report*, pp. xxv–xli; Vol. II *Evidence*, pp. 49–57; and *Immigration from the Indian Sub-Continent: the Government Reply* (Cmnd. 8725, HMSO, 1982).

8. Home Office, *Control of Immigration Statistics 1982* (Cmnd. 8944, HMSO, 1983).

9. *Ibid.*

10. The preceding powers are all to be found in the Immigration Act 1971, Schedule 2.

11. House of Commons Debates, 29th November 1983, cs. *439–440* (written answer).

12. Home Office, *Prison Statistics England and Wales 1982* (Cmnd. 9027, HMSO, 1983).

13. Home Office, *Control of Immigration Statistics 1982, op. cit.*

14. Home Office, *Report of the Committee on Immigration Appeals* (Cmnd. 3387, HMSO, 1967), p. 84. The 1981 Home Office discussion document, *Review of Appeals under the Immigration Act 1971* shows no change of attitude.

15. See NCCL evidence in *The West Indian Community*, Select Committee on Race Relations and Immigration (HC Paper 180, HMSO, 1976), vol. II, Minutes of Evidence, p. 219; and Grant and Martin, *op. cit.*, pp. 158–161.

16. House of Commons Debates, 29th November 1983, col. 439 (written answer).

17. *Zamir* v *Home Secretary* [1980] Appeal Cases, p. 930. See also A Nicol, *Illegal Entrants* (JCWI and Runnymede Trust, 1981); J Levin, *Second Class Justice* (1980) Legal Action Group Bulletin p. 178; C Blake, "The Death of Habeas Corpus", *New Law Journal*, 28th August 1980.

18. *Khajawa and Khera* v *Home Secretary* [1983] 1 All England Law Reports, p. 765.

15

WOMEN'S RIGHTS

POLLY PATTULLO

Women have never been able to take their civil liberties for granted. Even when progressive legislation has been passed or when attitudes seem to have mellowed, there is a reluctance to celebrate, for, with the knowledge of historical hindsight, women have learnt that the path to liberation is beset with obstacles. Often their story has been one of two steps forward, one step back.

The women's vote is a classic case. When women gained the vote, when the suffragists and suffragettes had expended that energy, skill, commitment and passion, what then? The legislation itself – although a tremendous achievement – was not enough in itself to effect, to protect or to extend women's rights.

The complex nature of women's rights and how they are to be achieved raises wide issues. Women's legal status – their right to full citizenship – underpins their relationship with the State. But the horizons of women's civil liberties stretch beyond this narrow definition. It is not just the political which defines women's rights; it is the private, too.

The ideal image of nineteenth-century, middle-class womanhood was such that it contrived to deny women any public role at all. The ground was cut from under their feet by the confines of domesticity. What Mary Wollstonecraft saw as the damage done to women by turning them into inferior social beings was what she called "false refinement", a distortion of their humanity. "Civilised women are therefore so weakened by false refinement", she wrote, "that, respecting morals, their condition is much below what it would be were they left in a state near to nature".[1] That dilemma of knowing what true femininity is, and how it is to flourish, without letting it be defined by men and for their needs, is relevant today to understanding why the issue of women's rights is so complex.

For women, then, civil liberty has ramifications at every level of life. It goes beyond the right to be an astronaut or a Prime Minister, although those rights must be implicit in any analysis. It is also about how women's relationship with the State is reflected in how men and women exist together both inside and outside the home. These are all parts of the same question.

We can see, to some extent, how this works today in so far as women's rights to full citizenship under our legal system are incomplete. We live in a society with the notion of equality under the law as one of its bedrock principles. Yet there are important pockets of the law which deny this to women. The time when women had virtually no rights at all and were the chattels of first their fathers and then their husbands is behind us, but the legacy of those assumptions lingers on in law.

The idea of women's economic dependence on men, for example, is prescribed by our social security legislation. The ideas behind it fuelled the Beveridge Report of 1942, which assumed that although marriage was a partnership, it was one in which the woman was financially invisible, tucked under the arm of her providing, protective husband. That view of married life bears little relation to today's reality when nearly 50 per cent of married women go out to work, as do around 30 per cent of women with children under five, albeit mostly part-time, and when one in seven of wives earn as much as or more than their husbands. Beveridge-style sentiments were endorsed in 1976, by a then Minister of State at the DHSS, who wrote to the Women's Liberation Campaign for Legal and Financial Independence with these views:

The number of instances of the wife having chosen to be the breadwinner, as opposed to having taken on that role, is still very small. Indeed, it continues to be a widespread view that a husband who is capable of work has a duty to society, as well as to his wife, to provide for his family.[2]

This view has been perpetuated in law until recently by denying married and cohabiting women the right to claim supplementary benefit or Family Income Supplement. Changes in the law were forced on the British Government by an EEC Directive. In November 1983, women were able for the first time, under certain circumstances, to claim supplementary benefit and be nominated the "breadwinner"; at the same time they became eligible to claim Family Income Supplement. By the end of 1984 women will also be able to claim contributory benefits for dependent children and extra sickness, unemployment and invalidity benefit for dependent husbands.

But there remain two important sticking points which will continue to discriminate sharply against married women: these are the non-contributory invalidity pension and the invalid care allowance. The former means that a woman with a long-term disability can only qualify if she is "incapable of performing household duties" (not, incidentally, a requirement demanded of men or single women). And, in the latter case, married women who care for dependent invalid relatives will still not be eligible for an allowance, despite the savings made to the taxpayer by their home care of the sick and old, on the grounds that they might well be toiling at home anyhow. By making full use of exclusion clauses allowed for in the EEC Directive, the Government has done its best to wriggle out of full equity in its social security law.

Our taxation system is a similar box of tricks, based as it is on the idea of the breadwinner husband. Single men and women are treated equally, but for a married woman the family's tax affairs are her husband's: he fills in the form for himself and his wife; he claims the married man's tax allowance and any rebates due to him and his wife. (Separate assessment, possible but unorthodox, is frustrating and time-consuming – and husbands must give their permission.) So the old tax anomalies remain, in a society which in no way conforms to the stereotype of the man at work, dependent wife at home with the children – the model around which the system was built. Indeed, according to the General Household Survey of 1978, only 5 per cent of the economically active population match this profile.

The twists and turns in immigration laws over the past 15 years or so demonstrate the racist and sexist stances of both Conservative and Labour Governments. The basic thinking has been crude – namely, to keep out as many non-white immigrants as possible. To this has been added the concept of women as dependants. Present Immigration Rules ban the fiancés or husbands of women who were not themselves born in this country or neither of whose parents were born here. This, effectively and neatly, results in thousands of women, mainly those of Asian origin, being forced to live apart from their husbands. Again, immigration officers have the power to refuse a husband permission to enter Britain if the authorities believe that the marriage took place primarily to effect his entry to this country, even if the woman was born here. He can also be refused entry as a fiancé if the couple have not met.

Challenges to the Immigration Rules continue: in 1982, five test cases of women deprived of their right to found a family because their husbands or fiancés were prevented from joining them in this country were taken to the European Human Rights Commission. Three of the cases were declared admissible which means that the British Government could be in breach of the European Convention on Human Rights.

If women have no right to be equal under some aspects of the law, how have they fared under legislation which does attempt to recognise women's rights? The equality laws, hailed as the most far-reaching in the world by then Labour Ministers, were ushered in like a new dawn in 1975. There, for the first time on the statute books, was the law, enshrined in the Sex Discrimination Act, which made it illegal to discriminate against women in training and employment, education, housing and the provision of goods, facilities and services. The SDA also embraces the important notion of indirect discrimination, which says that it is discriminatory to impose a condition which is more easily met by more people of one sex than the other. The other part of the package was the Equal Pay Act (this does not include the same notion of indirect discrimination – a serious shortfall for part-time workers, 93 per cent of whom are women). In the same year, the Employment Protection Act gave women the right to paid maternity leave and the right to return to their job after the birth of the baby.

These laws were a crucial step forward, and the stage had shifted. As Anna Coote and Beatrix Campbell put it in their book *Sweet Freedom*:

open disputes about whether or not women were men's inferior, worthy of unequal treatment, gave way to disagreements over what exactly constituted the equal rights that women were acknowledged to deserve, and how these could now be achieved.[3]

Achievement is the key, for what has been learnt since reveals not just serious weaknesses in the Acts themselves but also the incapacity of women to exercise the power to affect their rights. This was posited as long ago as 1976 by Counter Information Services (with reference to the Sex Discrimination Act):

The Act may well be important in terms of women's expectations, but there is little real hope of it changing women's role in society until women themselves consciously organise to do so – and in that situation the existence or otherwise of legislation is going to make little difference.[4]

In its first years, the Equal Pay Act did manage to jack up women's wages. But by 1982, seven years after its implementation, working women's average gross hourly earnings averaged only 73.9 per cent of men's. As the Equal Opportunities Commission noted in its Sixth Annual Report in 1981: "Improvements in women's earnings as a result of equal pay legislation have substantially ceased, and the ratio of women's hourly earnings to those of men has settled in the range of 73-75 per cent."[5]

One of the clearest examples of how the Equal Pay Act became a rather badly-botched cosmetic is that it failed to attack the issue of job segregation; and in a society where 45 per cent of working women work in segregated ghettoes this fact has featured as a serious omission, for under the law a woman must compare herself to a man doing like work in the same workplace to claim equal pay. Only then can she claim parity if her work is rated as equivalent to a man's in a job evaluation scheme. But even here there is a problem: what criteria are being used to assess job equality? The values put on male skills, for example dirty or heavy jobs, by both unions and management are often higher than those for traditional skills like manual dexterity. The web of assumptions about women and their "value" embroiders the map of equality laws.

The Government is now being forced to amend the Equal Pay Act to incorporate the concept of equal pay for work of equal value. In July 1982 the European Court of Justice ruled that Britain's equal pay legislation actually broke European law.[6] But introducing the concept of equal pay for work of equal value may not in itself solve women's low pay problems – for a start the problems of evaluation will remain.

The Sex Discrimination Act holds out a useful basis for challenging sex discrimination, but its effectiveness appears limited and its use unwieldy. One of the basic problems is that the burden is on the employee to prove discrimination: this is difficult. And the narrowness of the Act means that one woman who wins a discrimination claim wins victory only for herself – the broad range of women who might find themselves in that particular situation are stuck with it; good effect does not rub off on them.

The indirect provisions of the Act could, however, affect large groups of people. In one case, the law was used successfully by a civil servant who claimed that her appointment was blocked by the age bar (entry to executive officer grade was restricted to those aged 28 or under). This, she argued, was a condition more easily met by men since many women were in those years bearing and caring for children. She won her case[7] and the Civil Service has since raised its age bar in that grade to 45.

But few indirect sex discrimination cases have been heard. Not that occurrences of such breaches of the law are noticeably rare. The LSE's Equal Pay and Opportunity Project monitored 26 employing organisations and identified 16 cases of possible indirect discrimination.[8]

The number of cases under the equality laws which have been taken to Industrial Tribunals and the rates of success have declined over the years, most noticeably those under the Equal Pay Act. In 1976, 1742 applications were made under the EPA and of those heard nearly half were upheld. But by 1982, only 39 were made and of those heard under one fifth were upheld.[9] The large proportion of cases under both Acts which never actually reached court – in no year was this figure less than 50 per cent and usually a much higher percentage – is noteworthy, and there is some evidence to suggest that women are discouraged, either directly or indirectly, from going through with their claims.

The restrictive nature of the legislation is one side of the coin; the other is women's ignorance of their rights and their reluctance to pursue them. And while women are corralled in low-paid jobs on the margins of power they will not be able to begin to exercise those rights which do exist.

But there is another argument which raises more far-reaching questions. A research project carried out for the EOC by the Centre for Labour Economics at the LSE concludes that the Equal Pay Act has been an effective instrument in raising women's pay, but that women – even if legislation were "perfect" – could not hope to achieve 100 per cent of male pay because of the social circumstances that govern their lives, namely lower educational standards, less training and the years they stay outside the workforce looking after children. If this is so, a far greater and more fundamental realignment of male-female relationships is required.

Women's status is thus diminished by discriminatory legislation, the lack of ability to use positive legislation and the patterns of their domestic lives. But there is a more insidious aspect of discrimination, which highlights the problems of attitudes, in these examples, from within the judiciary.

Sachs and Wilson, in their impressive book *Sexism and the Law*, examined the "persons cases" in the last half of the nineteenth century in which judges were asked to decide whether "an individual's gender was irrelevant to his or her factual or legal capacity".[10] For six decades the judges deliberated and, until 1929, found otherwise, thus sustaining a concept of male monopoly, inherent in a system where laws were man-made and interpreted by men. "Without embarrassment or apology," noted Sachs and Wilson, "the judges painted a picture of women being too delicate and refined to undertake public functions, and accordingly classified them legally alongside the insane and insolvent, and even in one case alongside the inanimate".[11] If we have moved on from this set of images which denied women a public life "in their best interests", what interpretations of the laws that affect women do contemporary judges make?

It is useful to note that from inside the profession women lawyers are continually forced to appraise their marginalised position – corralled mainly into family law, undermined by the clubbiness of their male colleagues, and their professionalism sometimes called into question by insinuation. If that is how the male legal majority view their professional equals it is pertinent to ask how they perceive the other women who come into contact with the law as defendants, victims, witnesses and complainants. For it is at law that women's civil liberties are put to the test.

Claims under the Sex Discrimination Act illustrate, for example, some disturbing judicial views. Rosalind Coleman went to an Industrial Tribunal because she had been dismissed from her job as a travel agent the day after her marriage. Her husband worked for a rival firm and her employer, worried about the possibility of leaks, had, after conferring with her husband's employer, sacked Mrs Coleman. The tribunal found for Mrs Coleman on the grounds that her employer's assumption that her husband was the breadwinner constituted discrimination under the SDA. But on appeal, the judgment was overturned. Mr Justice Slynn commented that "there was really no material upon which the Tribunal could conclude that this employer treated Mrs Coleman less favourably than he treated or would have treated a man employed by him in the same situation". Finally, at the Court of Appeal, the case was won, but not before the dissenting judge called the claim "trivial and banal even when topped up with much legalistic froth".[12]

In another case, *Hurley* v *Mustoe*, heard under the SDA, Mrs Hurley had been sacked as a waitress because she had young children. The Industrial Tribunal found that her employer had acted out of justifiable "business necessity" and dismissed the claim. Women with small children were thus perceived as a liability and unreliable employees. At the Employment Appeal Tribunal Mrs Hurley eventually won her case. Compensation for injuries to feelings was set at £100 at the EAT, after the IT had awarded her a humiliating 50p.[13] As the EOC have pointed out, "The low level of damages awarded to successful complainants continues to give concern because aggrieved individuals have at present no incentive to engage in the protracted business of litigation."[14]

The outwardly trivial case against El Vino, the Fleet Street wine bar, highlights how women are faced with outmoded prejudice when they request equal treatment with men in a public drinking place. The court heard that women were denied service standing at the bar but were served sitting down – a "house rule". The case was brought by Anna Coote and Tess Gill, who claimed that this was discriminatory. But the judge quoted the words of Lord Denning sitting in the Court of Appeal: "It would be very wrong, to my mind," the now ex-Master of the Rolls had said, "if the statute were thought to obliterate the differences between men and women or to do away with chivalry which we expect mankind to give to womankind." The case was eventually won at the Court of Appeal.[15]

These three cases raise three images – woman as financial inferior, woman as professional inferior and woman as social inferior. The invoking of these outmoded stereotypes at a judicial level has serious implications for the opportunities of women to exercise their civil liberties.

Our laws and the legacy of the past have much to do, as we have seen, with how women's role in the family is defined. Women will be unable to make use of their civil liberties if, at the same time, the patterns of their private and sexual life are at odds with those rights. Much of the thrust of the contemporary women's movement has been to question the more personal dimensions of civil liberties. The debate about parenting and the need for men to share child care is not, narrowly defined, a field in which civil liberties might have much relevance. But, for example, the State's view on the issue of child care has far-reaching effects for women. Nearly 20 years ago it was estimated that more than one million mothers required day care places for their under-fives. But by 1981 there were only 129,000 full-time day care places for the under-fives, with the majority of these provided by registered childminders. A Government survey in 1968 on Women's Employment, by Audrey Hunt, which drew attention to the immense demand for child-care, elicited this response from the then Ministry of Health: "[Day Nurseries] have been provided by local health authorities since 1945 primarily to meet the needs of certain children for day care on health and welfare grounds. The service is not intended to meet a demand from working women generally for subsidised day care facilities."[16]

The provision of child care is a useful barometer for estimating government views on women's rights, or, more cynically, their market value. In wartime, for example, child-care provision is increased because women are needed in the workforce; such facilities decrease when peacetime comes.

The family has had, in popular thought, a charmed life – supportive against the outside world, inviolate behind closed doors. Privacy has been the key to its modern existence. In 1918, Alice Clark, in her book *Working Life of Women in the Seventeenth Century*, argued that as capitalism developed the State regarded the individual, not the family, as its unit, and "in England this State began with the conception that it was concerned only with male individuals. Thus it came to pass that every womanly function was considered as the private interest of husbands and fathers, bearing no relation to the life of the State, and therefore demanding from the community as a whole no special care or provision".[17] In a sense, any attempt to introduce regulation into family life has diminished individual male power, which may be one explanation of the reluctance of the State to appear intrusive. This has especially been true for laws that give women power rather than those which provide for their welfare as mothers or wives.

One of the social changes of the 1960s was the public acknowledgment of women's sexuality. The liberalisation of abortion and divorce laws, the less punitive legislation governing obscenity and greater access to contraception showed a willingness to "interfere" as a way of decreasing the State's role as moral watchdog. This climate of opinion engendered further possibilities for women, coinciding as it did with the emergence of the women's movement.

As the feminists moved in to force the State to acknowledge and protect women's "personal" rights, they uncovered issues which had long remained hidden. Violence in the family was one. It was not a new problem, but for the campaigners it was another dimension of how women's civil liberties could not be defined just in terms of the public arena. The Domestic Violence Act 1976 acknowledges that under certain circumstances an "Englishman's home is not his castle". It enables a married or cohabiting woman to obtain an injunction restraining a violent husband without first having to commence divorce or separation proceedings. The change was a modest but important one. Even so, there are problems in administering it for there is still reluctance from the police to intervene in "domestics" and from judges to recognise the serious nature of wife-beating. In another context, for example, a wife was refused permission to divorce her violent husband within three years of marriage because, as the judge said: "Before such assaults are said to inflict exceptional hardship, there must be something out of the ordinary in what happened."

The fear of violence in general, and sexual violence in particular, is one very real way in which women's lives are circumscribed. Rape invokes the historical legacy of a man's proprietorial right to a woman's body (indeed, rape in marriage is not a crime). The law relating to rape, together with the way it operates and the attitudes of those who administer it is one way in which society can measure how seriously rape is taken.

The nature of a rape trial poses specific problems. A jury must convict or acquit on the basis of the victim's evidence, but she is merely a witness and has no counsel to represent her. It can seem as if the woman herself is on trial. ("It is well known that women in particular and small boys are liable to be untruthful and invent stories": Judge Sutcliffe, 1976, at the Old Bailey.) Because the central issue is whether the woman consented or not, this has led to the idea that the woman should have injuries to show for it. But this is a double bind: there is always the fear of violence behind rape, and if a woman threatened with violence submits, she can be accused of not resisting fiercely enough. Judges' comments in various rape cases illustrate such assumptions.

The Sexual Offences Act 1976 offered a means to protect women rape victims. It restricted the practice of using a woman's past life and sexual history as evidence. This was a welcome reform, but research now suggests that a loophole, allowing the judge to decide whether such information is admissible, is being used extensively, thus negating its intent.

The problem, again, is in part about the image of women. Blaming a woman for being raped on the grounds of her life-style, her job, her sexual history can open the way to the dangerous assumption that it is only "good" women who are entitled to the protection of the law. Women's rights are again undermined when the old stereotypes are paraded.

One of the clearest ways in which the relationship between men and women and the State can be seen is when the family unit breaks down on divorce. Over the last century a body of reforms has improved women's legal position. Legislation has given women equal rights over their children and has recognised women's contribution to a marriage. The Matrimonial Proceedings and Property Act of 1970, for example, recognised that a woman caring for her husband and children should be entitled to a share of the family's capital and assets even when these are owned by the man. A woman's unpaid domestic labour is now also taken into consideration. The idea of blame has largely been removed while concern for the children's welfare has become paramount. And because it is considered natural that children should be with their mothers, custody normally goes to them.

All these changes have undeniably boosted women's position; some would even say they are now given preferential treatment. Yet none of these changes tackles the notion of women's dependency on men. Indeed, they reinforce it, for by insisting that it is the duty of husbands to maintain their ex-wives and children, the notion of the nuclear family in its traditional form as the only viable economic and emotional unit remains intact.

It is a view, too, that in a broader sense is being cultivated by the Conservative Government as it embarks on its second term of office. Its ideological base rests on reinforcing the family role at the expense of the welfare state, to make the family the repository of good as an alternative to what is seen as the perverting effect of the welfare state. But this family, which is spoken of in such reverential terms, is the family of the past locked into its old roles. Child care, as we have seen, is being cut back; and the allowance for the care of the sick is not extended to married women. Indeed, proposals from the Family Policy Group, leaked to the Press towards the end of the 1979-83 Tory administration, emphasise the need for families "to reassume responsibilities taken on by the state, for example responsibility for the disabled [and] elderly."[18] These burdens will be thrown back on women who will take on voluntarily what, in the past, they may have done as paid work in the community.

One of the keynotes in the FPG proposals was "to encourage mothers to stay at home", with the suggestion that the way to do this was "at least" to remove fiscal discrimination against them. Perhaps by amending the tax laws? One option would be to replace the married man's allowance with a single person's allowance for wives, which could be transferred to the husband if the wife did not work. This would mean that if a wife worked, her husband's tax allowance would be halved – a tempting incentive, perhaps, for some husbands to urge their wives to stay at home. An alternative scheme, rejected by the last Government, would be to abolish the married man's allowance but to use that money in some form of cash child benefit; this, in itself, might give a genuine choice to women about whether to go out to work or stay at home. Such a reform, though, would not appear to be on the agenda.

The inability of the Conservative Government to respond with positive and workable plans to EEC directives on equality legislation and part-time workers, who are not guaranteed the same rights as full-time workers, provides another indication of the Tories' broad thinking. The short debate on the draft Equal Pay (Amendment) Regulations in July 1983 demonstrated a wretched disregard for the whole subject. Tory backbenchers were openly contemptuous of women's rights: "Any trouble maker or potential irritated employee is going to pretend that her work is of equal value. It is an open invitation to any feminist, any harridan or any rattle-headed female with a chip on her bra strap to take action against her employer", said Northampton North Tory MP Tony Marlow.[19]

And by her silence, our first woman Prime Minister has made it clear over the years that she has little interest in or understanding of the way in which women's lives are circumscribed nor any notion of feminist thinking.

There are also specific clues which point up the definition on the political canvas. The tightening up of maternity rights in the Employment Act 1980, the Rayner Report's recommendations that women without adequate child care are not available for work and are thus ineligible to claim unemployment benefit, the abolition of 17 training boards which had begun to offer women equal access to skills training, dark hints about the future of the EOC, mutterings about abolishing the Wages Councils, which at least established minimum legal rates in many low-paid industries where women predominate, the change in the abortion notification forms which may now be making it more difficult for women to get NHS abortions on non-medical grounds – all these paint a picture which could restrict the breadth of women's lives.

But the economic landscape of the future may well have more thrusting side-effects than the political ones. If the days of full employment are over, there will be cases when women find work while husbands from the old industries remain unemployed. This will make new demands on family life: mothers at work, fathers at home may teach families new ways to live. We have hardly begun to investigate the effects of those new dynamics and how they could bring about new attitudes out of necessity.

Adjustments in the nature of work and how this spills over into the home must be an essential part of political thinking. With it must come more flexible working hours, greater help with child care and a real choice about who goes out to work and who stays at home by a restructuring of the basis of social security and employment legislation. At the same time, a real commitment to positive action (which is already allowed for under certain circumstances in the SDA) would allow some women to gain the equal opportunities which have evaded them. This could be applied not just in employment but in education where so many attitudes are formed and consolidated.

There is a tendency in hard times to retreat. The responsibility of all sections of the women's movement, which has been behind so many initiatives working towards women's civil liberties, must be to engage in the struggle for power, not to withdraw from it into side issues in a mood of defeatism and ideological dogmatism.

What the women's movement has achieved has been, at one level, to challenge the old assumptions and to inject a "women's angle" into every aspect of life. The campaigners have shown – even if they are forever fighting defensive actions – how the law can be used, and that it can be changed. Where legislation would seem to have minimal effect, attention has been drawn to the need to change attitudes which deny women their equal place in society. The recent exposure of the problems of sexual harassment in the workplace, for instance, is beginning to be taken seriously by employers and unions.

These are positive developments, and it is hard to imagine the dismantling of the forces which have created them. Attacks on women's rights – for example, the attempts to change the 1967 Abortion Act – have been met with widespread resistance: the campaigns aligning a broad alliance of women with both men and women within Parliament.

To rid society of discriminatory laws must be the first step: they are no accidents, for they underwrite specific definitions of women and the restrictive roles expected of them. Until there is a basis for equality no woman can find out what she is or what she is able to do. To function fully within society the law will provide a framework from which a change of attitudes can develop. Without such laws, women's civil liberties are endangered and the way is left open for the manipulation of women's self-doubt and powerlessness. The right of women to participate in society at all levels rather than existing on its fringes experiencing life through a distorted man-made mirror can only enrich the lives of both men and women and extend the boundaries of a democratic society.

NOTES

1. Wollstonecraft, *A Vindication of the Rights of Women* (1792) (Everyman Library, 1970), p.67.
2. "Disaggregation Now", *Feminist Review 2*, 1979, p.20.
3. Coote and Campbell, *Sweet Freedom* (Picador, 1982), p.107.
4. *Women Under Attack* Anti Report No. 15, Counter Information Services, 1976, p.4.
5. Equal Opportunities Commission *6th Annual Report*, 1981, p.73.
6. *Commission of the European Communities* v *UK* [1982] Industrial Relations Law Reports, p.333.
7. *Price* v *Civil Service Commission* [1977] Industrial Relations Law Reports, p.291 and [1978] Industrial Relations Law Reports, p.3.
8. "The Equal Pay and Sex Discrimination Acts", *Feminist Review 1*, 1979, p.50.

9. Figures taken from Equal Opportunities Commission Annual Reports.

10. Sachs and Wilson, *Sexism and the Law* (Martin Robertson, 1978), p.6.

11. *Ibid*, p.6.

12. *Coleman* v *Skyrail Oceanic Ltd* [1961] Industrial Relations Law Reports, p.398 (Lord Justice Shaw).

13. *Hurley* v *Mustoe* [1981] Industrial Relations Law Reports, p.208.

14. Equal Opportunities Commission, *7th Annual Report*, 1982, p.8.

15. *Gill and Coote* v *El Vinos Ltd* [1983] Industrial Relations Law Reports 206.

16. Hunt, *A Survey of Women's Employment,* Vol. 1 (Department of Employment, 1968), p.107.

17. Clark, *Working Life of Women in the Seventeenth Century* (Routledge and Kegan Paul, 1982 (reissue)), p.307.

18. *New Socialist*, May/June 1983, p.20.

19. House of Commons Debates, 20th July 1983, Col. 491.

16

GAY RIGHTS

PAUL CRANE

INTRODUCTION

Fifty years ago the Nazi Party was preaching the evil idea that "degenerates" must be exterminated. By 1935 a legal campaign of terror had been inaugurated against homosexuals during which more than 50,000 arrests were made by the police. By the end of the War between 100,000 and more than 400,000 gay people from Germany and the occupied countries had died from illness, medical experiments and in the gas chambers.

In many countries "rights" for lesbians and gay men remains as alien an idea as "rights" for women. There are still countries where it is extremely dangerous even to be known as a homosexual. In Argentina and Iran, for example, there have been documented cases of police terror culminating in executions and the disappearance of gay people.

In the wake of gains made by the social movements in the West during the sixties and seventies, gay women and men have moved from struggling for the right even to exist to a more complex struggle to establish an individual and collective identity beyond the limits set by prejudice and grudging tolerance. The revolution in attitudes among young people during the last fifteen years, and the impact of the gay and women's movements in particular, gave confidence and support to many to contest discrimination and oppression.

Yet the fight for gay rights through the legal system has produced few positive gains. The law has continued to provide some of the main intellectual rationalisations for the suppression of male homosexuality and lesbianism. It is one source of the stigma that shapes the meaning of "homosexual" in the public's mind, but as such the law has been and will continue to be affected by the presence of openly gay men and women and the campaigns around their cases.

This essay considers three of these areas of gay and lesbian civil rights struggles: the right to be openly gay or lesbian without fear of discrimination; the right to recognition for gay and lesbian relationships; and the right to respect for private life. These and other aspects are covered more comprehensively in my book *Gays and the Law*[1]

THE RIGHT TO BE OPENLY GAY OR LESBIAN
WITHOUT FEAR OF DISCRIMINATION

From its beginning in the late 1960s, gay liberation transformed the meaning of "coming out". Previously coming out had signified the private decision to accept one's homosexual desires and to acknowledge one's sexual identity only to other gay men and women. Gay liberationists recast coming out as a profoundly political act that could offer enormous personal benefits to an individual. The open affirmation of one's sexual identity, whether at work, at college, at home, in the media or wherever, symbolised the shedding of the self-hatred that gay women and men internalised, and consequently it promised an immediate improvement in one's life. To come out of the "closet" expressed the fusion of the personal and the political that was a cornerstone of the radicalism of the late 1960s.

Discrimination at work provides one of the clearest examples of the problems besetting gay people who do not want to hide their sexual orientation. For many lesbians and gay men, an open affirmation of their life-style has spelled the immediate threat of, or actual, loss of a job or opportunities for promotion. Those who decide to remain secret about their sexual orientation may find their jobs jeopardised by rumours that they are homosexual; this also happens to those who do not fit the stereotypes of the masculine man or the feminine woman. Still others whose orientation is hidden may be forced into the open by some crisis or legal trouble. The law in effect permits employers to refuse to hire, refuse to promote or even to dismiss or demote gay employees solely on the grounds of common prejudices.

The most significant issue of principle that derives from the many Industrial Tribunal cases since the mid-1970s is that the "general public" is entitled to hold "strong views" (i.e. prejudices) against homosexuals – and that the actual or supposed hostile views of customers, fellow workers or parents can justifiably be acted upon by an employer who wants to get rid of a lesbian or gay worker. This issue is refined according to the particular nature of the employment. In relation to employees working with children and young people hostile views are blatantly related to the risk of corruption and assaults on juveniles and the responsibility of employers to uphold the good name of their institution. With regard to workers who have contact with the general public, the reputation of the firm and the risk to profitability have been given as justifications.

Employees most vulnerable to discrimination on grounds of homosexuality are those who work in proximity to young people. It is crudely presumed that gay men are sexually uncontrollable and that young people in their care are at risk. Lesbians are also oppressed by similarly wild prejudices. In 1981 Susan Shell was sacked from her job as a night care attendant in a residential home for girls. A colleague had learned from her that she was lesbian, and had told her superior who forced Susan Shell to resign. In the following year Judith Williams, a residential social worker at a home for girls in care, was dismissed for being "temperamentally unsuitable" after it was discovered that she was a lesbian. Both cases were taken up in the gay and women's movement and drew widespread support.

Also in 1981 the courts decided that there was sufficient justification for an employer to act on the basis of popular prejudices about homosexuals. The hostel at which John Saunders had worked for about two years as a maintenance man was attended by young people of both sexes. One evening Mr Saunders had his wallet stolen by someone he met at a gay pub. He reported the incident to the police and in the course of the interview told them he was gay. Soon after, his employers were unofficially informed that John Saunders was a homosexual. Far from complaining about his work or behaviour at work, his employers sacked him because, to use their words, "information was received that you indulge in homosexuality. At a camp accommodating large numbers of school-children and teenagers it is totally unsuitable to employ *any person with such tendencies* (my emphasis). His appeals for a reasoned consideration of whether *he* had done or might do anything wrong fell on deaf ears at the Industrial Tribunal, the Employment Appeal Tribunal and the Scottish Court of Session.[2]

The injustice of the case and its implications for all gay people drew unprecedented support from the labour movement. Even *The Times* columnist Bernard Levin was moved to write

what happened to Mr Saunders is one part of the scandal; the greater part lies in the fact that if he does not get legal redress [which he did not] it will have been judicially established that a citizen who is wholly blameless may be punished because some people believe that *other* people, not including the citizen in question, might, in certain circumstances, behave wrongly.

When heterosexuals show off pictures of their spouse or their engagement or wedding ring, it is regarded as a socially acceptable public sharing of part of their personal lives. But when a homosexual does something similar or wears a badge instead of a ring, it is regarded as flaunting behaviour.

The case of Louise Boychuck[3] is a classic example of how little legal security is available to women and men who choose to be open about their sexual orientation. She was employed by a City insurance company as an accounts clerk. For three or four months before she was sacked she wore various types of gay badges on her work clothes. Things suddenly escalated when the managing director noticed one which read "Lesbians Ignite". She was told that he found it personally offensive, it would "offend the decencies of other people" and was "not a thing for clients to see". Normally her job would involve seeing the public only on about one day a week when she worked on the company's reception. She declined to remove this sort of badge and was sacked. During her case before the Industrial Tribunal, which was conducted by the NCCL, she was accused of trying to propagandise and encourage others to become lesbian. The fact that there was no evidence that any member of the public was *actually* offended was considered immaterial. As in the Saunders case, the Employment Appeal Tribunal came to a decision on the basis of possible beliefs of third parties who were not there to give evidence. The employer's paranoia was sufficient.

So often the process of self-realisation and openness by lesbians and gay men is seen not as proof of validity and self-esteem but as evidence of proselytisation. Social authoritarians and conformists assume that heterosexuality is the mainstream of thought and activity for everyone and that homosexuality is a sign of *interference*. Hence the obsessive hunt to remove the pebbles that might divert the stream.

The House of Lords has specifically identified the "encouragement of homosexuality" as the sort of thing that "reasonable jurors" should consider a "corrupt practice". In the course of upholding a conviction of the publishers of a radical youth paper called *International Times* which carried explicitly gay "lonely hearts" advertisements, Lord Reid said:

I find nothing in the Act [the Sexual Offences Act 1967] to indicate that Parliament thought or intended to lay down that indulgence in these practices is not corrupting. I read the Act as saying that even though it may be corrupting, if people chose to corrupt themselves in this way that is their affair and the law will not interfere. But no licence is given to others to encourage the practice.[4]

Since the ruling in this case there has been a continual public struggle over the right to free expression and representation of homosexuality. Films have been censored, magazines and papers seized and destroyed. In one notorious test case, moral order campaigner Mary Whitehouse tried to hobble *Gay News* for its publication of a poem by a distinguished academic which described a centurion's homosexual fantasies about the crucified Christ;[5] she also tried to pillory the director of Howard Brenton's *The Romans in Britain* for a 30 second scene of simulated anal sex between two men.[6]

THE RIGHT TO RECOGNITION FOR LESBIAN AND GAY RELATIONSHIPS

A second critical feature of the 1970s has been the appearance of a strong lesbian liberation movement. For many women who have discovered sexual desire for women in a feminist environment, lesbianism has had a very different meaning to conventionally defined homosexuality. Many lesbians regard their sexual orientation, perhaps unlike most gay men, as a rational response to male supremacy.

Attraction to the same sex may be experienced by some people more as a question of choice than as a disposition fixed before the onset of puberty. Consequently the parental rights of self-defined lesbians have emerged as a major civil rights issue. More and more women have refused to accept without a fight that they must choose between their sexual orientation and the custody of their children following the dissolution of marriage. The legal system in Britain has not accepted the notion that a good parent may also be openly homosexual and live with a same-sex lover. Several recurring themes emerge from court decisions on child custody involving lesbian parents.

First, there continues to be a substantial fear, despite the absence of any supporting evidence, that children brought up in a gay home will grow up to be gay themselves or will develop "improper" sex role behaviour. It has been openly suggested by the heterosexual parent that (in the case of a lesbian parent) the woman's lover will emasculate male children and seduce female children.

Second, it is widely presumed that, given a choice between a heterosexual and a homosexual home environment, the heterosexual home is unquestionably better for a child. Once again, no specific reason is provided to support the presumption. Occasionally courts take the position that a heterosexual home provides a better "role model" and a better moral environment than does a lesbian home. In the case of *W* v *W* in 1976,[7] the Court of Appeal made it clear that the lesbian mother was to be given custody of her two daughters only because the father had no suitable home to offer.

Third, there is the concern that being brought up in a lesbian household will stigmatise a child and create conflicts between the child and the child's friends. Even in cases in which a child has not experienced problems, judges, court welfare officers and psychiatrists have assumed that trouble will develop in the future, and therefore that the child would be better off living in a heterosexual home. Here the "best" interests of the child are crudely equated to the situation that appears most superficially "normal". In effect the courts are expressing fears concerning the challenge presented by an alternative home environment to the ideal of an isolated heterosexual family unit.

The current hard-line attitude of the courts was summed up by Lord Justice Watkins in *Re P* (1982):[8]

I accept that it is not right to say that a child should in no circumstances live with a mother who is carrying on a lesbian relationship with a woman who is also living with her, but I venture to suggest that *it can only be countenanced by the court when it is driven to the conclusion that there is in the interests of the child no other acceptable form of custody* (my emphasis).

The extreme fear and prejudice triggered by the notion of a homosexual parent is also shown in a number of cases involving the rights of non-custodial parents to visit their children. It is not uncommon to find, particularly in courts outside London, that the right to visit is given on an undertaking that the lover or any gay friends will be absent during the visit, or in some instances that a heterosexual adult will be present while the parent visits the children. In *Re D* (1977),[9] the House of Lords ruled favourably on an application by a mother and her second husband to adopt the son of her former marriage. The effect of this was to prevent all contact between the gay father and his son. One Law Lord stressed that the case was not one where "the father was only involved in homosexual incidents" but that "*his life-style is to keep a homosexual establishment*" (*sic* – my emphasis). *Re D* was a startling example of the prejudices judges hold against gay people. It was conceded that the father did not constitute any physical danger to his son, but nevertheless he should be separated from him. Although the case did not establish any general precedent against gay parents it was clear that having a stable home with a same-sex lover, having gay friends, accepting one's gayness fully were, to these judges, factors which count against homosexual parents.

Custody is not the only area where gay relationships have no validity. The same is true in immigration law where official decisions about the illegitimacy of gay relationships are crudely inhumanitarian.

"Eduardo" was born in Venezuela. For many years he had been abused, physically assaulted and ostracised because of his gayness. He was subjected to aversion therapy to alter his sexual orientation, which failed. Eduardo's mother then committed suicide and he suffered a nervous breakdown. Soon afterwards he left for Britain where he settled down and also formed a stable relationship with a man, the first he had been able to enjoy. Having outstayed his time in the UK, Eduardo was threatened with the breakup of that relationship. The Home Office Minister was presented with medical evidence pointing to the extreme likelihood that Eduardo would commit suicide if he returned to Venezuela. Nevertheless permission to remain was refused. When Eduardo left in 1980 his UK-born lover left with him.

The Immigration Rules for the UK recognise and accommodate emotional relationships between individuals of the opposite sex, usually, but not always, formalised in marriage. The Rules make provision for heterosexual relationships outside marriage albeit in limited circumstances.

By comparison a lesbian or gay man admitted to the UK for temporary stay, who develops a strong relationship with a UK resident, is not allowed to remain on the basis of that relationship. Neither does a gay person's emotional commitment provide any ground for admission to the UK. As a result some gay people have been refused entry or have had to leave Britain despite close emotional ties here.

The Home Office have claimed that they cannot devise criteria to assess the strength and stability of long-term relationships in the case of gay people. Even if it were possible to construct some alternative test the Home Office claim they would not want gays to "queue jump" ahead of legitimate fiancés.

It is hard to understand why the assessment of gay relationships should be more difficult than the checking of marriages, which are subjected to official investigation to assess their genuineness (marriage documents are never sufficient in themselves). Nor would acknowledgement of gay relationships as a basis for entry to stay here necessarily advantage gay relationships over heterosexual ones.

THE RIGHT TO RESPECT FOR PRIVATE LIFE

The criminal laws on male homosexuality are a dramatic illustration of institutionalised obsession with sex. There exists an archaic web of statutory provisions and judicial rulings to ensnare thousands every year. Compared with the position of heterosexuals the law gives the police overwhelmingly more excuses to intrude into the personal lives of gay people.

The right to a sexual life is recognised as part of a young person's emergence into adulthood. "Adult" for male homosexuals means only those aged 21 years and over. This breach of the right to respect for private life is justified mainly by the spurious rationalisation that an individual's homosexual orientation may be attributed wholly or in part to seduction by another man. Girls also face risks of seduction by men. In fact there are probably greater pressures on them to have sex. Yet women are not *made* heterosexual by seduction, nor is there evidence that men become homosexual by seduction. Most experts agree that primary sexual orientation is fixed early in life and certainly before the age of 16.

Couples of opposite sexes – and lesbians – are presumed by law to be adult enough to have sex from the age of 16 (or 17 in the North of Ireland). The bizarre attitude of male legislators towards women's sexuality is evident from parliamentary debates on a Bill which attempted to criminalise lesbianism in 1921. It was claimed that the proposals were undesirable because they would have brought lesbianism "to the notice of women who had never heard of it, never thought of it, never dreamed of it".

The question of whether it is lawful under the European Convention on Human Rights to discriminate over the ages of consent between heterosexuals and male homosexuals has now been taken up by an English gay teenager. At the time of writing, his case is in its preliminary stages before the European Commission.

The law defines privacy in relation to homosexual activity so tightly that gay men are more likely than heterosexuals to run foul of the law. For example, sex between two men wherever it takes place is a crime if a third person is merely present. This provision justified a raid, reported by the *Guardian* in October 1982, when police officers arrested, detained and questioned thirty-seven gay men who were guests at a private birthday party in West London. No charges were brought yet they had to answer humiliating police questions about the minutiae of their sex lives. The host of the party has subsequently filed an application with the European Commission. In Cardiff the police have even secured convictions against three men accused of having had sex together at the home where one of them lived. Their lovemaking had been filmed on video, and the tape was discovered there some weeks later when the police called at the house and searched the rooms. Neither of these cases would have raised similarly serious legal repercussions had heterosexuals been involved.

There is no special law prohibiting strangers of opposite sexes "chatting up" one another in public or making passes. But when gay men do this it attracts the charge of persistently soliciting or importuning in a public place for immoral purposes under section 32 of the Sexual Offences Act 1956. In 1981, Lord Chief Justice Lane confirmed that although it is ultimately for the jury to decide, the phrase "immoral purposes" applies even to *lawful* homosexual activity in private.[10]

It appears that the purpose of this offence (originally brought onto the statute book in 1898) may have been to protect women in the streets. Whatever its original intention the law has for a long time transformed behaviour which is acceptable for heterosexual men in public into a crime when it is between gay men. No complainant or victim need be produced in court; there is no need of evidence that a member of the public was actually offended. It is even unnecessary for the police to show that anyone – other than the police that is – actually saw or was affected in any way by the alleged soliciting. Consequently most court cases are brought as a result of plain-clothes officers enticing or inviting attentions from suspected men.

This law is not a dead letter: in England and Wales convictions rose from 488 in 1977 to 1208 in 1980, an increase of 247 per cent. The Court of Appeal has ruled that section 32 should not be used against men who "kerb-crawl" women. The only reported conviction of a heterosexual man soliciting females was in respect of 14-year-old girls with whom sexual intercourse is, of course, a criminal offence.[11]

The Criminal Law Revision Committee's Working Paper on Soliciting published in 1983 merely underlined the law's double standards. On the one hand it recommended that the law in relation to homosexuals should remain largely unchanged, whilst in relation to heterosexual men an offence of accosting a woman and causing her annoyance was thought impractical because "it might bring within the ambit of the criminal law the amorous advances which are often made by young men to girls where adolescents meet for the purposes of getting to know one another". Official concern of this sort is completely absent in discussions about gay youth.

Clubs and discos are equally part of heterosexual and gay social life. Yet the legal position of gay clubs appears to be exceptionally uncertain and insecure. In 1982 Mr Justice Leonard speculated that "under my reading of the law as it presently stands the proprietor of a gay bar who openly advertises it as such or even who does nothing about homosexuals meeting there possibly for sexual purposes could be acting improperly". He went on to suggest that two co-proprietors of a gay club could be indicted on a charge of conspiring to corrupt public morals.[12] A Luton publican was refused a licence in November 1982 after magistrates were told that he had advertised his premises in a gay magazine. The police claimed that young men might be "at risk from homosexual drinkers".

By comparison with the policing of similar clubs for hetero-sexuals, gay clubs have been raided by the police in a way that suggests harassment. For example, when Northampton police raided a local gay club in 1980 all 300 members present were made to pose for police photographs. Those who refused had their heads held while it was done. They were warned that if they did not co-operate they would be arrested and charged with breach of the peace. Complaints were made to the Chief Constable who replied that such methods were "normal procedure".

The Home Office published in 1979 research on sexual offences which showed that of those people convicted of a homosexual offence in England and Wales, the vast majority had been involved in consenting behaviour. By contrast a majority of those convicted of a heterosexual offence had been involved in behaviour in which the victim/partner was not a willing participant.[13]

It is unjust that crimes to which the "victim" freely consented should be prosecuted and hypocritical that double standards are applied to heterosexual and homosexual activity. In the light of subsequent developments the defects of the 1967 Reform Act are now apparent.

At best the legal position of gay men's sexual relationships or contacts is uncertain and unclear in many circumstances. At worst the Act and associated legislation have become effective tools for prosecutions, and large numbers of gay men of all ages remain "sexual outlaws".

CONCLUSION

Although discrimination and prejudice cannot be combated by civil rights legislation alone, it can be used as part of a strategy to achieve this end. As Peter Newsom, the Chairman of the Commission for Racial Equality, once remarked, "You can't legislate for what people think. That requires a change in attitude. But you can say 'whatever you *think*, there are things you will not *do*'."

A significant civil liberties initiative was taken in 1981 when the Parliamentary Assembly of the Council of Europe (a body comprising members nominated by all the major European political parties including those in the UK) passed the first international political resolution on gay rights.

The resolution urged Member States where homosexual sexual acts between consenting adults are liable to criminal prosecution to abolish those laws and practices. The states were also urged to apply the same minimum age of consent for homosexual and heterosexual acts. It was recommended that governments should act positively on a broad front of issues by (1) ordering the destruction of existing special records on homosexuals and abolishing the practice of keeping records on homosexuals by the police or any other authority; (2) assuring equality of treatment for homosexuals with regard to employment, pay and job security, particularly in the public sector; (3) requesting the cessation of all compulsory medical action or research designed to alter sexual orientation of adults; (4) ensuring that custody, visiting rights and accommodation of children by their parents should not be restricted on the sole grounds of the homosexual tendencies of one of them; and (5) asking prison and other public authorities to be vigilant against the risk of rape, violence and sexual offences in prison.

This important step can be seen in the context of positive action already taken by individual European states to remove discrimination. Holland, Denmark, Norway, Sweden and most recently France have made the age of consent equal for everyone. Legislation has been introduced in Norway and in Holland to make public statements encouraging hatred, persecution or contempt of homosexuals unlawful. In addition many European police forces have drastically reduced the amount of time wasted watching and harassing gay men.

The judgment of the European Court of Human Rights in 1981 in the Northern Ireland gay rights case brought by Jeffrey Dudgeon was a landmark, being the first international judicial ruling to condemn the use of law as a means of repressing homosexuality.[14] It remains to be seen whether the gay cases currently being considered by the European Commission will become pathbreakers in the rest of this country.

European libertarianism does create a positive pressure for change. In Britain, however, backward attitudes, particularly in

Parliament and the law, diminish the likelihood of spontaneous law reform. So, too, does the fact that many humanising concessions made in the sixties and seventies are being whittled away under the excuse of combating economic decline.

The law is sometimes the cutting edge of social attitudes and sometimes the tail-end. What one does in relation to the law is only part of a general approach. And to challenge discriminatory social attitudes is a very fundamental long-term task. On the question of gay rights, deep inroads will have to be made into public and Parliamentary ignorance, apathy and hostility before there is sufficient general support to outlaw discriminatory behaviour and promote equality.

The times ahead will be difficult on all fronts of civil liberties. As increasing attacks take up the resources of limited defences, it is still vital that the rights of gay women and men remain firmly and prominently on the agenda.

NOTES

1. Pluto Press, 1982.
2. *Saunders* v *Scottish National Camps Association Ltd* [1981] Industrial Relations Law Reports, p. 277.
3. *Boychuck* v *H J Symons Holdings Ltd* [1977] Industrial Relations Law Reports, p. 395.
4. *Knuller* v *Director of Public Prosecutions* [1973] Appeal Cases, p. 435.
5. *R* v *Lemon and Gay News Ltd* [1979] Appeal Cases, p.617.
6. See Paul Crane, *Gays and the Law*, (London, Pluto Press 1982), pp. 94-5.
7. *W* v *W*, Court of Appeal, 3rd and 4th November 1976, unreported.
8. *Re P (a Minor)*, Court of Appeal, 21st July 1982, unreported.
9. *Re D (an Infant)* [1977] 2 Weekly Law Reports, p. 79.
10. *R* v *Grey*, *The Times*, 27th November 1981.
11. *R* v *Dodd* (1978) 66 Criminal Appeal Reports, p. 87.
12. See Paul Crane, *op. cit.*, p. 31.
13. Home Office, *Sexual Offences, Consent and Sentencing* (London, HMSO, 1979).
14. *Dudgeon* v *United Kingdom* [1981] 4 European Human Rights Reports, p. 149.

17

CIVIL LIBERTIES AND YOUTH

NORMAN TUTT

The concept of *Youth* as a separate social category, whose members require specific protection or control by law, is a social construct which changes over time. Since it is a social construct, not clearly defined or described in any legislation or administrative guidance, but all the same generally accepted to exist, the boundaries of the definition are very loose and often contradictory.

The way in which changes occur over time is clearly demonstrated by the gradual raising of the minimum age at which children are allowed to leave school which has occurred throughout this century. It would be generally accepted that a person in full-time secondary education was not fully independent and that the transition from school to work has in the past been seen by British society as an important barrier between childhood and adulthood. In this century that barrier has moved from the age of twelve years by gradual stages to sixteen years; and with these moves, indeed most likely precipitating them, has been a changed view of childhood.

Yet these changes are not consistent across all social policy areas and therefore lead to marked contradictions. The age of majority by law is the eighteenth birthday and yet at the age of seventeen years youthful offenders are dealt with by the adult courts, and at the age of sixteen a young person can legally leave school and seek employment but not incur debts in his or her own name.

For the purposes of this essay youth will be defined as those aged up to seventeen years and will incorporate a span of life which covers both childhood and adolescence.

This statement itself reveals one of the anomalies involved in discussing the rights of children or youth, namely that the definition of "childhood" or "youth" is one made by adults and attributed to a

289

minority group of society, and yet it may be a definition not shared or accepted by that minority. Thus it is adults who decide at what age children and young people may indulge in sexual behaviours. This decision is not based on the evidence of either the individual youths' or youth's general sexual development but on adults' views on the propriety of sexual behaviours at certain ages. These adult views show little logic or consistency; for example whilst it is illegal for a girl under sixteen to have sexual intercourse, after her sixteenth birthday it is legitimate. Obviously an arbitrary age limit of this form takes no account of gradual sexual development. Why should the girl require the protection of the law because of her physical or mental immaturity one day and yet require no protection the very next day after her sixteenth birthday? Moreover for males the matter is even more irrational since whilst heterosexual intercourse is legitimate after the girl's sixteenth birthday, homosexual relationships are outlawed until after the age of twenty one, despite the age of majority being eighteen years.

The confusion created by arbitrary age definitions of childhood or youth must lead to asking the question "Is age a satisfactory classification upon which civil liberties should be based?" The different standards of rights which operate for children and adults may be justifiable but on what grounds? The major basis for the operation of different standards is that the undeveloped physique, intellect and maturity of the child require that it be protected in many ways. The United Nations Declaration of the Rights of the Child published more than twenty years ago clearly illustrates the case for protection, e.g. Principle 2:

The child shall enjoy special protection, and shall be given opportunities and facilities by law and by other means, to enable him to develop physically, mentally, morally, spiritually and socially in a healthy and normal manner and in conditions of freedom and dignity.

In general young people are seen as the responsibility of their parents and therefore have few rights of their own. The relationship between parent and child has however changed dramatically over the past four centuries. A study by Pinchbeck and Hewitt[1] illustrates the ways in which children were "legally the property of their parents" to be abused (Mrs Gaskell, the nineteenth century novelist, claimed to be an enlightened mother since it was not until her daughter Marianne was three and a half years and still failing to read that she disciplined her with a horse whip for her failures) or used and exploited by being put to work in dangerous and insanitary working conditions rejected by adults; for example chimney boys. There is no doubt that attitudes of parents have changed dramatically but the core concept of the child as the rightful property of the parent still flourishes. Mia Kellmer-Pringle, the former Director of the National Children's Bureau, summed up current parental attitudes cleverly when she wrote "a baby completes a family, rather like a TV set or a fridge . . . a child belongs to his parents like their other possessions over which they may exercise exclusive rights".[2] It is this attitude of the child as rightful property of the parents which has led to the stress on the significance of the "blood-tie" between parent and child which has been central to much psychiatric and social work thinking.[3] This stress on the "blood-tie" has operated against the development of a rational system of children's rights. For older children and youths the child-as-property argument has been shifted slightly to that of the child's behaviour being the responsibility of the parent. This stress on parental responsibility has been strengthened recently by the "Law and Order" policy adopted by the Conservative Government since 1979. This government continually stresses the need for parents to take more responsibility for the actions and behaviour of their children, so much so that sections 26–28 of the Criminal Justice Act 1982 place a duty on the court to order that any fine, compensation or costs be awarded against the child's parent or guardian unless that parent or guardian cannot be found or it is unreasonable to do so in the circumstances, and raise the amount of recognisances to be taken from parents to £500.

The general attitude that children are the responsibility of their parents means that civil liberties for children are obscured either in legislation binding on the parent or in more generalised approaches. A child therefore has no legal right to education but the parents by law have a responsibility to ensure their children receive an efficient full-time education up to a certain age. Where parents are unable to discharge their responsibilities for whatever reason the state is empowered to intervene. The courts can make orders under various statutes to remove the parental rights from the parents to the local authority. This in effect means that the child is still seen as a kind of "property" which can be transferred by law from an "incompetent" owner, the parent, to an allegedly competent owner "the state". Under the Children Act 1975 "the state" in the form of the local authority is now required to consider the wishes of the child or young person as to his or her placement. However in practice many of the children are seen as being too immature to express clear opinions.

Connected with the above power of the state to intervene in children's lives if parents are demonstrably unable to cope, is the state's powers to restrict certain activities of young people in order to protect the young person's physical or emotional development. The state has legislation to restrict the employment of children, to restrict children from consuming alcohol or smoking or indulging in sexual behaviour. However these powers to protect children are often closely connected with, and, at times, undifferentiated from, the major concern with older youth – that is the state's concern to protect its citizens from apparent unruly youth. Much legislation therefore shades rapidly from protection of children to the control of youth.

It would be easy to imagine that the problems created by boisterous adolescent behaviour in the community and the related problem of its control when it reaches unacceptable levels is a twentieth century phenomenon. The appearance of large scale "pop" festivals, riots at football matches, quasi-political marches, or disorders in inner city areas appear to be closely linked with the rise in the official statistics of violent crime by the young, and with the anxiety felt in the community about the control of violence. Social commentators ascribe the increase in violence variously to the breakdown of the family, the increase in viewing television, the raising of the school leaving age, or the decline in formalised religions, amongst a range of popular scapegoats.

However, many historians who take a rather more detached and perhaps longer term view than those who wish to rally popular feeling, are unconvinced that the problem is necessarily any greater now than previously; indeed a number believe that the real change is in the way society views violence as a social problem rather than a change in the real incidence of violence. For example John Robottom cites the following case:[4]

Mr T has been ten months out of work. He lives with his mother and explains that the cause of his distress was a quarrel with three friends in a train while leaving the races. They were all drunk, began to quarrel, and then he found himself on the line and an engine went over his hand . . . his last offence was breaking his mother-in-law's leg and assaulting his wife for which he received six months.

As Robottom points out:

The social homily given by the Charity Organisation Society on this case is not a condemnation of violent behaviour as the scourge of the period (1896), but a condemnation of betting. "To those who regard betting as one of the legitimate pleasures of the working class we recommend the study of the following case." It is interesting that the past eight decades have seen redefinition of betting as acceptable social behaviour, and the emergence of drunken brawling as a social problem of grave concern.

Robottom continues:

It requires only the quickest of skimmings through the novels of Dickens, the reporting of Charles Booth or Henry Mayhew or a modern account such as Kellow Chesney's *The Victorian Underworld* to recognise that violence was a predominant characteristic of life in the lower of the two nations of the time. Yet it is quite startlingly impossible to find any attempt to describe it as a distinct phenomenon or to ponder the causes and nature of violent behaviour as such.

Peter Marsh[5] makes a similar point in his chapter on "Aggro in History" namely that the problem of violence between young people and the community is a problem of some long standing. He also clearly illustrates that violent behaviour was not, as Robottom implied, the sole prerogative of the "lower classes". Marsh quotes:

As Knipe and Maclay point out in *The Dominant Man*, noble duellists did get killed. In fact, in the space of time between 1589 and 1608 some 8,000 were killed in France alone. But, "since the great majority of such affairs of honour were not fatal, these figures do not give a true reflection of the number of duels actually fought in France at that time".

Marsh, as with other commentators, (Pearson, Hall *et al.*)[6] goes on to describe the more recent fashions of adolescent or teenage problems, pointing out that the labels, mode of dress and language may change, but the basic problem of boisterous, at times even riotous, behaviour of groups of working class youth recurs with unerring frequency whether under the guise of teddy boys, mods and rockers, skinheads or punks.

To show that a problem has a long and established historical tradition does not of course make it any the less a problem, more especially since some form of action by state agencies is apparently required to contain and if possible control that problem in a different way. It may help us to accept that violence amongst the young is not the first stage in the destruction of our "civilised society". It may force us to question bland generalisations that the problem is on the increase. It may do all of these, but it does not remove the necessity for official action.

JUVENILE JUSTICE

Social policy for the control and treatment of youthful offenders is a useful illustration of what civil liberties are accorded to young people more generally. It is a useful illustration first because it is an area in which many young people will come into direct contact with the state agencies. It is known from self-report studies[7] that offending behaviour is in fact "normal" behaviour of young people living and growing up in urban conditions. It is known from the Official Criminal Statistics that approximately a third of all detected crime is committed by young people under the age of seventeen years. Thus for both the police and young people it is an area of constant contact and inevitably conflict. Moreover the juvenile criminal justice system neatly illustrates the dilemma of trying to protect the rights and civil liberties of the young person, and yet at the same time to exercise paternalism and protect the young people from their own behaviour and its inevitable social consequences. This is most clearly demonstrated by those behaviours which are dealt with by the court, which are only of significance because of the person's age, what is known in the USA as "status" offences – for example truancy, unlawful sexual intercourse, absconding from home and institutions. These are behaviours which have no adult equivalent.

Legislation affecting the control and treatment of young offenders over the past two decades has in the main been little influenced by the research that has been produced during the period. Instead the legislation has tended to be based on philosophies or ideologies which are deeply rooted in the culture of the United Kingdom.

Occasionally research has attempted to examine the relevance of the philosophy and comment on the effectiveness of policies developed from the philosophy. The two basic philosophies are those of justice or welfare. It is of great interest to analysts of social policy to observe that within the small geographical confines of the United Kingdom a range of systems exist. Northern Ireland has declared its future policy to be based firmly on the justice philosophy, Scotland has committed itself to welfare, and England and Wales has shifted within a decade from welfare to justice. This essay attempts to examine the implications of these two philosophies, their impact and effectiveness on social policy for youth.

However before embarking on an examination of the two philosophies it is worth noting that the differences in philosophies may be more substantive than the differences in outcomes.

The 1960s saw the major growth in the philosophy of welfare being applied to juvenile offenders. In the White Papers and discussions of that time the civil liberties of the child were almost totally ignored. The offence was not to be accorded any great significance but instead seen as "a cry for help", indicating that the child's needs were not being met. These needs were to be assessed by social workers and other professionals and the child allocated to services which would meet those needs regardless of the type or seriousness of the offence or indeed the civil liberty of the child. Thus the Children and Young Persons Act 1969 makes no mention of secure accommodation, its use or safeguards for children's civil liberties when placed in it, since children were to be placed in such units on the decision of professional social workers on the basis of the child's needs, and not on the basis of an offence. Moreover the young person could be kept in such accommodation for as long as necessary to meet his or her needs.

By the late 1970s the net outcome of this unrestrained welfare approach was that more young people than ever were locked up in secure accommodation and prison department establishments, and the growth of numbers in such provision was greatly out of proportion to the growth of juvenile crime. Therefore it seemed a matter of relatively simple logic that this trend could be reversed by merely placing greater emphasis on the judicial approach using the court to constrain social workers, and, by protecting the child's civil liberties through legal representation, to reduce the use of custody. This approach also fitted in neatly with the Conservative Government's greater emphasis on "law and order", since it stressed the significance of the offender, reinforced the powers of the court as opposed to social workers and reintroduced retributive sanctions – "short sharp shocks". This led to the passing of the Criminal Justice Act 1982 which embodies many of these views. The Act, in so far as it affects juveniles, was implemented on 24th May 1983. Unfortunately although it is early days to judge so soon after the legislation was passed, the net effect seems to be an even further increase in the numbers of young people going into secure units and prison department establishments. By returning powers to magistrates, the legislation has produced a backlash effect which is not overridden by increased stress on civil liberties.

The vast majority of offending behaviour by youth is dealt with in the juvenile magistrates court in England and Wales. These courts are charged with considering both the protection of the public and the welfare of the child. More recently with the passing and implementation of the Criminal Justice Act 1982 the emphasis has shifted to the protection of the public.

Since the outcomes of the justice and welfare approaches do not as yet seem spectacularly different it is worth examining the two philosophies to see if one or other gives greater scope for protection of civil liberties and the growth of a juvenile jurisprudence.

THE JUSTICE MODEL

Many of the arguments for a justice model derive from the American Bar Association's Commission on Juvenile Justice Standards. United Kingdom interpretations of these views can be found in Morris and Giller,[8] and Taylor, Lacey and Bracken.[9] From all of these sources certain features emerge.

Firstly, proponents of justice see offending behaviour as a matter of individual choice affected by opportunity. They stress the notion of free will, that the individual is in control of his own behaviour, that if an opportunity for criminal behaviour arises it is a matter of individual choice whether or not the individual commits an offence. Research support for this view can be found in the Home Office Research Unit Report *Crime as Opportunity* (1976)[10] where a number of research illustrations are given of the prevention of crime by reduction of opportunity. For example, the wide-scale introduction of steering locks on cars reduce the opportunity for car theft and therefore the amount of illegal driving and taking away. The use of lighting and vandalproof materials reduces the number of thefts from telephone kiosks.

Secondly, if offending behaviour is a rational response to certain situations then it is reasonable to hold the individual responsible and accountable for his actions. This view is qualified for certain people, most notably in England and Wales for those less than ten years of age who cannot be prosecuted for a criminal offence and for those adults able to show "diminished responsibility". The arbitrary nature of these exclusions is clearly shown by the fact that the age of prosecution in Scotland is eight years, in the Republic of Ireland seven years and yet in much of Europe as high as fifteen years. The difficulty in proving diminished responsibility within a court of law was recently illustrated in the trial of Peter Sutcliffe when the opinions of three psychiatrists were rejected by the jury.

Thirdly, the justice model accepts that proof of the commission of an offence is the sole justification for intervention and sole basis for punishment after a finding of guilt. This principle has certain crucial spin-offs since it leads to the necessity for legal representation of the accused and an adversarial courts system in which evidence is challenged and standards of proof demanded.

Fourthly, behaviour likely to attract legal intervention and associated sanctions under the law should be clearly and specifically defined in the criminal law. This leads to obvious difficulties since new deviant behaviour may emerge which does not figure in the current legislation; a recent example would be glue-sniffing, behaviour which in itself is not illegal and therefore cannot lead to judicial intervention.

THE WELFARE MODEL

Within the penal system the welfare model appears in its purest form in services for children and young people, but there are remnants of such thinking within the adult field. The welfare approach to youthful offenders is not, as it is often portrayed, an invention of the 1980s. It has a long and respectable history in legislation and action. For example in 1790 the "Philanthropic Society" was established; the Society existed "for the purpose of receiving the destitute infant children of convicts, and to rescue them from the vice and infamy to which the example and sentence of their parents exposed them, and for the reform of such young criminals whose youth gave promise of amendment by impressing upon their minds principles of morality and religion and instructing them in useful occupations to enable them to gain an honest livelihood and become beneficial members of society".[11] Also the 1908 Children Act, popularly dubbed the Children's Charter, was intended to establish a more child-orientated legal system with specialist juvenile magistrates who were required to consider the welfare of the children as well as administer the law. Moreover, the Act began the merger of the industrial schools for the "deprived" and the reformatories for the "depraved" by allowing transfer between the two types of institution without recourse to a court order. The main attributes of the welfare model are:

Firstly, criminal behaviour is clearly linked with social, economic, and physical disadvantage. Therefore any state intervention should be aimed at alleviating these disadvantages as much as, if not more than, punishing the individual offender. The bout of unrest by young people in inner city areas in 1981 clearly illustrates the principles of a welfare approach. The causes of the disturbances were put down variously to unemployment, poor housing, lack of recreational facilities and lead poisoning from exhaust fumes, all of which lead to an argument for amelioration of social conditions as opposed to punishment of the individual miscreants.

Secondly, in its extreme form the welfare approach would argue that delinquency is a "pathological" condition and therefore the individual should be exonerated from personal guilt. This underlies a plea of "diminished responsibility" for an adult but is common to much thinking about delinquency which suggests that children from deprived family and social backgrounds are inevitably impelled into delinquency and have little or no control over their own destinies. Research findings which support this view of delinquent behaviour are easy to find but perhaps the best validated were those of West and Farrington[12] in their study of over 400 boys growing up in an inner urban area. They found that the five factors most closely correlated with (but this does not mean causing) delinquency were: low family income, large family size, a parent with a criminal record, unsatisfactory child rearing by the parents and comparatively low intelligence of the child.

Thirdly, the welfare model, although accepting that social

conditions affect the individual, then adheres to the "medical" model of operation, going through stages of assessment (diagnosis) and treatment of the individual. This leads to a stress on assessing the child's problems, and the development of individual treatment plans, many of which focus on behaviour not shown to be directly related to offending – for example teaching the child to read, trade training, personal hygiene, social manners.

Fourthly, this approach advocates a single unified system of services for children and young people with no differentiation between offenders and non-offenders, since, it is argued, all children have the same basic needs, and the offending behaviour is seen merely as the presenting problem, which should not therefore lead to a fundamentally different treatment.

Fifthly, the model contains a paradox since it accepts that treatment to be effective must be voluntary but *in extremis* rejects notions of guilt and innocence and enforces treatment. For example the drug addict may be compelled to undergo treatment for *his own good* regardless of whether or not he is charged with an offence. The voluntary nature of treatment is also of long standing. Who could dismiss the words of the Reverend Turner writing in 1845 of the work of the "Philanthropic Society":

Voluntary, not forced good conduct must be the object we aim at; for this alone will last. If we render the boy dependent on the superintendence and discipline which we subject him to, he will be as but a child needing strings; and when the artificial support which he has been used to leaning upon is necessarily withdrawn on his going forth into the world, he will be liable to fall at every step he takes in life.

In summary the welfare approach stresses the offender as victim of circumstances, the importance of individualised treatment and therefore discretionary decision making and the need for intervention to be indeterminate and based on the progress of the individual.

No juvenile justice system is a pure example of the justice or welfare models; inevitably the operational system emerges as a compromise which attempts to be fair and differentiate for individual circumstances. Therefore even the most ardent proponents of a justice model (Morris and Giller)[13] allow for pleas of mitigation to explain individual circumstances, likewise the leading welfare systems (e.g. Social Work (Scotland) Act 1968) allow for pleas of not guilty to be determined in a court of law. However, in order that the debate continue in an attempt to refine the juvenile justice system, it is important to examine the criticisms that have been made of both models and to evaluate these criticisms.

A CRITIQUE

The justice model stresses the importance of an adversarial system, and to criticise such a system is to invoke the wrath of the legal establishment. However, it should be remembered that other systems are possible and seem to be as efficient. For example, in France the adversarial system is rejected in favour of an inquisitorial system in which the judge is responsible for uncovering the truth rather than the truth seen to emerge from a system of accusation and defence. The main criticism of the adversarial system is that it is not primarily concerned with establishing the "truth" of guilt or innocence, but instead places the onus on the prosecution to prove the offence. The defence lawyer's concern is to defend his client and not to uncover the truth; acknowledgement of this has come from some unlikely sources, who have as a result been massively attacked. The most obvious example is Sir Robert Mark, a former Commissioner of the Metropolitan Police, who caused a major stir in the legal dovecotes when in the Dimbleby Lecture in November 1973 he stated:

The criminal and his lawyers take every advantage of these technical rules (i.e. the rules of criminal law). Every effort is made to find some procedural mistake which will allow the wrongdoer to slip through the net. If the prosecution evidence is strong the defence frequently resorts to attacks on prosecution witnesses . . . In many criminal trials the deciding factor is not the actual evidence but the contest between a skilled advocate and a policeman or other witnesses.[14]

Such a system may be thought totally inappropriate for dealing with children and young people, more especially since the vast majority plead guilty.

The justice approach also stresses the principle of equality. It is difficult to see how this can ever be achieved. Firstly the constable apprehending the juvenile has, and will have, an enormous amount of discretion in determining both whether an offence has been committed and what offence the child or young person should be charged with.[15] This is merely the beginnings of discretion. It is known that there are marked variations in cautioning rates among police forces which cannot be explained by different patterns of crime. Moreover many of the decisions, particularly in civil as opposed to criminal cases, hinge on fine professional judgements, e.g. the definition of mental and emotional retardation, or physical abuse by the parent as opposed to reasonable punishment.

It may well be that ideally these variations would be reduced, certainly they could be by constraining the discretion by administrative control. For example the Report of the Parliamentary Penal Affairs Group[16] recommends that all first and second time offenders would receive an automatic caution, thereby reducing police discretion. However, other attempts aimed at reducing variations in sentencing have made little progress, for example an agreed sliding scale of fines for speeding offences. All this suggests that the principle of discretion, which is contradictory to that of equality in sentencing, is deeply maintained within the criminal justice system.

The principle of proportionality – the punishment should fit the crime – presupposes a consensus on a rank order of offences. There is some research evidence to suggest this is achievable. Sellin and Wolfgang,[17] working in the United States of America, were concerned to produce a scale which would be able to compare the crimes committed within one year with the differing crimes committed in another year in order to assess whether or not there had been an increase in the seriousness of the crimes committed. They produced a weighted scale of crimes that allowed different crimes to be compared with regard to their seriousness.

A high degree of concordance between raters was recorded, with homicide and crimes against the person ranking highest and damage to public property low. However, such rankings can be radically affected by changes in social attitude and publicity. For example changes in legislation and public attitude have affected views on homosexuality and recent publicity over cases of rape has led to demands for mandatory prison sentences. While there may be widespread agreement on the ranking of criminal acts, the agreement probably breaks down when circumstances of individual offenders are made known and when forms of disposal are linked with the criminal acts. For example the work of Thorpe *et al.*[18] in applying criteria to care orders suggests that no clear consensus on the factors crucial to the making of a care order exists even within the social work profession.

The welfare system can be criticised on the following grounds. Firstly, the view of the offender as a victim of circumstances. Although it may generally be valid that social, economic and personal disadvantage correlate highly with officially recorded juvenile offending behaviour, there is no evidence that this is an adequate causal explanation of crime. Thus the work of West and Farrington[19] along with other research accords with the everyday experience of police, probation officers and social workers, namely that the juvenile offenders who appear in court or before panels mainly come from deprived, socially disadvantaged backgrounds. However, the converse is not necessarily true, namely that coming from an equally disadvantaged background ensures a child becomes delinquent.[20] It may well be that the correlation between crime and disadvantage exists because of the different and discretionary response of the official agencies. The police may operate more strongly in areas of social disadvantage, and therefore catch more young people from those areas, courts may be more likely to find young people from those areas guilty, and social workers are more likely to wish to intervene in these children's deprived lives, and so on.

Secondly, the principle of individual treatment is a myth. It is argued that there is no proven treatment of delinquent behaviour and that the treaters tend to concentrate on behaviour that is open to intervention but has no proven connection with delinquent behaviour.

The final criticism of the welfare approach is that indeterminacy of sentence to allow for individual progress in treatment actually leads to longer periods of incarceration than determinate sentencing under a justice model. Moreover research on admissions to secure units suggests that the children referred to secure units were more likely to be the "failures" of existing institutions, i.e. those children who were persistently disruptive or persistently absconded from open local authority establishments, or List D schools (a prolongation of care) than children who posed a threat to the community through dangerous or violent behaviour.

The battle between the supporters of justice and welfare rages, but like all battles it is more on grounds of ideology than on empirical evidence. It is unlikely that research will ever be able to help resolve the battle by proving conclusively one approach is more effective than another, more especially since it is not primarily a research problem but an attitudinal or political problem. However, it may well be the battle is not only in vain but is in itself damaging, since it diverts all concerned from the reality of the current operation of the juvenile justice system.

It is interesting to note that in Scotland where a clear and committed welfare based system has been in operation for more than a decade there are two clear trends. One is the decreasing numbers of children being referred to List D schools, which has led to increased under-occupancy and moves to close establishments. The second is the small but significant increase in secure accommodation within the child care sector. In England and Wales, operating a confusion of welfare and justice, due to failure to implement fully the Children and Young Persons Act 1969, the numbers of young people referred to Community Homes with Education (the List D school equivalent) have declined rapidly and approximately 25 per cent of the 120 CHEs have now been closed. Alongside this there has been an increase in the number of secure units. This shift from traditional open training establishment to a mixture of unspecified community services and increased secure accommodation is also occurring in Northern Europe and Northern America. In Northern Ireland the Black Committee (1979)[21] recognised the reality of these shifts and recommended complete closure of all training schools, their function to be absorbed by community based services, backed up by a single secure unit.

The major difference between the English and Scottish experience is that in the latter the clear separation between the welfare and criminal justice system has blocked children passing into the penal system. In England and Wales where the welfare and justice systems intermingle a substantial number of young people have moved into the penal system, some 7,000 per annum.

The steady development both of the concept of childhood and youth, and their need for welfare approaches continued relatively unquestioned from the 1908 Children Act, to the 1933 Children and Young Persons Act on to the 1948 Children Act and the 1969 Children and Young Persons Act.[22]

However the 1970s saw the welfare approaches coming under

increasing attacks both from civil libertarians and law and order advocates. The first argued that welfare was too intrusive, allowing the state to intervene in individuals' lives on questionable pretexts, and also was in danger of backfiring – for example more and more children were being locked up in secure accommodation "for their own good" without being placed before a court of law (See Taylor, Lacey and Bracken, 1979).[23] The law and order advocates also attacked welfare approaches but on different grounds, namely that it had failed to stem rising youthful crime and had removed powers from "responsible" courts who were concerned to protect the public from irresponsible social workers whose only concern was the individual offender.

Those pressures led to the 1980 White Paper *Young Offenders*[24] – in which the consensus on welfare was finally broken and the social construct of youth dramatically redefined.

There are several features other than the content of the Young Offenders White Paper worthy of comment, since they indicate certain substantial shifts in thinking and policy. First, the very title is significant. In the 1960s White Papers were issued with the titles *The Child, The Family and the Young Offender* and *Children in Trouble*. Both titles indicate a view of juvenile offending, in which what is stressed is *the child*, with its connotations of immaturity and reduced individual responsibility. The title of the earlier White Paper hints at an underlying causal relationship between the child and his family and subsequent delinquent behaviour. The later White Paper plays down delinquency and uses the less emotive euphemism of "trouble", i.e. trouble at school, trouble with the police, emotional troubles. Both these White Papers referred continually to children and stubbornly refused to pander to public concern about juvenile crime. Thus, from the 1969 White Paper: "Much misbehaviour by children is part of the process of growing up, but some has more deep seated causes" (p. 16, para. 49). The 1980 White Paper not only devoted its first ten pages to the Young Adult Offender, but when discussing children it continually refers to juveniles, juvenile crime, and juvenile offending. The image of children misbehaving has gone; instead "The Government shares the general public concern about the level of juvenile offending" (p. 11, para. 34).

These features are extremely important. In the early seventies, when responsibility for Children's Services was transferred from the Home Office to the Department of Health and Social Security, consistent attempts were made to erode the division between the "deprived and depraved". Juvenile offenders were seen first as children with the same personal, social and educational needs as all other children; they were only secondly offenders who might need control. The emphasis on their immaturity has now been abandoned. The very fact that the 1980 White Paper dealt both with the young adult offender and the juvenile offenders without any clear differentiation suggests that offending is now the main focus rather than childhood.

The Criminal Justice Act 1982 clearly embodies these changed attitudes:

introducing determinate sentencing through: youth custody orders for 15–21 year olds; detention centre orders for 14–21 year olds; charge and control orders for children in the care of the local authority; and curfew orders on 10–17 year olds; and
limiting the discretion of welfare by: establishing criteria for the making of care orders; establishing criteria for the use of secure accommodation; and placement in a secure unit being dependent upon a court order.

Moreover one of the "spin-offs" from this return to justice is the young persons' right to legal representation before being removed from home either as punishment, in the case of a custodial sentencing, or for their own benefit, in the case of a care order.

The concentration in this essay is on the changes in the way society responds to disorderly youth. These changes however are important since they highlight an example of the changes which are occurring more generally in society's view of youth and their civil liberties.

It is clear, from the case study of the juvenile justice system, that whereas society some fifty years ago saw youth as an investment for the future who had the "right" of access to education and vocational opportunities and family or substitute family life, and that this consensus existed post World War II and into the early 1960s (see for example the Plowden and Robbins Reports on education, Albermarle Report on the youth leisure services and the Ingleby Report on child care), the 1980s see a fracturing of the consensus and greater stress laid on the need to control youth rather than provide opportunities. Much of this shift in attitude may have arisen from changes in the labour market. It is significant that throughout the European Community unemployment has fallen disproportionately upon the under-25-year-olds where it is estimated to be over 25 per cent. In the United Kingdom unemployment amongst 16-to-19-year-olds is very much higher. Therefore the need is not for the state to encourage and develop youth but instead for it to guarantee its control.

This pressure for control not only falls disproportionately on youth but further reinforces institutional inequalities already in existence. Thus while unemployment for school leavers generally is estimated at approximately 60 per cent, unemployment for black school leavers is significantly higher and in some regions or sub-regions estimated to be as high as 90 per cent. A similar phenomenon can be seen in the issue of crime control generally. Indeed in much discussion on youthful behaviour the term black youth has become synonymous with young offender and black youths are becoming further stigmatised and marginalised.

Moreover the increased demand for control can lead to restrictions on youth specifically, for example the introduction in the Criminal Justice Act 1982 of curfew orders; no equivalent exists for adults. A similar phenomenon can be seen in the debate over corporal punishment which, although outlawed long ago for adult prisoners and members of the armed forces, continues in schools throughout the country despite pressure from the European Court of Human Rights. This continuation is always justified by the need for control; it is argued that schools would rapidly collapse into chaos if corporal punishment were outlawed. This argument persists despite evidence to the contrary and appears to override any consideration that children should not experience greater punishments than those allowed by law for adults.

One protection for youth faced by greater controls is the development of rights for children and youth. The International Year of the Child precipitated the movement, and the establishment of the Children's Legal Centre which grew out of the IYC would seem to guarantee a momentum for the movement. Already the Children's Legal Centre has won some notable victories over the use of secure accommodation and corporal punishment by threatening to test government policies in the courts.

As the need for further control continues so does the need for clearer rights for young people emerge. Again if the juvenile justice system is an example it appears that greater controls are accompanied by pressure for greater protections. This may be best achieved by clearer statements of civil liberties for those who inhabit the limbo land between dependent children and independent adults. It is hoped that the future will see the development of a juvenile jurisprudence in which lawyers, courts and civil libertarians recognise the need that rules of law relevant to adults be tempered by the special circumstances and requirements of youth in Britain in the next two decades.

NOTES

1. I Pinchbeck and M Hewitt, *Children in English Society* (London, Routledge and Kegan Paul, 1973).
2. M Kellmer-Pringle, *The Needs of Children* (2nd ed., London, Hutchinson, 1980).
3. See, for example, J Bowlby, *Child Care and the Growth of Love* (Harmondsworth, Penguin, 1953).
4. J Robottom, "History of Violence" In N Tutt (ed.), *Violence*, (London, HMSO, 1976).
5. P Marsh, *Aggro: the Illusion of Violence* (London, Dent, 1978).
6. G Pearson, "In Defence of Hooliganism" In N Tutt (ed.), *Violence* (London, HMSO, 1976); S Hall and A Jefferson (eds.), *Resistance through Rituals* (London, Hutchinson, 1979).
7. W A Belson, *Juvenile Theft: the Causal Factors* (London, Harper and Row, 1975).
8. A Morris, H Giller, A Sinclair and C Green, *Juvenile Justice* (Lancaster University, Centre for Youth, Crime and Community, 1980).
9. L Taylor, R Lacey and D Bracken, *In Whose Best Interest?* (London, Cobden Trust, 1979).
10. P Mayhew, R V G Clarke, A Sturman and J M Hough, *Crime as Opportunity – Home Office Research Study No. 34* (London, HMSO, 1976).
11. J Carlebach, *Caring for Children in Trouble* (London: Routledge and Kegan Paul, 1970).
12. D West and D Farrington, *Who Becomes Delinquent?* (London, Heinemann, 1973).
13. *Op. cit.,* note 4.
14. R Mark, *In the Office of Constable* (London, Collins, 1978).
15. See N S Tutt, "Back on the Beat in Skem.", *Community Care,* July 1980.
16. Parliamentary Penal Affairs Group, *Young Offenders – A Strategy for the Future* (London, Barry Rose, 1981).
17. T Sellin and M E Wolfgang, *The Measurement of Delinquency* (New York, J Wiley, 1964).

18. D Thorpe, C Green and D Smith, *Punishment and Welfare* (University of Lancaster, Centre for Youth, Crime and Community, 1979).
19. *Op. cit.*, note 8.
20. H Wilson, "Parental supervision: a neglected aspect of delinquency" *British Journal of Criminology* 20 (1980), pp. 203-235.
21. *Report of the Children and Young Persons Review Group* (Belfast, HMSO, 1979).
22. *Op. cit.*, note 7.
23. *Op. cit.*, note 5.
24. Home Office, Department of Health and Social Security, and Welsh Office, *Young Offenders* (Cmnd. 8045) (HMSO, London, 1980).

18

MENTAL PATIENTS AND CIVIL LIBERTIES

TONY SMYTHE

In comparison with other citizens and consumers of health and social services, mental patients have suffered lower standards both of civil liberty and service provision.

Some random examples indicate the scale of the differences. They do not have the same access to the courts, their freedom can be removed by administrative and professional decision as well as judicial process, their evidence may be disregarded in court, they cannot in many cases choose or refuse treatment or a particular medical practitioner, they can be deprived of their driving licence and, when detained in institutions, be subject to restrictions on movement or social contact and control over their property. The discrepancies were even greater before the modest but hard-won reforms introduced by the Mental Health (Amendment) Act 1982 came into effect in 1983 – patients were denied legal aid to dispute their detention, could not register to vote and were subject to censorship of their correspondence and even less freedom to choose or refuse treatment.

There is a dimension of common sense which would justify these and other restrictions because of the nature of the mental illnesses, which may seriously impair the judgment of those they afflict, cause behaviour which may present danger to themselves or others or create an obvious and urgent need for care, protection or treatment. Certainly, few would argue that there should be no curtailment of classic civil liberties if there is a risk to life, property or the normal functioning of the community. Such situations are real enough if rare. However, the fear has been that the balance has been tilted too far against the individual's rights and expectations without sufficient safeguards such as the independent review of administrative and professional decisions.

This view was denied and fought strongly by Government, professionals and some relatives, but the extent of the reforms contained in the Mental Health (Amendment) Act 1982, which probably did not go far enough, indicate that the case for more and better safeguards could not reasonably be denied.

How was it that the injustices which have now been admitted were allowed to persist, who was responsible and who promoted change, are more reforms needed, and who are these mental patients anyway?

The language is replete with derogatory or widely mis-understood quasi-medical terms. Fashion, professional language and sheer abuse change but they have helped to sustain a climate of prejudice in which discrimination against individuals and mental patients as such has continued to flourish. Coupled with legal disadvantage, outdated institutions, the nature of some treatments and their unforeseen consequences, the considerable powers of professionals and the difficulties which many groups of patients have in representing their own needs and preferences leave a legacy of disadvantage which legislative reform of itself will not remove. Nevertheless the struggle to improve the status of mental patients has had the indirect consequence that mental health services have moved dramatically up the scale of Government priorities for health and social services even though performance has not matched intention because of continual public expenditure cuts and other obstacles to the provision of a different pattern of services.

The delivery of any public service requires a reasonably close definition of those who should be entitled to benefit from it. Mental ill health is manifested in a variety of forms from a complete divorce from reality to excessive unhappiness or an inability to function relatively normally without help. Distinctions between individuals, their needs and behaviour, and between groups of people who share diagnostic labels or common problems are blurred to give the impression that mental patients are a uniform class somewhat separate from the mainstream of humanity.

The misapprehension that there is a firm dividing line between normality and abnormality diverts attention from individual needs and capacities and the dangers of discrimination, paternalism and oppression. In fact there is no such line – more a grey area which is not entered by many of us, occupied permanently by some or crossed regularly or spasmodically by others.

Therefore, the working definition of a mental patient is wide and inexact but will include somebody who is receiving or has received care or treatment for an emotional or intellectual difficulty provided by mental health professionals either in the community or in a mental health facility on a residential, day or visiting basis. In addition, one-third of the general practitioner caseload relates to people with emotional problems, and many social workers and others who deal directly with people and their needs would recognise this aspect of their work. However, it is the people informally or formally (i.e. compulsorily) being cared for and treated in residential institutions – hospitals, nursing homes and prisons – or who receive regular professional help who represent the core of the civil liberty concern.

Under the Mental Health (Amendment) Act 1982, like the original 1959 Act, mental disorder means mental illness (not defined), arrested or incomplete development of mind (subdivided into mental impairment and severe mental impairment – the previous term was sub-normality), psychopathic disorder and any other disorder or disability of mind (which no longer can include sexual deviancy or dependency on drugs or alcohol of themselves).[1]

For the most part doctors decide on the precise nature of the disorder, and there are plenty to choose from within such broad categories as psychosis, neurosis and organic malfunctioning of the brain. More narrowly typical examples would be schizophrenia and endogenous depression, reactive depression, anxiety states and phobias, and senile dementia. Mental handicap or impairment is not generally regarded as a mental illness but a permanent condition present from birth or as a result of brain damage which is characterised by limited intelligence or learning capacity. Mental handicap is therefore not treatable in the sense of cure, but in most cases it does respond to measures designed to improve functioning. Schizophrenia, depression and senile dementia probably represent the main conditions with which a comprehensive mental health service has to deal.

In 1982 there were 65,000 people resident in mental illness hospitals or psychiatric units in general hospitals, 50,000 people including 2,500 children in mental handicap hospitals, and 2,000 people in high security "special hospitals" mainly for offenders or those thought to be a danger to the public. Half the mental hospital population is long stay, with a preponderance of elderly people.

The law provides a framework for the provision of services under professional supervision which may include the restraint or compulsory care and treatment of those who are considered to be a danger to themselves or the public. It covers admissions, detention for various periods and purposes, consent to treatment, discharges and transfers from one type of facility to another and the information and assistance made available to patients in the exercise of their limited rights. Within such a framework there are, however, areas of uncertainty, created partly by the vagaries of professional judgement, diagnosis and the state of the science. Principles can conflict, as when the exercise of a right could interfere with the duty to care or treat, where regulations and procedures appear to conflict with common sense or the availability of time and staff, or where resources simply do not match the pressure of demand.

Whilst civil liberty opinion will concentrate on safeguards against restrictions imposed on individuals, the experience of many patients and staff will lead them to give more emphasis to the delivery of suitable services of acceptable standards and the means of access.

If we were to accommodate both approaches the principles to be applied would include:

1. The right to have appropriate care or treatment and rehabilitation in a humane environment.

2. The right to care or treatment in the least restrictive setting.

3. The right to decide whether to consent to treatment, choose a practitioner or have a second opinion.

4. The right to retain normal civil rights and social opportunities.

5. The right of appeal, regular review and representation when restrictions are imposed.

In practice such principles have been strongly resisted for historical and professional reasons and, more lately, by governments which have traditionally preferred to sustain official discretion and have been increasingly wary of making new commitments involving public expenditure.

The care of the mentally ill has evolved from families and communities more or less coping through cottage industry, private madhouses, workhouses, public asylums and the now familiar mental hospitals to the, as yet, unfulfilled promise of community care. The process has been one of scandal, reform and consolidation. The Victorian preference for large isolated institutions gave way to legal regulation in the 1890s and from then until the 1960s the medical profession gradually took over. Voluntary admission to mental hospitals, which still left 70 per cent of the hospital population compulsorily detained, came in with the Mental Treatment Act 1930. But it is with post World War Two developments we are most concerned.

In 1946 the new National Health Service took over responsibility for the asylums, and the medical profession, which had learnt a great deal from its war-time experience, came into its own. Mental illness was already seen as similar to physical illness and therefore susceptible to physical treatments, many of them crude and frequently damaging. Insulin (sleeping treatment), psycho-surgery and electric shocks were all the rage. A handful of charismatic doctors whose treatment preferences ranged from the physical to the psychological began to open the hospital doors. Chlorpromazine (used for schizophrenia) was discovered in 1952 and came into use two years later, just after the mental hospital population had reached its peak. It was followed by a range of drugs which, whatever they did for the patient, induced unbounded optimism amongst the psychiatrists who were still struggling for recognition within an elitist medical profession.

Yet all this coincided with another scandal which was seized upon by the NCCL. Kathleen Rutty's case[2] was investigated. An NCCL report alleged that not only she but thousands of mental patients were detained in mental hospitals on dubious medical or legal grounds. The NCCL's fortunes were at a low ebb but the campaign for the civil liberties of mental patients became a major focus of activity. The Royal Commission on the Law Relating to Mental Illness and Mental Deficiency was set up in 1954, reported in 1957[3] and led to the introduction of the Mental Health Act 1959.

The Act was a momentous reform and so changed the balance towards voluntary (or rather informal) care that the proportion of formally detained patients fell to roughly 10 per cent. Doctors were given greater powers and influence but the trend towards the pioneering open door and multi-disciplinary team approaches were consolidated. Patients were given the right of appeal against formal detention for treatment, but not against short term compulsory admission in emergencies or for observation, to Mental Health Review Tribunals. However, while they were also given the right to be represented, legal aid and advice were not available to those who could not afford to pay for them. Some doctors remained sceptical, although on balance they were pleased to be free of inspection by the old Board of Control which had previously maintained oversight of mental hospital conditions. By and large the Act was welcomed although the optimism of some, significantly Enoch Powell, the Minister of Health, who in 1961 predicted the demise of the old mental hospitals within 15 years, proved in hindsight to have been misplaced.

Interestingly, the NCCL was left to implement its own recommendations concerning lay representation at tribunals. If not lawyers who else was to organise and provide the representation? With virtually no staff or resources, the NCCL's General Secretary, Martin Ennals, mastered the role and created a rota of volunteers who ranged from trade union officials and journalists, quite capable of mastering a difficult brief, to others whose competence did not always match their enthusiasm. The instruction to all of them was to avoid medical or social issues and concentrate instead on strictly formal arguments to represent the patient's own case for discharge. Insufficient weight was given to the social grounds for suggesting that a patient could be returned to his or her home or some alternative place in the community because the procedure itself restricted consideration to whether or not the patient remained a danger to self or others. There was no provision for conditional discharge or delay, whilst social arrangements could be made, if the application were granted.

One patient in Rampton represented by the NCCL was granted discharge having spent his entire life in institutions for the mentally subnormal. He arrived at the NCCL offices without money, literacy, or the experience of fending for himself in the community. He received personal support from the staff over many years and not only survived, but maintained a family.

The provision of skilled representation was difficult enough, but the NCCL was not equipped to provide social aftercare. Under the Act, local authorities were mandated to do so, but in generally unenforceable terms. They did not. Tragedies occurred; one man absconded from hospital, sought refuge in the NCCL office which was surrounded by a posse of police, and was escorted back to the hospital by an NCCL staff member. He was then represented at a tribunal, discharged and, having rejected any further help from the authorities or the NCCL, committed suicide within six months of securing his freedom.

Conscious of these difficulties, and aware of the fragility of a volunteer representation system, to which the only alternative was paid legal representation, which few patients could afford, the NCCL in the late 1960s commenced negotiations with the National Association of Mental Health to design a more sophisticated representation service which could combine advocacy with mental health expertise and aftercare provision. A scheme was devised but the funds to operate it were not found.

However, the alien concept of mental patients' rights penetrated the professionally dominated consciousness of the NAMH and, under the influence of David Ennals, who was for three years its Campaign Director during an interruption in his Parliamentary career, it published a campaigning report on the rights of mental patients. This may have helped to create an atmosphere which made possible the appointment in 1974 of a National Director (the writer) whose previous experience had been in civil liberties rather than mental health.

The Butler Committee on the mentally abnormal offender had been appointed by the Government in 1972 following a notorious case involving a discharged patient who then proceeded to repeat the offence (murder) which had led to his first incarceration in a special hospital.

MIND – the renamed NAMH – calculated that Butler was bound to recommend some change in the law and so decided to investigate the entire operation of the 1959 Act, which, curiously, had not been reviewed since its introduction. It recognised that a more civil liberty casework orientation would be necessary to accumulate sufficient evidence on how the Act was working in practice. The shift was difficult to achieve because the staff and volunteers, heavily influenced by care professionals, were more interested in therapy than rights.

By a fortunate coincidence a young American academic on a Fulbright Scholarship to review the mental health tribunal system contacted MIND for assistance on the advice of his supervisors. Although Larry Gostin was unusually offered an extension of his period of study in the UK, he succumbed to a MIND suggestion that he should become its full-time legal adviser to help the organisation develop new skills and a new approach. The initiative was not universally popular.

However, the appointment was decisive in promoting a new role for MIND and in starting a long process which led to the reforms of 1982. Gostin, with the benefit of his American experience and training, which covered both psychology and law, set about creating a conceptual basis for the recognition of mental patients' rights. The first volume of his *A Human Condition,*[4] which dealt with the sections of the 1959 Act applying to non-offender patients, created a sensation which was just about contained within MIND but, more important, divided the mental health professional associations and evoked outrage among prominent members of the Royal College of Psychiatrists. To suggest that mental patients had rights was bad enough, but to assert that psychiatrists were less than perfect in their diagnosis or ability to predict whether or not a patient was likely to be a danger to self or others, the key issue in depriving people of their liberty, was unforgivable.

Side by side with his research and writing Gostin started to advise and represent the growing number of patients, relatives and professional workers who wanted to dispute apparently arbitrary decisions, mistreatment and the deprivation of liberty. Thus practice and theory developed hand in hand.

As predicted, Butler recommended certain changes in the law on mentally abnormal offenders,[5] only to be ignored by Government, much to his annoyance, until after his death. Gostin then went on to produce a second volume of *A Human Condition*[6] on the abnormal offender, which took the Butler arguments and recommendations further and proved to be less controversial.

With incredible dedication and energy, Gostin, with anxious and sometimes less than enthusiastic support from MIND, developed a legal casework service and within this a test-case strategy which was to yield, eventually, the decisive results which made a more comprehensive review of the 1959 Act possible.

There were other consequences. Psychiatrists continued to be outraged. The mental health establishment expressed its distaste and some prominent figures publicly withdrew their support from MIND. Health Service unions were affronted when challenged in the courts. The enmity of the Prison Officers' Association, for many of the test cases involved special hospital patients and special hospitals are ruled by the POA, spread into political circles with the result that certain MPs indulged in scurrilous campaigns against groups of patients and MIND officials, sometimes under the protection of Parliamentary privilege.

The sheer irrationality of the attacks attracted more public attention through the media, and then both lay and professional sympathy. National and international attention was drawn to the experiences of MIND, so that, for example, other voluntary agencies dealing with social and medical issues began to use lawyers and adopt the rights/casework approach, while Gostin was asked to advise a UN Commission and comment on mental health law in many countries.

Test cases were pursued both domestically and internationally. At home the courts threw out most of them, thus demonstrating that the legal remedies for mental patients were inadequate and leaving no option but appeal to the European Commission on Human Rights, which declared a number of cases admissible. One of the earliest went on to the European Court of Human Rights where the UK Government suffered an ignominious defeat (*X* v *United Kingdom*).[7] This case successfully challenged the Home Secretary's powers over restricted patients in special hospitals and as a result, under the new Act, the Government has conceded the absolute right to discharge such patients to the tribunals. Following this, what has been described as the second generation cases continued and continue to wend their way through the European labyrinth, with a profound influence on the passage of the Bill during its Committee stages. Issues dealt with included the provision of legal aid, the need to speed up tribunal procedures and the removal of the Secretaries of State for Home Affairs and Social Services from the protection afforded by Section 141 of the 1959 Act which denied patients the right to sue anyone acting under NHS legislation without first gaining the consent of the High Court.

Many issues, such as censorship, "seclusion" and the discredited practice of using "unmodified" ECT (i.e. without muscle-relaxing drugs), were the subject of political and professional representations where there was little scope for litigation. On a more successful note remarkable victories were achieved in the

County Courts on the disenfranchisement of mental patients (or residents as they were redesignated) and in the Industrial Tribunals on the right of mental patients not to be discriminated against at work. Win or lose, political pressure or legal action, domestic or European remedies, the issues and the plight of patients concerned received enormous publicity which generated public sympathy. Television documentaries played a particularly important part. The Government and the psychiatric establishment were embarrassed and rattled. The politicians were put in the picture and in the mood to insist on change when the Bill came before Parliament. The "MIND" strategy which harked back to the Butler Report had worked.

These developments created much more confidence amongst mental patients who became more inclined to seek redress for their grievances. Many professionals, including social workers, psychologists and nurses, who had witnessed squalor and injustice without protest, began to see that conditions could be improved if they were exposed and contested.

The Labour Government, with David Ennals as Secretary of State for Social Services, had produced a White Paper on mental health which conceded some important changes but steadfastly maintained that the 1959 Act required adjustment rather than radical reform.[8] It seemed in 1979 that years of campaigning would yield some results even though the Secretary of State regarded MIND's first reaction to the White Paper as churlish and ungrateful. The general election robbed him of his chance to reform the Act, but his White Paper can now be recognised as a positive contribution to a process of awareness-building which needed more time to mature.

Late in the day the Royal College of Psychiatrists began to organise and exert its influence in Parliament. It was particularly successful in preventing any significant reduction in medical powers. Under the Conservatives a Bill emerged which was a small advance on the previous Government's White Paper but still defective in a number of respects. Lobbying became intensive as the Bill went into Committee. For once the all-Party legislative system began to work and clause by clause the Government proposals were refined or changed with the critical help of independently minded Conservative MPs who, like many of their Opposition colleagues, only began to appreciate the disadvantages faced by mental patients as they absorbed the information put before them by MIND, NCCL and other groups.

The new Act (1) required that social workers involved in admissions should be "approved", i.e. trained and certificated for mental health work; (2) gave the right of appeal to a tribunal to those admitted for 28 days for assessment (including compulsory treatment – an apparent retreat from the vague provisions of the original Act); (3) reduced the duration of admission for treatment by half (i.e. an initial six months instead of one year, and one year subsequently instead of two); (4) brought forward the time at which the right of appeal to a tribunal first applied; (5) introduced legal aid for tribunal cases; (6) reduced a legal guardian's responsibilities to essential powers on place of residence, attendance for treatment and access of professional workers to the home; (7) placed more strict conditions on detention of offender patients; (8) slightly improved the mental patient's right to litigate; (9) clarified to a degree the detained patient's obligation to accept treatment but with minimal safeguards in the case of treatments which gave rise to special concern, such as ECT and psychosurgery; (10) ended the Home Secretary's exclusive power to decide on the release of restricted patients.

A Mental Health Act Commission charged with keeping under review all aspects of the care of detained patients was established, and hospital managers were required to inform patients of their rights. Contrary to all reasonable expectations Gostin was not appointed to the Commission. Voting rights were extended to mental hospital patients with a home address (last address before admission or address where they would be if not in hospital) who could complete a registration form unaided.

When we are dealing with the state of civil liberties in an area which has recently been the subject of revised legislation but where the outcome in practice remains unknown, it is perhaps necessary to dwell on the process which brought about the changes, no matter how limited. We simply do not yet know if the new law will strengthen patients' rights sufficiently to satisfy their needs, sustain their dignity, halt the series of humiliations the UK has suffered at the hands of the European Commission on Human Rights, or fend off yet more cases in domestic courts and tribunals.

However, it would be reasonable to suppose that when one wave of passionate debate has subsided and the law is in operation, the disadvantages and injustices which mental patients have traditionally endured will once again attract public attention leading to further campaigns for yet more fundamental reform.

Matters covered in the amending legislation will make little or no impact on conditions in mental health facilities because of the impact of continuing public expenditure cuts, which seem likely to further reduce the quality of life in institutions and the performance of services in general and which will hold back the provision of alternative services more appropriate to the task.

It seems possible that the incidence of mental illness will increase because of the psychological damage done by unemployment, homelessness and comparative poverty and the growth of the elderly population until the late 1990s. We may also suspect that rapidly changing social conditions, the failure to give equality of opportunity to minorities and differing perceptions of sex roles influencing child care and security will all help to create vulnerability leading to conditions which demand help, support and treatment. The reality of mental hospital populations now is that they tend to be elderly, or damaged by long term institutionalisation. A new generation of "mental patients" may be less tolerant of bad conditions and more capable of expressing their own needs and concerns.

In a slightly less deferential age the power of doctors will not go unchallenged by patients and other mental health workers. It has long been clear that doctors cannot cope with managerial and planning responsibilities. Yet they exercise an influence beyond their specialist clinical responsibilities to the detriment of other professionals who should be playing a more prominent role and of patients whose non-medical needs following treatment have always been under-estimated.

While gross inequalities remain between mental patients and other consumers of the NHS and between mental patients in different units and districts, the standards which have come to be accepted by professionals and endured by patients are so inferior to those taken for granted in other circumstances at home and abroad, that this should produce renewed pressure for further reforms.

The accuracy of psychiatric diagnoses, given the state of the science, the efficacy of treatment, the divergent schools of thought on treatment and the continuation of treatments which may be shown to be damaging, should continue to provide fertile grounds for protest and litigation.

The scandal of the high security special hospitals for offenders remains. Protected by official secrecy, controlled by the POA, shunned by academics and innovating professionals, built as prisons, execrated by the press and public, they present a challenge which has yet to be faced by Government. Even the series of criminal trials which resulted from the Yorkshire TV investigation of allegations of brutality and malpractice in Rampton Special Hospital failed to persuade the POA to co-operate with the reorganisation recommended by two independent investigations. Faced with clean-up attempts by managements or scrutiny from outside, even police enquiries, the special hospitals staff simply close ranks with staggering contempt for legitimate authority or public concern. The pressures on the special hospitals are closely tied in to the crisis of the prisons, which because of the failure of health authorities to co-operate or to get on with providing medium secure units for which they have been given the money, are left to cope with mentally ill people without adequate treatment facilities. Yet one third of special hospital patients are non-offenders. Local hospitals, often backed by health unions, may refuse to accept transfers from prisons or special hospitals, which means that many patients are deprived of their liberty in the sense that they are contained in high security conditions they do not require. Moreover on some occasions an initial refusal to accept a transfer gives way to bargaining over bodies on the basis that we will take your chap if you will take another we want to get rid of.

The mental hospitals have always suffered from lack of resources and isolation. Many have continued to do a useful job in incredibly difficult circumstances, while others have languished and at least 30 hospitals, so far unnamed, have been characterised by the DHSS as being unsuitable for their purpose. Many who work in hospitals continue to defend them vigorously, either because they have not kept pace with current thinking on new patterns of care and treatment for mentally ill people, or because they are cynical about Government intentions to provide the resources and impetus for alternative provision, largely community based.

New admission policies and the discharge of many patients who, in former years, would have languished indefinitely in hospital, have brought about a steady decline in the mental hospital population. While some hospitals with 800-plus beds still remain, many others, also built in the Victorian era, are scarcely viable and are beginning to suffer from run-down blight. Staff morale declines, staff recruitment problems increase, as do the proportion of elderly and chronically disabled long-stay patients. In this situation standards will be even more difficult to sustain. A positive programme of replacement is needed if there is to be the slightest chance of maintaining the quality of life, still less of improving it. Mental hospitals have never been adept at monitoring and controlling standards while the agencies established by Government in recent years such as the Health Advisory Service and Community Health Councils, have had neither the teeth nor the influence to insist on change. Although civil liberties problems abound, the civil liberty approach is to some extent peripheral, in the sense that righting individual wrongs will do no more than add to the pressures for structural change.

The new Mental Health Act Commission, whose brief is limited to formally detained patients, is an unknown quantity, but it looks cumbersome and has enough of the characteristics of the Scottish Mental Welfare Board and the old Board of Control for there to be a doubt as to whether it can become a force for change rather than a palliative measure, dominated by doctors, ignored by Government and packed with the grateful recipients of establishment patronage.

The mental health movement, working in close collaboration with the civil liberties movement, needs to be revived and to make common cause with those concerned about other sectors of institutional care. The mental health establishment has had much to say about the civil liberty intrusion into its affairs. It may yet learn to appreciate that civil liberty pressure has strengthened the case for more resources, alternatives to large institutions and a better deal for both patients and staff.

NOTES

1. Sections 1 and 2, now consolidated in section 1 of the Mental Health Act 1983.

2. *R v Board of Control, ex parte Rutty* [1956] 2 Queens' Bench Reports, p.109.
3. Cmnd. 189 (HMSO).
4. Gostin, *A Human Condition*, Vol. 1 (MIND, 1975).
5. *Report of the Committee on Mentally Abnormal Offenders* (Cmnd. 6244, HMSO, 1975).
6. MIND, 1977.
7. (1981) 4 European Human Rights Reports, p.188.
8. *Review of the Mental Health Act 1959* (Cmnd. 7320, HMSO, 1978).

19

CIVIL LIBERTIES IN NORTHERN IRELAND

DERMOT P J WALSH

INTRODUCTION

It would not be an exaggeration to say that the development of
civil liberties has had a markedly different history in Northern
Ireland compared with that in Great Britain. While the problem in
Britain today may be one of traditional liberties coming under
increasing attack,[1] the difficulty in Northern Ireland is, and always
has been, the more fundamental one of developing a basic
awareness of civil liberties. It would seem that a civil liberties
consciousness has failed to take root in Northern Irish society, or,
if it has, it has failed to express itself. One possible explanation for
this lies in the fact that from its birth in 1922 until 1972 Northern
Ireland has had its own devolved government (Stormont) and
enjoyed considerable autonomy. Left to itself it developed its own
standard of civil liberties protection which diverged radically
from that prevailing in Britain. When Westminster resumed
direct control in 1972 many believed that British standards of
liberty and justice would follow. Although some advances were
made such hopes have since proved misplaced. What had happened
before and during Stormont rule left the Westminster administration with very little room for manoeuvre. An understanding of
the state of civil liberties in Northern Ireland today, therefore,
requires some reference to the practices and policies of the
Stormont government and the problems that it faced.

THE STORMONT CONTRIBUTION

When Northern Ireland first emerged in 1922 as a distinct political entity with its own devolved government (Stormont) within the United Kingdom, it inherited the centuries old cleavage between catholics and protestants in Ireland.[2] Within the new statelet the protestants enjoyed a comfortable two to one majority over their catholic adversaries.[3] Furthermore, because Stormont reflected the Westminster structure and because the electorate voted largely along religious lines the protestants held the reins of power without a break from the inception of the statelet to Stormont's demise in 1972. Nevertheless, they suffered from a deep sense of insecurity. The catholics in the rest of Ireland and those within the statelet itself resented its creation and so the protestants were constantly haunted by fear of attack from both quarters. Their response to this perceived threat over the following fifty years can be regarded as the most influential factor hindering the development of a civil liberties consciousness.

One of the earliest and most damaging attacks on the cause of civil liberties of the Stormont administration was the enactment of the Civil Authorities (Special Powers) Act (Northern Ireland) 1922-33 and the various regulations authorised by it. Some idea of its severity can be grasped from the comment made by Mr Vorster, then South Africa's Minister for Justice, when introducing a new Coercion Bill in the South African Parliament, that he "would be willing to exchange all the legislation of that sort for one clause in the Northern Ireland Special Powers Act".[4] Presumably he would have been more than satisfied with section 1, which permitted the Minister for Home Affairs, or any RUC officer designated by him, to "take all such steps and issue all such orders as may be necessary for preserving the peace and maintaining order". A leading authority on Northern Irish constitutional law, commenting on this section, said that it gave almost unfettered control to the Minister.[5] Other sections of the Act and Regulations made under it provided for:

1. internment without trial;
2. the Minister to impose curfews;
3. the RUC to arrest any individual without warrant and detain him/her for up to 48 hours solely for the purpose of

interrogation – no suspicion needed;

4. the army and the RUC to enter without warrant any home believed to be used or kept for any illegal purposes;

5. senior officers of the RUC to order any assembly of three or more persons to disperse if an officer making the demand believed that the assembly might lead to a breach of the peace;

6. the Minister to serve an order excluding a named person from all but a tiny part of Northern Ireland, thereby effectively excluding him from all of it;

7. the Minister to prohibit the publication or distribution of any newspaper, periodical, book or other printed matter;

8. the Minister to prohibit the holding of inquests;

9. the outlawing of various associations;

10. the death penalty for causing or attempting to cause an explosion likely to injure life; and

11. whipping for a number of lesser offences, mainly concerning explosives and firearms.

The framers of this legislation certainly were not going to make any concessions to civil liberties. This was confirmed by the terms of section 2 which stated that an individual was still guilty of violating the Act if he took certain actions that were prejudicial to the preservation of the peace even if those actions were not provided for in the Regulations contained in the Schedule to the Act.

The existence of such legislation on the statute book would, in itself, constitute a powerful disincentive to the development of a civil liberties consciousness among the rulers and the ruled. Harry Calvert points out that this is a particularly grave danger within the United Kingdom where the traditional safeguards to personal freedom are not entrenched constitutionally but exist rather as "principles of political morality depending for their efficacy upon the degree of sacrosanctity attached to them by legislators and administrators and the public at large".[6] If these safeguards can be so easily trampled upon by resort to the Special Powers Act then each successive rejection of them will undermine their status and prepare social attitudes for similarly harsh measures in the future. The existence of such legislation will also have an inhibiting effect on those sections of the community who perceive that they could be a target for it. As suggested by Calvert, the fact that they will

fear that innocent and inoffensive words, deeds and associations may, because of abuse or error or through excessive caution on the part of the civil authorities, result in fine or imprisonment is an evil in itself and may lead to a further one in the form of the curtailment as a matter of caution of socially beneficial activities.

The overall result, therefore, is to accustom those in government to the luxury of sweeping executive powers and to intimidate those who might oppose them into the begrudging acceptance of severe restraints on their liberties.

That, at least, would appear to have been the contribution of the Special Powers legislation to the development, or lack of it, of civil liberties in Northern Ireland. It remained in force without a break right up to 1972. The history of its application throughout this period suggests that its more important function was to suppress all forms of challenge, whether peaceful or violent, to the hegemony of its unionist sponsors. The sporadic bouts of republican and sectarian violence, which apparently it was introduced to deal with, could have been controlled easily by the ordinary law. It is the examples of its use in time of peace which revealed its true nature and, arguably, inflicted the most damage to the growth of a civil liberties consciousness.

A clear example of this occurred in October 1933. The authorities rounded up and detained between 40 and 50 republicans, but as there was no violent activity prevailing at the time they were reluctant to actually intern them. Accordingly, the minister for home affairs issued a Regulation under the Special Powers Act making it an offence to refuse to answer incriminating questions in a private examination by a magistrate. The men were examined, refused to answer and were duly convicted of an offence created subsequent to their arrest.

Nor was the Special Powers Act concerned solely with the republican threat. The Stormont administration also harboured a fear of labour unrest and had no inhibition about resorting to the Special Powers Act to deal with it. In 1925 and again in the 1930s – the only occasions in the history of Northern Ireland – the protestant and catholic working classes came together in a spirit of comradeship. The catalyst that brought them together was chronic unemployment coupled with the stark fear and reality of starvation and the workhouse. The government responded in the manner it had become accustomed to and resorted to the Special Powers legislation to ban marches, demonstrations and meetings. The "hunger marches" as they were popularly known were broken up by the RUC using brutal and, on occasions, deadly force.[7] When the veteran British communist, Tom Mann, came to Belfast to attend the funeral of one of the marchers shot dead by the RUC and address a rally he was arrested and served with a banning order under the Special Powers Act restricting him to Clogher in County Tyrone.

A similar intolerance to opposition was displayed towards printed matter. Here, the government were prepared to suppress even publications which reflected a different viewpoint. Republican publications were regularly banned, and on occasions communist papers. At one stage a catholic religious journal and the main local newspaper in Derry were banned.[8] It is not difficult to imagine the impact such incidents had on the activities of those who might have been inclined to advocate the cause of greater civil liberties.

One celebrated example of its use demonstrates not only its repressive nature but also the fact that it vested almost unreviewable powers in the hands of the government. The case concerned a Regulation issued by the Minister of Home Affairs in March 1967 under the Special Powers Act. It added to the list of unlawful associations: "the organisations at the date of this Regulation or at any time thereafter describing themselves as 'republican clubs' or any like organisation howsoever described". There was no suggestion at the time that republican clubs were involved in any seditious pursuits. The move seems to have been prompted more as a response to the growing civil rights agitation in republican circles. The only case arising from the ban was in the nature of a test case against a Mr McEldowney who was charged in March 1968 with being a member of the Slaughtneil republican club.[9] The local magistrates dismissed the charge on the ground that the club in question could not be held to be unlawful as constituting a threat to peace and order in Northern Ireland within the terms of the Regulation as they interpreted it. The Northern Ireland Court of Appeal reversed this decision on the ground that it was for the Minister of Home Affairs alone to decide whether a particular organisation should be deemed to be unlawful. The case was appealed to the House of Lords where the appeal was dismissed by a majority of three to two. The majority held that in the absence of proof of bad faith, which was not alleged, it was for the Minister alone to decide on the subversive nature of any organisation, and that in the circumstances the words "or any like organisation howsoever described" were not too wide to be supported.

As will be described later the Special Powers legislation was directed primarily against one section of the community and so its immediate impact on civil liberties was confined largely to that section. The Stormont government, however, did not display a very generous attitude to the freedoms of the rest of the community either. In law and order matters they constantly proved themselves more authoritarian than Britain. They retained the death penalty despite the fact that it was abolished in Britain in 1965. Up until 1970 the RUC always resembled a European gendarmerie much more closely than their British counterparts. Their officers were armed from the start, organised and trained along military lines and under executive control.

Progress in the social welfare field also dragged far behind that in Britain with the unionists, on occasions, openly opposed to some measures designed to improve the quality of life for all. They even voted against the introduction of welfare state measures at Westminster.[10] A similar negative attitude was displayed towards the introduction of judicial divorce, which was not made available at all in Northern Ireland until 1939.[11] Again when the law in England was changed in 1969 to make divorce more easily obtainable Stormont failed to follow suit. It was not until 1978, under Westminster rule, that some degree of parity was restored. A similar pattern recurs in the availability of legal aid. Despite the fact that the Legal Aid and Advice Act first appeared in England in 1949 it was not followed up in Northern Ireland until 1965. Other aspects of the greater relaxation in personal freedoms which emerged in Britain in the sixties were not followed at all by the Stormont government. For example, they adamantly refused to extend the provisions of the Sexual Offences Act 1967 and the Abortion Act 1967 to Northern Ireland.

The foregoing indicates the extent to which a lack of respect for civil liberties in Northern Ireland prevailed, at least until Westminster resumed an interest in 1969–70. What it does not explain, however, is why organised pressure for reform only emerged in the sixties, and then largely from one section of the community. The answer to this is important because not only does it help explain how the Stormont administration enforced such a reactionary regime for so long unchallenged but also why there is still little effective pressure for reform despite the persistence of such a regime. A large part of the answer lies in the unequal application of the laws and the enforcement of policies which discriminated between the two religious divides.[12] For example, when internment was introduced in 1922 and in 1971, it was used initially against republicans alone although they were by no means the only ones engaged in violence. More remarkable was the electoral law and practice which actually denied the democratic principle of one man one vote in local government elections right up to the seventies. When the Labour Government at Westminster abolished the restricted franchise for local government in Britain by introducing universal suffrage, the Stormont government ensured that Northern Ireland was excluded. They introduced their own Representation of the People Bill in 1946 which not only confirmed the restricted franchise but restricted it further by taking votes away from lodgers who were not ratepayers. Some 10,000 young married couples lost the vote in Belfast alone.[13] The Bill also retained the extraordinary principle of company voting whereby limited companies received up to six votes according to their rateable valuation; the votes to be exercised by the company directors.

These measures operated primarily to the disadvantage of the catholic minority, thereby reinforcing the view that their rights and freedoms were even more tightly constrained than those of their protestant neighbours. This was confirmed by an amazing gerrymander of local government constituencies which produced such absurd results as a unionist majority of 12:8 in Derry city where the catholics were in a majority of 2:1.[14] This policy of discrimination also reflected itself in public sector housing allocation and, in particular, employment and industrial investment. Today exclusively catholic and protestant housing areas are common and can be distinguished easily by the consistently high unemployment rates in catholic areas compared with the relatively low ones in protestant areas.

These policies and practices had the effect of increasing the burden of the general restrictions on civil liberties for catholics while ameliorating them for the protestants. The latter generally escaped the bite of the Special Powers legislation while their allegiance was secured by the benefits to them of the discriminatory housing and employment policies. Little wonder then that when the civil rights campaign finally burst into public prominence in 1969 it was primarily a catholic movement. Few protestants felt sufficiently aggrieved to bridge the sectarian divide to support their catholic neighbours. In fact it would be fair to say that most were convinced by their unionist overlords that the harsh measures were necessary to keep the rebellious catholics in check. So successful were they in this that instead of joining in the campaign for greater civil rights for all in the late sixties, the protestants, in many quarters, confronted the marchers with violence in a determined attempt to prevent reform.

There were additional factors which prevented the growth of a civil liberties consciousness during the Stormont reign. Primary among these is the fact that for most of their reign the Government did not come under any influential and sustained pressure to introduce reforms. The catholics' political representatives at Stormont were never capable of presenting a coherent, united voice. Even if they had done so it is unlikely that they could have achieved anything given the permanent, in-built, unionist majority. The catholic church, potentially their most capable champion, for the most part similarly failed them in this respect. Although vociferous and successful in protecting its own institutional interests, such as in education, it was seldom heard or seen advancing the cause of civil liberties either for its own adherents or for Northern Ireland generally. Nor was the trade union movement any more prominent in this sphere. Despite the fact that sectarianism and discrimination showed itself most openly in the workplace it continued to ignore these potentially volatile issues and generally accepted the status quo.[15] In many ways this was the price it had to pay for its own legitimacy in the eyes of the state and the protestant working classes. To campaign against discriminatory policies or for greater civil liberties would be interpreted as being pro catholic or republican and anti the Northern Irish state. To maintain protestant support, therefore, the trade unions had to turn a blind eye to the civil liberties issue.

The British Government for its part remained aloof from the whole affair. Under the Government of Ireland Act 1920, Stormont was nothing more than a devolved government. Section 75 explicitly states that the "supreme authority of the Parliament of the United Kingdom" remains unaffected by the creation of Stormont. The practice developed, however, that Westminster would resort to section 75 only in the most exceptional circumstances and, furthermore, that discussion of matters relating to Northern Ireland which were within the competence of the Stormont Government would not normally be permitted at Westminster.[16] The British Government hid behind these practices as a justification for non-interference with Stormont rule: at least until the outbreak of the current violence forced them to take an interest.

An important element which impeded (and is still impeding) the development of civil liberties is violence. Northern Ireland as a political entity had a violent and bloody birth in 1922; a fact which was largely responsible for the enactment of the Special Powers Act. In the thirties, forties and fifties republicans mounted sporadic, ineffective and ill-supported campaigns in an attempt to overthrow the statelet. Although these never posed even a remote threat, they kept alive the protestant fear of internal and external attack, thereby entrenching their siege mentality. These activities reaffirmed their belief in the necessity for the Special Powers legislation and harsh, discriminatory measures against the catholics. When the latter took to the streets in 1969 demanding equality and basic civil rights their action was wrongly interpreted by the authorities as another attempt to overthrow the government. They responded not with reforms but with violence which provoked counter-violence. As this spiralled the unionist majority demanded increasingly tough security measures. The Stormont administration willingly responded, but the level of violence continued to increase. Eventually, the British Government felt they had no option but to prorogue Stormont of its powers and resume direct control over Northern Ireland's affairs.

THE WESTMINSTER CONTRIBUTION

Westminster intervened initially in 1969 with the aim of quelling the violence and reducing catholic grievances by promoting reform. The task of introducing, or prompting the Stormont Government to introduce, British standards of justice was a forbidding one. The catholic minority, which had suffered the worst excesses of the Special Powers legislation, wanted nothing short of its repeal and the elimination of discriminatory policies in housing allocation, employment opportunities, industrial investment and voting rights with an end to the gerrymandering of constituencies. The protestant majority considered that the state was under threat from a subversive catholic minority and that more draconian security measures should be introduced. They viewed concessions in this field or in the discriminatory policies as concessions to the enemy. To complicate matters further violence was escalating. The prospects of implementing British standards of civil liberties in this environment were remote if not impossible.

Nevertheless, the general thrust of Westminster's initial intervention in 1969 was designed to ease the burden on the catholics and could be viewed, therefore, as a concession to greater civil liberties. It must be said, however, that it concerned only the most basic of civil liberties. In the course of the next couple of years a Commissioner for Complaints and a Parliamentary Ombudsman were established, local government was reformed, central agencies were established to administer housing and education and, perhaps most significantly from a libertarian point of view, the police force was radically reformed. The notorious and hated B-Specials were abolished – but the Ulster Defence Regiment was set up immediately afterwards. The RUC itself was reorganised along civilian lines and modelled on its counterparts in Britain; it was disarmed, removed from the direct control of the Minister of Home Affairs and placed under the supervision of a police authority, and strong efforts were made to repair its tarnished image among the catholic community. But the notorious Special Powers Act remained unaffected. In the event these reforms proved too little too late, and many of them were swept away in the tide of violence which had begun even before they took effect.

The turbulent history of Northern Ireland from 1969 to the present day is well known. Westminster resumed full and direct responsibility for Northern Ireland in 1972 and has retained such control since, apart from a short interlude in 1974. When the state of civil liberties today is considered it is ironic to reflect that there was a widespread belief in 1972, at least among the catholic community, that Westminster rule would bring Westminster standards of liberty and justice. It is true that improvements have occurred in some fields. A Fair Employment Agency was set up to combat discrimination in employment, an Equal Opportunities Commission was set up to combat discrimination on the grounds of sex, the Housing Executive has overcome the discrimination problem in the public housing sector, and a degree of parity with Britain has been achieved in the matters of divorce, legal aid and homosexuality. But all of these advances have been grossly overshadowed by the record in the law and order field.

When Westminster resumed control violence was at its most intense level in the history of the statelet. The Unionist majority bitterly resented losing Stormont and would only be placated by a rapid improvement in the security situation. For them this meant the continuation of harsh, repressive measures against what they regarded as a rebellious, catholic minority. Westminster believed that violence must be eradicated if a lasting solution to the centuries old problem was to be found. Their method of achieving this, however, although different in formal appearance, was markedly similar in substance and effect to the Stormont military approach. Far from dismantling the Special Powers legislation Westminster renamed it, revitalised it and, arguably, made it more permanent. Today it exists as the Northern Ireland (Emergency Provisions) Act 1978 (EPA) and the Prevention of Terrorism (Temporary Provisions) Act 1976 (PTA). This legislation is designed not only to counteract the violence by harsh, emergency measures, but also to undermine the political nature of the violence by characterising it as mere criminality; the hope being that that will diminish the level of public support for those involved.

Accordingly, the Westminster government have constantly striven to play down the military aspect of their security policy and emphasise the primacy of the police and the courts. This policy was given a major boost by the Gardiner Report.[17] In line with that policy internment was phased out during the seventies, the army was reduced from its high profile strategy to a back-up role to the RUC and top priority was given to securing convictions through the court system. The change from a military to a civilian police strategy, however, has been more apparent than real. The RUC is anything but a civilian police force. Its officers are armed and have been suspected of operating a "shoot-to-kill" policy recently, following a series of incidents in which a number of unarmed republicans have been shot dead at RUC road-blocks. They have also resorted to lethal force in the form of plastic bullets in riot-type situations. In certain areas they wear bullet-proof vests, travel in military-style armoured Land Rovers and operate in a military fashion. In fact their role in republican areas is almost identical to that of the British army and the UDR; the only apparent difference being their uniforms.

The notion that the authorities are relying on the ordinary

criminal process to combat the violence is further contradicted by the scope of the emergency arrest powers and the manner in which they are used. Under section 11 of the EPA a police officer can arrest anyone whom he suspects is or has been involved in terrorist activity. There is no need for the suspicion to be reasonable, nor must he suspect the person of having committed any offence. On making the arrest it would appear that he need not tell the person anything more than that he suspects him of involvement in terrorist activity. Under section 11 the arrested person can be held for up to three days without ever knowing what he is supposed to have done wrong or when he is supposed to have done it. A police officer can also arrest him under section 12 of the PTA in the same circumstances but then he can be held for up to seven days, although the initial suspicion must be reasonable. The army has its own special arrest power under section 14 of the EPA. This allows a soldier to arrest anyone whom he suspects of having committed or to be committing any offence no matter how trivial. He need not comply with the common law requirements of a valid arrest and can hold the arrested person for up to four hours. In practice these powers are interpreted as authorising arrest for general questioning.[18] They are primarily used for screening purposes, intelligence gathering, surveillance and harassment.[19] As many as 90 per cent of the persons arrested under these powers are released without charge after having been detained for anything from four hours to seven days. For many individuals the experience is repeated several times a year, thereby constituting a serious infringement of their personal liberty, disrupting the lives of their families, often preventing them from complying with requirements for obtaining welfare benefits and effectively making them unemployable. In the vast majority of these cases no crime is suspected – the substance of the questioning often does not touch on any particular offence at all but rather on personal details about the individual's life and about members of his family and associates. Also, in many cases the purpose would appear to be to put the individual out of circulation for a short while and for harassment. Frustration over such practices is fuelled by the current tendency to use the power to detain for seven days more often.

It is worth emphasising the part played by the army here and the supplementary role of the power to stop and question at random conferred on both police and army by section 18 of the EPA. Not only is the army, strictly speaking, acting illegally in using its section

14 power for mere intelligence gathering purposes but, in so doing, it is imitating the police. This makes it even more difficult to differentiate between police and army in Northern Ireland. The power to stop and question under section 18 of the EPA allows a police officer or soldier to stop anyone, without prior suspicion, and ask their name, address, where they are coming from, where they are going to and what, if anything, they know concerning any recent, serious terrorist incident. It is an offence to refuse or fail to answer to the best of one's ability. This power is most commonly used at random road checkpoints both by the police and army, and it is the one aspect of the emergency legislation which most members of the general public experience. Equally, perhaps, it is one of the clearest indicators of just how submissive the Northern Irish public have become to restrictions on their freedom. It is common practice at these checkpoints for persons to be asked their age and their occupation and for the answers to be recorded in writing. Despite the fact that these questions are not directly related to controlling terrorism it would appear that the answers are willingly volunteered, thereby contributing to the massive intelligence gathering operation on the Northern Irish population which has been going on now in one form or another since the early seventies. Although there is no legal requirement to answer questions on one's age or occupation the refusal by the author to answer them at such checkpoints has invariably led to heavy-handed treatment by the police or soldiers concerned. It would appear that many of the personnel manning the checkpoints believe there is a legal obligation to answer any question they care to put – another indication of the lack of consciousness about civil liberties.

The emergency powers of arrest are also used as a step in bringing persons before the no-jury Diplock courts. This is a particularly invidious exercise of the power and, as will appear, is part of an apparatus designed to give the appearance that suspect terrorists are being dealt with fairly by the courts. In fact the apparatus is nothing short of a conveyor belt designed to ensure a high level of convictions, not just of suspect terrorists but of all who get entangled in its net. The use of sections 11 and 12 in this context is particularly objectionable because in many cases the police reasonably suspect the accused of a particular offence and so are in a position to arrest him or her under their ordinary powers.[20] Resorting to the emergency powers in these situations denies the accused the protection of the Judges' Rules while he is in police custody, allows the police to detain him much longer, allows the police to keep him in ignorance of what offences they suspect him of, restricts his right to a solicitor and permits a much harsher regime of interrogation. This last factor is crucial because under section 8 of the EPA any statement made by the accused may be admitted in evidence against him unless he can raise a prima facie case that he made the statement as a result of being subjected to torture, inhuman or degrading treatment and the prosecution fail to prove beyond a reasonable doubt that he was not subjected to such treatment in order to make the statement. This gives much greater latitude to officers in the interrogation room than would otherwise be available to them under the ordinary law. They can use bribes, threats, false promises, long debilitating interrogation sessions, verbal abuse and, according to one Lord Justice, even a certain degree of physical force in order to extract a confession without such a confession necessarily being ruled inadmissible.[21]

There is little doubt that throughout the latter part of the seventies the RUC was using section 8 to the full and even going beyond it by brutalising suspects in the interrogation room to extract confessions.[22] Disturbingly, the vast majority of convictions in the Diplock courts during this period were based on confessions. Although the worst excesses of the interrogation policy of the late seventies appear to have diminished it is still the case that administrative rules and regulations introduced in an attempt to curb abuse are not being fully enforced.[23] That the interrogation system is still a harsh, rigorous regime geared to securing a high confession rate is suggested by the latest figures available which show that convictions are still heavily dependent on confessions and in a substantial number of cases accused people are confessing in the interrogation room to offences they were not initially suspected of.[24] It should be remembered here that the convictions based on these confessions are resulting in very long prison sentences for many of those concerned.

At the end of the conveyor belt are the no-jury courts (Diplock courts). Lord Devlin once said that trial by jury "is the lamp that shows that freedom lives". For many in Northern Ireland the lamp has gone out and they are by no means all suspected terrorists. It would appear that as many as 40 per cent of individuals tried before the Diplock courts are accused of offences which are not directly related to the current violence.[25] The vast majority of these have already been processed through the emergency arrest, detention and interrogation procedures before arriving at the door of the Diplock court. If they had been accused of committing the same offence in Britain with exactly the same motive, the likelihood is that most would be acquitted as their confessions would be ruled inadmissible. As it is the vast majority are convicted by virtue of section 8 and the no-jury system. This, more than anything else, reveals the extent to which the harsh emergency apparatus, with its contempt for personal freedom and liberty, has become an integral part of the Northern Irish legal system and, therefore, society. No action has been taken to remedy this "loophole" in the emergency law and there has been no public outcry to demand its remedy.

Nor is the system any more excusable for the terrorist suspect. It is he who is most likely to be charged with serious offences carrying very long prison sentences. Government attempts to argue that he is afforded a fair trial by due process of law ring hollow when the law and practice of arrest, interrogation, the rules of evidence and the no-jury trial are considered together. That the system is designed not to ensure him a fair trial but to secure a high rate of convictions is suggested by the fact that there has been an almost continuous decline in the acquittal rate in Diplock courts since their introduction, and that the acquittal rate is running well below that in the ordinary Crown Courts.[26] Various explanations have been put forward for this. The most common are that it is the result of judges becoming case-hardened and that the RUC has perfected its intelligence and interrogation techniques to such an extent that it always gets the right man. Whatever the truth of the phenomenon the fact remains that the emergency justice process is weighted heavily in favour of the prosecution, it is producing an abnormally low rate of acquittals and the checks and balances which encourage confidence in the outcome of the ordinary trial process are absent. This must be a source of some concern to those who operate the system, to those against whom the system operates and to those who may experience it in the future. It is worth remembering that the last two categories are by no means confined to suspect terrorists.

The authorities prefer to use the Diplock courts as opposed to internment without trial as the former tend to escape the approbrium attached to the latter. Nevertheless internment remains an option for the government, as it is still on the statute book.[27] One draconian measure which the government has not been reluctant to use in recent years is the exclusion order.[28] An individual served with one of these is prohibited from entering or living in Britain or Northern Ireland or both. The Secretary of State may serve an exclusion order simply if he is satisfied that an individual has been, is, or intends to become involved in terrorism and is not a citizen of the United Kingdom who has been living in the proposed exclusion area for more than 20 years. The individual is never informed of what it is he is alleged to have done to give rise to the suspicion; nor, indeed, is it necessary that he be convicted of any offence. The Secretary of State acts as judge, jury, prosecution and defence. The sentence normally consists of the individual digging up his and his family's roots, leaving home, job, friends and country to move to another country, or alternatively separating from his family. That, at least, has been the usual impact of its use against people from Northern Ireland who had set up home in Britain. It has also been used, however, for political purposes. The most publicised example of its exercise was the recent exclusion of Sinn Fein elected representatives who attempted to enter Britain to fulfil a number of speaking engagements.

The emergency apparatus also provides sweeping powers of entry, search and seizure available to both the police and army. As with the other powers they, too, constitute a gross invasion of the freedom and privacy of the individual. For example, a police officer or soldier, if authorised by a senior officer, may enter any individual's home and search it for any munitions or transmitters if it is suspected that they are there unlawfully. There is no requirement that the suspicion be in any way reasonable. It is normal practice, following a terrorist attack on the security forces in a residential area, for the army to cordon off the area and carry out a house to house search for the weapon used or those involved. In some areas, therefore, it is a regular occurrence to have one's house searched by RUC officers or soldiers. The legality of such operations is suspect given that the weapon or individuals involved cannot be suspected of being in all the houses. Another frequent practice in certain areas is the random street search. Under section 15 of the EPA a police officer or soldier may stop anyone in a public place, whether pedestrian or motorist, and physically search him or her for unlawful munitions or transmitters. Incredibly, there is *no* need for any suspicion whatsoever; the police officer or soldier can act on a mere whim and the citizen must comply. Needless to say this power is regularly used in working-class, republican areas where it is interpreted as just another example of legalised harassment.

But perhaps the most blatant example of civil liberties infringement is the blanket physical searching of citizens entering Belfast city centre. Permanent steel security fencing blocks off every route into the city centre and every single individual entering through the various gates is bodily searched by either civilian or military personnel. For this Belfast must be unique among the capital cities of the world. Equally unusual is the unquestioning acceptance of such methods of control by the public; yet another example of the sorry state of civil liberties consciousness in Northern Ireland today.

Freedom of association and expression have also suffered under the emergency measures. An interesting feature here is that many of the restrictions on these are now incorporated in public order legislation which does not even attempt to portray itself as temporary. In fact this permanent legislation adds significantly to the restrictions imposed by the so-called emergency measures. Together they provide the authorities with the power severely to curtail any organisation or show of dissent to government policy and actions. The Public Order (Northern Ireland) Order 1981, for example, requires five days' notice of a march before it will be lawful. A senior RUC officer may impose certain conditions as he feels necessary for the preservation of public order if he has reasonable grounds for believing that the march may occasion a breach of the peace or serious public disorder. The conditions would concern such things as a change in the route or starting time. The Secretary of State, if he feels that the police will not be able to prevent serious public disorder resulting from any march in any area, may make an order prohibiting all marches or a particular class of march in that area for a period of not more than 12 months.

These provisions afford very broad discretion to the authorities, and it would appear that the discretion is not always applied impartially. During the recent "H-block" crisis the government refused absolutely to permit peaceful marches against government policy on the issue outside the republican ghettoes. This was enforced by the Secretary of State using his power to prohibit and by the police using their extensive arrest powers. It was also marked by hundreds of convictions for taking part in marches which did not comply with the five day notice requirement. This contrasted sharply with the decision to grant permission and protection to provocative loyalist marches on two recent occasions in the catholic town of Downpatrick, the first of which provoked serious violence.

And so one could continue listing the restrictions on freedom of movement, association and expression which emanate directly or indirectly from measures intended to deal with the current violence. Indeed, one could go further and consider direct attacks on basic human rights such as the right to life. The use of plastic and real bullets on the streets of Northern Ireland in recent years has resulted in the deaths of men, women and children in circumstances where the victims were posing no threat to the security forces or anyone else.[29] Lately, the sinister practice of individuals and whole families disappearing has become part of the scene in Northern Ireland. This is directly related to the increasing reliance of the authorities on supergrasses in an attempt to break the paramilitaries. The disappearances are engineered by both the security forces and the paramilitaries. In either case it is virtually impossible for the relatives to find out anything about the whereabouts, health and well-being of the missing persons.

Westminster's contribution, therefore, has done little to advance the cause of civil liberties in Northern Ireland. Certainly it has achieved some success in curtailing the discriminatory policies of the Stormont administration and has encouraged progress in fields such as divorce and legal aid. These advances, however, are overshadowed by its record in criminal justice and by the extensive discretionary powers over freedom of movement, expression and association which it has reposed in the executive. In fact, little has changed in this field since Westminster first took an interest in 1969. The emergency apparatus is still alive and well and making its presence felt most keenly in the catholic areas. The division between the two communities is as deep as ever with the unionists constantly pressing for even more severe measures to combat republican violence. The violence, itself, continues; no doubt fuelled by the harshness of the measures used to combat it. The prospect of encouraging a civil liberties consciousness generally is now no greater than at any time throughout the 50 years of Stormont rule.

CONCLUSION

Some would argue that curtailment of civil liberties and human rights in Northern Ireland is necessitated by the overriding need to restore peace and normality; that the restrictions are justified to protect the right to live in peace and security; that when normality returns so also can the traditional freedoms. Even if one accepts the principle of this argument – and it should be remembered that the "restrictions" themselves are operating as a denial to some of the right to live in peace and security – it has no application in Northern Ireland. It is not possible to return to a state of things which has never existed. Northern Ireland has not had a tradition of civil liberties protection. Throughout its 62 year history, whether under Stormont or Westminster rule, it has been governed by permanent emergency legislation. The freedom of the individual has always depended for its existence on the uncontrolled discretion of a police officer, soldier, Minister of Home Affairs or Secretary of State. The last 15 years is abnormal only in that there has been serious violence. The harsh measures which are being used to tackle the violence do not exist simply because of the violence: they or their like have always existed in Northern Ireland and have been used in time of peace and unrest; they are synonymous with the Northern Irish statelet.

This situation gives rise to a number of evils. Firstly, as Harry Calvert had feared, the administrators will become accustomed to trampling upon civil liberties in the daily running of the State. As has been seen, both Stormont and Westminster have been grossly guilty of this in their administration of Northern Ireland. Recently, the latter even went so far as to alter the law on the eligibility of successful candidates to take their seats following election to the United Kingdom Parliament. This was in response to the election of convicted IRA hunger-striker Bobby Sands for the Westminster constituency of Fermanagh and South Tyrone. Rather than tackle the underlying problems that produced such a result the government blandly introduced the Representation of the People Bill which denied the right of those sentenced for more than one year to membership of the House of Commons during their detention. This was duly enacted in 1981.

Secondly, society itself comes to accept severe restraints on traditional liberties as normal. As has been seen, the majority in Northern Ireland have come to accept without question such measures as being stopped, questioned and searched at random, being arrested and interrogated for up to seven days at a time, being searched on entering Belfast city centre and being charged, tried, convicted and sentenced in a court where many of the most important traditional safeguards for the accused are absent. It is true that such measures are deeply resented and opposed in republican areas where they are felt most keenly. But even there it is considered a normal, everyday event to be taken out of bed by soldiers at five o'clock in the morning, arrested under section 14 of the EPA, taken to an army base, questioned about personal, family and other innocuous matters and released four hours later.[30] This apparent lack of awareness of a right to live one's life free from harassment by the State or its officers is mirrored in the absence of any significant demand for greater freedoms generally. Issues such as divorce, abortion, gay rights, the provision of legal aid, Sunday licensing laws, etc., have never attracted any significant popular concern in Northern Ireland. What progress there has been in any of these fields stems more from Westminster initiative; usually many years after the equivalent has been implemented in Britain. This can be partly explained by the preoccupation of one section of the community with much more basic issues such as equal opportunity in housing and employment, and the preoccupation of the other section with the supposed vulnerability of the state to internal and external attack.

A contributory factor also, however, has been the conservative stance of the churches in Northern Ireland. Their opposition to the legalising of homosexual acts between consenting adults in private stopped the British Government from extending the provisions of the Sexual Offences Act 1967 to Northern Ireland and resulted in Britain being held in breach of its obligations under the European Convention on Human Rights. When these factors are considered together it would not be unfair to conclude that there is a general lack of civil liberties consciousness in Northern Ireland.

A third evil could be of more concern to Britain than Northern Ireland. This is that the low status accorded to civil liberties in the latter will soon become the norm in the former. This prospect can be discerned already in the criminal law enforcement field. The Police and Criminal Evidence Bill introduced just before the end of the last

Parliament, and reintroduced in October 1983 contains a number of features similar to the emergency apparatus in Northern Ireland. The proposals to allow the police to stop and search suspects, to set up road blocks, to extend powers of arrest to situations not previously covered, to relax the restrictions on the length of time that the police can hold a suspect for questioning and to change the rules on the admissibility of confessions from the "voluntary" test to one of oppression, which is to include torture, inhuman and degrading treatment, all represent a significant tilt in favour of the prosecution. They will produce a criminal law enforcement system for Britain which is very unlike that currently prevailing there, but very similar to that to which Northern Ireland has grown accustomed.[31] It is not difficult to imagine the exercise of these powers in the inner city areas of Britain producing the same reaction they provoke in the riot-torn areas of Belfast and Derry. The next step will be to adopt more of the North's repressive emergency measures in order to contain the violence.[32] Bit by bit the ignorance of, and lack of respect for, civil liberties and human rights, prevalent for so long in Northern Ireland, will be transported to Britain.

What can be done to reverse this process and encourage the development of a civil liberties consciousness in Northern Ireland? The major obstacle is, of course, the emergency apparatus. A return to trial by jury, controls over police and army powers of arrest, search and seizure, a relaxation of the constraints on freedom of movement, association and expression would encourage a greater respect for civil liberties generally among the administrators and society at large. This could be compounded by the adoption of a Bill of Rights along the lines of the European Convention on Human Rights.[33] This, in turn, would help to dissipate the notion that the State has or should have complete control over the freedom of the individual and would encourage individuals to recognise that they have rights and to enforce them against the State. The State, for its part, would be forced to have due regard to the fundamental rights and duties of the citizen in both its legislative and administrative actions. This, in itself, would not transform Northern Ireland into a liberal democracy but at least it would assist it to progress in that direction from its current status as little better than a totalitarian police state.

NOTES

1. For an up to date critique on the state of civil liberties in Britain today see: Patricia Hewitt, *The Abuse of Power* (Law in Society Series: Martin Robertson, Oxford, 1982).
2. For an historical account see: Robert Kee, *The Green Flag* (3 volumes, Quartet Books, 1976); Roger H Hull *The Irish Triangle* (Princeton University Press, Princeton, NJ, 1976).
3. Throughout this chapter the terms catholic, republican and minority are used interchangeably to denote one side; and protestant, unionist, loyalist and majority are used interchangeably to denote the other.
4. Michael Farrell, *Northern Ireland: The Orange State* (Pluto Press, London, 1976) p.93.
5. Harry Calvert, *Constitutional Law in Northern Ireland* (Stevens & Sons and Northern Ireland Legal Quarterly, 1968) pp.279-80.
6. *Ibid.*, p.383.
7. Farrell, *op. cit.*, ch. 6.
8. *Ibid.*, p.94.
9. *McEldowney* v *Forde* [1969] 3 Weekly Law Reports, p.179; see K Boyle, T Hadden and P Hillyard, *Law and State: The Case of Northern Ireland* (Martin Robertson: Law In Society, London, 1975) pp.14–15.
10. Farrell, *op. cit.*, p.189.
11. Northern Ireland Legal Quarterly, *Divorce Law Reform in Northern Ireland* (NILQ, Queen's University, Belfast, 1978).
12. Harry Calvert refers to the possibility of relying on the constitutional guarantee against discrimination in the Government of Ireland Act 1920: see Calvert, *op. cit.*, pp.334–5. For various reasons this option was not exercised by the minority: see Boyle, Hadden and Hillyard, *op. cit.*, pp.9–17.
13. Farrell, *op. cit.*, p.85.
14. See the *Report of the Commission of Inquiry into the Disturbances in Northern Ireland* (Belfast, HMSO, Cmd. 532, 1969) (Cameron Report).
15. O'Dowd, Rolston and Tomlinson: *Northern Ireland: Between Civil Rights and Civil War* (CSE Books, London, 1980), ch. 3.
16. Calvert, *op. cit.*, ch. 6.
17. *Report of a Committee to Consider in the Context of Civil Liberties and Human Rights, Measures to deal with Terrorism in Northern Ireland* (Cmnd. 5847, HMSO, London, 1975) (Gardiner Report).
18. *Ex parte Lynch* [1980] Northern Ireland Law Reports, p.126.
19. See generally Dermot P J Walsh, "Arrest and Interrogation: Northern Ireland 1981", *Journal of Law and Society*, 1982, and *The Use and Abuse of Emergency Legislation in Northern Ireland* (Cobden Trust, 1983).

20. *Ibid.*
21. *Per* Lord Justice McGonigal in *R* v *McCormick* [1977] Northern Ireland Law Reports, p.105; doubt has been cast on this by the Lord Chief Justice in the case of *R* v *O'Halloran* (1979) Northern Ireland Judgments Bulletin.
22. See generally: Peter Taylor, *Beating the Terrorists* (Penguin, 1980); K Boyle, T Hadden and P Hillyard, *Ten Years On in Northern Ireland* (1980); *Report of an Amnesty International Mission to Northern Ireland* (1978); *Report of the Committee of Inquiry into Police Interrogation Procedures in Northern Ireland* (Cmnd. 7497, HMSO, London, 1979) (Bennett Report).
23. Walsh, *The Use and Abuse of Emergency Legislation*, ch. 3.
24. *Ibid.*, chs. 3 and 4.
25. *Ibid.*, chs. 1 and 4.
26. Boyle, Hadden and Hillyard, *Ten Years On*, pp. 59-62.
27. Section 12 and Schedule 1 to the EPA.
28. See Catherine Scorer and Patricia Hewitt, *The Prevention of Terrorism Act: The Case for Repeal* (NCCL, London, 1981) chs. 3 and 6.
29. See, for example, Denis Faul and Raymond Murray, *Plastic Bullets Maim and Kill* (Dungannon, 1981).
30. Walsh, *Journal of Law and Society, op. cit.* note 19.
31. On this see: Paddy Hillyard, *From Belfast to Britain*, Power and Politics No. 4 (Routledge and Kegan Paul, London, 1982).
32. It is significant here that a number of police forces in Britain already have their stock of plastic bullets at the ready.
33. See: *Do We Need a Bill of Rights?*, edited by Colin Campbell (Temple Smith, London, 1980) for a discussion of the merits and demerits of a Bill of Rights for Northern Ireland.

PART V

A Wider Perspective

A TRANSATLANTIC VIEW OF
CIVIL LIBERTIES IN THE UNITED KINGDOM

NORMAN DORSEN

It is a chancy business to appraise the institutions and health of another country, and I do so with trepidation. That I do so at all is a tribute to more than the kind invitation of the editor of this volume. For I hope that this paper reflects, in addition, my deep professional and personal concern for civil liberty – which should be a birthright for all peoples everywhere – and the affection that I developed for the United Kingdom during many visits, in particular my years at the London School of Economics as a graduate student during the mid-1950s and as a visiting professor in the late 1960s.

Our two countries are Western industrialised democracies, whose legal systems are each rooted in the common law of England. And both countries are "free", with a healthy measure of individual autonomy and personal security. But the contrasts between the countries are greater than the similarities, and not only because, as one wag has put it, they are divided by a common language. Britain is an old country, with a tradition of limited government tracing to the thirteenth century; and the United States is still relatively young. The United States is much larger and richer, it contains a far greater number of ethnic, racial and religious groups, and it has no Established Church. In terms of structure, the United Kingdom is essentially governed by a single set of laws (although there are variations in Scotland and Northern Ireland), while the United States is composed of 50 states each of which retains strong elements of sovereignty, including its own legislature, court system and laws. Perhaps most important, the United States and each of the states has a written constitution containing a Bill of Rights that is judicially enforceable.

These important differences in our two societies might be

expected to lead to sharply varying problems of individual liberty, or solutions to these problems. There are examples of such differences, some of which will be discussed below, but the essays in this book on the whole reveal more common ground – including ground for concern – than differences. I shall first discuss certain civil liberties issues, common and distinctive, and then briefly comment on the controversy surrounding the proposed Bill of Rights for the UK, a controversy which sheds light on alternative means of securing individual liberty. Before any of this I should like to pay richly deserved tribute to the NCCL on its 50th anniversary.

1

The most striking feature of the NCCL from an American vantage point is its persistent effectiveness, given its limited size and its inability to rely on entrenched constitutional principles that can be judicially enforced against arbitrary Parliamentary laws. In contrast to the resources available to the NCCL, the American Civil Liberties Union is fortunate enough to have more than a quarter million members, functioning units in all 50 states (each of which has its own board of directors and in most cases paid staff), and a combined annual budget of more than $15 million. That the NCCL has achieved all it has, and emerged in the past half century as the most visible champion of liberty in the UK, is an extraordinary achievement.

The absence of a mechanism to invalidate legislation through judicial action has meant that many of NCCL's greatest victories must be at the bar of public opinion, to be fully reaped later, it is hoped, in ameliorating legislation. As I survey the record, it seems plain that NCCL has led the public to a greater awareness of women's rights, police accountability and freedom of information about the actions of government, even if these sentiments have not yet been adequately transformed into law. This is not to overlook NCCL's imaginative support of test cases to a far greater degree, and with more success, than other British human rights organisations.

Despite the great disparities between the NCCL and the ACLU, there are common problems. One is the constant struggle to define civil liberties persuasively – neither so narrowly as to exclude novel issues thrown up by new social attitudes or developments in community life nor so broadly as to dilute or trivialise great principles. In the effort to remain current, the ACLU in recent years has studied government regulation of commercial advertising, the police use of undercover agents, the scope of the insanity defence to criminal conduct, university research undertaken for the CIA, patients' refusal of medical treatment, and claims of newspapers to special access to prisons and institutions for the mentally ill. Both NCCL and ACLU are seeking to come to terms with the civil liberties implications of nuclear power. In the United States we are particularly troubled by the pervasive secrecy that surrounds decisions relating to nuclear energy and by the surveillance of private citizens whom the authorities regard as a threat to this secrecy.

Perhaps the most difficult definitional area for civil libertarians concerns economic rights, such as the right to a minimum standard of living. The ACLU has never adopted an across the board principle of economic rights as distinguished from rights of speech and association, privacy and due process, but in recent years we have extended our concept of civil liberties to include poverty-related rights – for instance the termination of welfare or unemployment benefits, or the foreclosure of a farm mortgage without a proper hearing (which we view as raising due process issues) or the unequal expenditures of funds on public education among school districts (which we view as an equal protection question).

In both countries there are times when enthusiastic – and sometimes prescient – staff may seem to wander beyond the policies enunciated by boards of directors. Although the problem is complicated in the US because of the substantial autonomy of our state affiliates (which sometimes take inconsistent positions), NCCL as well as ACLU apparently finds itself from time to time preoccupied by internal differences over the application of certain organisational policies.

NCCL apparently shares some of the ACLU's difficulty in attracting members of minority groups. A poll taken in 1981 showed that racial minorities comprised less than 2 per cent of the ACLU membership although they comprise about 20 per cent of the population at large. This concerns us deeply, since minorities are often the brunt of arbitrary official action and their point of view is important in sensitising directors and staff to problems that might otherwise be overlooked. Like NCCL, we have been far more successful in recruiting women, who were previously under-represented, as members and into positions of responsibility and leadership.

In short, NCCL, like ACLU, has faced and will continue to face the inevitable organisational problems common to institutions whose mission encompasses the volatile subject of civil liberties. In doing so, NCCL has every reason to take pride in what it has accomplished over 50 years.

2

Turning to the substance of civil liberties, it is striking that the vast majority of pressing issues in the UK, as identified by contributors to this book, are similar to those in the US.

The police and the courts are where the average citizen most frequently confronts the state, and the litany of issues is familiar. At the police level, there are coerced confessions, illegal searches of private dwellings, electronic wiretapping and eavesdropping, the use of agents provocateurs, and detention without the filing of charges. At the judicial level, there are arbitrary denials of bail, questionable decisions to prosecute, inadequate client access to lawyers, improper panelling of juries, excessive delays before trial, and invasions of the right of defendants to remain silent.

One serious problem of fairness exists in somewhat different form in our two countries. May evidence tending to prove the guilt of an accused be heard in court if it was unlawfully obtained by the police? In England, such evidence is admissible and may form the basis of a conviction. That was the American law prior to 1961, when in *Mapp* v *Ohio*[1] the US Supreme Court declared that all such evidence must be excluded. But in recent years, as a result of popular agitation about the crime problem, there has been a whittling away of this rule as the definition of "unlawful" has been considerably narrowed. In 1984 the Supreme Court may decide whether evidence that has been seized unlawfully can nevertheless be received if the police error was made in "good faith",[2] – for example, if an officer mistakenly but "reasonably" thought his search warrant was based on probable cause or if he guessed wrong on a novel question concerning the legality of the search. The ACLU fears that if a good faith defence is upheld the practical consequence will be a return to the era when convictions based on illegally seized evidence will be the routine. The experience in Scotland, where this is currently the rule, apparently suggests that the fear is well-grounded.

When one examines the ubiquitous problem of inequality, it is important to bear in mind that in the United States, if government is involved in any way, improper discrimination violates the Constitutional provision guaranteeing all persons the "equal protection of the laws".[3] *Private* discrimination, by contrast, is prohibited by statute (both Federal and State), as in the UK.

These legal prohibitions have not ended bigotry in either country. Racial discrimination in particular remains widespread. The use of the law to eradicate deepseated prejudices is expensive, time-consuming, and often humiliating. The results are also unpredictable because of the unreliability of witnesses, the availability of alternative explanations for the challenged conduct ("we rented the apartment just before the plaintiff arrived", "there were others more qualified for the job"), and the reluctance of most fact-finders to attribute improper motives where a possibility exists that the defendant acted in good faith.

A major arena of controversy in the US concerns "affirmative action" designed to help previously victimised minorities. This can take the form of programmes to hire or promote minority members, or to admit them into schools or housing. Sometimes a plan is adopted voluntarily, in other cases it is ordered by a court after a finding of unlawful discrimination; in some cases it is a government programme, in others it is introduced by a private employer or school; and in some cases it includes a rigid quota, in others merely a percentage "target". In all cases it means some disadvantage to white persons who are usually not themselves guilty of wrongdoing. This has naturally led to charges of unconstitutional "reverse discrimination" in favour of minorities. In the famous *Bakke* case[4] a sharply divided Supreme Court held that the Fourteent'. Amendment barred a University of California medical school from reserving a fixed number of places for minority students, but not from using minority status as a "plus" in considering the qualifications of an applicant. More recently, the Court has upheld employment quotas self-imposed by a private company[5] and a federal statute setting aside a portion of government contracts to minority owned concerns.[6] These complex and emotion-ridden issues have been discussed in the

UK in the context of the Scarman Report and, if American experience is a guide, they may one day preoccupy the country and therefore the NCCL.

Discrimination against women is also widespread. Although women have made major advances since Victorian days, when females were denied any public role, gender continues to shape the limits and experiences of both men and women, and generally to predict economic and political status.[7] The UK apparently faces the same sort of issues we do – job discrimination, sexual harassment, unequal pay, social security disparities, uneven application of the immigration laws, and the like.[8] A problem coming to the fore in both countries is to assure equal pay for work of "comparable value" even though the jobs differ. The virtual exclusion of women from certain positions has created the impetus for this sort of remedy. For instance, to give women bank presidents the same pay as men in that position is almost meaningless because there are extremely few female bank presidents. To determine comparable worth for different jobs may be sensible in theory, but it is extraordinarily difficult in practice since many subjective variables are involved in deciding what is comparable work. The problem has not yet been solved in either country.

Discrimination against part-time workers is apparently an important sex discrimination issue in the UK, because of the large percentages of women who are relegated to marginal employment. That issue has not assumed the same importance in the US, probably because of different economic circumstances. The ultimate goal in both countries should be to eliminate the separate spheres in which men and women are required, by custom and attitudes, to move in economic life, with the sexual asymmetry ordinarily disadvantaging the female. The disappointing statistics under the UK Equal Pay Act do not presage an early solution to this problem, which seems to afflict all contemporary societies.

Other forms of discrimination exist. Prejudice against homosexuals is rife in both societies, and is yielding only slightly to the efforts of gay liberation movements. Former mental patients bear a stigma not easily removed by a certificate of cure, and this is reflected in their unequal access to lawyers and courts and their limited employment opportunities. The civil liberties concerns of both these groups, as described in this book, are familiar to Americans. So also are the excruciatingly difficult issues relating to youth. In 1967 the US Supreme Court held that young people accused of delinquency were entitled to due process under the Constitution,[9] and a few years later it ruled that young people possessed cognisable rights of free speech.[10] But these rights were not found to be co-extensive with those of adults, and American courts in trying to determine the precise protections young people can rely on have grappled with issues similar to those the courts have faced in the UK – curfews, pretrial detention, indeterminate sentences, and above all the apparently intractable issues spawned by epidemics of violence. Unfortunately, sociologists and psychologists on both sides of the Atlantic have failed to make much progress in predicting antisocial behaviour, and neither society has had the insight or resources to reform youthful offenders. Norman Tutt's comment that "the principle of individual treatment is a myth" is sadly recognisable to an American observer.

Passing from issues of discrimination to those of free speech, one may observe that few citizens of either the UK or the US would deny the abstract proposition that a fair opportunity to express oneself and to understand what our democratically elected governments are doing is fundamental. Despite such assent, it is evident that there are serious problems in both countries, only a few of which can be noticed here.

The first is an aspect of freedom of association – the right of individuals to attend public or private meetings, and to participate in rallies or demonstrations. On the face of it, the law in the UK is clear and permissive. Thus, Lord Scarman stated in 1975 that "The right [to demonstrate] of course exists, subject only to limits required by the need for good order and the passage of traffic".[11] But apparently this is an overstatement. Patricia Hewitt has recently described the reality.[12]

Far from being a reasonably clear area of freedom in which to act, subject only to specific restrictions imposed by law, the freedom to demonstrate is at the mercy of arbitrary decisions by the police and the executive, often unchallengeable in the courts. The common law recognizes a freedom to move along the highway in a procession, but that freedom is subject not only to an ill-defined law of obstruction of the highway but also to the power contained in the 1936 Public Order Act to ban processions, including those in connection with which no threat to public order is envisaged. The freedom to hold stationary demonstrations in a public place is even less well protected by common law; the police have extensive discretionary powers to disperse groups of people, to limit the numbers present and to bar access to the place chosen, against which the would-be demonstrator has no legal protection whatsoever.

As Americans know from bitter experience, this state of affairs is highly prejudicial to an open society. "Demonstration" cases – like cases involving police misconduct – are a perennial ingredient of the ACLU's case docket, as apparently of the NCCL's.

Racist marches or protests are an acute example of the genre. There is much respectable opinion that would ban public meetings of the National Front in the UK and the Nazi Party and the Ku Klux Klan in the US. While such appeals are superficially attractive, in my opinion it would be a serious mistake to adopt that position. Many sorts of ideas are repugnant to members of the community, and if government is allowed to ban some ideas it will surely ban others – including those that opponents of racist speech might find attractive. Democratic premises require protection of all points of view, even the most hateful. Furthermore, from a practical standpoint, if the marketplace of ideas cannot be trusted to winnow out the hateful, there is no reason to believe that censorship will do it. The ideas will persist, and martyrs to an ugly cause will be created by operation of law.

In the UK, the law permits restriction of the right of protest if there is a threat of "serious public disorder", but even this standard could be mischievous. If there is such a threat, the proper remedy is to restrain those who would interfere with speech, not those who wish to express themselves. In the US the ACLU adhered to this position several years ago when a "Nazi" group sought to demonstrate peaceably in the town of Skokie, Illinois, where many Jewish survivors of Hitler's death camps resided. ACLU lawyers represented the Nazis in extensive court proceedings, and eventually secured their right to march.[13] At the time several thousand ACLU members resigned, and there was a severe financial drain – indeed at one point the organisation seemed in jeopardy. But the *Skokie* case has turned out to be a longterm benefit for the ACLU. Many members who resigned have returned, and many new members were moved to join because of a perception of the organisation as sufficiently principled (as one woman wrote us) to "put its money where its mouth is". Above all, the general membership sharply enlarged their contributions to manifest their support. As Justice

Oliver Wendell Holmes once wrote, "If there is any principle of the Constitution that more imperatively calls for attachment than any other it is the principle of free thought – not free thought for those who agree with us, but freedom for the thought that we hate".[14]

Another perennial issue stems from pornography, which is censored almost everywhere, in part because of fear the "filth" will find its way to the young. Given the variety of human tastes and standards, it is not surprising to find that the law in both the UK and US is a mess. Not very long ago, Supreme Court Justice Potter Stewart, frustrated by the inability of the Court to define "obscenity" with any precision, threw up his hands and pronounced a judgment relying on his ability to "know it when I see it".[15] In the UK, there is far greater film censorship than in the US, and apparently more systematic attempts to suppress gay and lesbian publications. The House of Lords' ruling that upheld the conviction of *Gay News* on the ground that it was blasphemous libel to publish "material calculated to outrage and insult" Christian religious principles[16] has no American counterpart. On the other hand, the pressures in the US from elements of the feminist movement to censor materials that "degrade women" have not, as I understand it, been widely replicated in the UK. In America, the effort fortunately has borne little fruit, largely because of the extraordinary difficulties in defining the class of material that should be censored on this ground. But the alliance between some feminists and reactionary groups has aggravated an already unsettled situation by increasing the general pressure to restrict circulation of certain books, magazines and films.[17]

The final aspect of free expression that I would discuss represents, in the long run, the greatest threat to democracy. Throughout history, princes have sought to operate in darkness, shrouding actions so that their subjects are unable to criticise or revolt in the face of incompetence or corruption. An American President, James Madison, once commented that "Knowledge will always govern ignorance". Ignorance can be contrived as well as intrinsic; it can be a method of subjugation. Unfortunately, the instinct for secrecy in government persists to this day.

In the UK, the 1911 Official Secrets Act seems to keep information from the public more thoroughly than anything in American law. Section 2 of the Act, which makes it an offence to communicate *any* official information to an unauthorised person has, not surprisingly, permitted prosecutions of breathtaking scope. Fortunately from the vantage of an open society, a proceeding brought in 1971 against the *Sunday Telegraph* for publishing a report on the war in Nigeria failed, as did another proceeding in 1978, the *"ABC"* case, against the investigative journalist Duncan Campbell and two others. Indeed, in the *Telegraph* case the judge issued a stinging rebuke to those who would restrain information "not concerned in the slightest with national security".[18] But the deportation of Mark Hosenball, an American journalist, apparently for his probing of official secrecy, was upheld by the courts in 1977.[19]

The failures, in the last years of the Labour Government, to reform the Official Secrets Acts and to enact a suitable Freedom of Information Law (despite active lobbying by NCCL), are regrettable above all because they left an open field to the present Government to enact in the name of "reform" even more restrictive measures than those currently on the books. The Thatcher Government's attempts to make use of this opportunity with a Protection of Official Information Bill were fortunately thwarted by the explosion of the Blunt spy scandal at a crucial time. In my view, there can be no higher priority for the NCCL than to continue to oppose such measures vigorously and, when the time is ripe, to support the sort of legislation that would permit maximum sunlight to be beamed on official actions.

The history in the US is rather different, and until fairly recently there was some warrant for pride in the containment of government pressures towards a closed society. In 1971 the Supreme Court rejected censorship by upholding the right of the *New York Times* and other journals to publish the Pentagon Papers,[20] a harmless history of decision-making during the Vietnam War. Later the Supreme Court rejected President Richard Nixon's attempt to withhold White House tapes that incriminated him and others of criminal conspiracy during the Watergate affair.[21] Earlier, in 1966, the Congress enacted a Freedom of Information Act which, as subsequently amended, provided substantial (if not ideal) public access to government records.[22]

Recently, however, the Government has taken steps to tighten the secrecy laws which, if allowed to become effective, will create severe problems. Among the actions completed or proposed are the refusal of visas to foreign scholars whose views the Administration finds unpalatable; restriction of publication and dissemination of scientific research; prohibitions against travel by Americans to certain countries; widespread use of lie detectors against government employees whether or not leaks of classified information have occurred; attempts to gut the Freedom of Information Act; and a requirement that all government officials sign lifetime agreements to submit future writing for Government clearance.[23]

The trend towards greater secrecy began in the US before 1981, but the Reagan Administration has accelerated it enormously and seems to regard restriction of information as a central strategy of government. It sees the free flow of information to the public as a threat and seeks increasingly to insulate government decisions from public scrutiny and debate. This recently was manifested in an unprecedented way by the total barring of the press from Grenada during our invasion in October 1983.

An informed observer has written that "The United Kingdom has rightly been described as one of the most secret countries in the Western world".[24] Regrettably, the US is moving rapidly in a similar direction.

3

There are some issues of civil liberty that, for historical, cultural or legal reasons, persist in either the UK or the US but not in both countries. In the US, capital punishment still may be imposed for murder in half of our states, and more than a thousand men and women live in death row under sentence of death. The Supreme Court has laid down complex rules for determining when execution is constitutional,[25] and each individual facing this punishment is vigorously represented by lawyers from the ACLU or the NAACP Legal Defense Fund. American civil libertarians have concluded that the death penalty is prohibited by the Eighth Amendment to our Constitution as "cruel and unusual punishment", because it is final – the innocently convicted have no remedy; it is applied with no apparent consistency ("freakishly" as one judge termed it); and it is used far more often against racial minorities than against whites. The NCCL is fortunate that this troubling issue is not on its docket.

Another major civil liberties concern in the US that is not viewed in constitutional terms in the UK is abortion. In 1973, our Supreme Court held, to the surprise of many observers, that women (in consultation with their physicians) had a constitutional right of privacy that included an absolute right to an abortion during the first trimester of pregnancy and that until the fetus was viable the right could be limited only to promote the mother's health.[26] Certain religious groups and their allies immediately organised to reverse this decision by constitutional amendment. They have been unsuccessful until now, but they have through legislative action managed to cut off Federal and most State funding for poor women who seek abortions while continuing to fund childbirth and other operations. To its discredit, the Supreme Court upheld the constitutionality of these restrictions although their effect was to deny millions of American women an opportunity to enjoy a right ostensibly proclaimed for all.[27] The source of the anti-civil liberties impulse in this area, as in so many others in the US, is grounded in the excesses of religious fundamentalism, some of the leading advocates of which have perverted Christian humanitarianism into a monolithic and cramped morality.

For its part, the UK lives with a singular problem without counterpart in the US–Northern Ireland. Dermot Walsh's essay portrays a police state in which elementary guarantees of individual liberty are lacking. An overseas observer is amazed that within the UK there might be a place where the police have untrammelled discretion to invade dwellings and to make arrests, where for many of the gravest offences trial by jury does not exist, where freedom of association is denied, and where even the right to vote has been circumscribed by the disqualification of hunger strikers from the ballot paper. The explanation, of course, lies in the continuing violence and the hard attitudes prevailing in the two religious communities. The territory seems the victim of a vicious circle, in which violence begets repression, which in turn infuriates its victims and stimulates further violence, apparently ad infinitum. It is not for an outsider to suggest a way out of this morass, especially since a tradition of civil liberties has apparently not been notable in Ulster. Although there is no comparable situation in America, complacency on our part would be inappropriate since the condition of the Catholic minority in Northern Ireland today is not so very different from the status of blacks in much of the United States until the 1960s.

The suggestion in Mr Walsh's essay that some amelioration might take place by the adoption of a Bill of Rights along the lines of the European Convention on Human Rights leads naturally to a broader inquiry concerning the desirability of an entrenched guarantee of rights for the UK.[28] In the United States we have lived with a Bill of Rights from the beginning, although only in recent decades has it been interpreted to restrain state and local governments (in addition to the Federal Government in Washington).

Although the ACLU would not fully endorse constitutional doctrine as enunciated by our Supreme Court, it is nevertheless true that a functioning Bill of Rights has permitted our judges to expand liberty dramatically, especially since Earl Warren became Chief Justice of the US in 1953.

This familiar history may lead some to forget that for a century the Supreme Court, far from enhancing civil liberty, tended to crush it. In the infamous *Dred Scott* decision, which helped to precipitate the Civil War, the Court ruled that even blacks who were no longer slaves could not be admitted to American citizenship; in the *Civil Rights Cases* of 1883 and *Plessy* v *Ferguson* in 1896 it upheld and legitimated a system of racial apartheid.[29] In the spheres of criminal justice and free expression the results were similar, as the Supreme Court rejected virtually all claims of individual right.[30] This was true also from the standpoint of economic justice. Until 1937, the Court emerged as a truly reactionary institution, invalidating the first attempt at a national income tax (which had to be authorised by constitutional amendment a generation later), striking down laws seeking to improve the lot of workers as inconsistent with "liberty of contract", and ruling that unions were criminal conspiracies unprotected by the law.[31] The modern image of the US Supreme Court is misleading if not seen in historical perspective.

The debate over a Bill of Rights for the UK is fascinating to Americans in part because it divides many whose goals are similar. My impression is that civil libertarians in Britain differ on the desirability of a Bill of Rights depending on their optimistic or pessimistic view of how the American experience would be transposed to British soil. That is, some believe that, given the rapid pace of modern life and law, a Bill of Rights would soon encourage British Courts to approximate the current US Supreme Court in protecting civil liberties. Sceptical opponents believe that British judges, chosen from a much narrower class than their American counterparts, would in fact resemble, for the foreseeable future, the pre-1937 or at least the pre-1953 Supreme Court, protecting property rights by striking down, for example, a wealth tax or nationalization statute, while refusing to protect civil and political rights of concern to the NCCL and its supporters.

Inspection of the decisions rendered by Lord Denning, a judge widely regarded as the champion of the individual against the state, muddies the waters still further. He upheld the right of peaceful assembly and opposed improper jury vetting. But he denied the right of a black immigrant and an American journalist to a fair hearing, the right of social security claimants to judicial review of adverse administrative decisions, and the right of trade unionists to take part in peaceful industrial action. Lord Denning issued these rulings while rendering other judgments that protected the rights of "television licence holders, tax evasion suspects, a Conservative education authority and a private airline company".[32] Even those trained in British law apparently find it difficult to make sense out of this pattern of decisions.

The situation in the UK is complicated still further by the different models of a Bill of Rights that have been proposed. These include complete entrenchment, with a Constitutional Court that could as the US Supreme Court; a Bill of Rights that would have a favoured me powers status over other legislation short of full entrenchment; and a Bill of Rights that would have favoured status only over earlier legislation.

While a Bill of Rights is seen by some as a hope for the tangled life of Northern Ireland – in the words of one writer, to "protect a settlement, not produce one"[33] – it appears unlikely in the near future that an entrenched instrument will be legislated for the UK as a whole. Whatever the fate of a Bill of Rights, it seems plain from the essays in this commemorative book that there will continue to be incursions on civil liberty in the UK, as in other countries, and that the gallant and valuable work of the NCCL must continue as a bulwark of a free society.

NOTES

1. 367 US Reports, p. 643 (1961).
2. The pending cases are *Massachusetts* v *Sheppard*, 82–963; *Colorado* v *Quintero*, 87–1711; *US* v *Leon*, 82–1771.
3. US Constitution, Amendment XIV.
4. *University of California Regents* v *Bakke*, 438 US Reports, p. 265 (1978).

5. *Steelworkers* v *Weber*, 443 US Reports, p. 193 (1979).
6. *Fullilove* v *Klutznick*, 448 US Reports, p. 448 (1980).
7. For an insightful analysis of gender discrimination see Estrich and Kerr, "Sexual Justice", in N Dorsen (ed.), *Our Endangered Rights* (1984).
8. See generally the ACLU handbook, S D Ross and A Barcher, *The Rights of Women* (revised edn., 1983).
9. *In Re Gault*, 367 US Reports, p. 1 (1967).
10. *Tinker* v *Des Moines School District*, 393 US Reports, p. 503 (1969).
11. *The Red Lion Square Disorders: Report by the Rt. Hon. Lord Justice Scarman, OBE* (Cmnd. 5919, HMSO, 1975).
12. P Hewitt, *The Abuse of Power* (Oxford, Martin Robertson, 1982), p. 115.
13. There were two proceedings: (i) *National Socialist Party* v *Skokie*, 432 US Reports, p.43 (1977) and 439 US Reports, p.916 (1978), and (ii) *Collin* v *Smith*, 439 US Reports, p. 916 (1978).
14. *US* v *Schwimmer*, 279 US Reports, p. 644, at pp. 654–5 (1929).
15. *Jacobellis* v *Ohio*, 378 US Reports, p. 184, at p. 197 (1964).
16. *R* v *Lemon* [1979] 1 All England Law Reports, p. 898.
17. The National Coalition against Censorship, 132 West 43rd Street, New York, NY 10036, maintains comprehensive records on all aspects of the subject.
18. Both cases are unreported. The quotation is from P Hewitt, *op. cit.*, p. 82.
19. *R* v *Home Secretary, ex parte Hosenball*.
20. *New York Times* v *US*, 403 US Reports, p. 713 (1971).
21. *US* v *Nixon*, 418 US Reports, p. 683 (1974).
22. See US Code, Vol. 5, para. 552, for the current version of the law.
23. *Free Speech, 1984: The Rise of Government Controls on Information, Debate and Association* (ACLU, July 1983); Halperin, "National Security", in N Dorsen (ed.), *Our Endangered Rights* (1984).
24. Hewitt, *op. cit.*, p. 106.
25. See Gillers, *Deciding Who Dies* (1980) 129 University of Pennsylvania Law Review, p.1.
26. *Roe* v *Wade*, 410 US Reports, p.113 (1973).
27. *Harris* v *McRae*, 448 US Reports, p.297 (1980).
28. See generally P Wallington and J McBride Civil Liberties and a Bill of Rights (London, Cobden Trust, 1976); M Zander, *A Bill of Rights?* (2nd edn., Chichester, Barry Rose, 1979); and J A G Griffith, *The Politics of the Judiciary* (2nd edn., London, Fontana, 1981).
29. The citations to the three cases are 60 US Reports, p.393 (1857); 103 US Reports, p.3 (1883); and 163 US Reports, p.537 (1896).
30. See generally L Tribe, *American Constitutional Law* (1978); G Gunther, *Cases and Materials on Constitutional Law* (10th edn., 1980).
31. Citations to the three leading cases are *Pollock* v *Farmers' Loan and Trust*

Co., 158 US Reports, p.601 (1895); *Lochner* v *New York*, 198 US Reports, p.45 (1905); and *Coppage* v *Kansas*, 236 US Reports, p.1 (1915).

32. These and other examples are discussed in P Hewitt, *op. cit.*, p.243.
33. K Boyle, "Emergency Conditions", in C M Campbell (ed.), *Do we need a Bill of Rights?* (Temple Smith, 1980).

INDEX